REMEMBERING TO FORGET

REMEMBERING TO FORGET

HOLOCAUST MEMORY

THROUGH THE CAMERA'S EYE

BARBIE ZELIZER

THE UNIVERSITY OF CHICAGO PRESS

Chicago and London

BARBIE ZELIZER is associate professor at the Annenberg School of Communication at the University of Pennsylvania. A columnist for the *Nation,* she is
the coauthor of *Almost Midnight: Reforming the Late-Night News* and author of
*Covering the Body: The Kennedy Assassination, the Media, and the Shaping of Collective
Memory,* the latter published by the University of Chicago Press

The University of Chicago Press, Chicago 60637
The University of Chicago Press, Ltd., London
© 1998 by The University of Chicago
All rights reserved. Published 1998
Printed in the United States of America
07 06 05 04 03 02 01 00 99 98   5 4 3 2 1

ISBN (cloth): 0-226-97972-5

Library of Congress Cataloging in Publication Data

Zelizer, Barbie
    Remembering to forget : Holocaust memory through the camera's eye /
Barbie Zelizer
        p.   cm.
    Includes bibliographical references and index.
    ISBN 0-226-97972-5 (alk. paper)
    1. Holocaust, Jewish (1939–1945)—Pictorial works.   2. Holocaust, Jewish
(1939–1945)—Press coverage.   3. World War, 1939–1945—Concentrarion
camps—Liberation—Europe—Pictorial works.   4. World War, 1939 1945—
Concentration   camps—Liberation—Europe—Press   coverage.   I.   Title.
D804.32.Z45   1998   98-18164
940.53`18—dc21   CIP

CONTENTS

CONTENTS

VI

Remembering to Remember
Photography as Figure of Contemporary Atrocity Memories
171

VII

Remembering to Forget
Contemporary Scrapbooks of Atrocity
202

ACKNOWLEDGMENTS

This was not an easy book to write. The topic captured me somewhat unawares, as I was trying initially to produce a broader investigation of the tension between images and words in news. I clearly remember the point at which I realized that my broader investigation would have to wait, and that I was about to commit myself to a full-scale exploration of the photographic record of the liberation of the Nazi concentration camps. I was ambivalent about my ability to address a topic that was both so appealing and so horrific. This was made no easier by my own proximity to the subject at hand. As a Jew who had lived in Israel for many years, and whose father's extended family near Lodz, Poland, perished during the Holocaust, I was uncertain of my ability to research a topic that resonated for me in such disturbing ways. And although my father is no longer alive to read the fruits of the research that resulted, I remain confident that he somehow knows, or knew, of my gradual gravitation toward this topic.

I was fortunate to have extensive help in launching this project. For technical help, I remain the grateful recipient of a fellowship from The John H. Simon Guggenheim Memorial Foundation, a research fellowship from the Freedom Forum Media Studies Center at Columbia University, and a recipient of a Goldsmith Research Award from the Joan Shorenstein Center on the Press, Politics, and Public Policy at the John F. Kennedy School of Government at Harvard University. Temple University provided me with initial grant money to get the project under way. The Annenberg School for Communication at the University of Pennsylvania offered extensive financial and technical assistance that enabled me to conclude the project with the same degree of enthusiasm with which it was begun. I also thank The Annenberg School for generously assisting in the procurement of photographs and photographic credits.

Numerous people have offered their expertise in reading parts of the manuscript and supporting its evolution. I thank Roger Abrahams, Dan Ben-Amos, Carol and Richard Bernstein, David Cesarani, Richard Clurman, Natalie Zemon Davis, Daniel Dayan, Everett Dennis, Sidra Ezrahi,

Saul Friedlander, Larry Gross, Geoffrey Hartman, Richard Heffner, Nick Hiley, Andreas Huyssen, Kathleen Hall Jamieson, Amy Jordan, Tamar Katriel, Elihu Katz, Volkhard Knigge, Yosefa Loshitzky, Carolyn Marvin, Victor Navasky, Marion Rodgers, Itzhak Roeh, Pamela Sankar, Michael Schudson, Marsha Seifert, Robert Snyder, Sari Thomas, John Tryneski, Lucette Valenci, Liliane Weissberg, and Annette Wieviorka. For technical and research assistance, I thank Terry Anderson, Chanan Beizer, Sharon Black, Debra Conry, Janice Fisher, John Huxford, Daiwon Huyun, Richard Isomaki, Selcan Kaynak, Oren Meyers, and Sharon Muller. I thank the various forums that have invited me to speak on the topic, including Swarthmore College, Loughborough University, University of Colorado at Boulder, Northwestern University, Syracuse University, the Adirondack Work-Study Center, L'Ecole des Hautes Etudes en Sciences Sociales, University of Pennsylvania, Temple University, the Photographic Resource Center at Boston University, University of Maryland, the Shelby Cullom Davis Center for Historical Studies at Princeton University, and Tel Aviv University. I thank my mother, Dorothy Zelizer, and my sister, Judy Shifrin, as well as other members of my extended family for helping to keep me focused. I also thank numerous friends who inevitably popped up when life intervened, as it tends to do when one least expects it. Although I cannot thank them all, they know that this book would not have been completed without their incredible friendship and support through difficult times.

I dedicate this book to my three children—Noa, Jonathan, and Gideon Glick. As always, their presence grounds my academic pursuits in a very real fashion. Their vitality, joy, and hopes for the future justified this project in urgent ways. It is for them and others like them that we must consider the representation of atrocity in its fullest form. And it is for them that we must figure out how to stop Remembering to Forget, so that our representations of atrocity can make a difference for generations to come.

I

Collective Memories, Images, and the Atrocity of War

IN WRITINGS PUBLISHED POSTHUMOUSLY AFTER WORLD War II, the cultural critic Walter Benjamin contended that images of public events merit attention because they offer a compressed moral guide for the future. "Every image of the past that is not recognized by the present as one of its own concerns," he said, "threatens to disappear irretrievably."[1]

This book stems from Benjamin's observation. It begins with a number of questions about visual memory and examines that memory's role in representing one of the most disturbing phenomena of the twentieth century—war atrocity. Through U.S. and British media coverage of the liberation of the World War II Nazi concentration camps, the book considers how haunting visual memories of the Holocaust and war atrocity were produced by the photographic record of the camps' liberation. These memories linger, in scholar Saul Friedlander's words, as an "indelible reference point of the Western imagination."[2]

Yet what kind of reference point did they provide? As we stand at century's end and look back, the visual memories of the Holocaust set in place fifty-odd years ago seem oddly unsatisfying. The mounds of corpses, gaping pits of bodies, and figures angled like matchsticks across the camera's field of vision have paralyzed many of us to the point of critical inattention. But they have provided only a thin veneer of knowledge about the camps and the atrocities that took place inside. How were those first images of the camps produced and presented? By whom and under which circumstances? How were they received and to what effect? And most importantly, when, why, how, and to what purposes were they co-opted into memory? In what ways have they persisted as vehicles of collective memory, both about the Holocaust and about the ravages of war?

Questions like these are worth answering because the images of the concentration camps—called the World War II "atrocity photos" by postwar critics—have become a lasting iconic representation of war atrocity and human evil. But the questions are difficult to answer because they underscore a broader lack in our scholarship on images and image making. We still do not know enough about how images help record public events, about whether and in which ways images function as better vehicles of proof than words, and about which vehicle—word or image- –takes precedence in situations of conflict between what the words tell us and the pictures show us. Moreover, as the technologies for photographic manipulation have changed and public skepticism about photos has grown, the questions themselves have changed too.

We know even less about how images function as vehicles of collective memory. Beyond recognizing that they conveniently freeze scenes in our minds and serve as building blocks to remembering, we do not yet fully understand how images help us remember, particularly in circumstances we did not experience personally. In an age where the media have become ever-present agents of collective remembering, this is no small problem. And it threatens to loom larger as image-making technologies become more sophisticated and diverse over the coming century.

This book addresses the mechanics of visual memory and historical record at their broadest level. Admittedly, studying images and collective memory through the concentration camps' liberation generates its own problems, because it is doubtful whether any change in the record would have affected the atrocities themselves. But the moral questions raised here about an image's viability to prove and disprove the past go beyond the Holocaust, to other cases where images might kindle outrage. Today, atrocities in places like Bosnia and Rwanda readily provoke comparisons with the Holocaust, suggesting that the earlier atrocity photos do more than simply document the Nazis' systematic extermination of the Jews and other persecuted groups. The photos' broad resonance suggests that images have enigmatic boundaries which connect events in unpredictable ways. Like a familiar sequence of musical notes that seems to appear from nowhere, images creatively pop up in ways that challenge what we think we know about the past and how we think we know it. It is with this challenge that *Remembering to Forget* is concerned.

THE SHAPE OF COLLECTIVE REMEMBERING

When cultural critic Susan Sontag recalled seeing the atrocity photos as a young girl, she claimed that experience had divided her life into before and after periods. "When I looked at those photographs," she wrote, "something broke. Some limit had been reached, and not only that of horror; I felt irrevocably grieved, wounded, but a part of my feelings started to tighten; something went dead; something is still crying." This book explores how others, like Sontag, have used the World War II atrocity photos to link past and present. It takes its cue from work on collective memory, which sees memory as a fundamentally social activity, and follows the scholarship of French sociologist Maurice Halbwachs, who argued that memory is accomplished not in one's own gray matter but via a shared consciousness that molds it to the agendas of those invoking it in the present. The book thereby views collective memory as a tool "not of retrieval but of reconfiguration [that] colonizes the past by obliging it to conform to present configurations."[3]

How might work on collective memory shed light on visual memories of the Holocaust? When viewed as a collective activity, memory takes on characteristics that distinguish it from individual remembering. It opens up the terrain that is remembered and turns it into a multiple-sided jigsaw puzzle that links events, issues, or personalities differently for different groups. Unlike personal memory, whose authority fades with time, the authority of collective memories increases as time passes, taking on new complications, nuances, and interests. Collective memories allow for the fabrication, rearrangement, elaboration, and omission of details about the past, often pushing aside accuracy and authenticity so as to accommodate broader issues of identity formation, power and authority, and political affiliation. Memories in this view become not only the simple act of recall but social, cultural, and political action at its broadest level, "not things we think about, but things we think with, [possessing little] existence beyond our politics, our social relations, and our histories." As scholar Geoffrey Hartman has observed, collective memories constitute "a gradually formalized agreement to transmit the meaning of intensely shared events in a way that does not have to be individually struggled for."[4]

Because we do not know enough about the mechanics of collective memories, however, an analysis of the Holocaust's visual memories might prompt us to know more. We know, for instance, that collective memories lack an identifiable beginning and end, are ever changing, and are often accomplished amid the ruins of earlier recollections—as when history books are rewritten or statues of former heroes taken down to accommodate new targets of emulation. Collective memories implicitly value the negation of the act, where forgetting reflects a choice to put aside what no longer matters. We also know that collective memories are unpredictable, often appearing when least expected. Because they are not necessarily stable, linear, rational, or logical, memories take on pieces of the past in unanticipated ways, as when former U.S. president George Bush unexpectedly invoked World War II—not Vietnam—to justify the U.S. involvement in the Persian Gulf in 1991. We know too that collective memories are partial. No single memory reflects all that is known about a given event, personality, or issue. Instead, memories resemble a mosaic, where they generate an authoritative vision in repertoire with other views of the past. For instance, the Yitzhak Rabin assassination in Israel in 1995 produced talk of various U.S. parallels that depended on which aspect of the assassination was being discussed—the Civil War, the American Revolution, the Lincoln assassination, and the Kennedy assassination; while no association comprised the total response to the event, together they made a powerful composite statement about the variegated meaning of Rabin's death.[5]

What else do we know about collective memory? We know that collective memories are usable, facilitating cultural, social, economic, and political connections, establishing social order, and determining belonging, exclusivity, solidarity, and continuity. Decorating housefronts for Halloween, displaying wedding rings, and wearing red ribbons on National AIDS Day all signal community membership for certain persons and community exclusion for others. Collective memories are also both particular and universal. A memory can invoke a particular representation of the past for some while taking on a universal significance for others: the word *Auschwitz* has certain meanings for Holocaust survivors' children that are not necessarily shared by contemporary genocide scholars. This follows from the rather basic fact that everyone participates in the production of memory, though not equally. As Iwona Irwin-Zarecka has observed, the term *collective* suggests an ideal rather than a given.[6]

We also know that collective memories are material. They have texture, existing in the world rather than in a person's head. We find memories in objects, narratives about the past, even the routines by which we structure our day. No memory is fully embodied in any of these cultural forms, but instead bounces to and fro among all of them on its way to gaining meaning. Memory's materiality is important, for it helps offset the fluctuations that characterize remembering. And finally, we know that collective memories are plural. Dependent on interpretive groups called "memory communities" to gain meaning, memory "depends for its existence on the social codes that prevail in a group, a time, or place." Individuals might thereby share memories of the past with certain persons with whom they share ethnicity, with yet others via a shared age bracket, and with still others through a common nationality. Certain vehicles of memory help communities address significant collective agendas more effectively than others, and which vehicle "we resort to to represent our witness of the times, depends on who we are, and what we need to know, which facts we wish to verify, and which to obscure."[7]

Around each of these axes for remembering, collective memories

"vibrate." Dissipating the notion that one memory at one place and one time retains authority over all the others, collective-memory studies presume multiple, often conflicting accounts of the past. The important issue becomes "not how accurately a recollection fitted some piece of a past reality, but why historical actors constructed their memories in a particular way at a particular time." Recognizing conflicting renditions of the past necessitates a consideration of the tensions and contestations through which one rendition wipes out many of the others. Memories become not only the construction of social, historical, and cultural circumstances, but a reflection of why one construction has more staying power than its rivals. The study of collective memories thereby represents a graphing of the past as it is woven into the present and future.[8]

Despite its popularity, however, the study of collective memories has been plagued by a broad range of unaddressed issues. Some have had to do with memory itself: Which memory? What kind of memory? How complete or authentic a memory? Others have focused on the activity of remembering: Who remembers? Why do we remember, how, and with what resources? For whom is remembering being accomplished? And others have targeted the status of remembering: How does the power of memory persist over time? How does it act as evidence for things and events of the past? How does it prove or disprove remembered events? And is the issue of proof more or less relevant as time passes?

IMAGES IN COLLECTIVE MEMORY

Much of our ability to remember depends on images. Hailed in classical Rome as a mnemonic device for personal remembering, the images of social memory borrow from a broad tradition of pictorial depiction that used painting, photography, and ideographic systems of communication to make its messages public.

How images work depends largely on their complex linkage with words. In W. J. T. Mitchell's view, words and images offer not only two different kinds of representation but "two deeply contested cultural values." As modes of representation change, both the relationship between words and images changes as well as how we understand images and words independently of each other. Images have in part always depended on words for directed interpretation. William Saroyan comments that "one picture is worth a thousand words but only if you look at the picture and say or think the thousand words"; the image "invites the written information which alone can specify its relation to localities, time, individual identity, and the other categories of human understanding." This dependence on words is enhanced and magnified in memory, where words provide order and connection. But pictures also function differently from words; consider the rush of emotions driven by Picasso's famous painting, *Guernica*. In dealing with the most realistic image—the photograph—this has particular importance. For there, the visual, aligned with the camera, produces a powerful interpretive tool that derives strength from both its mechanical aura and the verisimilitude that it conveys.[9]

The link between words and images becomes even more complex in memory. While words function much like the "index cards" of shared memory, with phrases from the Gettysburg Address, jingles on advertisements, and opening statements in memorable court cases cluttering our memory banks, images depend on their material form when operating as vehicles of memory. Our ability to remember the past is facilitated by photographs, paintings, and snippets of films that are readily available in the public sphere. A 1963 image of a dazed and newly widowed Jacqueline Kennedy, staring into space as Lyndon Baines Johnson was sworn in as the next president, is seen nearly thirty-five years later in multiple contexts—a New York City exhibit on memorable news photographs, a Dallas museum commemorating the slain president, and malls across the United States featuring Andy Warhol's version of the image.[10] Visual memory's texture becomes a facilitator for memory's endurance.

Thus, materiality renders visual memory different from other kinds of remembering. Images help stabilize and anchor collective memory's transient and fluctuating nature in art, cinema, television, and photography, aiding recall to the extent that images often become an event's primary markers. In George Washington's crossing of the Delaware River, the raising of the flag on Iwo Jima, and the Kennedy assassination, one specific image of the event has come to symbolize its broader recollection.[11]

Yet difficulties arise when using images to collectively shape the past. Images, particularly photographs, do not make obvious how they construct what we see and remember. Often, they arbitrarily connect with the object or event being remembered. As scholars James Fentress and Chris Wickham have noted, the "relation between a remembered image and the meaning or event to which this image supposedly refers is inherently arbitrary; yet nothing in the nature of the remembered images themselves gives this away." Moreover, the images of collective memories are composites, constructed "from a mixture of pictorial images and scenes, slogans, quips, and snatches of verse, abstractions, plot types and stretches of discourse, and even false etymologies." Even the frame of the depicted image hides its own constructed nature; in one British study of the 1970s, the aggressive aura of antiwar protesters increased as a photograph of the demonstration was cropped more closely. Electronic image tampering also shows the ease with which composite images can be made to appear natural. In today's mediated age it is easy to disembody images in ways not made apparent to audiences.[12]

The images of collective memories are also both conventional and simple—in Fentress and Wickham's view, "conventionalized, because the image has to be meaningful for an entire group; simplified, because in order to be generally meaningful and capable of transmission, the complexity of the image must be reduced as far as possible." Photos in the *National Geographic* fastened Third World peoples over the past century in a primitive stage of development that overstated their exotic nature and understated their poverty, hunger, sickness, and oppression. *Life's* depictions of the American family of the fifties offered cozy, two-parent, suburban anchors who constrained the instability of social and cultural life. The impulses toward conventionalization and simplification often render resulting memories trite and overplayed. Pictures of war, for instance, often go no further than shots of anonymous heroism, as Paul Fussell has shown. Yet paradoxically, this thrust helps make images one of memory's most effective carriers.[13]

Finally, images of collective memories are schematic, lacking the detail of personal memory's images. Few of us remember the name of the South Vietnamese village where children ran screaming from their napalmed homes into a photographer's field of vision. Nor do many of us remember the date or circumstances under which the photograph was taken.[14] But its resonance as an image of war atrocity—and invocation by U.S. antiwar groups during the sixties and seventies—stabilized its meaning precisely along its more schematic dimensions. Collectively held images thus act as signposts, directing people who remember to preferred meaning by the fastest route.

Each feature of collective visual remembering depends not only on an image's strategic relay but also on its storage, and it is here that the media are key. In events as wide-ranging as the *Hindenburg* explosion, the *Challenger* disaster, and the O. J. Simpson car chase, our ability to collectively remember through images depends on a recognized means of storage that allows us to appropriate images with others. Today's capacity to freeze, replay, and store visual memories for large numbers of people—facilitated by museums, art galleries, television archives, and other visual data banks—has thus enhanced our ability to make the past work for present aims.

Discussions of visual memories thereby become at some level discussions of cultural practice—of the strategies by which images are made and collected, retained and stored, recycled and forgotten. By definition this connects visual memories with a culture's socially, politically, and economically mandated and sanctioned modes of interpretation, with how certain uses of images are set in place, challenged, and legitimated. With photography this is crucial, for it turns the mechanical process of registering light on paper into a cultural representation of events beyond our grasp. Photographs turn somewhat magically into iconic representations that stand for a system of beliefs, a theme, an epoch. As photography critic Vicki Goldberg observed,

> Although photographs easily acquire symbolic importance, they are not merely symbolic. . . . for photographs intensely and specifically represent their subjects. The images [that are] iconic almost instantly acquire symbolic overtones and larger frames of reference that endow them with national or worldwide significance. They concentrate the hopes and fears of millions and provide an instant and effortless connection to some deeply meaningful moment in history.[15]

Acting as "remnants of light captured from another time," photographs tell "us not only about what the world looks like, but also something of what it means." We can thereby link a photo of a Buddhist monk's self-immolation with antiwar movements or recognize a shot of a just-freed African-American rapist as sufficient evidence for legal reform. As Hans Kellner has contended, "even when memorials take the form of photographs or museum objects, their sense will depend upon a discourse that articulates them."[16] The compelling weight of the photograph, then, is determined by a linkage between its material and discursive dimensions, and the power created by that linkage draws us to a photo's many meanings, both now and then.

NEWS IMAGES AS VEHICLES OF MEMORY: TRUTH-VALUE VERSUS SYMBOLISM

Photos of the liberation of the Nazi concentration camps appeared primarily in the news, and their role as memory carriers is made interesting by photography's contested status in journalism. Although images have been incorporated in news since the inception of journalism, they have long been regarded as secondary to and supportive of the accompanying words.[17] That regard has conflated what were essentially two sources of the photograph's power—its truth-value and its symbolic force:

> [There are] two levels of belief in a news photograph. One is a confidence that what is depicted was not staged but actually occurred and that the depiction has not been tampered with. . . . The second level of belief is acceptance of the interpretation the culture places

on the photograph, the meaning that adheres to an image within a particular society at a particular time.[18]

The recognition of the photo's truth-value was of greater service to journalism than was its symbolic power, for truth served journalism's own aspirations for objectivity. As Walter Lippmann said in 1922:

> Photographs have the kind of authority over imagination today, which the printed word had yesterday, and the spoken word before that. They seem utterly real. They come, we imagine, directly to us, without human meddling, and they are the most effortless food for the mind conceivable. . . . The whole process of observing, describing, repeating, and then imagining has been accomplished.

From the mid-1800s onward, the photograph's technical and mimetic qualities established it as a successful tool for gathering empirical evidence. Photography became lodged in the imagination as a vessel of accuracy, authenticity, verisimilitude, and truth. It came to be seen as realistic and objective, a support for

> the written stories derived from the kind of proof it is supposed to offer—the proof of 'being there.' This is invested with the sanctity of truth value. . . . The idealized version of the photojournalist is someone who stands outside the event—a neutral eye.

Thus photographic realism helped journalism prove and establish its own on-site presence by grounding the assumption that photographs captured the scene as it was. It conveyed the experience of having-been-there to the entire newsmaking apparatus.[19]

A second dimension of the photographic image has helped legitimate news photos. While photography ascended in journalistic importance primarily because "seeing is believing," the image also derived power from the interpretive and symbolic dimensions surrounding that act of seeing. The photo's significance here evolved from the ability not only to depict a real-life event but to position that depiction within a broader interpretive framework. Invoking issues like scale, scope, and magnitude, photography's symbolic dimension gave the news image context because its interpretation was "malleable [and] rearranged by information, belief, even wishful thinking . . . [leaving] the viewer outside the frame of the photograph but inside the frame of its meaning."[20]

How does the news photo's dual function figure into memory? As Alan Trachtenberg has observed, all photographs of the past pose a "double question of comprehension: how were they understood at the time and how should they be understood today?" In analyzing photos, we must thus ask, not

> What do these photographs authenticate? but: How were they artic-
> ulated in and how did they articulate an argument? Whose was this
> argument? How was it validated? Who spoke it? To whom? Under
> what conditions? To what ends? With what effects?[21]

As tools of memory, then, news photos need to be considered as mark-ers of both truth-value and symbolism. They need to be examined both for their denotative or referential qualities and for the broader set of features through which that referentiality is made meaningful. An analysis of atroc-ity photos becomes not just a graphing of what was seen, but a considera-tion of how and why, and in what ways it has been remembered.

USING PHOTOGRAPHY TO BEAR WITNESS TO WAR ATROCITY

Perhaps at no other time is humankind as in need of integration and reas-surance as during war, and war atrocity places publics in particular need of reassurance. Atrocities are so named because they challenge standards of decent and civilized behavior, violating expectations of what falls within the purview of so-called appropriate war practices. Because they challenge assumptions of appropriate behavior, issues of proof almost always accom-pany their articulation. Furthermore, when atrocities are directed against civilians, the discussion of standards of behavior tends to intensify. It is thereby no surprise that twentieth-century Western accounts of atrocity have evolved in conjunction with broader notions about truth telling, mak-ing the act of testifying against atrocities one of the paramount political acts of this century.

Photographs are of particular importance here, for the act of giving tes-timony against atrocity tends to go beyond the mere authentication of hor-ror and to imply the act of bearing witness, by which we assume responsi-bility for the events of our times—"not merely to narrate but to commit oneself. . . . to take responsibility for history or for the truth of an occur-rence." Bearing witness constitutes a specific form of collective remember-ing that interprets an event as significant and deserving of critical attention. It suggests assuming responsibility for the events, which are often perceived as "aberrations or ruptures in the cultural continuum—[that] demand retelling." In a sense, then, bearing witness calls for truth telling at the same time as it sanctions an interpretation of what is being witnessed. Bearing witness implies that there is no best way of depicting or thinking about atrocities, but that the very fact of paying heed collectively is crucial.[22]

Bearing witness calls for a specific use of photographic images. And indeed, although people have borne witness to atrocity for as long as wars have been waged, bearing witness has changed with technology. In his analysis of Holocaust literature, for instance, James Young demonstrated that witnessing became a critical attribute of prose:

> the more realistic a representation, the more adequate it becomes as testimonial evidence of outrageous events. . . . the closer writers came to the ghettoes and death camps, the more likely they were to redefine their aesthetic mission as one of testifying to the crimes against them and their people.

Images have also been particularly instrumental in shaping the act of bearing witness, for, in Julia Kristeva's words, the "art of the image excels in the crude exposure of monstrosity." The mission today is "no longer to bear witness to inadequately known events but rather to keep them before our eyes. Testimony is to be a means of transmission to future generations."[23]

But images can come into play only at a certain point in the evolution of assumptions about atrocity. While photos are important tools for constructing moral consensus, particularly about events newly named or classified in public discourse, they tend not to be displayed until the cultures and nations involved are prepared to call the atrocities by name. As Susan Sontag has remarked:

> A photograph that brings news of some unexpected zone of misery cannot make a dent in public opinion unless there is an appropriate context of feeling and attitude. . . . Photographs cannot create a moral position. But they can reinforce one—and can help build a nascent one. . . . The contribution of photography always follows the naming of the event.[24]

Indeed, the photographic record produced at the time of the concentration camps' liberation depended on larger impulses to call the atrocities by name, and its appearance was first of all a mechanism of governmental persuasion. As with other events of World War II, photographs were used as propaganda tools for both the Allied and Axis sides, providing stereotypical representations and "restricting the memory of war to a few recurring themes."[25] Yet unlike the case with other events of World War II, propaganda was accomplished not through a small and selective filter of atrocity images but through a seemingly endless display of photographic shots of the camps. The record of the camps' liberation was mandated to be seen. Over a three-week period in April and May 1945, photographs—produced to convince a disbelieving public that what the liberating forces were seeing was real—were splashed in prodigious numbers across the pages of the daily and weekly press in the United States and Britain. They were displayed to such a degree that many observers held them responsible for shocking both nations out of their skepticism and processing the unbelievable atrocity story into plausible interpretive schema.

But the atrocity photos were important for the media as well, for they signaled significant changes in the status of news photography. As one Holocaust scholar told it, "the significance of the Holocaust is that it not only confronted humanity with a previously inconceivable horror, it also marked the beginning of documenting that horror." The images' display was so unusual that it required a lifting of censorship restrictions, changed expectations about how photography was thought to function in news, and facilitated the photographic depiction of atrocity. Unlike other events of the war, it also played to the skills of nonprofessional photographers. As one scholar noted, "with Holocaust photography, a new dimension is added to the history of [war photography]. We have thousands upon thousands of non-combat photos taken by non-professional picture-takers." The atrocities thus offered a somewhat modified free-for-all, in which newspapers, journals, and magazines used photos with considerable liberties, sanctioned by military and political leaders and unmatched in other events of the war. The liberation of the camps can therefore be looked at as a critical incident in the tentative but evolving status of news photography. It offered a forum for words and images to compete and images to emerge triumphant. Though not the only event to do so, the atrocities helped facilitate modern photojournalism's coming of age.[26]

It is no surprise, then, that nearly all of us share some memory of the atrocity photos of World War II. In the years since the camps' liberation, the atrocity photos have undergone strategic recycling, and the photographs that appeared on the camps' liberation have reappeared over the past half-century in history textbooks, commemorative journals, and documentary films. These memory practices make clear that those of us who did not experience the Holocaust personally now know it in part through its photographs. In her 1993 review of the movie *Schindler's List*, *New York Times* film critic Janet Maslin anchored her discussion of the film to the status of Holocaust photographs. She began by telling the story of a steel tin of photos that had been buried secretly in a park outside Vienna and unearthed decades later. The "real photographic record," she argued, provided the basis for the Steven Spielberg film, allowing him to present "the subject as if discovering it anew." In that tension—between the familiar and the rediscovered—the "Holocaust threatens to become unimaginable because it has been imagined so fully."[27] It is there that the power of the photograph as a vessel of memory resides. A powerful building block to the past that connects the unimaginable with the imagined, photographs permeate nearly every recollection of the Holocaust, often to the extent that they have become entwined in our capacity to remember.

As befits the workings of collective memory, however, the atrocity photos of World War II have not only helped us remember the Holocaust. For bearing witness, as a type of collective remembering, goes beyond the events it depicts, positioning the atrocity photos as a frame for understanding contemporary instances of atrocity. When viewing extensive pictorial spreads, photographic supplements, and special photographic exhibits about the atrocities of Rwanda or Bosnia, we often use our memories of World War II atrocities as a backdrop or context against which to appropriate these more contemporaneous instances of barbarism.

This raises moral questions of no small significance. How have these earlier images changed the way in which we "see" each new instance of politically sanctioned death and slaughter? How have they altered the act of bearing witness in the contemporary age? In connecting the atrocity photos to events as wide-ranging as contemporary barbarism, AIDS, urban poverty, and political suppression we may have forgotten how to navigate the terrain that connects them with real action. It may be that we have learned to use our Holocaust memories so as to neglect our response to the atrocities of here and now. As Leon Wieseltier recently noted in the *New Republic:* "In the contemplation of the death camps, we must be strangers; and if we are not strangers, if the names of the killers and the places of the killing and the numbers of the killed fall easily from our tongues, then we are not remembering to remember, but remembering to forget."[28] Paradoxically, then, it may be that Holocaust photos have helped us remember the Holocaust so as to forget contemporary atrocity.

ORGANIZATION OF THE BOOK

This book tackles the issue of memory and atrocity by examining the visual representation of one specific historical incident—the liberation of the concentration camps of the Western front of World War II. It argues that photographs became the main event of the journalistic record for one of the few times in the history of the daily and weekly press in the United States and Britain, and that these photographic images created collective memories about atrocity of such impact that they may be neutralizing our ability to attend to contemporary atrocities.

The early part of the book focuses on how the U.S. and British media covered and documented the liberation of the camps on the Western front. Plumbing the archives of both the popular and professional trade press, chapter 2 traces the unclear and ambivalent relationship between photographers and journalists on both continents. At the time the Allies entered the camps there were few photographic standards of practice regarding attribution, credits, captions, and other identifying information. Equally important, the youth of photojournalism as a field—and the antagonism showed it by reporters—created a fundamental uncertainty about the specific roles words and images should play in reporting.

Chapters 3 and 4 analyze the actual record of the atrocities as conveyed through the verbal and visual accounts of the liberation of Buchenwald, Dachau, and Bergen-Belsen. Having downplayed earlier rumors of atrocities due to a lack of corroboration and the sheer unbelievability of the stories, reporters now faced the seemingly impossible task of conveying the unbelievable in a situation where the normal standards for news gathering—confirming stories, providing background details for sources, locating sources of high rank—were generally unavailable. Journalists compensated by framing their stories as eyewitness accounts of the liberation, trying to concretize the details of Nazi atrocities yet constantly noting that "words cannot describe them."

More powerfully than the initial narratives describing the camps, the flood of photographs that soon followed helped turn collective disbelief into the horror of recognition. One did not need to be at the camps; the power of the image made everyone who saw the photos into a witness. At the same time, though, photographs were presented with few identifying characteristics, such as place, date, and relationship to the texts accompanying them. The images took on a universal, symbolic quality with captions that told of generalized phenomena rather than of specific events—*a* mass burial, *a* shower, *a* survivor. Images succeeded where words did not, confirming the atrocities at the most generalized level.

Chapters 5 and 6 address the patterns by which the atrocity photos were recycled and made part of Holocaust memory. There were three waves of memory in which the salience of the atrocities rose and fell in the public imagination. First was an initial period of high attention that persisted until the end of the 1940s; then a period of relative amnesia that lingered until the 1970s; and finally a renewed period of intensive memory work that began in the late 1970s and continues until today. Each wave produced its own mode of bearing witness to the atrocities that was linked to certain atrocity images.

The book's final chapter explores the broader implications of relying on images to remember and understand war atrocity from World War II to the present day. Stock images of Nazi atrocities—the neat rows of bodies, the haunted faces behind barbed wires—are echoed in the photos taken in

Bosnia, Rwanda, and Cambodia; Nazi atrocity photos are often run side by side with depictions of more recent horror. This recycling of photos from the past not only dulls our response to them but potentially undermines the immediacy and depth of our response to contemporary instances of brutality, discounting them as somehow already known to us.

No other instance of atrocity has been depicted in as full and wide-ranging a fashion as the brutality of World War II. That circumstance alone should make us pause—not only for what it suggests about the Holocaust but for what it also suggests about contemporary atrocity in the public imagination. Walter Benjamin was prescient when he remarked that

> the past can be seized only as an image which flashes up at the instant when it can be recognized and is never seen again. To articulate the past historically does not mean to recognize it. . . . It means to seize hold of memory as it flashes up at a moment of danger.[29]

The atrocities of World War II provided one such moment, and atrocity's recurrence in the contemporary age bears testament to the importance of examining their depiction in memory.

Before the Liberation

Journalism, Photography, and the

Early Coverage of Atrocity

THE NAZI ATROCITIES FORCED THE U.S. AND BRITISH media to rise to the challenge of documenting what they saw when the concentration camps of Nazi Europe were liberated in the spring of 1945. Few knew, however, how to cover the horror that emerged, raising questions about accommodating in coverage the strengths and limitations of two representational codes—words and images.

While the war had catalyzed reporters' acceptance of photographers and enhanced the need for photographic documentation, the camps' liberation brought reporters and photographers face to face over a story with no parallel or precedent in contemporary media history. In both form and content, the atrocities crystallized professional tensions surrounding the legitimation of news photographs. Not only did the scenes of the camps' opening stretch the limits of the imagination. But standards for depicting atrocity left over from previous wars now needed to be reworked so as to recount the horror in a plausible fashion. The fact that early hints of the atrocities had failed to compel belief about what was happening made this more difficult.

ISSUES OF FORM:
A LEGACY OF ANTAGONISM BETWEEN
JOURNALISTS AND PHOTOGRAPHERS

Journalists and photographers approached the liberation of the camps in World War II through a legacy of professional antagonism. Such a legacy, tangible during the thirties, was brought to a head by the war.[1]

The thirties had promised different things to journalists and photographers. While the decade's early years should have ensured professional advancement, with the depression giving reportage—in word, image, or both—the aura of an essential social duty, in fact different kinds of media workers were pitted against each other. As one wire-editor opined in 1932, "to dig themselves out of depression, people must think and they cannot think unless they are reliably informed."[2] Yet who was to give the public its most reliable information for thinking—photographers or reporters? Which tool—photographs or words—was better suited to achieve that aim? And if both modes of documentation were to play a role, then how were they to work together?

Although attempts had been made since photography's invention to include images in news, journalists and photographers had not yet established a tradition of full professional cooperation. As late as the 1940s, photographs—still derisively labeled the work of "newspaper illustrators" or "pictorial reporters"—remained a source of conflict for editors in the United States and Britain. Conflict derived in part from the different professional stature experienced by journalists and photographers. On the one hand, journalists—criticized in the United States for belittling evidence of the depression and for experimenting with tabloidlike journalism and excessive commercialism, and critiqued in Britain for pandering to caution once the war mandated "fighting journalism"—were suffering a "loss of momentum" and decline in public credibility. U.S. public-opinion polls reported that at least one in three persons did not believe what they read in the daily and weekly press, while British journalists were demoralized by numerous merging and folding news organizations. On the other hand, photographers were experiencing a surge in popularity. Strides in documentary photography, such as those associated with the U.S. Farm Security Administration, and photography's co-optation in films and newsreels, in novels such as Christopher Isherwood's *I Am a Camera* and in the "Camera Eye" sections of John Dos Passos's *U.S.A.* trilogy, and in the tabloid press, piqued popular interest in a visual culture and showed it was possible to use images for important social aims. The popular picture-magazines of *Picture Post, Look,* and *Life* (and the shorter-lived *Click, Focus, Mid-Week Pictorial, Picture,* and *See*) proved that images could depict daily life differently from the accounting of verbal narrative. By the decade's end, much of the public on both continents saw images as an accessible and trustworthy alternative to words.[3]

Changes in technology necessitated a certain degree of cooperation between journalists and photographers, when long-range airplanes, extensive and faster wire connections, additional news bureaus, faster film, smaller cameras, the flashbulb, and better lenses all made it easier to use images in news. In particular, wirephoto's arrival in 1935 made it possible to transmit images as quickly as words. But as the thirties gave way to the forties, journalists had not yet recognized photographers as full newsmaking partners, nor were photographers looking with great interest at journalism. In fact, it would take a full decade before press photographers would be called anything but "journalism's poor relation."[4] Only as the war turned the world into one great battlefield and the potential surrounding photographic documentation became clearer did newspapers, magazines, and journals provide a more hospitable home for pictures.

Journalists on Photography

What did U.S. and British journalists think about photography on the eve of World War II? Journalists were generally ambivalent, both needing and resenting photography, and this was reflected in a series of uneven practices for using photos that they employed throughout the war.

On the one hand, the photo's use in the daily and weekly press was on the rise in both continents. By the beginning of the 1940s photographs had become an increasingly frequent feature of the press, with U.S. dailies reporting an increase of nearly 40 percent in the use of photographic cuts. Newsmagazines such as *Time* and *Newsweek* began to highlight photographs regularly alongside compartmentalized texts, and by 1937 leading news editors were requesting picture files for their archives. Photographic services expanded, adding new beats, photographers, and bureaus, while news organizations opened subsidiary photographic agencies, such as World Wide Photos, ACME Newspictures, United News Pictures, and International News Photos. Trade forums on both continents debated photographers' membership in professional associations and photojournalism's introduction into journalism schools.[5]

Yet the rising use did not enhance journalists' comfort with photography, and their discourse revealed considerable ambivalence about the idea of photographic representation in news. Many journalists feared that the image's power might circumvent that of the word. They knew that the photograph could bolster verbal narratives, but they perceived it as the unwanted intrusion of an additional language that might take the word's place. Many voiced a professional resistance that denied photography an autonomous status and recognized it primarily in ways that upheld the supremacy of the word.

Resistance had many forms. Photographs were sometimes codified as a problem, photojournalism "a mechanical side-line to the serious business of fact-narration—a social inferior." The few reporters who advocated using photos were treated derisively, and their discussion at professional meetings met with protest. "Too great an emphasis on pictures . . . might pull down the dignity of the press," one editor told an applauding convention of the Associated Press's Managing Editors Association in 1935. It is "one thing for a cameraman to take a photo," observed a photographer watching the proceedings, "but another for the publication of it."[6]

Photography was sometimes denounced outright, due to both the cost and the quality of its resulting images. Wirephotos in particular had no "recognizable features," lamented one editor. Most "would have been discarded without a second glance had they come by mail," said another, adding ironically that "the paper could have used the captions and pictures interchangeably throughout these months with no one the wiser." Editors were sometimes bothered by the photograph's broader popularity, castigating the picture-magazine for taking mankind "well on the way backward to a language of pictures . . . to the Stone Age of human intelligence."[7]

Photographers were a frequent source of additional discontent. One British reporter likened photographers to machine typesetters and scoffed that photography involved no act of creation. "I am not prepared to receive [photographers] as journalistic colleagues," he declared. Their "work is important and valuable but it is *not* journalism." In 1935, one British trade forum—the Institute of Journalists—debated the admission of photographers, but readers of the institute's main organ, the *Journal,* immediately tore the idea to shreds, arguing, under titles like "Two Different Professions" and "Not Journalists," that the press photographer's admission into journalistic organizations was "indefensible."[8]

Some journalists resisted news photography by claiming for themselves the role of taking pictures. They favored a disembodied photography—photography without the photographer. Professional committees set up to address news photography included no photographer, while editors, hoping to make photography yet another reportorial skill, set up courses to train reporters in photography and instructed reporters to carry cameras. The "day is coming," predicted one observer, "when a reporter who can't operate a camera will be as helpless as one who can't use a pencil." Yet as time passed, the plan lost enthusiasm. Editors began to instruct reporters to take three shots of every object of coverage in hopes that one would produce a good photo. Not surprisingly, photographers protested proposals to arm reporters with cameras, claiming that they would lead to the staff photographer's extinction. But the idea was dismissed for more pragmatic reasons, once reporters produced shots of "headless men, chinless women, and tipsy buildings"; certain cameras were even discarded because they proved too complicated for reporters to handle.[9]

In resisting photography, most journalists took the role of pragmatists who turned the growing presence of photographs and photographers to their own advantage. For instance, members of the American Society for Newspaper Editors discussed photography's growing presence in three separate annual meetings—in 1935, 1938, and 1941: in the first, they decried the news image, but by the last they saw it as a necessary evil that would benefit journalism by being positioned secondary to words. As one photographer complained:

> newspapers generally are not giving enough thought to pictures. . . . I think that is largely due to the fact that the average publisher or editor has accepted the fact that pictures today are a necessary evil, the studio is a necessary evil, the photographers are a necessary evil. He has accepted it and he says, "well, all right, the general public wants pictures and we will give them pictures" and he is giving them pictures today, granted, but without regard to how they are being printed.[10]

For most journalists, photography was constructed as a medium of record, viewed as a medium not of symbolism, interpretation, generalizability, and universality but of denotation, recording, indexicality, and referentiality—the ability of photographs to "tell things as they are." "We tell our photographers," said one editor, "that what we want is realism," a photography that is "hard, cold, exact, detached, and sometimes cruel." Photography offered "a new instrument . . . for factual reporting," an "adjunct of the daily news" that would help journalists report the news better. Even the ascendance of *Life* was seen fleetingly as an opportunity to uphold the image's referential or denotative power, its editors claiming that the magazine would operate "on the journalistic principle of *reporting objectively* the folk and folkways of the world—in pictures" (emphasis added). The emphasis here on referentiality was important, for it allowed journalists to sidestep ambivalence about photography while using it to credential their own discussions of the "real world." In effect, they found solace in the assumption that images would continue to need journalists' intervention to make sense.[11] And such sentiments would persist throughout the war.

Recognition of photography by journalists, then, was weak-hearted. Those journalists who did recognize photography played primarily to its referential or denotative qualities and ability to reference reality. If photography were to be a part of news, these journalists reasoned, it should offer a visual expansion of journalistic practice that could extend the adage "the camera does not lie" to the larger journalistic community. Regardless of whether or not this view encompassed all that photography could offer journalism, defining it so made sense to journalists. Referentiality thus became the dominant frame through which modern photography was consolidated as part of the daily and weekly press in Britain and the United States. Photography was seen as a medium of record not only because such a view emphasized what was most salient about the image but also because it helped journalists bolster their own authority in telling stories of the "real world."

Photographers on Journalism

Journalists' limited welcome of photography was supported by photographers' own ambivalence about making inroads in news. Photographers and photographic trade journals at first ignored the camera's journalistic potential altogether. In 1939, the author of one U.S. photography textbook lamented that his own colleagues had said "little or nothing . . . in favor of press photographers." Characterizing news photography as a "passing phase," trade journals published only one or two articles a year on news photos, advertisements remained unconnected to current events, and even the most compelling news story—the war—failed to draw interest. One 1941 U.S. trade advertisement entitled "Why Join?" referred not to the military but to a camera club; similarly, a March 1939 British article entitled "With a Camera in Spain" addressed not the Spanish war but tourist photography of Toledo and Madrid.[12]

As World War II expanded, however, photographers found they had no choice but to consider documenting its battlefields. In 1941 trade journals on both continents began to address news photography and widespread military call-ups by 1942 forced attention, although the war's proximity to Britain had an urgency missing in the United States. Feature articles began addressing wartime photography, the logistics of shooting military pictures, censorship regulations, and wartime press credentials; advertisements for photographic equipment promoted equipment that could produce good wartime shots; and photographic materials were adapted to wartime use, such as washing camera papers in sea water. Civilian newspapers began training military photographers, and *Life* magazine formed its own school for army photographers. As the president of the Royal Photographic Society of Great Britain said in 1943, "the value of photography is at last being recognized as an asset of the greatest importance in our modern life, but it has taken a war to bring about this recognition."[13]

As the war broadened in scope and generated interest in photography, it did so by playing primarily to notions of photographic realism. News photography was expected to remain "scrupulously honest," "accurate," and "as dependable as are the laws of chemistry and physics upon which it is based," photographers as "efficient with their machine as the sharpshooter with his rifle." This meant that the photograph's referential dimension— earlier emphasized by journalists for their own reasons—now became a part of linking news to the war and propaganda effort. "Seeing is believing, but its truth cannot be more clearly demonstrated than by the newspicture," one early article had said in *Photo-Era Magazine,* and as the war effort increased, this became more rather than less the case.[14]

The Playing Field of War

Documenting World War II offered a way for journalists and photographers to test their coexistence. Broader goals about helping the war effort forced a degree of cooperation, and the different vehicles for communicating information—photographs, radio broadcasts, and newspaper articles—helped produce complementary coverage rather than competition. Scoops were infrequent, and even those who wanted to deviate found that structural arrangements, such as photographic or journalistic pools and censorship, facilitated cooperation.[15]

Journalists and photographers experienced the opportunities for coverage differently. Although both comprised one of the most widespread press corps in contemporary history, spread over five continents, coverage was hindered by censorship and unprecedented problems of manpower, expense, transport, logistics, and communication. In the United States uneven attempts were made to balance propaganda with the flow of information about a geographically distant war. Members of the British press, closer to the war than their U.S. colleagues, faced considerable constraints, with more than a third of British journalists enlisted by 1944 and only skeletal journalistic staffs operating. Paper shortages reduced the size of British newspapers, and reporters learned to write more tersely.[16]

For photographers in both countries the logistics for photography were unusually difficult. Here, the U.S. photographers fared better than their British counterparts. Drawn from various quarters—photojournalists, photographers with the U.S. Signal Corps, adjuncts to military units, and representatives to service organizations like the Surgeon-General's Office and the American Field Service—they were organized into a still-picture pool that circulated both civilian and professional photos and made picture-scoops obsolete. By 1942, nearly every U.S. fighting unit on land, sea, and air had its own photographic team, soon earning nearly every photographer in the war zone the designation of "War Department Photographer." Many soldiers carried their own cameras, and by 1944 the Signal Corps shot 50 percent of all still images published in U.S. newspapers, books, and journals.[17]

In contrast, the British armed forces initially had few photographers among their ranks. Photography was complicated by the need for special permits, limitations on accreditation, an inability to reach the front lines, and what observers called "severe censorship." Although British photographers were accredited both to the War Office and to a small British Pool of Photographic Services, few allowances were made for roving photographers, and the British picture pool proved cumbersome. Photos required approval by representatives of the armed services, the government, and the Ministry of Information, all of which created long delays in publication. As one photographer later told it, the military "wanted soldiers to be trained as cameramen rather than cameramen to be in combat." These circumstances prompted complaints that the majority of British photos were thrown out by the War Office, and as late as April 1945, 90 percent of all British photographs still depicted U.S. soldiers in action, not Britons. British photography continued to be called "sloppy and amateurish."[18]

Yet photography in both countries had its payoffs, as photographs increasingly became harnessed to the war machine. As photographer Margaret Bourke-White later said, recording the war was a "twilight of the gods. No time to think about it or interpret it. Just rush to photograph it, write it, cable it. Record it now, think about it later. History will form the judgments." By D-Day, the U.S. armed forces was lauded for being picture conscious, and by April 1945, fifty-five thousand still photos had been taken on the European front. One observer happily declared that "ranking officers have conceded that news photographs are of great importance." World War II in effect offered a forum for consolidating the importance of photographs, constituting "not only the most photographed war in history but the best photographed."[19]

All of this had immediate effect on the professional forums on the home front. More newspapers developed pictorial pages to accommodate the steady flow of images, and pictorial supplements, beaming the news that photos could be transmitted from London to Washington in only seven minutes, sold widely at newsstands. In 1942, the term *photojournalism* was coined for one U.S. university's sequence of journalistic training, and other universities set up training sequences and special photojournalism seminars. The following year, the British Newspaper Society and the Institute of Journalists agreed to recognize photographers as journalists. By late 1944, the Photographic Society of America opened its first Press Division; one year later U.S. photographers formed their first association of photojournalists—the National Press Photographers' Association, duly labeled an organization of "reporters with cameras." By the war's end, then, photography emerged as a more integral tool of daily and weekly news. Photography developed into a profession of recognized stature, with the news photographer—at least in some views—having earned a status equal to that of any reporter.[20]

Yet problems with incorporating photographs in news lingered. As late as the end of the forties, photographers still claimed that they comprised "forgotten men" no better than the "doormat of journalism," and they complained that editors continued to pay lip service to pictures, regarding them as "fillers and story illustrations but not as a principal method of telling the news." Bitter that not all newspapers were developing photographic facilities, photographers questioned why they were still not classified as "newspaper men." Why, asked one photographer resentfully, did a difference persist between "the men who report a story through the photographic lens and those who use a typewriter?"[21]

Equally important, the burst of enthusiasm for photographs in war generated problems with consolidating a profession under pressure—an uneven use of photographs that had not been sufficiently developed in the prewar years and did not see further development during wartime. As the war interceded and photography expanded rapidly, photographers did not think through the full range of practices by which news photography could be effectively developed. In a sense, the need for images in wartime outpaced the ability to standardize their usage.

ISSUES OF FORM:
USING PHOTOGRAPHS IN NEWS

The uneven standards for using news photos dated in part to the battles of earlier eras, when photos had been used to meet broad interpretive goals. In wars as wide-ranging as the Crimean War, Civil War, Spanish-American War, and World War I, photos had been accompanied by limited referential data, captions and credits had appeared without sufficient standardization, and the degree of permitted explicitness had limited depictions of war's horror. Particularly in World War I, images connected events to broader themes of heroism, patriotism, and honor far more than they depicted identifiable scenes of war. Photos were zealously miscaptioned and highly censored; their captions "rarely identified the precise battle or location pictured in the images." Dates and places were not mentioned, and individual photographs remained unaccredited. For the defeats of the war to become bearable, "the war had to be represented in a way which would transcend the contingent details in photographs."[22]

But World War II differed from earlier conflicts, because photography was co-opted as an active tool for garnering support for the war effort. This meant that newspapers, magazines, and journals needed guidelines for deciding which images to use, how many, in what format, and in what size. The lack of such guidelines facilitated a neglect to "produce spontaneous or interpretative news coverage originally in photographic form and allow it to compete on an equal footing with word news." The press made insufficient efforts to "develop staff skills in selecting pictures and in relating words to them in such a way as to get more out of the mediums in combination."[23] Thus, as the events of the war created a need for photographic documentation, the press had few guidelines for addressing that need.

Captioning Photographic Images

One practice that remained uneven through World War II was captioning images. Thought to anchor a picture's meaning, there remained throughout the war a simultaneous dismissal and worship of captions. In photographer Carl Mydans's view,

> The captions were just as important as the film. Many of us making very good pictures of action in very difficult circumstances were unable to get sufficient captions down between taking our film out of our camera and giving it to someone to take in for shipment. Then, even though the film got to New York, if someone could not make head or tail out of what you had, it was not usable.[24]

But while captions told people what they were seeing, they were also often dismissed as "afterthoughts" and "tags for convenience." In one picture editor's view, if they were needed "to inform the beholder of intention or to tell part of the story, then the picture has in some respects failed in its mission." Not surprisingly, there was thus little discussion of how they should look. Photographers were told only that captions should "relate to the pictures," "show the reader what to look for and give basic facts," and comprise between one and six lines. Few directives were provided about what captions should say, how they should be written, and what relationship they should bear to photographs.[25]

When guidelines did exist, they rarely addressed the full mechanics of writing captions. Certain military services composed captioning procedures and handed out caption sheets, or "dope sheets," for photographers to complete. Yet other than stipulate that each caption be typed and shipped with the negatives, the guidelines provided little more than general advice to "contain all the information necessary." When British photographers joined the Army Film and Photographic Unit, they were told only to give the name and details of those they photographed so as to add "personal interest." Other directives offered lists of things *not* to do: not to start the caption with unremarkable words like *the* or *a* and not to use too many adjectives. It was also unclear how to rewrite captions that did arrive with pictures in a style that resembled that of the newspaper or journal. Picture editors, photographers, and members of photographic agencies could all affix captions to an image in any given instance.[26]

When compared with the captions to photos of earlier wars, the images of World War II appear highly documented. But when compared with their main competitor, the word, they lacked definitive detail and were often inaccurate. Not surprisingly, then, after the war trade forums continued to debate how to write news captions. Photographers needed to be told through the forties that "captions, which require lively selling words just like headlines in news story leads, are more than labels." Organizers of the 1947 convention of the Associated Press's Managing Editors Association offered guidelines for caption writing in newspapers and newsmagazines but later admitted that they were not being followed. Captions "still did not contain enough facts or description" and sometimes did not agree "on details or spelling of names." By the end of the forties, *American Photography* was still trying to establish guidelines and cautioned photographers against using "only general terms as caption material." A "photograph can be sold to a newspaper editor only if it carried his kind of caption. . . . [It] should have all the pertinent facts" and should never be faked, "for you can almost be hanged for it." Caption writing, summed up one observer, "is a neglected art [that] must be corrected before newspapers will be doing a real job in pictorial journalism."[27]

Accrediting Photographic Images

Another uneven practice throughout World War II was the issue of photographic credits. How to assure the accreditation of photographers and how to credit photographers for the publication of their images were questions central to consolidating the news photographer's stature. Yet here too, the issue was not explicitly discussed or evenly practiced.

Although credits had substantially improved from previous eras, particularly the World War I photos accredited by the general phrase "Passed by the Committee on Public Information," the practices of World War II still fell short of accrediting those responsible for an image. The U.S. War and Navy Departments purposefully imposed the anonymity of combat photographers as a security move, invoking the "ancient tradition that the closer to the fighting a man was, the less anyone knew about him." The world beyond the military was no help. Newspaper editors and photography textbooks remained indifferent to the issue: some textbooks said nothing; others defined credits as the "photographer's counterpart of an author's byline" or as the "name of the person *or* organization responsible for the making *or* sale of a photograph" (emphasis added); little mention was made of the mechanics involved in their production.[28]

But questions surrounded those mechanics, such as who was to receive accreditation. Often only correspondents affiliated with the major newspapers and journals were accredited, but during the war that rule penalized those photographers working without professional affiliation. As photography scholar Marianne Fulton later recounted, wartime accreditation brought "access to transportation and shipping—crucial elements to a photographer in the field. A great war picture is useless if it arrives too long after the action, is lost on the way, or arrives with no caption." Whose name was to be included in a credit was also unclear—that of the individual photographer or that of the syndicate. Confusion over who was to issue the directive bounced responsibility among relevant agencies. Most newspapers printed syndicate credits only part of the time, and some provided no credit at all. Where a credit was to appear also lacked resolution. Credits often did not appear or were relegated to back pages, although in the case of extraordinary photos they sometimes appeared next to the image. As one observer saw it,

> now and then a credit line is given to a photographer who has obtained some unusual photos and in some instances some stories have been written about cameramen who performed outstanding deeds. However, the men who do yeoman service day in and day out are treated anonymously.

One need only imagine how such anonymity would have been challenged if applied to reporters in the popular press. As late as 1944, the War Still Picture Pool, picture syndicate heads, picture editors, and military officials all blamed each other for not standardizing accrediting practices.[29]

For many photographers, the lack of credits underscored their second-class status in journalism. "The war cameramen," complained one, "expose themselves to all the dangers of enemy fire [that correspondents do] yet receive little of the glory." Photos are "enriching the history of modern journalism," pleaded another. "Let them be recognized." All news photographers, wrote *Editor and Publisher,* feel "some resentment at the differentiation between writers and themselves" and see themselves as "equally deserving as byline writers." In the early forties, *U.S. Camera* published a two-part piece that denounced the failure to accredit. So as to illustrate their point, the editors set aside a two-by-five-inch white square with only the words: "This space is typical of the size allowed for the photographer's credit lines for an entire issue." Yet the lack of recognition persisted throughout the war. Photographers continued to complain that their work was being presented anonymously, and as late as 1947 still called for systematic accreditation.[30]

Presenting Photographic Images

Photographic presentation was also uneven in the wartime press. The common view held that editors "print anything so long as it's type but reject all pictures unless they rate among the year's best." Thus, how a photograph was to appear on a page of news text—where, in what position, size, and angle—was virtually ignored. Artistic expression was absent from the discussions; one news photographer cautioned his colleagues to forget aesthetics altogether, because news editors "care very little for artistic balance in spot news pictures." Instead, the precise relationship between image and text remained undetermined, and press photography constituted a "potent, if restricted, factor in the space-cramped newspapers. . . . The official hand-out stuff is thrown into the paper without thought to presentation." Not surprisingly, then, photos were positioned in varied ways in newspapers, magazines, and journals. Images were sometimes placed alongside unconnected texts, and pictures stretched somewhat indiscriminately across columns of news text. Pictorial pages, increasingly on the rise, grouped images in nondescript ways. Even picture-magazines, then heralded for innovative ways of presenting photographic images, employed layouts displaying "stodgy, nonnarrative clumps of photographs."[31]

The inability of photographers to affect their images' presentation exacerbated the problem. Wartime photographers generally knew little about whether or which images were being published on the home front; one commented that photographers were seen "as a race of talented children, to be humored and pampered until their picture-taking is done, and then pushed out of the way." Even picture editors—who were to decide "what shall be printed and how it will be presented" but whose "side of the picture seems to escape notice"—were often excluded from final decisions. One picture editor for the British *News Chronicle* left his job publicly because "there were no further prospects. It was pointed out to me that the *Chronicle* was a newspaper and not a picture paper."[32]

The situation did not substantially improve through the war. As late as 1947, picture editors, by then seen as "proven misfits in another department," were held responsible for slowing the progress of photojournalists; photographers asked them to take courses in basic photography. Images often depicted events not represented in the accompanying texts. Good pictures continued to be unjustly tossed aside by picture editors, badly cropped, and generally handled as "nuisance jobs"; editors did "not make the same study of cropping or reproduction or news value of pictures that they make of the written word."[33] Even when photographers and picture agencies provided vital information about the images they transmitted over the wires, the picture editors of newspapers often left such information out of their papers to accommodate the lengthier narratives of reporters.

Photography into Journalism: A Missed Opportunity

All of this suggests that the press's standards for using photographs in news, uneven during World War II, were often informally adjusted to circumstances as they arose. Standards were also insufficient to deal with the enormous influx of pictures that arrived on the doorstep of nearly every newspaper, journal, and magazine in the U.S. and Britain during the war. This left unanswered a slew of questions about technological adaptation: on breaking stories, would reporters follow the lead of photographers, or photographers that of reporters? How would the claim to space be negotiated between words and images? How would the newspaper or magazine organize photographers alongside the regular news staff? These and other unaddressed questions left news photographs—and the photographers who took them—somewhat on the margins of the journalistic world. As one observer said in 1947, photojournalism has "grown so rapidly in the last few years and to a large extent without form or guidance" that there remain "few specific new laws governing the use of pictures." This circumstance persisted both during the war and afterward, rendering the incorporation of news photographs a missed opportunity. In the eyes of the editor of one photographic journal, "the conditions and prospects [facing photographers] are extremely mixed. Everywhere adjustment and adaptability are called for."[34] His words, however prescient, were not adequately translated into practice.

Errors in photographic documentation did not help matters, and each time a photo was found faulty, fears about the authenticity of all photographic documentation were augmented. When one photographic shot of a dogfight over Dover was found to have been faked, it prompted immediate fears "that authentic pictures would be questioned hereafter." Similarly, when the British journal *Picture Post* admitted using the same shot—a Frenchwoman bidding farewell at a train station—to document two separate events, its editors conceded that

> nothing is easier than to make a mistake in dealing with the thousands of pictures that face an Art Editor every week—particularly in the case of pictures said to have been "smuggled out" of this country or that. We print this explanation not as an attack, but in order to keep the record straight.[35]

Significantly, however, the uneven standards for using images directly undermined the photograph's anticipated referential force. Photos sometimes appeared without any precise delineation of what they were depicting or how they connected to the accompanying news story, and that lack

of attention was rarely corrected as the war's urgent events pressed photographers to continue. Photos in many cases were thus deprived of their
referential status for depicting events of the war. Yet at the same time their
interpretive and symbolic dimensions were inadvertently highlighted. This
would have particular effect when the press had to document the war's
more challenging events, such as the Nazi atrocities.

Thus, regardless of the degree of wartime co-optation surrounding photographs, the legacy of antagonism between photographers and journalists
left its impact on the practices by which the war's main events were recorded. As one key photojournalism text of the time saw it, the inclusion of photography in news took place "so inevitably" that "it may be said to have happened in spite of . . . the old newspaper school."[36] The press accommodated
news photography in a way that highlighted the photograph's symbolic and
interpretive dimensions because it insufficiently standardized the uses of
photos in news. The standards employed before and during the war exacerbated a lingering uncertainty about the linkage of words and images in the
press that would affect the atrocities' documentation.

ISSUES OF CONTENT:
TRADITIONS FOR DEPICTING ATROCITY
IN WORD AND IMAGE

The conflicted professional backdrop connecting reporters and photographers did not make it easier to cover the unprecedented story of Nazi
atrocities. Although atrocity stories had been around as long as war itself,
never before had the press come face to face with such extensive evidence
of mass brutality and such an ability to document it. Covering the scenes
of horror in the camps required overcoming both assumptions about earlier atrocity stories and the inadequate standards that existed for depicting
violence in word and image.

Tales of atrocity had long documented the horrors inflicted on civilian
nationals of occupied countries. The U.S. press reported far-reaching
atrocity tales during the U.S. Civil War that pitted North against South.
During the Boer War, the British press ran reports of Boers massacring
pro-British citizens, flogging natives, and executing Boers who wanted to
surrender, all creatively illustrated by artists; one early British newsreel
even simulated one such scene, employing actors from a London suburb.
The fictions underlying the atrocity tales that circulated during the Spanish-American War were hard to separate from the yellow press's declared
aim of inflaming public opinion in favor of Cuba's independence from
Spain. Four-inch headlines topped articles, and the "correspondents' copy,
often grossly exaggerated, had to match the headlines."[37]

But by World War I, atrocity tales reached new heights. Tales of so-called bloodthirsty Huns mutilating their victims circulated widely, and from 1914 onward the Germans were said to have tied up the dead "in bundles like asparagus." Reports accounted for the mass mutilation of Belgian nuns, nurses, and infants, and for a "corpse-conversion factory" where Germans were said to have boiled human fat and bones into lubricants and glycerine. The latter story was eventually found to be a fictionalized part of a massive Allied propaganda campaign, its inventor a British brigadier general who had linked a description of making horses into soap with a photograph of a boxcar of dead soldiers. As one reporter who searched for evidence of brutality recalled:

> I couldn't find any atrocities. . . . I offered sums of money for photographs of children whose hands had been cut off or who had been wounded or injured in other ways. I never found a first-hand Belgian atrocity story; and when I ran down the second-hand stories, they all petered out.[38]

The exaggerated nature of the World War I atrocity story set in place an aura of fakery that greeted the initial reports of atrocities in World War II. In fact, the resemblance of later atrocity reports to the false World War I atrocity stories generated such skepticism that until proven true, atrocity reports were assumed false; they were regarded first as narratives of exaggeration and propaganda and only later as potentially credible accountings of the ravages of war.

This meant that during much of World War II the press lacked a frame for making sense of atrocity. Part of the difficulty in eliminating skepticism emanated from the inability to confirm whether the stories were true or exaggerated. Throughout the war the press persisted in trying to confirm each news item it dispatched, and when it could not, difficulties were noted publicly.[39] But as the atrocity stories persisted, so too did the inability to more authoritatively gauge what was happening. Atrocity reports heightened in intensity alongside journalists' inability to report them and unwillingness to believe them. As a chronicle about wartime, then, the atrocity story challenged reporters' dependence on proven newsmaking routines and played upon the lack of a precedent for credibly reporting atrocities.

Similar problems faced photographers. While a tradition for visualizing atrocity was as old as war itself, it nonetheless fell short of capably portraying the horrors that would characterize World War II. The Crimean War, portrayed by British Royal Photographer Roger Fenton, was depicted as a series of battles in which "everything looks ship-shape and everyone happy." During the Civil War, the battle to secure belief about atrocities was fought primarily by editorial artists, who produced pictures of imagined atrocities on both sides. Engravings of the emaciated bodies of Yankee soldiers incarcerated at Andersonville Prison also circulated widely throughout the late 1800s, their presentation thought to be "a thousand-fold more impressive than any description. . . . No evidence is like these pictures." But these images were not made available in the daily press, finding instead a smaller audience from stereo cards, photographic exhibitions, and wood engravings in *Harper's.* Pictures of British dead in the Boer War—a scene later characterized as a "field of massacre"—were not published because they were thought to be "revolting Boer propaganda." During the Spanish-American War, the yellow press's embellishment of atrocity stories depended in large part on photographs: one such shot appeared in *Leslie's Illustrated Weekly* in December 1896 with a lengthy legend that told readers precisely what they were looking at: "The bodies of six Cuban pacificos lying on their backs, with their arms and legs bound and their bodies showing mutilation by machetes, and their faces pounded and hacked out of resemblance to anything human."[40]

Levels of explicit depiction changed abruptly during World War I, when rigid censorship restricted what was seen of the war. Official British photographers were forbidden to photograph "gruesome scenes." In one view, the war simply

> never showed up. With few exceptions—and those often turned out to be faked or staged pictures—the photographs that were allowed to pass the censor were mundane and uninspired . . . [with] a near-total absence of either a sense of the horror or the thrill of the danger.[41]

Significantly, one set of World War I stories that did receive photographic documentation was the false tale of German crimes. The same British brigadier general who circulated rumors of German atrocities also sent photographs of a wagon of dead bodies to the newly formed Department of Information, which used them for propaganda purposes. For the press of later wars, this aligned the use of atrocity photos with propaganda.

Moreover, photographers had tolerated a long tradition of photographic tampering, which caused many to immediately suspect unbelievable photos. Memorable scenes during the Civil War—such as the battle at Gettysburg—were found later to have been staged, and even the more reputable press sometimes tampered with photographic images. In 1918, *Collier's* ran a two-page spread that interspersed real and fake images under the headline "Real War Pictures—and the Other Kind." Noting that the faked pictures looked more "like war" than the real photographs, the magazine called on readers to recognize photographs that had been changed for propagandistic aims. Later, the tabloid and yellow press routinely altered images and generated disbelief whenever improbable photos appeared.[42]

The visual depiction of atrocity took a more complicated turn in World War II. Broader patterns for visualizing violence at first undercut the potential for explicitly depicting atrocity. At the time of the camps' liberation, U.S. and British publics were largely unaccustomed to viewing violence in the popular press, which tended toward benign pictorial elaboration. Through the early years of the war, for instance, the depiction of nude corpses was so restricted that U.S. audiences were prohibited from seeing the naked bodies of victims of natural disasters or accidents. Such images were routinely subjected to touch-ups, and artists drew clothes or blankets to cover naked bodies. As late as 1943, the British *Picture Post* ran a one-page piece entitled "Pictures We Would Rather Not Publish." The first bold sentence read: "They offend us. They will offend everybody else. But we have a duty to recognize what has happened." Ironically, the photos dealt not with the atrocities but with the famine in India. Reticence about explicit wartime images thus derived from a censorship that was in part self-generated.[43]

But there was also censorship of a more official kind. The images of World War II tended to be more suggestive of devastation than revealing of its details. In the war's early years, the press rarely published gruesome images or printed photos that portrayed a dark vision of their own side. In covering D-Day, censors held back numerous images of the Omaha Beach landing on the grounds that they showed the U.S. destruction of French property. The first photographic shots of Pearl Harbor showed nothing more explicit than distant spirals of billowing smoke. More graphic images—the sunk shipwreck of the U.S.S. *Arizona*, burning airfields, and soldiers clad only in their underclothes—did not appear until February of the following year. And it was a full year later that *Newsweek* and *Life* ran the official U.S. Navy photographs of the devastated airfield. Even as late as Hiroshima, photographs depicted the explosion in the sky rather than the devastation below, suggesting that "photographs of that strange new landscape had no referents." Such depictions, initially delayed for publication and then released simultaneously with the Japanese surrender on August 11, were contextualized against the story of the war's end, so that representations of a peace forced by the bomb took over depictions of the bomb itself. In such a light, *Life* depicted two shots of mushroomlike clouds under the general title "The War Ends." There were "no injured Japanese in these photographs, no doctors and nurses treating the ill and wounded, no funeral pyres, no one mourning": the shots were important not because "such moments existed or were now possible to retain on film, but [because] photographers and editors during World War II wanted to evoke emotions about this war that could be connected to traditional attitudes about combat."[44]

Thus, photographs offered a different portrayal of wartime and violence than that provided by words. The image's potency derived from a lesser, rather than greater, degree of explicitness about its details. Faces were blackened or obscured by shadows. Names—identified on uniforms— were smudged from view. As Paul Fussell argued about all images of World War II, the "more significant and 'authentic' they were, the less they rendered [culturally] identifiable." The dead were rarely identified; the wounds shown in most photographs were neat and clean. There was no visual agony, no bleeding, no mutilation. Simply put, the "photographs did not tell the whole truth. They avoided acute nastiness, were often artistically composed."[45] They were referentially incomplete.

But there was a broader significance to these images of violence. The photos offered broader parameters for visualizing atrocity that went beyond the explicit details of a given instance of death or mutilation. They linked with the broader interpretive themes that justified the war effort. The potency of these images thus derived from their invocation as symbols—from representational strategies connected with generic representation, anonymity, connotation, generalizability, and universality. Such dimensions made photographs particularly suited for anchoring the preferred interpretations of the war in place.

To a large extent, the symbolic force of photographs had positive effect, for alluding to the broader dimensions of the war story was one way of accounting for the scope of the German horror. One typical photograph that originally appeared in *PM* ran widely across the United States, not so much because of its referential force—that is, what it told audiences about a specific time and place—but because of how it more generally symbolized the war effort (fig. 1). Taken by photographer John Florea, the picture portrayed an emaciated U.S. prisoner of war who still appeared severely malnourished four months after his release by the Germans. As the *Stars and Stripes* told it a few weeks after it first appeared, the photograph produced

> a wave of great revulsion toward the German nation. . . . The most powerful factor forcing people toward remembering again and again—and burned into the brains of many people—is the picture of the living skeleton, the American prisoner of war in Limburg lying on a cot, which was front-paged in every tabloid in the country and in almost every other newspaper.[46]

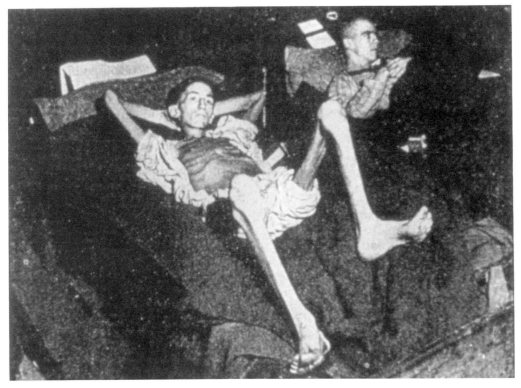

Figure 1. Joseph Demler, April 11–April 30, 1945, by Keystone/Sygma.

In contrast to usual norms of news presentation, the picture ran consecutively for two days in the *Observer* of Charlotte, North Carolina.[47] The second time, it was used as a visual foil to pictures of well-fed German soldiers in U.S.-run camps, emphasizing the disparity of treatment accorded POWs and providing the visual evidence needed to shore up support for the war effort.

As the war broadened and its scenes offered increasingly graphic depictions of violence and horror, standards of appropriateness inched toward greater latitude in pictorial depiction. The level of violence depicted in photographs seemed to increase as the war became more all-encompassing, though some observers remained uncomfortable with the increasingly explicit use of images. The British minister for coordination and defense castigated the press for publishing "horror" pictures of the war in China—lamenting the same reasoning later invoked to justify publication of pictures of the camps—and deplored the "tendency which, in time, would come to justify by custom the reproduction of anything so shocking and terrible."[48] But as the war broadened, officials and publics on both continents became increasingly hardened to the idea of viewing violence.

Subtle additional changes in the shape of permissible photographic presentations also changed the depiction of violence, as military officials and censors increasingly recognized the image's ability to legitimate—and delegitimate—war claims. The United States led Britain in this regard, with a decision in 1943 that the U.S. home front should have a more accurate portrayal of the hardships being experienced abroad. While the administration felt that "photographs which accurately depict the terrible strain of our wartime conditions" would support the war effort, it was ambivalent about how realistic that portrayal should be. "There is no simple precise rule to be worked out," wrote editor William L. Chenery of *Collier's,* who counseled Navy officials to engage in "restricted realism" and spare ordinary citizens exposure to harsh images. Not long after, *Newsweek* published one of its first graphic photographs of American war wounded. Under the headline "Photo with a Message," it showed a picture of a bleeding marine receiving emergency medical treatment; that shot was soon followed by another graphic image—a frontal view of a soldier's amputated leg.[49]

It took another six months of negotiation before the press was allowed to publish pictures of U.S. war dead. *Life* led on this count, publishing two images in close sequence: the first in the beginning of August depicted a dead soldier concealed by a blanket, with only his foot protruding. The second and better known, taken by George Strock and published in late September, was captioned "Three Dead Americans on the Beach at Buna": it showed three anonymous bodies sprawled face-down on the sand (fig. 2). The image's importance was underscored not only by the accompanying text—which told readers that it had been finally "decided that the American people ought to be able to see their own boys as they fall in battle"— but also by the photograph's presentation. Set off from the magazine's other stories, it stood on its own and stretched across two full pages of the magazine. An editorial that ran opposite discussed the decision to print the picture, asking "Why shall we print this picture? . . . The answer is that words are never enough." That same week *Newsweek* published an image of dead paratroopers in Sicily. By D-Day, photographs of Americans killed in battle were appearing regularly. And a Gallup poll in 1944 revealed that a majority of readers wanted photographs "showing all the grim, hard realities of the war."[50]

Britain remained more reticent than the United States about displaying violent pictures of war. This was for a variety of reasons: it was closer to the front and so more sensitive to war violence; it also possessed a clearer memory of the World War I propaganda that had involved atroci-

Figure 2. American dead at Buna Beach, September 1943, by George Strock, *Life Magazine* ©Time Inc.

ties. Extensive British restrictions thereby necessitated special permits, rigid censoring, and lengthy delays in the publication of images. One 1942 editorial in a British trade journal complimented the press for putting shots of Royal Air Force damage of German towns on its front pages—calling it a mark of "faith in the news value of the picture"—yet simultaneously lambasted the quality of the official pictures that had been provided. Said the editorial:

> The picture has been the Cinderella of the war from the press point of view. Before September 1939 the trend was to more and more pictures in the press. But when war came the services did not realize the influence of the picture as a propaganda weapon.

British newspaper editors—and individuals writing letters to the press—lamented the lack of explicit photographs. As one article in *Picture Post* complained in July 1944, "where are the pictures? Why are they not being taken? If they are being taken, why are they not being issued?" Trade journals lamented as late as April 1945 the lack of pictures of Britain's war dead, complaining that the War Office "seems to pursue the policy that no British soldier is killed in this war and that it is all a nice neat little affair."[51]

Yet on both continents the traditions for depicting war and its violence fell short of the scenes requiring depiction once the concentration camps were opened in 1945. The visualization of the war moved onto new stages of graphic depiction with the liberation of the camps.

ISSUES OF CONTENT:
HINTS OF ATROCITY BEFORE THE LIBERATION

The ambivalence about incorporating photography in news and the inadequate precedent for depicting atrocity provided only part of the context relevant to covering Nazi atrocity. For Holocaust scholars have long argued that Western journalism did not report sufficiently in either word or image what was happening in the concentration camps during the preliberation period. Despite repeated hints of atrocity before the camps' opening, the story remained a back-page curiosity, rarely given full play. From the mid-1930s onward, both U.S. and British reporters tended to discount what they heard about Nazi atrocities.[52] The press's neglect in giving the story full attention created a backdrop of professional failure, which the camps' liberation would rapidly make evident. Covering the atrocities would require not only persuasion to change public disbelief but repair work by which the press could institute its own professional corrective.

Verbal Hints of Atrocity

The U.S. and British press both received and processed verbal hints of the Nazi atrocities in the years preceding the liberation, although not always in immediate sequence. Treatment of those hints was far from adequate. Three issues of credibility came to the fore as the press neared the camps. One issue had to do with the rationale that reporters used to downplay the atrocity stories before the camps' liberation. Ambivalence over the story had many origins in the broader population, including anti-Semitism and an assault on basic premises of liberal thought—notions of toleration, progress, a confrontation with difference, and the acceptance of diversity.[53] For the journalistic community, however, a persistent association between atrocity stories and governmental propaganda had direct impact. In particular, skepticism about the atrocity rumors of World War I left many wary of any similar account, and numerous reporters simply did not believe the preliberation accounts of brutality.

But the reticence to publish had other origins too. In many cases, reporters had no workable frame against which to contextualize the atrocities, and they thus misunderstood what was happening. Certain journalists, like *Chicago Daily News* reporter Edgar Mowrer, strategically underplayed the horrors: Mowrer deleted from his stories descriptions of the camps received from escaped survivors for fear they would exacerbate an already bad situation. In January 1935, *Harper's* painfully misread the horror when it declared that the Nazi persecution of the Jews would at least "break that century-old, unnatural alliance between Jews and money, which . . . has formed the most prolific source of anti-Semitism." Others discounted the accounts that they heard. The *Los Angeles Times* reported that the "amazing tales of oppression" from Germany were "exaggerated," while *Time* glibly referred to the "'atrocity' story-of-the-week." And as late as 1944, the *Christian Century* dismissed reports of unusual degrees of Nazi brutality by maintaining that "war always generates atrocities."[54]

In other cases, reporters saw what was taking place, but their observations were discredited at home: a 1943 U.S. Gallup poll still counted a full third of its respondents who dismissed the news of two million Jews killed. Writing in *Journalism Quarterly* in September 1942, reporter Vernon McKenzie decried "a hangover of skepticism" from World War I and "a refusal to accept" atrocity accounts because of a stubborn tendency to equate atrocity with propaganda. But his voice, like that of others, went largely unheard. As scholar Deborah Lipstadt has argued, the "chasm between information and belief was one of the major obstacles to the transmission of this news. . . . Reliable sources told at least a portion of what was happening, and those far from the scene and unfamiliar with Nazism discounted the news as exaggerated or dismissed it as not quite possible."[55]

Much of this had to do with a second issue of credibility—the fact that even standards of journalistic practice worked against attempts to cover the atrocity story. Because reporters were largely denied access to the camps prior to liberation, most could not rely on their own methods of news gathering to recount what was happening. Unable to personally verify circumstances or events, they depended on others to tell the story for them. This meant either incorporating the words of various bystanders—witnesses or prisoners who had escaped persecution—in their own reportorial chronicles or giving the bystanders their own bylines. Some of the best-known instances of the latter case were eyewitness reports from the Warsaw ghetto and other locations published in *Collier's* and other periodicals. But the lack of objective eyewitnesses and the difficulty of obtaining confirmation from impartial sources made the press question the content of what it was being told. Editorial boards complained that "the stories which trickled through cannot be checked and officially verified." In many cases, "details were . . . missing, sometimes the number of victims . . . exaggerated or underestimated, and the size and specific function of particular death camps were not publicly revealed until relatively late." All of this made the story of mass extermination and death a sidebar to more general wartime coverage. Lacking the criteria of sound coverage, the atrocity story was relegated to the inside or back pages of the press.[56]

When the reports persisted, a third issue of credibility came to the fore: the magnitude of the atrocities and the sheer number of victims. In one view, "it was almost more rational to dismiss [the news] as untrustworthy than to accept it as true." Although the publics of Allied countries had been informed of the camps' existence and of Nazi intentions to eliminate the Jews, no rumor or other verbal description offered by persons who had escaped confinement could convey the full extent of horror associated with the camps. Only with their liberation did the public grasp the magnitude of what had been happening in Nazi-occupied Europe. As one news editor of the time admitted, "the occasional trickle of news, the testimony of fugitive eyewitnesses, seemed somehow exaggerated." Against such disbelief, journalists often read the wrong signs and processed the signs that they read in the wrong ways. Some tried to maintain balance and modulate the tone of their reports so as not to be accused of fomenting hysteria; others "leaned backward in reporting the truth," trying to "verify the minutest particulars of what they wrote." Wary of overstatement and exaggeration, the press produced reports so reserved that they told a story of moderation ill suited to what was happening.[57]

Yet despite a general failure to bring the atrocity story to public attention, early hints did trickle out. By the end of the thirties, official reports
on Nazi brutality had emerged from quarters as varied as the Polish gov-
ernment-in-exile, the British government, and the Vatican, bolstered by
the accounts of released prisoners or reports smuggled from the camps. By
1939, one U.S. newsmagazine was able to comment that "too many alum-
ni have emerged from concentration camps with the same story to leave
any further doubt that sadism and brutality are part and parcel of the concentration camp routine." That same year, the British White Paper, a thirty-
six-page official document on the camps, generated a flurry of press interest in Great Britain and the United States; by that time, though, the *New York
Times* correctly observed that the "sickening" truth had "long since been
established."[58]

Certain books by reporters posted to the area also began to appear, documenting what was happening in Germany. Frederick Oechsner of the
United Press flatly stated that the Jewish position had become one of "complete hopelessness" as "wholesale exterminations" were taking place across
the occupied territories. Associated Press correspondent Louis Lochner,
following a visit to a camp at Sonnenburg, recounted his fears that the Jews
were overly optimistic about their chances for survival. And in 1944, Sigrid
Schultz detailed how the Nazis were successfully playing upon the Western
dislike for propaganda, telling their agents abroad to "brand any report of
crimes an untrue atrocity story, reminiscent of the propaganda campaigns
of World War I. . . . they knew that anything labelled 'propaganda' is disbelieved in America." In February 1943, the American Jewish Congress issued
its detailed report of Hitler's accelerated program of mass murder, and the
press filled with stories suggesting the widespread nature of what was happening; the *New York Daily Mirror,* for instance, now spoke of the "actual
obliteration of a people by accelerated murder." The following year, initial
reports from Auschwitz underscored the situation's severity, and they were
soon followed by the War Refugee Board's detailed report on the camp.[59]

Yet the reports were neither methodical nor consistent, and public disbelief persisted. Writing in the *New York Times Magazine* in late 1944, Arthur
Koestler lamented the findings of opinion polls, which claimed that nine of
ten U.S. citizens still viewed accusations against the Nazis as propagandistic lies.

> There are a few of us, escaped victims or eyewitnesses of the things
> which happen in the thicket and who, haunted by our memories, go
> on screaming on the wireless, yelling at you in newspapers and in
> public meetings, theaters and cinemas. Now and then we succeed in

reaching your ear for a minute. . . . We, the screamers, have been at
it for about ten years.

The *Christian Century* responded that "screaming" about the atrocities
against the Jews would only sideswipe eventual peace efforts.[60]

Thus, before the liberation there was insufficient accounting of the horrors that would become evident with the camps' opening. Until then, the
atrocity story did not have a recognizable place in public discourse. For
even the sketchy reports that did emerge only hinted at the magnitude and
scope of what was happening, making the details that surfaced with the
camps' liberation that much more shocking. Equally important, a documentary tool that could convey the scope of what was happening at the
same time as it documented was needed. In this regard, photographs
would prove an able tool.

Photographic Hints of Atrocity

The ability to photograph the camps before the liberation was characterized by a fundamental problem: how to depict in photographs circumstances that were not only unbelievable but basically inaccessible. Even the
earliest atrocity reports called for photographic proof of what was taking
place in the camps. In late 1944, *Collier's* ran an "eyewitness story" of Belzec
by Polish patriot Jan Karski, whose first-person narrative shocked even the
most casual reader. The account recounted in explicit detail Karski's horrific journey around the camp, where he witnessed crushing mobs of
starved people and their forced crowding and death in train cars. Like others who later entered the camps, Karski recognized the limitations of his
own reportage and admitted as much in words: "I have no proofs, no photographs," he said. "All I can say is that I saw it, and it is the truth."[61]

Yet who was to procure such proof, such photographic images? How
were they to be taken? How were they to be safely retrieved from the
camps? And who would stand behind their documentation?

Photographic hints of the atrocities existed from the midthirties,
although they were given even less credence by the U.S. and British press
than were the verbal reports. As early as 1933, the German illustrated
press ran a story about Oranienburg under the title "A Visit in a Concentration Camp." The one-page story used minimal text and presented nine
images that depicted what was supposed to be daily camp routine.
Although the Western press did not follow up the story, it changed its
approach when the Nazis later treated the concentration camp of Dachau
as a propagandistic triumph and the German illustrated press ran on it
three separate stories. In 1937, the *New York Times Magazine* reprinted some

of the Dachau photographs, explaining that both the images and their captions were reproduced exactly as they had appeared in the German press, yet noting that their innocuous portrayals—such as "a pond built by prisoners last year"—did not capture the camp's true atmosphere. In the images, prisoners marched in clean, scrubbed uniforms, accommodations appeared comfortable and tidy, and no photographs were made of the beatings and deaths that were already becoming camp routine. *Life* scathingly called the story and the pictures a "whitewash."[62]

By the early 1940s, the Polish Ministry of Information, independent journalists, and underground groups released photos of corpses tumbled into graves or stacked onto carts. One such depiction, which appeared in the *Illustrated London News* in March 1941 under the headline "Where Germans Rule: Death Dance before Polish Mass Execution," portrayed victims digging their own graves or facing the death squad. The journal told its readers that "behind these pictures is a story of cold-blooded horror reminiscent of the Middle Ages," reminding them that the six unaccredited images were "the first published to show the workings of German justice in Poland." Although the pictures' publication was protested by the Germans, it was justified as a countermove to Nazi propaganda.[63]

Other images that suggested persecution but revealed little of the atrocities already being committed also appeared. In February 1941, *PM* ran a five-page series of year-old photos smuggled out of the Warsaw ghetto. The photos—all grainy, dark images—were collectively titled "Inside Poland: Smuggled Pictures Show Nazi Persecution." The *New York Times* ran a shot of a man in a suit gesticulating to soldiers under the caption "Victims Tell of Nazi Brutality in Italy." In October 1943, *Picture Post* ran a pictorial spread on survivors of a concentration camp in Italy. One photograph, which showed a dozen women just released from the camp smiling and balancing laughing children on their knees, appeared with the reminder that "*ten years ago* the world was stirred to horror by the stories of the concentration camps that Hitler had opened" (emphasis added).[64] It offered a calm depiction of civility and decency, totally unlike that which would be seen following the liberation of the Western camps two years later.

Not all of the early depictions of atrocities reached the West, but those images that did suffered from a number of problems. One was an issue of scarcity. While over one and a half million images documenting the Nazi brutalities in occupied Europe have been dispersed today over thirty archives in a dozen nations, at the time the photographic recording of events in the camps was scarce.[65] Until 1941, Western photographers with the neutral nations, the press associations—including the Associated Press, United Press, Wide World Photos, and the *New York Times*—and the civilian service organizations—such as the American Friends Service Committee or the children's relief agency, the Oeuvres de Secours aux Enfants (OSE)—were stationed across Europe and snapped photographs of wartime conditions. Once the war broadened, however, pictures of atrocity became more difficult to procure. Photographic access to the atrocities, and particularly to the concentration camps as the site of extreme Nazi brutality, was denied. Much of the atrocity story was placed strategically beyond the reach of photographers associated with the Allies.

A photographic record of the atrocities did emerge, however, though it was not taken by Western photographers. That record's existence highlights yet another problem surrounding these early photos—the photographer's identity and the circumstances of the photographic shot, both crucial yet unarticulated pieces of referential data. As scholar Sybil Milton has shown, the preliberation photographic documentation of the camps was provided by a wide span of individuals who could gain entry. Members of the underground, escapees from the camps, and sympathetic civilians provided one set of images; soldiers at the front snapped souvenir images with their own private cameras; and German photographers serving with the PK (Propaganda Kompanien) produced numerous commissioned and uncommissioned photographs.

Yet most photographs of the concentration camps were made by the most organized of documenters—the Nazis themselves. Their "snapshots were part of the administrative records of the camp, of its architecture and routine, of the medical experiments, the prisoners, and the commandant's household." Using photography as part of their propaganda arsenal, the Nazis meticulously documented the deportation of Jews to the East until their death in the camps, though most of these images did not turn up in public until many years later. Indeed, the penchant for intimidating and harassing through photographs was evident as early as the thirties, when posters threatening punishment through photographic recording were found on the streets of Germany; one such poster cried "Jewish Business. Whoever Buys Here Will Be Photographed." That penchant continued throughout the war, as the visual evidence of Nazi crimes accumulated. One particularly vile example was found in the possession of a Treblinka commander, who parodied the idea of the photo album by subtitling his collection of camp images as the "Best Years of My Life." The brutality of his images and others like them, though not always set in print at the time, reflected the most authentic portrayal of life in the camps before liberation. In Gerhard Schoenberner's words, the Nazis "photographed themselves at work. . . . The [victims] had no choice but to have their photographs taken. As they went to certain death . . . they saw the enemy's camera turned on them."[66]

In Sybil Milton's view, numerous crucial issues surrounding a photographer's identity and the circumstance of the shot remain unclear. Who had taken a given photograph and under what circumstances? Was it a neutral passerby, a Nazi who photographed and then killed his or her victim, a resistance fighter, or, later, a liberator? And for what purpose had he or she taken the image? Was it to record, to mock, to remember, to exploit? Was the picture a freak incident or was it representative of a larger pattern of violence?[67] Each of these questions, none of them with available answers, linger uneasily around the photographs.

Most images taken by this wide range of photographers were not published in the daily and weekly press of the time; indeed, many did not enter the public domain until years after the war ended. But for those images that did draw notice, a fundamental unevenness of documentation constituted a third problem. Images taken by the Nazis displayed high technical quality but provided primarily staged information about the atrocities. Some were printed in the U.S. and British press. For instance, images released by the Nazis, depicting lines of inmates being questioned in detention, were published with the 1939 release of the British White Paper. Similarly, the British press reprinted some of the Nazi pictures as reminders of why the Allies were fighting.[68] Such depictions, however, were sporadic and partial representations of what was happening in the camps.

Other images that reached the West had high informative value but failed to meet recognizable standards of photography. Grainy and smudged, they lacked "precise identification, accurate dating, and intelligent interpretation." Only some were published: when the American Jewish Congress published its 1943 report on the camps, the *New York Post* appended an image of dead bodies and Nazis under the generic caption "A Common Grave." Similarly, in September 1941, a manifesto signed by the "Leaders of the Working Masses of Poland" was smuggled out of Poland and published in Britain. Following some discussion over its authenticity, the *Picture Post* hailed the report, calling it

> the bravest document of the war. Side by side with terrible photographs of unbridled terror (rows of corpses freshly shot, firing squads at work, a Jew being tortured, women and girls being led blindfolded to execution) is the confidently written story of unbroken resistance and unshaken faith.

Finally, even the resonance of photographs smuggled out by professionals was limited because they were often mistakenly captioned. One photo of the 1938 expulsion of Polish Jews from Germany was listed as a record of the 1941 deportation of Posen Jews; similarly, photographs of collaborators in Vichy, France, were labeled depictions of a Jewish detention.[69] Smuggled out of Europe, the early images often lacked specific explanations of what was being depicted, and readers of unaccredited, captionless photographs were told little more than that they were looking at the Nazi atrocities in some form.

Against all of these circumstances, the U.S. and British press provided inadequate visualization of what was happening in the camps. One picture-spread, which appeared in *Picture Post* in October 1941, conveyed the broad parameters by which the experience of Nazi oppression was being typically depicted. Affixed to an article entitled "The Terror in Europe," the text used eight unaccredited images to illustrate life under the Nazis, none of whose origin was made clear to readers and each of which depicted a moment of oppression captioned by one-word phrases, such as "Starvation!" or "Hanging!" The first image was in fact a reprint of an eight-year-old photograph of Nazi policemen on the roof of a building, and its legend told readers, "This is an old picture. The date on its back is 1933. We publish it just because it is a picture of 1933. For in that year, Nazis . . . began to hold down the free elements inside Germany."[70] Here, then, the photographic image was deployed less for its news value than for its cogency as a symbol.

Two other photographs in the series bear closer examination. One picture showed two weeping women, under the general caption "Horror!" Its legend read: "Their homes burnt. Their men killed. Their country crushed under the jackboot. These Polish women weep, as millions weep in the occupied territories" (fig. 3). The photograph had no identified place or date, no definitive details about the individuals being depicted, no credit or other information about the individual or agency who took the shot, and no direct relationship with the text that accompanied it on the larger page of the journal. In other words, the lack of definitive or referential detailing created an ambiguous impression as to how the pictures came together— *other* than that they illustrated the German war machinery. The images thereby made better sense within a broad interpretive scheme about Nazi brutality than within a tight frame documenting a specific instance of violence. Yet another photograph in the series showed a similarly generic depiction of brutality—a close-up shot of a Nazi guard facing down a group of prisoners. The legend told readers of "The concentration camp! The rule of the rubber truncheon! The rule of the barbed wire fence. Inside the Third Reich alone, there were 100,000 victims in concentration camps in 1938. Now there are camps all over Europe."[71] The image lacked referential indices, as nowhere did the caption specifically mention a certain

HORROR! *Their homes burnt. Their men killed. Their country crushed under the jackboot. These Polish women weep, as millions weep in the occupied territories.*

Figure 3. Polish women weeping, October 1941, by AP/Wide World Photos.

camp, a certain action, a certain date. In retrospect its almost civilized pose of Nazi guard and prisoners conveyed little of the horror that would soon characterize photos of the camps. But at the time the photograph was typical of the available documentation.

All of this means that even when the first atrocity photos did reach the West, the press did not know what to do with them. Often it failed to use the photographs in a way that might have lent credence to the sketchy atrocity reports circulating at the time. Instead, images were used as symbolic markers of an as yet incomplete and unarticulated atrocity story, largely because an even or consistent record of what was going on in the camps had not yet been compiled. The absence of a gradual accumulation of photographs during this period created a disjuncture that would make the photographic record provided on liberation that much more unsettling. Moreover, the delayed emergence of that record and the lack of a frame for presenting images of atrocity made the camps' liberation an important site of persuasion: it was only on seeing the camps that the press would understand that it needed to report the unbelievable. As the *New Republic* said during the Allied thrust across Europe the following April, "only now, after Allied correspondents report what has been going on behind the walls of these Nazi camps, are all the hideous stories, doubted for so long, confirmed."[72]

But the camps' liberation was important for the press too. The general tensions between reporters and photographers that had inadequately addressed how best to use images in news, a tradition for depicting atrocity that had emphasized benign over explicit representation, and a failure to report hints of the atrocities during the preliberation period all made the opening of the camps an important setting for displaying the different representational forces of images and words. In covering the atrocities made evident with the camps' liberation, the word took backstage to the image for one of the few times in the history of the U.S. and British press. That relationship would shape the record of Nazi atrocity at the time as well as in memory.

Covering Atrocity in Word

AS WORLD WAR II MOVED TOWARD THE LIBERATION OF the concentration camps, U.S. and British journalists and photographers faced one of the most trying forums in professional memory. Against a mountain of skepticism and disbelief about Nazi atrocity, the press made its way across a war-torn landscape, ill prepared for what it would find. By the time it reached the camps of the western front—among them Buchenwald, Bergen-Belsen, and Dachau—it needed to process the story of the atrocities into a plausible narrative. Doing so required extensive repair work, which involved correcting, altering, and redoing reports that had been already filed.

Earlier reports of the concentration camps freed on the Eastern front of the German occupation helped shape the story the Western media produced. In particular, reports from one such camp, Majdanek, freed by the Russians months before the U.S. and British forces neared the camps of the West, offered a dress rehearsal for coverage. The act of bearing witness also facilitated the press's attempts to make sense of what it saw. But both dimensions of coverage underscored the limitations of words in shaping the atrocity story.

COVERING MAJDANEK:
A DRESS REHEARSAL FOR RECORDING
THE UNBELIEVABLE

The camps of the eastern front were liberated by the Russians almost a year before those freed by the British and U.S. forces. In July 1944, the Russians liberated the camp of Majdanek and occupied the already evacuated camps of Belzec, Sobibor, and Treblinka; other camps on the eastern front—including Auschwitz and Birkenau—were liberated the following winter. Because the main thrust of the U.S. and British forces' activities did not begin until the spring of 1945, when a string of camps, including Buchenwald, Bergen-Belsen, and Dachau, was freed, the Russian liberation of Majdanek offered one of the first opportunities for the press to see what was happening inside the camps of Nazi Europe. Moreover, the liberation of the eastern camps established a standard of coverage against which the U.S. and British press could measure its own performance.[1]

The experience of liberating the eastern camps was chilling. When the Soviet army came upon Majdanek on July 23, 1944, it found a location already depleted of most of its inmates. Although over half a million persons had been killed there, only seven hundred emaciated but living prisoners met the Russians. They showed their liberators mass graves, gas chambers, and warehouses filled with shoes, children's toys, eyeglasses, and clothing. From Majdanek, the Red Army continued west across Poland, where it overran the camps of Belzec, Sobibor, and Treblinka, all emptied of survivors and artifacts. On January 25, 1945, the Russians entered Auschwitz. With estimates of over a million killed, fewer than three thousand persons, most of them Jews, greeted the liberators.

The Russians were curiously uneven in their attempts to make public what they found when they liberated the camps. They issued no press releases on Belzec, Sobibor, and Treblinka. And they did little to publicize Auschwitz's liberation until after the liberation of the western camps. Yet to Majdanek they invited a select group of Western correspondents to tour the camp. This made Majdanek the one camp that drew Western attention. But even that attention was less than wholehearted.[2]

Reports of the Majdanek atrocities failed to kindle public notice. The first eyewitness accounts appeared in the Russian press in August 1944, and although the U.S. and British press reported these accounts within days, they were not given full play. The *New York Times* cautiously attributed the story of the execution of "several hundred thousand persons" to the Russian army newspaper *Red Star*, which in turn cited "witnesses and official German records" as its source; the *London Times* reported even less information one day later, and the BBC refused to cover the story at all in its Russian version. *Time* reprinted parts of the eyewitness account of Soviet war correspondent Roman Karmen as part of its foreign news roundup, placing it alongside a piece of equal length about the Polish constitution and enclosing its eight paragraphs with quotation marks. *Time*'s presentation of Karmen's piece not only appeared to dispense with the newsmagazine's responsibility for the account but also deflated the institutional voice of the Soviet correspondent: the piece read like the distanced recounting of an eyewitness telling the story of one isolated incident, rather than a reporter recounting an event representative of the Nazi reign of terror. At the end of August *Life* published a pictorial spread from Majdanek that provided pictures of ovens with granulated bones. Yet that visualization too was undercut by the picture-magazine when it displayed its ambivalence about the source of the report by referring to the "circumstantial Russian story" that accompanied the photos.[3]

Much of the press's ambivalence toward the story had to do with the circumstances mentioned earlier—the willingness to disbelieve, the tendency toward benign representation, the experience of false World War I atrocity stories, and traces of anti-Semitism. But additional antipathy derived from a broader skepticism about Russian reporters, particularly a dislike for the Russian literary news-writing style and tendency to exaggerate. When the *New York Times Magazine* ran an early piece by an *Izvestia* correspondent who provided details about the methods of execution being used in the camps, it foregrounded ambivalence about his journalistic credentials by introducing him as a "noted novelist and war correspondent." His "somewhat unreal literary style" made many discount his writing as propaganda.[4] That skepticism made the Western press regard the liberation of the eastern camps as a story in need of additional confirmation. Its dismissive attitude was exacerbated by the fact that the U.S. and British forces by and large had been denied access to the camps of the eastern front. For professional reasons, then, it was easier to regard the information trickling out as Russian propaganda.

This somewhat changed when the select group of reporters and photographers was invited into Majdanek in August and September 1944. Thirty foreign correspondents were brought into the camp under the auspices of the Russian-backed Polish Committee of National Liberation. So unprepared was the press for what it found there, that decisions had not yet been made about how to designate concentration camps in the news. Nearly every newspaper, journal, and magazine reporting on the camp employed a "Lublin" dateline, marking the town two miles away rather than the camp itself. One article in the *Chicago Tribune* never once mentioned the camp by name. The decision not to employ a dateline from Majdanek had the curious effect of deflating the significance of this site of German brutality, and it persisted for months after the camp's liberation.[5]

The encounter with the camps shocked members of the press. "This is the most horrific story I shall ever have to write," began a reporter for the British *News Chronicle.* He went on to say that

> It gives me no pleasure to tell you all this. What I have seen I shall never forget—the horror of this camp will live in my mind until I die. I wish one of you could see it for yourself, all the same. I wish every German could see it for, wickedly though the Germans have behaved as a nation, I do not think the mass of the German people know what is being done in their name. I hope soon they will be told fully and convincingly.[6]

That scenario was not to be, for the initial reports of Western journalists from Majdanek were generally dismissed or minimized at home. Briton Alexander Werth's report was rejected by the BBC as "Russian propaganda" but found its way a month later into the *Christian Science Monitor*. The *New York Herald Tribune* warned that "maybe we should wait for further corroboration of the horror story that has come from Lublin . . . [for] this tale sounds inconceivable." One U.S. news editor admitted only that "this terrible story of Maidanek *may* be true" (emphasis added). And the *Christian Century* ridiculed those papers that did run the story, noting that the parallel between the "alleged killing" of 1.5 million persons at Majdanek and the "'corpse factory' atrocity tale of the First World War" was "too striking to be overlooked." Each report lacked the accoutrements of regular coverage, particularly its verification by credible eyewitnesses.[7]

Certain newspapers, magazines, and journals did sustain some belief in their reporters and printed the Majdanek story with supporting evidence. Editorial appeals to readers bolstered the reportage's credibility, as when the editors of the *Saturday Evening Post* implored audiences to just "read the simple and moving report" of the journal's correspondent. Bill Lawrence of the *New York Times* ran a lengthy story—published at some delay from its reportage—with a memorable lead claiming, "I have just seen the most terrible place on the face of the earth." But the following day, the *Times* took the rather incredible step of assuring its readers Lawrence was not prone to overstatement: he "is employed by this newspaper because he is known to be a thorough and accurate correspondent." The evidence, it went on to say, "is visible and Mr. Lawrence saw it." Later, Lawrence complained that "never before or since have I seen the *Times* so describe one of its reporters."[8]

Yet regardless of the editorial supports offered, telling the Majdanek story underscored the limitations of journalists as chroniclers. As an editor with the *Saturday Evening Post* observed,

> once in a while you run across a story . . . so loathsome as to make the meanest beast seem clean and wholesome by comparison, that it renews itself through the continued interest or incredulity of the public, and through the subjective experience of the reporter. Maidanek is such a story.[9]

Reporters struggled against odds to present their narratives in a way that would make people believe what they had to say.

Telling the Majdanek story showed the press how difficult were the atrocities to cover. Although the physical evidence surrounding Majdanek was tame in comparison with what reporters would find on the western front, even if the story were no less horrific, its coverage underscored for the press the difficulty of processing the atrocities into a plausible narrative. It was here that the larger aim of bearing witness helped journalists accommodate their own limitations.

Majdanek as a Standard for Bearing Witness

The Western coverage of Majdanek was important because it established a standard by which reporters and photographers could later bear witness to Nazi atrocity, that is, take responsibility for what they saw. Even though reporters and photographers entered Majdanek in small numbers and at a considerable delay, coverage of what they found there would help shape their story of the western camps. It was no accident, for instance, that when the *New York Times* documented the liberation of Natzweiler in eastern France in December 1944, it titled its reportage "The Lublin of Alsace," in reference to earlier coverage of Majdanek.[10] Covering the camps, then, established a reportorial and photographic standard that would be put to repeated use during the remainder of the war.

In helping the press recount Majdanek's liberation, images and words shaped the atrocity story in different ways. Words grounded the story by concretizing the details by which the camp had functioned. Photos generalized the story by taking it beyond the confines of Majdanek. Though scarce, photographs hinted already in Majdanek that they could compensate for some of the inadequacies displayed by words. While photography's function of providing a medium of record had made it appealing to reporters, its referentiality was not what figured in the Majdanek coverage. Rather, the image's ability to link the scenes of Majdanek with a broader interpretive scheme for comprehending what was happening suggested how photography might be particularly suited to documenting the camps. And in so doing, it would also facilitate the act of bearing witness.

Thus, as the horror of the camps appeared to transcend the ability of reporters to capture it in words, images assumed a role that went beyond merely illustrating the words at their side. But this did not happen at once. For the relative absence of vivid documentation of Majdanek only hinted at the role that photographs could play. Rather, it took shape in conjunction with the press's entry into the western camps, where scenes of massive decay and death could be photographed more easily. The ability of images to bring home the horror more capably than words by underscoring the scope and magnitude of Nazi atrocity would prove itself with the flood of photos made available with the western camps' liberation. Yet already at Majdanek, there were suggestions that the atrocity coverage would be most effective by playing toward images and away from words.

Majdanek in Word: The Eyewitness Report

For as long as the press had reported on war, it had chronicled wartime through the eyewitness report. Seen as an effective way of upholding credibility and authority, the press favored the eyewitness report because it offered nonanalytical, noninterpretive recountings of "what reporters saw." In fact, the "further the story is taken from the eyewitness source, the weaker the proof that it ever occurred." This semblance of authenticity and on-site presence compelled reporters to use eyewitness reports for stories that they find difficult to contextualize and for which audiences have no firsthand knowledge.[11] From the beginning, then, the eyewitness report had an appeal for reporters covering Nazi atrocity.

In covering Majdanek, the press turned immediately to the eyewitness report. Reporters' accounts provided grounded chronicles of what they saw, referential evidence they hoped would help the public back home bear witness to the atrocities. Reporters struggled to piece together plausible accounts of the horror they found, as in the following narrative about the camp's gas chamber:

> Hot damp air was found to give the best results—hence the showers and the hot air fan. I made a mental note that the room could (I repeat could) really have been used for the innocent purpose of disinfection. But what of the next room which I saw? This was a hermetically sealed concrete room, seven feet high and about fifteen feet square, with an iron gaspipe leading into it from a smaller whitewashed room where was an apparatus for attaching cylinders of carbon monoxide. Between one room and the other was a small glass peephole with a grating over it. You would not need a peephole to watch clothes being disinfected.[12]

The eyewitness reports of Majdanek took on a highly standardized form. Nearly always identified by byline, the reports provided terse, blow-by-blow chronicles that wandered little from the most obvious and concrete details of the scene at hand. The prose was simple and direct, its language marked by repetitiveness. "This is a place that must be seen to be believed," went the refrain. "My eyes cannot deceive me." Edgar Snow of the *Saturday Evening Post* admitted taking two trips around the camp so as to double-check his details before writing his report, and *New York Times* reporter Bill Lawrence's account filled a full page of prose with paragraphs that began with the words, "*I have seen* . . . This is Maidanek as *I saw it*" (emphasis added). A *Newsweek* correspondent told of how "*I went* through this immensely efficient human slaughterhouse" and "*I saw* lethal chambers into which new arrivals were invited to go for baths" (emphasis added). Generally tendered in first- or third-person narratives that focused specifically on what reporters saw, these accounts made little attempt to analyze, generalize, or interpret. They thereby remained highly referential.[13]

The content of the reports was no more varied. The reports were structured through two main narrative foci—territory and the act of witnessing. Touring the camp's territory was a useful way for reporters to carefully account for what they saw. Reporters led their readers from the bathhouse to the crematorium to the open graves to the warehouses filled with possessions, the camp comprising "an impressive collection of buildings . . . neatly laid out." Readers were taken around the camp in directed word-tours: "We got out to inspect the bathhouses. . . . We walked back into the sun. . . . We rode a little distance to some cabbage patches. . . . We came to a large unpainted warehouse." Word-tours sometimes focused on one particular scene, as when *Time-Life* correspondent Richard Lauterbach reported on the shoe warehouse.

> I stepped up and went inside. It was full of shoes. A sea of shoes. I walked across them unsteadily. They were piled, like pieces of coal in a bin, halfway up the walls. Not only shoes. Boots. Rubbers. Leggings. Slippers. Children's shoes, soldier's shoes, old shoes, new shoes. They were red and grey and black. Some had once been white.

Concretizing a camp's places of torture, reporters used the particulars of the terrain to document the horror it embodied. One reporter with the *New York Herald Tribune* simply outlined how "I went through this camp." The accounts read almost like tour guides for the blind, concretely and dispassionately retracing the physical steps taken to cross the camp.[14]

The Majdanek reports similarly focused on the act of witnessing. They did so by citing the witnesses whom reporters encountered in the camps, witnesses who were valuable parts of the story both because of the information they supplied and for the depth their silent presence lent the narratives. Witnesses introduced an indexical dimension to the atrocity story and, like the territory, authenticated the story's horror by grounding it in the here and now.

The most authoritative, though most distanced, act of witnessing was enacted by the reporters themselves, who not only needed to piece together the story but also to underscore the depravity of what they saw. Yet because the depravity was so overwhelming, reporters needed witnesses with greater authority to authenticate their accounts. They found them in the ranks of victims, survivors, German bystanders, other foreign nationals, and perpetrators. The words and responses of these witnesses gave

Majdanek accounts a sequencing that took readers from one act of witnessing to another—from a dialogue with an S.S. man in Majdanek who had "glassy, expressionless eyes" to a former prisoner incarcerated for black-market meat operations, from interviews with four German prisoners of war to three officers associated with the camp. Not surprisingly, errors of interpretation easily found their way into these verbal narratives, largely because journalists did not have the reportorial frame, worldview, or expertise to evaluate what they were seeing. One reporter for the *Daily Telegraph,* for instance, maintained that the Germans left Lublin so quickly that they left behind "abounding evidence of their ghastly crimes." In fact, the Nazis had systematically cleansed the camp, but that would only become evident once reporters experienced the western camps where the Nazis left behind mounds of evidence. Horror, it seemed, gained perspective most effectively through more horror.[15]

Thus, by relying on the eyewitness report, until then the most surefooted way of recording what the reporters were seeing, the press fashioned its own professional corrective for not having reported the atrocities earlier. Doing so concretized the atrocity story and ensured that words would function referentially. On that basis the press had some assurance that its reports would be believed. Yet the referentiality of words inverted professional expectations held of the image. For if words were to provide the referential force of the message, what role would photographs play? That became clear with the liberation of the western camps, when words could offer only a partial vehicle of persuasion about Nazi horror. It was then that images took over the primary role of convincing disbelieving publics about the atrocities.

Majdanek in Image: The Photograph as Symbol of Atrocity

The potential role of photography in documenting Nazi atrocity became most vivid when the press entered Majdanek. The camp's scenes were so unbelievable that they required visual representation to help secure public belief. But photographers did not have much to work with at Majdanek, for although photos were taken of the camps, they were limited in target of depiction and restricted in number, a far cry from the images that would circulate later with the liberation of the western camps.

Perhaps because the depictions provided less evidence than was required to dispel disbelief, they were published unevenly and infrequently. Not all of the major newspapers even included photographs. The British *Daily News* presented three uncaptioned pictures—one each of a crematorium, a group of weeping Lublinites, and an open pit. No corpses, victims, or survivors were depicted. Singular images of cremation ovens that had been distributed by the Russian Sovfoto Agency were published. The *Chicago Tribune* printed two photographs from the "concentration camp at Lublin, Poland": one shot offered a frontal view of a cremation oven, the other scores of "containers in which ashes of prisoners at Lublin were sold for fertilizer."[16]

The most graphic set of images from Majdanek appeared a full two months after the camp was liberated, in October 1944, when certain recycled Sovfoto images made their way back into the Western press and accompanied the images of Western photographers. The *Saturday Evening Post* published shots of accumulations of possessions—shoes, cans of human ashes, family snapshots. The *Illustrated London News* published the largest display of images—eleven photographs (fig. 4). Next to the photos the newspaper apologized to its readers, not for the delay but for the gruesome nature of the images.

> It is not the custom of the *Illustrated London News* to publish photographs of atrocities, but in view of the fact that the enormity of the crimes perpetrated by the Germans is so wicked that our readers, to whom such behavior is unbelievable, may think the reports of such crimes exaggerated or due to propaganda, we consider it necessary to present them, by means of the accompanying photographs, with irrefutable proof of the organized murder of between 600,000 and 1,000,000 helpless persons at the Maidanek Camp near Lublin. And even these pictures are carefully selected from a number, some of which are too horrible to reproduce.

More than the earlier photographs, these images hinted at the scope and industrial nature of the Nazi atrocities. The photos depicted prisoners' cells, the interior of barracks, the building housing the torture chamber, and heaps of personal possessions—photos, luggage locks, boots.[17]

How was Majdanek seen in image? The camp's photos revealed only schematic detail of the atrocities themselves. Most displayed inanimate artifacts—mounds of objects, warehouses, gas chambers, strings of cremation ovens—and few provided depictions of survivors or victims. Unlike the images of later camps, few pictures of dead corpses were as yet published, and the images that did appear tended to be cleansed of human bodies. The emphasis was instead on the accoutrements of atrocity—gas cells, hanging ropes, furnaces, and cans of Zyklon B, the gas used for extermination—while portrayals of enormous quantities of objects associated with the victims—mounds of shoes, passports, and luggage locks— suggested how widespread and systematic was Nazi brutality and how numerous its victims. Though the photos did not furnish the visual proof of masses of corpses that would later be supplied with the western camps,

THE MOST TERRIBLE EXAMPLE OF ORGANISED
MASS MURDER BY THE GERMANS AT

(Continued.)

barbed wire, it
never intended to
vide permanent acc
modation for the
mates, and the
racks were cleared
as fast as the priso
could be killed
Some, it is true,
of hunger and dis
but the favou
method of extermi
tion was by po
gas. In the f
concrete cells is prov
for the purpose,
victims were pa
so tightly that
died on their fe
the gas was pur
in. Fifteen mi
after the introdu
of the gas, the ex
tioners entered the
and removed the e
In the centre of
camp stands a
stone buildin

LUBLIN'S "CAMP OF ANNIHILATION": THE BARRACKS' INTERIOR,
SHOWING REMNANTS OF ROPES USED TO HANG VICTIMS.

THE EXTERIOR OF THE TORTURE CHAMBER
AT THE MAJDANEK "ANNIHILATION CAMP,"
SITUATED SOME TWO TO THREE MILES OUTSIDE
LUBLIN.

THE GAS CELLS INTO WHICH THE PRISONERS WERE PACKED SO TIGHTLY THAT THEY DIED ON THEIR FEET
AS THE POISON GAS WAS PUMPED IN.

A FEW OF THE CYLINDERS CONTAINING POISON
THIS WAS THE NAZIS' FAVOU

IT is not the custom of "The Illustrated London News" to publish photographs of atrocities, but in view of the fact that the enormity of the crimes perpetrated by the Germans is so wicked that our readers, to whom such behaviour is unbelievable, may think the reports of such crimes exaggerated or due to propaganda, we consider it necessary to present them, by means of the accompanying photographs, with an irrefutable proof of the organised murder of between 600,000 and 1,000,000 helpless persons at Majdanek Camp, near Lublin. And even these pictures are carefully selected from a number, some of which are too horrible to reproduce. The Majdanek camp was called by the Germans themselves "the camp of annihilation"; built over an area of 20 square kilometres and surrounded by

(Continued above.)

THE FURNACES IN WHICH THE GERMANS CREMATED THE BODIES OF THE MEN AND WOMEN
THEY HAD DELIBERATELY ASPHYXIATED BY POISON GAS.

THE OPENING IN THE ROOF OF THE GAS CHAMBE
THROUGH WHICH "CYCLONE" CRYSTALS WERE POURE

Figure 4. "The Most Terrible Example of Organized Cruelty," *Illustrated London News,*

CRUELTY IN THE HISTORY OF CIVILISATION.
THE MAJDANEK "CAMP OF ANNIHILATION."

world's biggest
...torium. In this
...torium are five
...ovens, where five
...es were never
...d to go out.
...and night, pillars
...ck smoke belched
...the chimneys, as
...bodies of the
...ers were dragged
...he gas chambers
...urnt. Even in
...most horrible of
...ck the Germans
...methodical : a
...of bodies, then
...of logs, another
...of bodies, an-
...ayer of logs ; and
...One thousand
...undred corpses
...o disposed of
...twenty-four
...and the ashes
...he furnaces were
...y collected and
...o Germany as
[Continued below.]

AN ENORMOUS QUANTITY OF LOCKS FROM THE PRISONERS' LUGGAGE WAS FOUND IN THE CAMP: FOREIGN CORRESPONDENTS VIEWING THESE LOCKS.

SOME OF THE PASSPORTS AND IDENTITY CARDS BELONGING TO THE VICTIMS OF NAZI BRUTALITY AT MAJDANEK CAMP.

...OR THE WHOLESALE SLAUGHTER OF PRISONERS.
...OF EXTERMINATION.

THOUSANDS OF PAIRS OF BOOTS AND SHOES, ONCE BELONGING TO FREE MEN AND WOMEN, HERE COLLECTED FROM THE VICTIMS FOR CONSIGNMENT TO GERMANY.

[Continued.]
fertiliser for Nazi kitchen gardens. This story as it stands is almost incredible in its bestiality, but German cruelty went further still at Majdanek. Prisoners who were too ill to walk into the camp—there to strip and neatly hang their clothes on pegs specially provided for the purpose before going to their death—were dragged alive to the furnaces and thrust in alongside the dead. And the man chiefly responsible for these mass murders ? Herr Mussfeld was his name, the camp commandant. And yet no one man can be held responsible for these mass murders, not even Himmler : the whole German nation is involved, for it has chosen its leaders and presumably ad-mires them. This camp, as it stands to-day, is a grim reminder of that streak of utter inhumanity which is found in every German.

...OF "CYCLONE" CRYSTALS : SUCH CANS WERE
...D BY THE SCORE IN THE MAJDANEK CAMP

THE CRYSTALS OF THE POISONOUS CHEMICAL KNOWN AS "CYCLONE." THE GERMANS USED THE WORD CYCLONE—"ZYKLON "—AS THE TRADE NAME FOR THIS GAS.

they pointed to the carefully planned nature of the atrocities and suggested that death in the camps was meticulously arranged, not thoughtlessly
implemented. The photos also lent a visual dimension to the two narrative
foci that had been most instrumental in conveying the atrocity story in
words—the camp's territory and the act of witnessing.

The camp's territory was visually presented in ways that metonymical-
ly referenced the atrocities happening elsewhere. Most images were presented without credits, telling readers little about who had taken them,
and captions offered only generalized interpretations of what the images
depicted: alongside a disarrayed assembly of tin cans was the note, "Cans
for Human Ashes." A collection of documents was captioned "Passports and
Identity Cards Belonging to the Victims of Nazi Brutality," a stack of shoes
"Thousands of Pairs of Boots and Shoes, Once Belonging to Free Men and
Women." The words alongside the images authenticated the depictions at
their side, but they did so in broad language that rendered them generic
representations of the atrocities.[18] A warehouse of shoes or a string of
ovens thus told less about the camp itself than about the nature of Nazi brutality. Instead of providing word-tours around the camps, as reporters did
in their verbal narratives, these images invoked the broader scope of Nazi
horror by depicting one scene of the camp's territory and making it representative of all Nazi barbarism. Because readers needed a broader context
to understand that the images depicted mechanisms central to the Nazi
death machinery, the photographs guided publics to the broader story of
atrocity. The photos thereby were set in place as symbols of that context.

In a like vein, photographs focused not on the survivors—for there
were few to be photographed—but on the act of bearing witness. Photo
after photo showed individuals examining evidence of the atrocities in Majdanek: the *Saturday Evening Post* portrayed unidentified observers, presumably male civilians from Lublin, inspecting a battery of incinerators. Behind
them stood a line of women—second-order witnesses—who squeamish-
ly watched them. The *Illustrated London News* depicted a group of "foreign
correspondents *viewing the locks* taken from prisoners' luggage" (emphasis
added). In both cases the images marked not only the atrocity's documentation but also the response to it, separating the act of witnessing from the
actual circumstances being witnessed.[19] Unlike reporters' narratives,
where witnessing was made part of a chronological sequencing of events,
images made the act of witnessing into a part of the atrocity story that was
equally important to the depiction of the atrocities themselves. The
salience of photographs facilitated such a transformation. Here too, photography pushed aside the actual details of brutality in Majdanek so as to
accommodate the broader act of bearing witness to atrocity. Even when

the witnesses' gaze was not particularly newsworthy or significant, the act of witnessing received photographic coverage. This suggested that the press would be able to use similar images of other camps to link them together in a broader story about atrocity.

Thus in both word and image, reporting Majdanek provided a dress rehearsal for the Western press's entry into the camps. Although depictions of the Majdanek story were tame in comparison with what would follow, confirming the Russian reports of the camp somewhat prepared the press to bear witness to the camps of the western front, where it would be first to record the sights. The dress rehearsal had one further important effect as well: it revealed the extent to which the Western world was not prepared to believe what the Allied forces would find the following spring.

As a measure of the power of that disbelief, skepticism lingered following the reports of Majdanek's liberation. It may have been the lack of explicit and repetitive visualization of the Majdanek atrocities—that is, the relative absence of photographs of dead bodies and other gruesome scenes—that facilitated that disbelief. For the Majdanek story "had little impact on public opinion in the West. Those who believed were confirmed in their belief; those who did not believe remained skeptical." As one officer of the British Psychological Warfare Division wrote as late as January 1945: "The British and American people are still not as a whole willing to believe that the German atrocities . . . have been anything like they are." Noting that many still thought that the reports were "Russian propaganda," he recommended publishing a special photographic record to quell their disbelief. Incredibly, public knowledge and awareness about Nazi atrocity actually declined between 1943 and the end of the war, when disbelieving publics, in the view of *Washington Post* correspondent Edward Folliard, continued to "have to be shown" in order to believe the stories. That would become possible only following the liberation of the camps of the western front—when photographs of atrocity would become readily available. For it was "not until the liberation of Dachau, Buchenwald, and above all, Bergen-Belsen, that the skeptics finally and unequivocally acknowledged that the Russian accounts were accurate. The truth about the camps was, if anything, worse than the most extensive of rumors."[20]

THE WORDS OF ATROCITY:
COVERING THE CAMPS OF THE WESTERN FRONT

Bearing witness to Nazi barbarism was dramatically complicated with the entry into the camps of the western front, for the atrocities that became evident on their liberation were like no other in the memory of the press corps. In media scholar Philip Knightley's view, "correspondents of exceptional ability [were required] to convey the full horror of the concentration camps."[21] Reporters, however, were unclear about how to convey that horror.

At the heart of their discomfort was the irrevocable nature of the evidence that they confronted. Having emphasized moderation in their accounts for so long, they now needed to produce powerful documentation that could not only convince disbelieving publics of an insufficiently reported story but could help them repair their own earlier coverage. Anxieties, shock, horror, and a lingering sense of disbelief complicated reporters' own professionalism and placed them in the odd circumstance of having to work against their own carefully crafted standards of credibility. But how were they to do so? And through which tools would they be able to convince publics of what they were seeing?

The U.S. and British role in the liberation of the camps on the western front started in earnest in April 1945. From the first week of April onward, the U.S. forces entered a series of camps in rapid succession, including Ohrdruf, Nordhausen, Buchenwald, Dachau, and Mauthausen. At about the same time, the British forces entered Bergen-Belsen. The Allied troops who entered these camps were often accompanied by reporters and photographers, whose words and photographic images constituted the first sanctioned record of what was happening inside. For those who had covered Majdanek's liberation even from afar, the experience immediately proved worthwhile: without explicitly stating it, the press was now able to invoke the standard earlier established in covering that camp. Although the liberation of the camps forced a revelatory role onto the Western press that Majdanek had not called for—in that here the reporters entered the camps *as* they were being liberated, forcing them to report rather than corroborate the accounts of others—the record of the western camps confirmed the earlier Majdanek reports. Admitting the skepticism that had greeted the Russians on their liberation of Majdanek, the editor of the *Boston Globe* put it succinctly when he said: "Now we know that the Russians told the truth."[22]

As with Majdanek, the press here activated images and words differently in the act of bearing witness. Using Majdanek as a clear standard, it turned to the eyewitness report as a way of offering publics their first detailed verbal encounter with what had been happening in the camps. The eyewitness report's grounded and nonanalytical prose offered a valuable guidepost in verbally shaping a story that was unbelievable even to those responsible for telling it. And although images had played so little a role in covering Majdanek, their anticipated use here was also clear; for as the press entered camp after camp, it recognized that images could help report the scenes of horror and decay that it was seeing. The dress rehearsal of Majdanek was proving its mettle months after the experience in guiding the press to the core of the atrocity story. From the outset images were expected to play an active part in its shaping.

Like other war coverage, coverage of the camps drew upon the implicit rules of wartime cooperation that had been set in place with the broadening of the war effort. Not intent on competing, journalists were able to bear witness by repairing to this cooperative mode of journalism, even if it undermined familiar practices of newsmaking. As they struggled to piece together a comprehensive and comprehensible account of the harsh evidence of Nazi brutality, journalists found that their cooperation with each other acted as a tool of confirmation of what they were seeing, both for themselves and their reading public. They shared sources, used other reporters for confirmation, and generally pooled their resources in their attempts to make sense of the story.[23] Few of the stories differed from each other, and many of the same tales, persons, and scenes repeatedly resurfaced in coverage.

The Content of Bearing Witness: Chronicles of Liberation

When the press entered the camps of the western front, it found that the most effective way to tell the atrocity story was as a chronicle of liberation. This shifted the coverage from the somewhat abstract accounting of the heretofore unconfirmed reports that had existed prior to entering the camps into a record that would focus on a concrete site and explode with horrific details of every kind imaginable.[24]

The liberation of Buchenwald, Bergen-Belsen, and Dachau took place over a three-week period in April and May 1945. Buchenwald was liberated on April 11, 1945, when the U.S. forces—members of the Sixth and Fourth Armored Divisions—found some twenty thousand male inmates of the camp, including approximately four thousand Jews. Most of the camp's prisoners had been forcibly marched out days earlier, followed by scores of fleeing Germans. Bergen-Belsen was liberated on the afternoon of April 15, when British troops entering the camp were met by approximately forty thousand prisoners, two-thirds of them women. Another fifteen thousand prisoners were in the temporary camp at the Panzer Training School along with a number of German soldiers and loyalists—approximately eighty S.S. personnel, among them Commandant Josef Kramer, several Hungarian soldiers, and some German army regulars. Dachau was liberated on April 29 by several divisions of the U.S. Army—the Twentieth Armored Division, the Forty-second Infantry Division (also called the Rainbow Division), and the Forty-fifth Infantry Division. A few German gunners who had remained

behind in the camp unknown to the U.S. forces exchanged fire with the soldiers during the liberation. Approximately seventy thousand persons
imprisoned within the Dachau system greeted the liberators.

With the liberation of all three camps, the press immediately faced its
own limitations. Unlike other events of the war, the camps' liberation was
accompanied by a military decision to make available its scenes to the
world. A shocked General Dwight Eisenhower saw scenes of horror in the
camp at Ohrdruf on April 12, and he immediately proclaimed that "the
things I saw beggar description." He demanded mass witnessing of the
atrocities: members of the U.S. military were ordered to tour the camps,
and photographers and reporters stationed within a one-hundred-mile
radius were directed to change their destination so as to provide coverage.
Tours of politicians, news editors, and other officials were arranged so as
to facilitate the act of bearing witness, and a strident denazification campaign forcing German nationals to tour the camps was begun, with the
Overseas Branch of the Office of War Information mandated to reeducate
the Germans about responsibility for the war.[25] In Eisenhower's view,
bearing witness was a necessary response to the atrocities, and extensive
actions were taken to accomplish it.

On the one hand, the official interest in providing access to the camps
made it easier for reporters to cover the story. Unlike other events of the
war, many reporters entered the camps much like the troops whom they
accompanied. Often donning military uniforms and presenting passes
when needed, they were at times distinct from the accompanying soldiers
only by their minimal equipment—notepads and pens. Many entered the
camps with few military restrictions and were able to tour the terrain and
speak with whom they encountered. And although some reporters sus-
pected the sudden lifting of military restrictions—restrictions that extended to the procurement of identity cards, passports, health cards, and uniforms—they were relieved at the easing of red tape.[26]

But confusion abounded, and little could prepare the press for what it
would find. The camps were so numerous that the U.S. and British forces
often came upon them by accident. Commanders themselves did not
always know of their existence, as they were not marked on most maps,
and divisions received little intelligence about the camps before they got
there. As one correspondent later remembered, "patrols of the British Second Army . . . stumbled without warning on Bergen-Belsen." Some
reporters realized the "category" of their destination but knew little more:
in one correspondent's words, he was entering "another hell-hole of a
camp."[27] The name of a given camp, its history, the nationalities of its
inmates or victims, the differences between camps—these were all details

that eluded even the military and were thus often missing or wrongly represented in the coverage that resulted.

Other problems faced reporters once they entered the camps. They received few guidelines on how to cover the atrocities, yet they lacked a frame for improvising on that coverage. As one reporter later said, "this was obviously no routine assignment to be covered briefly and then forgotten."[28] Yet how were they to corroborate sources for a story that blew apart not only reportorial expectations but moral ones as well? How were they to confirm the unbelievable numbers of tortured, imprisoned, and dead? Normally surmountable problems—such as language differences—here became paramount, as prisoners mumbling in foreign languages fell dead before interpreters could be found to record their words. Even as they faced the dead piling up around them in courtyards, on train tracks, and on roads, many journalists still naively expected proven journalistic methods to help them record what they were seeing. After visiting Buchenwald but filing from Paris, one editor wrote that "obviously in the short time given editors for inspecting the camp there was little opportunity to weigh evidence and decide on the reliability and creditability of witnesses."[29] The disjunction between his practiced notions of newsmaking and what faced him on the ground was telling.

Reporters covered the carnage by fashioning their coverage into chronicles of liberation, which catered to proven newsmaking practices. Both at the time of entry into the camps and in the accounts that unfolded over the following weeks, journalists used the grounded and nonanalytical prose with which they had discussed Majdanek to describe what they saw here. In carefully tendered eyewitness reports, they relayed in meticulous detail the scenes that they saw as the prisoners of the camps were freed: the masses of wasted humanity, the sick crumbling at their feet, the officials struggling to instill order. Even when the press entered the camps after liberation, as was generally the case, it provided extensive details of the postliberation scenes. As one chronicler of Dachau wrote, the reports were "a plain straightforward account of what I saw."[30]

In all three camps, journalists struggled to find metaphors powerful enough to capture what they were seeing in words. Survivors were likened to "whipped dogs," "miserable wrecks," and "creatures," the camps seen as "the ultimate in human degradation," a "hell carefully planned and executed," and "death reduced to a state of ordinariness." Often the horror was communicated in the juxtaposition between the everyday and the atrocious, as when correspondent Martha Gelhorn wrote that in Dachau "the clothing was handled with order but the bodies were dumped like garbage rotting in the sun."[31]

From the first tentative accounts of the camps through their fuller recording, the tale of the camps' liberation traveled across newspapers, magazines, and journals in a journey that reflected its ascent as a credible accounting in the public eye. Though the story appeared initially on the interior pages of the daily and weekly press, where it was structured as a sidebar to the broader war story, during the height of military activities in the camps it merited front-page coverage.

For three weeks the camps' liberation drew widespread coverage that proceeded with the logic of a substitutional rule: the accounts of a camp previously liberated were replaced by the reports of a newly liberated camp. Items about Ohrdruf and Nordhausen gave way to accounts of Buchenwald, followed by stories of Belsen, and then to accounts of Dachau. All told, the story of the camps' liberation filled the pages of the U.S. and British popular press from April 9 until the end of the first week in May 1945. Depending on the time slot, reporters covering the liberation of different camps found themselves in different parts of the larger atrocity story. In mid-April, for instance, the front pages of many newspapers, magazines, and journals featured second-round accounts of Buchenwald, compiled by reporters who had been on extended stay in the area, alongside initial reports of Belsen's liberation. Two weeks later, second-round accounts of Belsen were accompanied both by reports of the official delegations on Buchenwald and initial reports of Dachau's liberation. Chronicles about the liberation of different camps were thus presented side by side.

The first identifiable thrust of detailed reporting came immediately after the first camps were liberated during the second week of April, when brief wire service dispatches told of stacks of bodies and gruesome scenes of brutality and death. They were followed within days by lengthy, blow-by-blow accounts of what reporters were seeing. From Buchenwald came the accounts of reporters like Gene Currivan, Percival Knauth, and Harold Denny, from Belsen Edwin Tetlow and Ronald Monson, from Dachau Marguerite Higgins and Martha Gelhorn. Most reporters filed more than one article from each locale and often more than one in a given day—detailing not only what they saw but what they were told about life before they had arrived: stories of death counts, torture regimens, and horrific daily routines.[32]

Reporters and photographers entered Buchenwald shortly after the U.S. troops. Among them was *Time* correspondent Percival Knauth, whose actions were recounted by one biographer as follows:

> The courtyard was "alive with a kind of subdued noise"; no energy existed to make more. In the yard a truck was heaped high with the

naked, angular corpses of the recent dead, their feet and heads abruptly thrust out at passersby. . . . [I] spotted the body of an S.S. man stacked along with the others. . . . "I don't even remember writing about it back at the press camp."

One reporter, admitting that he had not intended to write about Buchenwald, said he ended up doing so anyway because "I merely wanted first-hand knowledge so that if anyone ever asked me about German concentration camps, I could tell them the unexaggerated truth."[33]

Belsen was recorded with similar difficulty. "I saw Belsen," wrote one wire service reporter whose account appeared in the *Boston Globe,* the *Washington Post,* and the *Los Angeles Times.* "I saw these dead. . . . I saw the living beside these dead. . . . I saw children walking about in this hell." Recounting the stories of witnesses, he ended with the simple statement, "I heard more but I cannot go on." A *Daily Telegraph* reporter admitted that after two visits to Belsen, "I am further than ever from a solution."[34]

Dachau too struck reporters with the limitations of their ability to file the story. One wire service reporter who entered Dachau while the S.S. guards were still firing into the crowd carefully recounted the grasping movements of the near-dead. For him, the greatest horror came from juxtaposing a trainload of corpses with civilians who passed it "with no more than curious glances. . . . Children even pedaled past the bodies on bicycles, and never interrupted their excited chatter. Looted clothing hung from their handlebars." Marguerite Higgins was one of the first correspondents to enter Dachau as the camp's main gate was being rushed by the U.S. soldiers. Over twenty of the remaining S.S. officers in the camp surrendered to Higgins and *Stars and Stripes* correspondent Peter Furst. Speaking in French, English, and German, Higgins informed the prisoners that they were free. Her affirmative nod to the question "Are you American?" caused near-pandemonium. By the time that reports about Dachau began to circulate in the U.S. and British press during the first week of May, the liberation of the camps was sustaining attention in most newspapers, magazines, and journals.[35]

A second thrust of reporting accompanied the delegations who visited the camps on Eisenhower's suggestion over a three-week period in April. The effortless fashion in which reporters had entered the camps immediately on their liberation was repeated now as delegations of parliamentarians, congressional representatives, and news editors streamed into the camps with relative ease. The junkets to the camps provided additional instances of eyewitness testimony for reporters to record. They tracked the responses of British parliamentary members and U.S. congressional representatives who toured the area in mid-April, of other delegations—labor leaders, clergymen, and members of the United Nations war crimes commission—who inspected the camps during the last week of April, and of an eighteen-member delegation of U.S. newspaper editors and publishers that toured both Buchenwald and Dachau. Through it all, streams of German nationals were forcibly brought in, often helping to bury the dead.

Chronicles of liberation, then, constituted for reporters the obvious way to shape their stories around the act of bearing witness, and the eyewitness report offered them a way to do so in an authoritative and credible fashion.

The Form of Bearing Witness: Concretizing Atrocity through the Eyewitness Report

In an oft-cited formulation, Holocaust scholar Saul Friedlander has contended that the insufficiency of "traditional categories of conceptualization and representation" rendered the Holocaust an event "at the limits of representation."[36] Perhaps nowhere was this as evident as in the press's initial attempts to cover the scenes of the camps.

Paradoxically, bearing witness to the atrocities somewhat neutralized the professional expectations of reporters covering the story. Bearing witness changed the shape of the liberation chronicle—and the expectations of the journalists responsible for the story—even before they reached the camps, though it did little to mitigate the horror that they needed to process. Because there was no one best way to bear witness, and each new report was couched in ways that both substantiated the claims of earlier reports and confirmed scoops already won, much of the onus for providing coverage paled alongside the broader need to bear witness. Bearing witness somehow made the fact of simply having seen the atrocities meaningful in the long term. As one reporter explained, his own reportage was a means of supporting the reports of others, "a way of bearing witness to what responsible eyewitnesses have already written."[37]

Invoking proven patterns of reportage helped journalists adjust their coverage to this aim. Not only did reporters structure their accounts of each camp as chronicles of liberation but they turned to the eyewitness report, proven at Majdanek, as a way of accommodating the difficulties in representing scenes of carnage. Reports of firsthand seeing emphasized how "*I saw the blacked, rotting bodies of the victims*" (emphasis added). A lengthy article in the *Philadelphia Inquirer* began every other paragraph with details of what "*I saw . . .*" (emphasis added). One British reporter commented that "we few who have the opportunity to view this atrocity have the right to demand your attention [and] our word, our honor must suffice that this may be known to all the world."[38] The eyewitness report was a particularly helpful way of bearing witness in that as a genre it underscored a reporter's authority derived simply from having been there. Reporters reasoned that by stressing its two main narrative foci—territory and the act of witnessing—the horrific could be made more concrete and imaginable.

In this vein, the first articles that reporters filed tended to describe the camps' terrain, while on the second and third rounds concrete detail was provided by the accounts of people who had been victimized inside. Territory led to witnesses, and together they provided a frame for bearing witness. For instance, Associated Press correspondent Howard Cowan dispatched a number of reports from Dachau: initial coverage of the camp's liberation was followed by separate reports about boxcars of corpses nearby and other reports that recounted the responses of witnesses.[39] Such coverage facilitated the act of bearing witness, though the chronicles of liberation into which it was collapsed offered a precarious and sometimes insufficient fit.

TERRITORY. The territory of the camps constituted a topography of atrocity through which journalists provided detailed verbal maps, or word-tours, of what they were seeing. The atrocities appeared to become more real through close descriptions of the physical terrain on which they had taken place, concretized through details that were relentlessly provided and particularized. As one *New York Times* reporter wrote about Buchenwald,

> The deathhouse had been built conveniently close. It is a neat brick building. To enter it you walk through a courtyard where stand the gibbets on which a dozen men could be hanged at once. . . . At the side of the death house is a stairway leading into a basement. This basement is paved with concrete sloping toward drains and equipped with hoses. Beside the stairway a chute led down into this basement on the outside.

The *Manchester Guardian* regarded the word-tours as sufficiently important to subtitle its ploddingly horrific piece on Buchenwald "A Conducted Tour of the Camp."[40]

Though focusing on the details of the terrain presumably produced discomfort among readers, repulsing at the same time as it captured their attention, the detailed presentation was a necessary step to bearing witness to the atrocities. "This is what I saw in the four tours I was on in the camp," wrote one reporter of Belsen, and he then drew intricate verbal portraits of the camp's places of torture and the routes taken to reach them. "The only way to get an appreciation of the place is to take the revolting journey that our party took," wrote another of Dachau. "We went on," recalled a *Time* correspondent.

> We went around this building and came to the central cemetery. The rooms here, in order, were: 1) the office where the living and the dead were passed through . . . ; 2) the *Brausebad* (shower) room, where the victims were gassed; and 3) the crematory. . . . We were lured on and on, from building to building.

From the "crematorium and shower-room at Dachau" to the "shacks of hell" at Belsen and the research block at Buchenwald, reporters pounded readers with the detailed horror of what they were seeing. As *Collier's* correspondent Martha Gelhorn wrote, "in Dachau, when you want to rest from one horror, you go and see another." Forcing attention to these word-tours compelled readers to bear witness to the atrocities. The concrete descriptions of the crematoria, strangling rooms, scientific and medical laboratories, and torture chambers left little to the imagination and drove home the need to react to what had been transpiring in the camps.[41]

Some reporters broadened the word-tours somewhat by accounting for the changing territory of the camps over time. After visiting Buchenwald on April 21, a correspondent for the *London Observer* noted that "the camp today is vastly different from what it was ten days ago, when it was overrun by the Third Army. It has been cleaned." The increased decay was at issue for other reporters, such as one who noted of Belsen that "I spent yesterday, last night, and today here. The worst horrors I described in yesterday's dispatch are far exceeded by what I have seen since." The camps were also compared with the larger terrain outside—where flower-beds, churches, and rippling brooks posed a cruel contrast. The camps' territory received a second run with the arrival of German civilians and U.S. and British officials. Readers of the *London Times,* for instance, read of a group of Weimar civilians who were forced to tour

> the crematorium with its blackened frames of bodies still in the ovens and two piles of emaciated dead in the yard outside, through the huts where living skeletons too ill or too weak to rise lay parked in their three-tier bunks, through the riding stables where thousands were shot, and through the research block, where doctors tried new serums on human beings.[42]

Some word-tours were highlighted by certain scenes of horror that were contemplated in detail, usually by combining the mundane and everyday with the atrocious as at Majdanek. For instance, one reporter went into considerable detail about the deceptions through which inmates were brought to a gas chamber at Dachau.

> The gas chamber . . . had a peculiarly false front. Twenty-five or thir-ty prisoners at a time would be told they could take a shower. They would enter a pleasant building where a matron welcomed them in a reception room. Flowers were on her desk and an atmosphere of serenity prevailed. They would be handed soap and a clean towel in a practically unprecedented surge of hospitality and would enter the shower room. The shower heads were false, however, and when the doors were sealed it was only a few minutes until the prisoners' bod-ies were ready for cremation.[43]

In fact, that scenario was more representative of gas chambers at other camps than an accurate description of a gas chamber at Dachau, which appears not to have been used.

Why was the focus on the camps' physical terrain significant? Not only did the word-tours fulfill a reportorial function by concretizing the atroc-ities, but they allowed journalists and publics to bear witness by making the horrific more imaginable. In one reporter's view, this put journalists in a mode of automatic relay, by which they could record details of the atrocities without forcing themselves to make sense of them. After tour-ing one camp, he admitted, "I staggered out, unable to see or speak." Sim-ilarly, a reporter with the *London Evening Standard* said that while touring Belsen his car brushed the uniforms of a number of Wehrmacht soldiers. "How I would have liked to have swung the wheel into their ranks," he admitted. Yet both immediately filed their reports, mechanically process-ing the scenes of the camps into narrative. As reporter Edwin Tetlow later told it:

> I hurried as quickly as I could out of Belsen to my jeep for the jour-ney back to base, to write everything I had seen that terrible day while it was all fresh in my mind. I felt better after that duty had been accomplished. Writing my story emptied me of emotion, restoring me to a realization that I was not a participant in the hor-ror but a professional observer with the duty of telling others what Belsen was like.[44]

For many, providing coverage had a compensatory effect that restored some perspective to the horror.

THE ACT OF WITNESSING.   Reporters also were able to bear witness by recounting the words and actions of witnesses whom they met inside the camps. The responses of these witnesses concretized the atrocities and lent the authority of personal experience to the chronicles.

Reporters cited four categories of witnesses in their chronicles: the prisoners and victims of the camps; German nationals, including civilians who lived nearby and former S.S. officials; soldiers with the liberating troops; and the officials of foreign governments and news organizations.[45] All four groups bore witness to the scenes of the camps during the first week or two after liberation. And while each added a different dimension to understandings of the act of witnessing, deepening and complicating its meaning, in narrative they were often presented in a chronological sequencing that flattened the larger atrocity story.

In an article entitled "Nazi Horrors Too Awful for Belief," *Philadelphia Inquirer* reporter Hal Boyle told readers that "you don't have to look at it through a reporter's eyes," as he recounted the statements of numerous people he had encountered in the camps. "I spent four hours today talking with the living skeletons who survived," said one reporter. "First I'll tell what Andy Rooney, reporter for the *Stars and Stripes,* and I, the first American correspondents, saw," said another journalist with the *New York Times.* "Then I'll recount what a survivor of the S.S. carnival of blood told us had happened." "They Say 'We Didn't Know,'" read the headline in the *Daily Telegraph* somewhat disbelievingly, as it repeated the words of the reluctant German bystanders.[46]

The most common way of representing the act of witnessing was in layers: liberated inmates watched German civilians, reporters watched officials, and everyone watched the corpses. One reporter watched a U.S. soldier who in turn watched a group of German civilians.

> The horror of it caused many women to faint. Others sobbed and put their hands to their eyes to blot out the things that confronted them. An American M.P. ordered them to take their hands down. He told them to have a good look and never to forget what they had seen.

Another reporter recounted how at the same time as German civilians were marched around, "all around them were thousands of liberated 'slaves,' just brought in. Even the barracks roof was crowded with them. They watched silently."[47]

As befit the eyewitness report, reporters acknowledged their own act of witnessing, documenting what "I saw." As a correspondent for the *Philadelphia Inquirer* told it, "I realize before starting that you can't and won't believe, and I know the old shrug that accompanies atrocity stories. But I've been there." Sometimes the reporter's shift to the role of witness occurred in curious ways. One wire service reporter tendered his entire report of Dachau in third person except for the paragraph recounting his sighting of the train cars with dead bodies. At that point in the narrative he switched to first person, telling readers that "when *I reached* the camp shortly after the battle, *I saw* a train" (emphasis added). His shift to first person enhanced the narrative's credibility by muting his professional role as neutral observer, signified in third person, and acknowledging instead his role as witness.[48]

But journalists also focused on the responses of prisoners and survivors of the camps. *New York Times* reporter Harold Denny recounted how the prisoners of Buchenwald "seemed hardly human and some had lost their minds. Some stared at me with piercing eyes from shrunken faces. Some looked idiotically ahead, their eyes seeing nothing, their mouths gaping." Survivors remained anonymous, though some were at times identified by name and country of origin. One such witness hobbled up to *Life* photographer George Rodger in Belsen and "spoke to me in German. I couldn't understand what he said and I shall never know, for he fell dead at my feet in the middle of his sentence." When they could, reporters sought out persons who had achieved stature in their prewar lives—doctors, university professors, authors, diplomats, military officers. One newspaper called the prisoner list at Dachau "a European Who's Who."[49]

Even when reporters found reputed individuals, they were not always able to process their responses into words. After commenting on the anonymity of corpses at Buchenwald, one correspondent noticed a sign of vitality among the living dead. It was "a white-haired Frenchman, 73 years old, who . . . told of punishments inflicted by the S.S. guards so depraved and so obscene that I could never tell them except to other men in whispers." The everyday was again combined with the atrocious, and the very fact of survival was recounted alongside mundane details. One survivor recalled a forced march from Buchenwald to Dachau alongside a description of his prewar past. Some reporters reflected on the identity of victims who had disappeared in captivity or were thought dead: the *Manchester Guardian,* for instance, investigated rumors about former French premier Léon Blum or Princess Mafalda, the daughter of the king of Italy. Speculation about the fate of these individuals and others like them turned up in a number of accounts. While the search for recognizable names lent referentiality to the narratives, here too reporters were limited in their ability to gain confirmation. Reporting on the disappearance of a Czech author, one writer concluded somewhat defensively that he had died three weeks earlier, "according to fellow prisoners *whose word I have every reason to believe*" (emphasis added).[50]

Journalists also reported the actions of German nationals in the camps.

Many reporters showed little hesitation in holding them responsible for the atrocities—either directly as perpetrators or indirectly as bystanders. Because the Germans were invoked in a largely voiceless capacity, readers received instead extensive details of their physical reactions to the atrocities. When civilians were brought forcibly into Buchenwald by the Allied forces as part of its denazification campaign, reporters told of how "twelve hundred men and women of Weimar walked unwillingly . . . and wept, retched, fainted." Report after report chronicled how the Germans cried, fainted, and were made sick by what they saw. "I watched," wrote reporter John Wilhelm, "as these German burghers, clad in their best Sunday clothes, some with stiff white collars and neat black ties, picked up these emaciated, mutilated corpses and placed them side by side with their own German ancestors." Reporters were also quick to point out irreverent behavior: the S.S. women, said one, were "unmoved by the grisliness of their task" and "one even smiled as she helped bundle the corpses into the pit." The article's subhead underscored the inappropriateness of the woman's reaction, recounting in bold black print, "She Smiled." Harold Denny of the *New York Times* focused on one young German member of the Hitler Mädchen organization, who, made to sit before the camp's open furnace doors, cried, trembled, and moaned. When fleetingly given a voice, she referred to the horrific nature of what "they" had done. At that point, Denny muted her voice, observing that the "girl showed no sense of personal responsibility, though she had been a sworn supporter of the regime."[51]

Another second-order witness was the soldiers, the "G.I. sightseers." Their witnessing was important because it signified a military response to the scenes made evident by the camps' liberation and stood in for the lack of military response before the liberation. Percival Knauth of *Time* told of his entry into Buchenwald nine days after it was liberated:

> we came up from the cellar and passed into another yard fenced in by a high wooden wall. There was a pile of bodies there, stacked more or less the way I stack my firewood back home, not too carefully. . . . Their mouths were open as though in pain and little streaks of blood flowed from their noses. "Some kind of hemorrhage," said a medical corpsman. "Hell, those guys died of starvation," said another G.I. He stared and stared and couldn't get that thought out of his mind, repeating it over and over.

Readers were told of how the "soldier wept," the "soldier turned his head," and the soldier "stared vacantly"—all suggesting lapses of military professionalism. Conversely, reporters also noted demonstrations of toughness among the soldiers. In an article entitled "Yanks Make Germans Dig Up Murdered Prisoners by Hand," *Stars and Stripes* reporter Wade Jones said that "American troops arrived with hate in their eyes." While supervising grave digging by German civilians, one soldier shouted, "Shut up and get going. You're all responsible." Edward Folliard of the *Washington Post* followed "thousands of American soldiers to the concentration camp." One soldier,

> a fine, clean-cut youngster, looked on the spectacle [of bodies] and murmured, "Good Lord." After a moment of silence, he said something about a thing like this being hard to believe when you read about it. Then he added, "But there it is."

Folliard supported the soldier's observation: "Yes, there it was," he wrote. The soldier's act of witnessing was complemented by that of the reporter, and both reflected the larger collective response of bearing witness to atrocity.[52]

Sometimes, the words of certain soldiers were repeated across the press, as was the case with a British medical officer from Belsen, whose comments were reprinted in the *Los Angeles Times,* the *London Times,* the *Daily Mail,* and the *Daily Telegraph.* Women's bodies at the camp, he said, "were piled to the height of a table. I saw four girls carrying a body which was thrown on a pile. And I saw a woman carry her dead baby to it." Others published accounts of their experiences, such as one U.S. soldier who wrote a letter to the editor of *Newsweek:* "Yesterday," he commented, "I saw something that unless seen cannot be believed."[53]

A third-order witness involved the officials who toured the camps in back-to-back visits in late April. Groups of U.S. congressional representatives and British parliamentarians "got shocked eyewitness proof of the atrocities." Told to "see for yourselves and be the spokesmen," these officials' testimony brought few revelations but instead authenticated the earlier accounts of reporters and military personnel—they were, after all, "to look at horror," a pure act of witnessing. Said one M.P.: "there has been no exaggeration. It beggars description," while another commented that "we heard atrocity stories from the last war which were not verified, but now we have seen them with our own eyes and they are the most sordid I have ever imagined." Reporters focused closely on the official reactions, regardless of how much there was to report. One correspondent, for instance, recounted over and over how "the visitors froze with horror," another how the parliamentarians cried on seeing the victims.[54]

Some attention was paid to the role played by women as witnesses. In relaying the list of British parliamentarians who would visit the camps, one article was topped with the headline, "Woman, M.P. to See Horror Camps," in reference to parliamentarian Mavis Tate. Both *PM* and *News Chronicle* ran a Reuters dispatch that chronicled the fact that Tate, the only woman in the British delegation, wept when she saw Buchenwald. The *New York Times,* discussing the U.S. congressional delegation, similarly focused on the only woman in that delegation—Clare Boothe Luce—who "spared herself none of the grisly spectacle."[55]

A final round of witnessing accounts came after Eisenhower assembled a fact-finding mission of eighteen American newspaper and magazine editors. The press printed extensive accounts of the tour, and newspapers, magazines, and journals, whose own editors made the trip, gave special prominence to their comments. Both Malcolm Bingay of the *Detroit Free Press* and Leonard K. Nicholson of the *New Orleans States and Times-Picayune* put together pamphlets containing press clippings and diary excerpts. Here again, witnesses' words were ones of confirmation rather than revelation, with editors affirming the earlier reports of their own correspondents. *Los Angeles Times* editor Norman Chandler told his readers that

> the American war correspondents were accurate in their reports, that this was not propaganda but the plain unvarnished truth. . . . There is no need of going into details. They have all been told. My purpose is merely to testify as to the accuracy of the American correspondents—they have told the truth. They have not exaggerated. Exaggeration, in fact, would be difficult.[56]

One report, published in the *Bulletin* of the American Society of Newspaper Editors (ASNE), attended less to the atrocities and more to their inscription as public record. "American reporters," it began, "had accurately and fully reported the atrocities of Buchenwald and Dachau." They

> went in with the liberating troops and had an opportunity to see at first hand much more than was left for our observation. . . . What we saw, however, was enough to convince anyone of the Nazis' systematic program of starvation, torture and debasement. If our reporters erred at all it was on the side of understatement, because words are inadequate to describe the utter horror and degradation of those establishments.[57]

Because the different categories of witness were not able to tell the complete story of Nazi atrocity, the more witnesses who could corroborate a given story, the stronger was the evidence for the press. This meant that for as long as reporters were stationed in the camps, they continued to search for additional sources, regardless of whether or not they had new revelations to offer. Congresspersons were depicted as having fallen "into the pattern already described in appalling detail by newsreels and correspondents." U.S. Representative Clare Boothe Luce admitted, "I am one person, and among many others, who will be able to say that she has seen examples of these atrocities with her own eyes."[58] There appeared to be a curious strength in numbers of people validating the same details—curious because it worked against journalistic objectives of "scooping" the opposition. Yet reporters appeared to find solace in producing additional reports to confirm earlier ones. This was because a focus on witnessing helped authenticate the broader aim of bearing witness to atrocity.

On the Importance of Bearing Witness

As an aim of coverage, bearing witness required certain adaptations on the part of the press. Scoops remained less important than the ability to confirm what had been reported elsewhere. Bits of the story of the camps' liberation were pieced together in eyewitness reports that stretched across time, circumstance, news organization, and individual reporter. Given the horrific scenes of the camps, this not only made moral sense but it had practical implications too: the press was able to vouch both for the authenticity of what was being reported and for its ability to tell the story, despite less than ideal newsmaking circumstances.

Editors recognized this altered mission of the atrocity coverage, and they applauded the efforts of their reporters. Recognizing that it mattered more that the story was told than who told it and how, they viewed the coverage as an accomplishment shared by all. Editorial statements, banner headlines, subheadlines, and bold print positioned the camps as a story demanding reader attention. The *New York Times* reprinted the words of its reporter in Buchenwald as part of its weekly review section. The *London Evening Standard* positioned a small boxed comment from the editor alongside a piece on the liberation of Belsen. Titled "For the Record," it went as follows:

> "I have seen the effect of pestilence in India. . . . But as I have always been a truthful correspondent with an eye to fact rather than an ear for hearsay, believe me when I tell you that what I saw this day was worse than anything I have ever seen anywhere." That is an extract from this report on the Nazi concentration camp of Belsen by *Evening Standard* Correspondent Ronald Monson. His story supplements the existing record of Nazi infamy in this camp.

Not only did this editorial statement draw the reader to the story nearby but it vouched too for the authenticity of the ongoing chronicle about the camps. *PM* appended a similar editorial comment to one of its items which proclaimed that "of all the stories we print in *PM,* those about Axis death camps are the ones we like least. It is our duty to print them because they are the facts of life."[59]

Reader attention was also compelled in more innovative ways, as one newspaper that reprinted the radio broadcast of Edward Murrow: "Permit me to tell you what you would have seen and heard, had you been with me on Thursday," he implored listeners. Editorials corrected the invalid claims of earlier articles, such as when the *Christian Century* admitted that "we have found it hard to believe that the reports from the Nazi concentration camps could be true [but] the evidence is too conclusive." The *Daily Mail* displayed a particularly creative use of headlines: it cut and pasted the headline to a report on Belsen, entitled "The Most Terrible Story of the War," onto the next day's front page; in its second use, it functioned as a caption for a photograph of Belsen's commandant, Josef Kramer. The headline not only stood in for the resonant story of atrocities it had brought with it and eliminated the need for a caption the next day, but it credentialed the story from the preceding day and created a context within which readers could connect the two articles and decode them as matching pieces of a larger story about atrocity.[60]

Accounts also made their way into the journalistic trade literature. The British trade journal *Newspaper World* discussed how the atrocity stories walked a fine line between decency and "the object of rousing the public to the full realization of what Nazism means." The *Bulletin* of the ASNE devoted the first few pages of its June 1945 issue to the subject. Titled "Reflections on Atrocities," the account printed the reactions of three editors, one of whom recalled "with horror" the strangling rooms and "medical experiment building" at Buchenwald. Following the official visit of newspaper editors to Buchenwald, the U.S. trade journal the *Quill* ran a series of articles on the camps. One editor's account was introduced as follows:

> A man who has been on major newspaper desks for nearly 20 years knows how quickly John Q. Public forgets. When the man happens to be one of the small group of American editors chosen to inspect Nazi concentration camps while the horror was still fresh, he has extra reason to fear this short memory. E. Z. Dimitman saw Buchenwald and Dachau and he will see them all his life. He wants American newspapers to help make sure we do not forget.[61]

In this case, bearing witness to the scenes of the camps was contextualized not only as a professional practice of the first order but as an act of moral importance. In bearing witness, then, the press looked at itself as having fulfilled responsibilities that went beyond journalism.

On the Limitations of Bearing Witness

Using words to bear witness, however, had a more problematic side, and it involved an inadequacy in narrativizing what was happening—both in terms of what reporters saw, how they reported and evaluated what they saw, and how they appraised their own performance in doing so.

A reliance on the eyewitness report and an emphasis on "liberation" rather than "atrocity" offered a grounded way to authenticate the scenes of the camps that made sense within the aim of bearing witness. But this was not "good" journalism, per se, for it produced other problems in constructing a record of the camps' liberation. In pitching the story so closely to the details of what they were seeing, many journalists did not regain sight of the larger picture. And in concentrating simply on what they saw, many left unaddressed a space in which to interpret the horrific events that they witnessed.

BEARING WITNESS AND THE INTERPRETIVE WORK OF JOURNALISTS. Bearing witness was firstly problematic for the press because it undermined much of the interpretive work by which coverage is often fashioned. The lack of interpretation exacerbated numerous errors of coverage that were set in place as the reporters entered the camps. Not only did most reporters not engage in sufficient interpretive work about the scenes of the camps, but the schema that had made sense concerning the details of one camp no longer applied as the liberation of the camps continued.

This had the effect of normalizing the scenes of carnage. Presenting the camps as a series of eyewitness reports that focused on the act of liberation introduced a revolving standard of evaluation, by which each camp was compared with the camp previously liberated. The camp at Nordhausen came to be called the "Maidanek of the East," Dachau "the most dreaded camp," Belsen "the largest and most terrible." As the liberation of other camps continued, they too were labeled in comparison with camps freed earlier—"another Buchenwald" or a "second Dachau." Such a standard had the effect of mainstreaming the horror at the same time as it described it. "There have been so many camps," one correspondent wrote, "each worse than the one before it, that they are hardly news anymore, and it takes something pretty revolting to rate another story."[62]

This consolidated certain errors of reportage. For instance, the scenes that reporters saw were immediately characterized as "the worst" of Nazi brutality. While they were certainly the worst that the reporters had seen until then, they had no way of knowing that far more gruesome stories awaited them in other camps. And reporters were unable to imagine circumstances that were substantially worse than what they were seeing. Yet stories of unmatched horrors would emerge at some delay from the camps that had already been liberated on the eastern front. Similarly, the issue of surprise—certainly an understated frame of reference for the shocked members of the press—was overplayed as reporters constructed their narratives, which continually recounted how no one had known what was taking place in the camps. Yet the emphasis on surprise downplayed the official foreknowledge of the camps in both U.S. and British circles. As scholar Robert Abzug has contended, "the liberations were shocking, but they did not reveal the first real evidence the Allies had of the Nazi plans to destroy Europe's Jews. Nor were those camps liberated in the spring of 1945 the killing centers. They were not even the first to be liberated."[63]

In some cases journalists erred by failing to differentiate between what had been reported correctly, inaccurately, and left out of the coverage altogether. Errors of coverage that had been picked up by certain reporters and used in their own coverage were rapidly cemented into the general journalistic record. Camps were wrongly identified, both by name and category. The camp of Nordhausen, for instance, was given four separate names, all of which continued to be used. The labels of "death-camp" and "extermination center," wrongly used to describe places like Buchenwald, confounded distinctions between the concentration camps of the western front and the death camps of the East. Furthermore, anti-Semitism—so strong in the U.S. and Britain of 1945 that more than half the polled population thought that the Jews possessed "too much power"—created problems surrounding the reporting of Jewish victimization. Believing that Jews were "problematic victims" and that "reference to their persecution might not elicit popular sympathy," sentiments persisted "that to acknowledge how many of the victims were Jews might dampen indignation" about the atrocities. The overwhelmingly Jewish nature of victimization by the Nazis was thereby strategically understated.[64]

A somewhat faulty understanding of the camps was thus set in place. As Tony Kushner has demonstrated, even after the camps were liberated, the horror was often misread because it was wrongly codified in conjunction with what was known about the camps during the thirties. All of this produced a slew of inaccuracies—concerning what the scenes of the camps signified, the point at which governments, citizens, and soldiers knew about the camps, the degree to which the camps represented the worst of

Nazism, the relationship between the camps liberated by the Allies and the far more gruesome death camps of the East, and the Jewish nature of victimization.

Given the aforementioned difficulties inherent in reporting the camps' liberation, the shortcomings of the press performance were somewhat understandable. Yet they suggest that as a verbal template for journalistic coverage of the atrocities, bearing witness had certain limitations. Not only did it generate a record of the camps that was inaccurate vis-à-vis the larger atrocity story. But in accommodating the need "to see" the scenes of the camps, it adopted a frame for telling the story in content—the liberation of the camps—and in form—the eyewitness report—that was incapable of addressing the broader story of Nazi atrocity. This would have tremendous bearing in memory, where the broader story would emerge as the more effective way of remembering Nazi barbarism.

BEARING WITNESS AND PROFESSIONAL NEWSMAKING PRACTICES. While the act of bearing witness muted recognition of the interpretive work involved in reporting the story, it in many ways glossed over additional difficulties that reporters experienced in newsmaking itself. In large part just the fact of having been in the camps was enough to merit coverage, and there seemed to be little need to discuss the practices through which such coverage was provided. Yet in fact much reportorial work in the camps was of an improvisory and compensatory nature. Because reporters were forced to process their own horror at the same time as they gathered information for their stories, many moved rapidly back and forth between shock, disgust, and fear for their own health. In Edwin Tetlow's brutally honest words, he moved through Belsen overcome with pity. But as horror after horror presented itself,

> I have to confess, I was beginning to feel repugnance. Pity had been replaced by a fear that I might become contaminated. I found myself treading a way round the rest of the camp with heightening nervousness and unwillingness, not even wanting my boots to touch more heavily or more often than was absolutely necessary the diseased soil of Belsen.[65]

Words were found repeatedly incapable of conveying what reporters were seeing, and proven practices of coverage continuously came up short. For instance, a reliance on recognized sources, the provision of background detail, and the verification of fact were either inadequate or irrelevant practices for covering this particular story. Many reporters were unable to provide even the simplest details of the story they were covering. Accounting for the identity, name, or nationality of a camp's victims and survivors was generally impossible or untenable. One Associated Press correspondent admitted that reporters sometimes elected *not* to ask the questions that they would normally pose as journalists. "There are times," he wrote following a conversation with a woman at Belsen, "when even a reporter may not ask questions—I not only do not know what became of the boy [about whom he had been told]—I still do not know the madame's name." Approached by a sobbing young girl, a reporter with the *Daily Mail* later recalled stifling "the professional urge to ask questions, so wrung was I by pity for this child."[66]

Other difficulties had to do with news telling. Once faced with compiling their notes into narrative, journalists often fell short of establishing an authoritative voice. In account after account, reporters voiced their own inability to find the proper tone in which to tell the story. The inability to find the proper tone, of course, reflected a far more basic inability to comprehend what had happened. One British reporter dispatched a cable to his newspaper's editorial board that began as follows: "I have the duty now to report something beyond the scope of human understanding."[67] Yet it was unclear how they were to proceed with such an initial point of inarticulation.

Sometimes the press tried to correct the blinders of journalistic work. *PM* magazine, for instance, took pains to establish the seemingly objective stance of one of its "non-correspondents," a soldier acting as an observer.

> Gordon Walker is not a war correspondent. He is a trained observer. He did not write a story. He took notes of what he saw and what he was told. He went to investigate, and these next words are his report.[68]

But on the whole the importance of the camps' coverage offset any discussion of its limitations. Just the fact of having been there was enough, and there seemed to be little need to discuss the practices through which coverage was provided.

Many reporters admitted later that they broke down while inside the camps. During much of his time at Belsen, United Press correspondent Richard MacMillan remembered being "forced to peep through his fingers like a frightened child." Marguerite Higgins convulsed with nausea when she saw the boxcars of dead bodies outside Dachau. Edward Murrow spent much of his time at Buchenwald numbly pressing the winnings of a poker game into the hands of the emaciated prisoners who clutched at him. Unable to contain his anguish, correspondent Alan Moorehead asked for permission to leave Belsen. Popular BBC broadcaster Richard Dimbleby recalled five instances of his own weeping in the midst of recording from Belsen. Remembering how he had struggled with the BBC over its reluctance to let him recount the full story, he recalled insisting,

> "I must tell the exact truth, every detail of it, even if the people don't believe me, even if they feel these things should not be told.". . . It was the BBC who refused to believe it, or to broadcast it, insisting on confirmation from other sources, so that Dimbleby, in rage and anguish, telephoned the newsroom with the ultimatum: unless his report went through, he would never again broadcast in his life.[69]

Fortunately for Dimbleby, confirmations were coming through at a rapid pace, and the BBC broadcast his report. Yet few admissions of reporters' weaknesses were made public at the time of the camps' liberation. The need to be professional compounded the anguish of reporters in reporting the unbelievable carnage.

All of these difficulties had to do with a fundamental paradox in telling the story: once reporters recognized that existing standards of journalism fell short when helping them bear witness, by definition they recognized too their own inability to process what they saw into a plausible narrative. As suggested earlier, the circumstances of the camps were so far beyond journalists' own experiences that the plausible narratives that they generated were at best incomplete. The solution, then, was to admit their own insufficiency as chroniclers.

BEARING WITNESS AND JOURNALISTIC NARRATIVE. Bearing witness in word was characterized most dramatically by journalists' repeated admissions of the limitations of their own capacity to chronicle what they were seeing. One reporter began by claiming that "unless you personally have seen Buchenwald, you won't, you can't believe it." Another noted, "What we have seen with our own eyes confirms every dreadful story and adds frightful details we had not heard."[70] In hinting at the underside of its own telling, the story of the camps thus emerged as a chronicle of journalistic insufficiency, which explained how journalism fell short at the same time as reporters documented what they saw.

The insufficiency of journalistic narrative had many roots. One insufficiency had to do with the choice of words themselves, seen as inadequate carriers of the information they were expected to bear. "The word 'appalling' does not define the living-death scene I witnessed today," said one reporter. "Anything you hear . . . will be understatement," said another. "Buchenwald," in most views, was "beyond all comprehension. You just can't understand it even when you've seen it." An editor with the *Saturday*

Evening Post admitted that although "the war correspondent did a good job of factual reporting, there is a limit to what can be said," and Clare Boothe Luce declared that the camps "are even more horrible than the printed description." Perhaps the most famous recounting of Buchenwald's liberation came from neither word nor image but from sound. Broadcast on April 15 and reprinted in newspapers around the world, CBS Radio correspondent Edward R. Murrow observed that "the stink was beyond description. As we walked out into the courtyard, a man fell dead. Two others, they must have been over 60, were crawling on the ground." Yet he "begged his audience to believe him," saying that "I have reported what I saw and heard. But only part of it. For most of it, I have no words."[71]

Other reporters emphasized the generic inadequacy of the eyewitness report. "It is impossible to tell a connected story of the horrors of Buchenwald," said one *New York Times* reporter. Another wrote that "in this war we have had more than our share of atrocity stories, but Buchenwald is not a story." After seeing Belsen, a correspondent for the British *News of the World* admitted, "I have told you only part of the story. I dare not, I cannot write the whole story. It is too utterly sickening." One Reuters correspondent was quoted as saying that his story "would offend public morality if given in any other form than a medical report," while a reporter with the *News Chronicle* admitted that "horror is the hardest thing to write about I know. . . . I did not see it until today." The press underlined its disgust with the story in additional ways. The *Washington Post* datelined a United Press dispatch from Belsen as having emanated from "Belsen Hell Hole, Germany." *PM* headlined a pair of photographs, "This IS the Enemy," and painted thick black arrows atop the pictures so that no reader could miss the point.[72]

Yet other reporters addressed the general inadequacy of news language, claiming that the content of the atrocity story challenged existing standards of language appropriateness. This often meant citing a quote but qualifying alongside it what had been left out. The *Daily Mail* recounted the story of one senior medical officer in Belsen only after conceding that "much of what the officer said cannot be printed, but here is the rest of his statement as told a few minutes ago." One news story began with the claim that "if you tried to tell the actual facts of the Buchenwald horrors, you would get a story of obscenity and filth that would be unprintable." A *New York Times* reporter, admitting that "even a hint of the present hygienic conditions would be unprintable," said that "writers have tried to describe these things, but words cannot describe them, and even if they could, there are details too filthy to be printed anywhere." Edward Murrow told his listening public that what he was about to report "will not be pleasant listening. If you are at lunch, or if you have no appetite to hear what Germans have done, now is a good time to switch off the radio." In discussing the behavior of camp inmates around a camp latrine, Murrow admitted that "I saw it, but will not describe it." As one editor told it, the media were experiencing a case of language failure: "In the presence of these German horror camps, language breaks down."[73]

The journalistic coverage of the liberation of the camps thus had many sides. Journalism accomplished the important aim of bearing witness to the atrocities, in that reporters provided numerous and extensive details that were necessary to concretize the story of Nazi atrocity in the public imagination. Yet reporters were unable to fully concretize the story and ended up chronicling their own insufficiencies at the same time as they reported on what they saw. When viewed as a persuasive documentation of what had been happening in the camps, journalistic coverage thus generated mixed reviews.

The difficulties experienced by U.S. and British reporters in recording the camps had many origins. Primary here was the nature of the object being reported and the fundamental problem of how to translate an event experienced as totally unprecedented into the humble tools available for reporting the world. But in addition to the difficulties surrounding the event itself, proven standards of news gathering and news telling also proved problematic. The normal routines of gathering news—confirming stories, providing background details for sources, locating sources with high rank—were generally unachievable. The tone, mood, and authority of daily-news reportage offered insufficient news-telling strategies to document what reporters were seeing, and standards of appropriate language, genre, and word choice were all unable to fully convey the larger story of atrocity. Finally, journalists chose to frame their stories as eyewitness accounts in form and as chronicles of liberation in content. These choices provided considerable referential documentation but offered little leeway for engaging in interpretive work about the broader atrocity story. All of this meant that the reportorial mission in the camps was short-circuited by the larger aim of bearing witness.

Yet the public needed proof of what the liberating forces were seeing. Hence, the limitations of the reportorial mission pushed the documentation of the atrocities in other directions. If words were not up to the task of representing the atrocity story in the daily and weekly press, the press needed better devices through which to bear witness. And it was here that photographic images would come into play.

Covering Atrocity in Image

U SING IMAGES TO BEAR WITNESS TO ATROCITY required a different type of representation than did words. Images helped record the horror in memory after its concrete signs had disappeared, and they did so in a way that told a larger story of Nazi atrocity. As the U.S. trade journal *Editor and Publisher* proclaimed, "the peoples of Europe, long subjected to floods of propaganda, no longer believe the written word. Only factual photographs will be accepted."[1]

While words produced a concrete and grounded chronicle of the camps' liberation, photographs were so instrumental to the broader aim of enlightening the world about Nazi actions that when Eisenhower proclaimed "let the world see," he implicitly called upon photography's aura of realism to help accomplish that aim. Through its dual function as carrier of truth-value and symbol, photography thus helped the world bear witness by providing a context for events at the same time as it displayed them.

ATROCITY PHOTOS AS TOOLS OF DOCUMENTATION

The photographs that became available on the liberation of the western camps were too numerous and varied to be published together by any one U.S. or British publication. This was because scores of photographers in different capacities—professional, semiprofessional, and amateur photographers as well as soldiers bearing cameras—accompanied the liberating forces into the camps, and most were placed immediately under the aegis of the U.S. Signal Corps, the British Army Film and Photographic Unit, and other military units. Making available numerous atrocity photos already in the first days after the camps' liberation, these photographers displayed horror so wide-ranging and incomprehensible that it enhanced the need to bear witness, forcing an assumption of public responsibility for the brutality being depicted.

How did photographers record the scenes of barbarism that they encountered? Like reporters, photographers accompanying the liberating forces received few instructions concerning which camps they were entering or what they should do once they arrived; they were given even fewer guidelines about which shots to take or how to take them. This meant that for many the so-called professional response to the event was simply one of "making do," an improvisory reaction to often faulty equipment, bad weather, and uneven training and experience. As one photographer with the British Army Film and Photographic Unit said simply, "we did what [we] saw at the time."[2]

The atrocity photos played a complex role in recording the atrocities. Like words, the images were of limited representativeness, providing only a partial picture of the consequences of years of forced torture, harassment, and eventual death—not the Holocaust per se but a partial depiction of its final phase. As British M.P. Mavis Tate commented, "you can photograph results of suffering but never suffering itself." But photography also offered graphic representations of atrocity that were more difficult to deny than with words. Photographers, one reporter claimed, sent pictures bearing such "irrefutable evidence of Nazi degradation and brutality" that were "so horrible that no newspaper normally would use them, but they were less horrible than the reality." Photographs thus pushed the authenticity of unbelievable camp scenes by pitching depictions closely to the events being described at the same time as they signaled a broader story of Nazi atrocity. It is no surprise, then, that photographs flourished for the press as an effective mode of documenting what was happening.[3]

Photographing Atrocity

Like reporters, photographers found the camps a horrifying experience. Photographers struggled with their own necessary intrusion on the dignity of their cameras' targets. Whether depicting victims or survivors, dead or living, perpetrators or traumatized, the photographers' normally prying behavior proceeded with a certain insensitivity to the boundaries between public and private that was intensified by the challenge posed by the scenes of the camps to common standards of decency and civility. Certain photographers associated with recording the camps' liberation—Margaret Bourke-White, George Rodger, John Florea, Lee Miller, Dave Scherman, and William Vandivert of *Life* are among the best known—later claimed that the experience had irrevocably changed them as professionals. Faced with scene after scene of human carnage, they found it difficult to come to terms with their role in its documentation yet forced themselves to continue photographing. Regardless of the continent from which they came, the photographers shared pool arrangements that facilitated the appearance of the same shots in both the United States and Britain. This created a shared visual record for both countries, somewhat neutralizing the differences between the nearby war in Britain and the more distant one experienced in the United States. The record produced was massive yet uniform.

Margaret Bourke-White was perhaps the most well known of the group, and she accompanied the U.S. liberating forces first into the camp of Erla and then Buchenwald. On assignment for *Life,* she took shots from within a "self-imposed stupor" that veiled her mind: "In photographing the murder camps, the protective veil was so tightly drawn that I hardly knew what I had taken until I saw prints of my own photographs," she later wrote. "It was as though I was seeing these horrors for the first time." Bourke-White knew the limitations and cogency of the camera in normal circumstances, and it was as if the camp survivors had altered those dimensions at will. As one biographer told it, the camera could not be used to force self-consciousness on its subjects, for "Buchenwald had stripped away self-consciousness and ordinary response." Yet Bourke-White forced herself to "map the place with negatives," convinced "that an atrocity like this demanded to be recorded." As "difficult as these things may be to report or to photograph, it is something we must do. . . . Our obligation is to pass it on to others." Bourke-White later admitted that her visit to Buchenwald had changed her to such an extent that it prompted her book on Germany, *"Dear Fatherland, Rest Quietly."*[4]

Similar tales of British photographer George Rodger circulated in association with Bergen-Belsen. Rodger, who also worked for *Life,* was so affected by the scenes of the camps that he decided temporarily to abandon photojournalism after he toured Belsen. Thought to have been the first war photographer to enter the camp shortly after the British forces toured the area, he did so totally unprepared for what he would find.

Struck by the mounds of human bodies, piled alongside people eating, washing, and cleansing utensils, Rodger initially reeled from the carnage. But he forced himself to take photos and to his horror soon found himself inspired by the grotesque spectacle he was witnessing. He started to shoot frantically, "subconsciously arranging groups and bodies on the ground into artistic compositions in his viewfinder." That revelation—that he was "treating this pitiful human flotsam as if it were some gigantic still-life"— so disgusted and appalled him that he promised himself "never again to photograph a war." Disillusioned, he later recalled,

> It wasn't even a matter of what I was photographing as what had happened to me in the process. When I discovered that I could look at the horror of Belsen. . . . and think only of a nice photographic com-

position, I knew something had happened to me and I had to stop. . . . I said this is where I quit.

Decades later he turned his repulsion for what he had seen at Belsen into a broader mission to visually document atrocities elsewhere.[5]

Lee Miller, on assignment with *Vogue,* was one of the first photographers to enter Dachau with the U.S. liberating forces. Ironically, for she produced some of the most memorable shots of the camp, she originally pronounced the atrocities beyond the parameters of her "fine Baedecker tour of Germany."Yet she too forced herself to take pictures, and noted that in the few minutes it took her to do so, "two men were found dead, and were unceremoniously dragged out and thrown on the heap outside the block. Nobody seemed to mind except me." Miller also displayed a toughness that was not always shared by others: while the U.S. soldiers initially had been encouraged to tour the camp, "by midday, only the press and medics were allowed in the buildings, as so many really tough guys had become sick it was interfering with duties."[6]

The photographers of the camps were alike in their will to record the scenes they witnessed—not only for the next day's press but for posterity. Bearing witness thus became part of the mission that captured the photographers recording atrocity. For most, shooting the camps was like "driving uphill with the brakes on," yet few turned away from recording the scenes. As one said, "I took pictures of a soap factory because if man can do it then man must be strong enough to have a look at it. You can't pretend it didn't happen."[7]

The Images of Atrocity

The atrocity photos taken by the U.S. and British photographers streamed in so quickly that the press back home had little time to debate their impact. Turning out roll after roll of black-and-white film, photographers relentlessly depicted the worst of Nazism in stark, naturalistic representations of horror: bodies turned at odd angles to each other, charred skulls, ovens full of ashes, shocked German civilians alongside massive scenes of human carnage. Within days of photographers' arrival in the camps, the wires were flooded with scenes of explicit and gruesome snapshots of horror, the likes of which had never before been presented on the pages of the U.S. and British popular press.

Some of the first atrocity photos appeared on April 9, when three British newspapers—the *London Times, News Chronicle,* and *Daily Mirror*—printed pictures of a group of Russian women who had been victimized by the Germans; the *Daily Mirror* explained that its staff "went out on this

Figure 5. U.S. major and corpses in Ohrdruf, April 1945, by NARA (National Archives and Records Administration); Acme Newsphotos/Corbis Bettman Archives.

story deliberately in the belief that our readers ought to see these pictures." Although corpses did not appear in all of these initial shots and the *Daily Express* justified its selection of a general view of the camp without bodies as "the only picture fit to print," a more graphic set of photos nonetheless was made available the following day, when U.S. papers such as the *New York Times, Los Angeles Times, Washington Post,* and *PM* all depicted a stack of corpses in Ohrdruf, discovered when the camp had been liberated on April 4. Those shots also appeared in the British *Daily Telegraph, Daily Sketch,* and *Daily Mail.*[8]

One particularly memorable shot from this set circulated the first week of April (fig. 5). It showed a U.S. Army major, who looked pained and stiff, hunched in a wooden shed behind a stack of nude, lime-covered corpses, which spread into the camera's field of vision. The corpses spilled out of the frame on one side, suggesting a horror that went beyond the depicted scene. The photo was one of the first showing a graphic portrayal of nude bodies, and it was widely circulated. Interestingly, this series was accompanied over the wires by extensive verbal documentation that provided the army major's name and hometown (fig. 6). That documentation, which was divided into general information about the events leading up to the shed's discovery, more specific information about the bodies and reaction to their discovery, and very particular details about the depicted soldier, was typical of the information accompanying most wire photos. Unlike later photos, most of it was printed in the captions accompanying the photo's initial oS MURDER CAMP

The swift advance of the Thi...
famous Fourth Armored Division uncovers
horror of a Nazi SS murder camp at Ohrd
entered April 4, 1945, after the fall o:
eight miles to the north. American sold.
who seized the camp found the courtyard littered
with the bodies of Czechoslovakian, Russian,
Belgian and French slave laborers, slain because
they were too weak to be evacuated. In a shed,
they found a stack of 44 naked and lime-covered
bodies.

According to survivors, 3,000 to 4,000 prisoners
had been killed by SS troops, 70 being slain just
before the Americans reached the camp. The 80
survivors had escaped death or removal by hiding
in the woods. They reported that an average of
150 died daily, mainly from shooting or clubbing.
The Nazi system was to feed prisoners a crust of
bread a day, work them on tunnelling until they
were too weak to continue, then exterminate them
and replace them with another 150 prisoners
daily.

Led by Colonel Hayden Sears of the Fourth Armored
Division, prominent German citizens of the town of
Ohrdruf saw with their own eyes the horrors of SS
brutality during a conducted tour of the Ohrdruf
charnel house April 8, 1945. As they stood over
the slain prisoners, Colonel Sears said: "This
is why Americans cannot be your friends..." The
enforced tour of the Germans ended with a visit
to a wood where 10 bodies lay on a grill, made
of railway lines, ready for cremation. Colonel
Sears asked a uniformed German medical officer:
"Does this meet with your conception of the
German master race?" The officer faltered and
at last answered: "I cannot believe that Germans
did this."

S & G 61324

THIS PHOTO SHOWS: Major John Scotti of Brooklyn,
New York (left), points out the unmistakable
evidence that many of the men died of beating to
Colonel Hayden Sears. Major Scotti is a medical
officer with the Third U.S. Army's Fourth Armored
Division. British Combine — Acme Photo F 15477
from Sport and General.
WAR POOL PHOTO, NOT FOR USE IN BRITISH ISLES,
FRANCE OR WESTERN HEMISPHERE
SERVICED BY LONDON OWI TO LIST B
CERTIFIED AS PASSED BY SHAEF CENSOR

Figure 6. Signal Corps wirephoto copy, April 1945, by NARA.

appearance. But detailed captions were quickly discontinued with the atrocity images, even though such information routinely arrived with the photos. And in fact as this particular photo continued to surface in *Time, Newsweek,* and elsewhere, such information was routinely eliminated from the caption. By the middle of the month, the same picture bore generalized captions such as "Nazi Horrors."[9]

Over the next few days, more and more shots became available, and atrocity photos rapidly proliferated in the press of both countries. As the British trade journal *Newspaper World* observed at the time, "Probably never before has the press set out so deliberately—and although each newspaper made its own decision, so unanimously—to shock the public by the publication of stories and, above all, pictures of atrocities." The first images of Ohrdruf were soon followed by numerous shots of Buchenwald—both within days of its liberation on April 11 and when officials and editors separately visited the camp over the following weeks. In mid-April, images began arriving also from Belsen. And ten days following the display of the Belsen photos, on April 30, pictures from Dachau appeared in the daily and weekly press. Thus, over an approximately three-week period between April 9 and the end of the first week of May, the U.S. and British publics were exposed to an explicit and ongoing photographic display that visually documented the atrocities. Women handling the images in the Office of War Information in London became ill processing the U.S. Signal Corps images into news photographs. Audiences on both continents were "sickened and horrified by [the] pictorial evidence of the iniquities."[10]

From the beginning, the photos appeared in both Britain and the United States without much attention to the content of the stories at their side. While the reporters' narratives had progressed chronologically from camp to camp, photographs were presented with little regard for when they had been taken. Photos that appeared within days of a camp's liberation in one newspaper resurfaced days and weeks later elsewhere; one image of three Dachau survivors appeared on May 2 in the *Washington Post* and reappeared a week later in the *Boston Globe,* one survivor cropped from the frame. While that practice in itself was unusual for the press, even more telling was the failure to mention the time lag. This lack of attentiveness to the actual day on which an image had been taken suggests that time, as referential data, was not particularly relevant to an atrocity photo's presentation. Rather, the story's visualization was primarily nonsequential. That nonsequentiality facilitated the use of visuals to illustrate the broader strokes of the atrocity story rather than the contingent details of one specific instance of violence.[11]

Atrocity photos were similarly presented with little attention to the place where they had been taken. Photos documenting one camp were appended to stories of another camp. *Time,* for instance, ran one article on the camps that was illustrated with a picture of Nordhausen, which was not discussed. Often, the public was told little or nothing about the place being depicted, leaving the photo to function instead as a generalized spot of Nazi horror. Unlike the narratives of reporters that provided the minute details of the camps' topography of terror and left little doubt as to how the camps were physically set up, the visual representation of the camps left their physical spaces unnamed and void of verbal elaboration. Paradoxically, however, this facilitated the use of visuals in illustrating the broad atrocity story.[12]

What did the photographs portray? "This Is the Enemy," proclaimed the *Daily Telegraph* on April 19 beneath a set of photographs that stretched starkly across the top of one page. Said to depict "Horror Unequalled throughout the Centuries," the shots portrayed German civilians digging trenches, examining a crematorium, and viewing dead corpses at Buchenwald. The accompanying text spoke of how "other pictures, too terrible to reproduce, show bodies lying in the long trenches dug by the Germans."[13]

Those other images—"too terrible to reproduce"—appeared elsewhere. They included piles of human ashes, mounds of corpses, crematoria and hanging pits, dazed looks of barely alive skeletons, faces framed by wire, gaping pits of bodies. One, a long view of hundreds of bodies lining the pavement of Nordhausen in a manner reminiscent of a tidy field of crops, appeared in the *Boston Globe* on April 17, while a closer view of the same scene appeared two days later in the *News Chronicle, London Times,* and *Daily Mirror.* Presented in the latter as part of a two-page photographic spread entitled "World Demands Justice," the photo brought the following cautionary note from its editors:

> On pages four and five you will see pictures of German civilians being shown the horrors which existed in their midst. And there is one picture which gives some greater realization of the evil inside Nazi Germany. It is one of many terrible pictures from photographers following up the Allied advances. It is by no means the worst.

On the same day, the *Daily Mail* featured a graphic midview image of a row of human corpses at Nordhausen under the proclamation, "This Is the Evidence," while *PM* ran a more suggestive picture of a closed coffin with a trapdoor bottom, captioned "Always Efficient, the Germans." The *Illustrated London News* published its first two of four atrocity supplements already in mid-April. In each case, editorial comments justified the publication of the photos in a way that left little doubt about their relevance as atrocity documentation.[14]

From the beginning, then, images of the camps presented a varied and wide-ranging display of atrocity. That display, however, persuaded both the skeptical and the ignorant with believable evidence. In negating the usual linkages to time and space that were typical of news photos, images were presented differently than were the words of news reports. An individual photo's status as evidence mattered less than the ability to simply document what the Nazis had done. Photography thereby provided a collective body of visual documentation that facilitated the act of bearing witness to Nazi brutality, even if photos were not given specific captions and were not presented in association with the times and places in which they had been taken.

Assessing Atrocity Photos

Although the atrocity shots appeared in greater numbers and more frequently than did photographs of most other events in contemporary memory, they did produce immediate discussion among those who processed them. As the first atrocity photos flooded the Office of War Information, the British and U.S. trade press recognized their immanent power as tools of persuasion. Showing an unusual degree of cooperation with Eisenhower's instructions to "let the world see," most editors did not entertain the idea of *not* publishing any photos at all. Rather, they began to debate how, when, and which pictures to publish, and with which types of editorial rejoinders.

Taking the lead in the United States, the trade journal *Editor and Publisher* immediately declared that "a good strong measure of pictures of the Nazi atrocities is good for the American public. Newspapers should print all that space will allow." *Popular Photography* declared that "because photographs have shown, people believe. . . . Yet the larger fact is that we already [know] these things to be true. The photographs just [remind] us with a horrible impact." The British trade journal *Newspaper World* ran a series of brief articles entitled "To Print or Not to Print?" just as images of the camps at Ohrdruf and Nordhausen began to circulate. Firmly advocating in favor of printing the images, it ran the following editorial:

> A spate of horror or atrocity pictures dealing with German crimes against humanity have reached London newspapers from the Western front during the past week and editors have once more been faced with the problem of to print or not to print. . . . There was the conflict of bringing home the realism of German brutality and sadism with the desire not to offend against the standards of good taste and cause offense to readers.

The journal admonished those who hesitated about publication: "Shocking readers on certain occasions into the realization of some outrage by the publication of pictures which in the more normal way would be withheld is justifiable," it argued, "so long as such a step is taken with a full sense of the responsibility involved."[15]

Members of certain editorial staffs voiced discomfort with the fact that children would be able to see the images. *Vogue* at first refused to publish Lee Miller's images of Dachau but then relented and did so under the title "Believe It." The *Illustrated London News* solved the dilemma by printing its main presentation of atrocity photos in a four-page detachable supplement, which it told readers was "intended for our adult readers only." Subscribers with young families, it counseled, could remove the shots. Others were more direct about the need to see. In a leader, the *Daily Mirror* proclaimed how glad it was that the pictures were being published. "One reason for publishing is to *protect* the children. It is better that they should be 'nauseated' now than mutilated later on" (emphasis added).[16]

As with words, the press positioned the atrocity photos in ways that proclaimed their significance. Using captions, headlines, boxed-in notes from the editor, and accompanying articles, the press played up the role of images in proving Nazi brutality. Alongside verbal accounts of Belsen, the *London Times* reminded readers that "Pictures taken in the camps at Nordhausen, Buchenwald, and Ohrdruf, which confirm the published accounts of German brutality, appear on page 6." Similarly, the *Daily Telegraph* accompanied a photo of Nazi torture methods with this comment:

> The weight of pictorial evidence of the ghastly conditions in the German concentration camps continues to mount. More than a dozen photographs, each giving indisputable testimony of the bestial cruelties inflicted on civilians, reached the *Daily Telegraph* yesterday; but they are of such a revolting nature that it has been decided not to reproduce them. Here, however, is one that can be printed.

Midway through a story of Belsen, the *Daily Mail* italicized its proclamation that "a full photographic record of the terrible sights has been made for historical record and future evidence." The *Philadelphia Inquirer* told its readers that "these are pictures made inside German concentration camps where thousands died under almost unbelievable Nazi cruelty," and the *News Chronicle* caught the attention of its readers with an editorial statement entitled "Indisputable Proof":

> Here, and in pictures on the back page today, the eyes of British men and women may behold for the first time some of the more revolting

Figure 7. Heap of ashes and bones in Buchenwald, April 18, 1945, by NARA, courtesy of USHMM.

features of Nazi guilt. These are official pictures and the *News Chronicle* has decided to print them, because it is right that the world should see at close quarters indisputable proof of Germany's crimes against the human race.

It went on to say that "other pictures, still more horrible in detail than these, have been circulated by the military authorities, but the selection here published tell their own story plainly enough."[17] The *Daily Mirror* devoted a full quarter-page to a close-up shot of a pile of incinerated bones. "Heaped Evidence . . . ," read the headline, and the caption underneath the image told readers to "Look Well at This Picture—and Remember" (fig. 7). As with other pictures, the frame cut off the sides of the picture, making it appear as if the bones went on forever.

Comments such as these were important because they called on readers to attend to the atrocities. But they also contextualized the scenes presented against the scenes that had been edited from public view. Atrocity photos were presented as a subset of images that did *not* make it into print. And instead of presenting the camps in a way that claimed to be complete and comprehensive, readers received a continuous inventory in words of what they were *not* seeing. While such a presentational mode resonated with the nature of the story and the fact that no one image could really capture its core, it went against journalistic standards for presenting information as fully as possible. Instead, it repaired to an alternative mode of cooperative journalism, already seen with reporters, by which photographers joined forces in documenting the atrocities. That alternative mode suited the aim of collectively bearing witness.

As already suggested, bearing witness implied that there was no single way to depict atrocity. Rather, the very fact of depiction was sufficient because it documented the act of witnessing, even in cases where the atrocities were not portrayed. It was not surprising, then, that no one image emerged as the best way to depict atrocity. Nor was it unusual that even when photographs earlier looked over by the press turned up later, disparaging remarks were rarely made about the delayed display. Bearing witness therefore made allowances for unusual judgments by which the press selected images for presentation.

Displacing the Eyewitness Report

The atrocity photos accommodated a broader story about atrocity through a wide range of presentational strategies. Primary among them was photography's ability to supersede reporters' preferred chronicle of documentation—the eyewitness report. That ability made the atrocity photos more effective than words in shaping the act of bearing witness.

Images addressed the territory and witnessing activity that had been so central to the eyewitness report, but they did so via visual equivalents that at times appeared to supplant the verbal cues supplied by reporters. The most frequent early objects of depiction were among those that later resurfaced as Holocaust iconography—skulls and corpses, barbed-wire fences separating survivors and victims from the outside world, camp courtyards, accoutrements of atrocity such as crematorium chimneys and furnaces, the victimized mother and child, and abandoned possessions.[18] But there were other types of photos that disappeared from view, even though they initially filled the pages of the press.

IMAGES OF TERRITORY. Images captured the camps' territory in a way that had not been possible with words. While reporters' narratives had squeezed the territory into plausible, chronological word-tours, photographers visualized territory in a way that simultaneously accommodated its details, magnitude, and scope of horror. Camps were visually presented as general sites of suffering, without the definitive detail that marked them as a portrayal of one location. This helped the images stand in for German war atrocity at its broadest level.

Textual interfaces gave the press a way to achieve this kind of interpretation. Even when images focused on specific scenes—such as an entry to a building, a stack of bodies, or a string of ovens—accompanying texts characterized images as more general than the scenes they depicted. At times, the press augmented stories about certain locales and atrocities by providing images of other locales and atrocities: a Belsen photo accompanied a Buchenwald article, or a Buchenwald picture illustrated a Mauthausen story. Often images of a camp were simply left out of chronicles about that camp, such as one Buchenwald story whose accompanying images—of emaciated American soldiers at Marktreidwitz, carnage at Gardelegen, and Soviet infantrymen storming a German position—bore no particular connection to Buchenwald but fit together in a broader discourse about Nazi atrocity. The press also used specific visual markers—such as one picture each from Buchenwald, Ohrdruf, and Belsen—to illustrate general atrocity stories, even if the photos had little to do with the accompanying textual discussion: *Newsweek* ran a full-page story about the Nazi policy of mass extermination and appended four photos, all of which portrayed German civilians in activities around unidentified mounds of bodies, whose relation to the story was never made clear. And finally, the press neglected to identify a photo's location: photos commonly bore generalized place-markers, like "Inside Conquered Germany," "In a German Labor Camp," or "German Concentration Camp."[19]

One early photo of the Nordhausen courtyard, published in both the United States and Britain, displayed the press's idiosyncratic use of photos. The photo offered a long view of what were reported to be nearly three thousand bodies awaiting burial at the camp; the bodies lay in long corridors across the camp's courtyard, like apparel laid out to dry in the sun. Bounded on three sides by a white sky and large, crumbling buildings, the bodies were spread neatly across the photo's midsection, stretching from foreground to background. The image in effect had more than one life. It was not always identified as being from Nordhausen, and in at least one case it illustrated an article about another camp altogether. Though published by the *London Times, Washington Post,* and *Boston Globe* over an eight-day period in April, the time differential was not mentioned by the press. The same scene also reappeared in an unexplained second round of print-

Figure 8. Nordhausen courtyard, April 12, 1945, by NARA.

ing at the end of April, when the same bodies, still strewn across the courtyard, were now interspersed with U.S. soldiers and German civilians who
walked among them (fig. 8). Many of the figures walked away from the
bodies, not looking at them, making the courtyard in the photo's center
with its thousands of corpses seem almost inconsequential, a visual reflection of their lack of status within the Nazi belief system. Such idiosyn-
crasies suggested how irrelevant was the referential data surrounding the
photo's time and space and revealed a leap to its use as symbol. The courtyard at Nordhausen stood in for the larger terrain of suffering under the
Nazis, where images of mass death brought home the scope of atrocity in a
way accomplished less effectively by words.[20]

Scenes of outdoor horror were particularly effective in capturing the scope of atrocity, and they surfaced to this end frequently. Each camp produced its own degradation of public space—the wagons of Buchenwald, the pits of Belsen, the train tracks of Dachau. Dachau was represented by numerous views of corpses spilling out of train cars outside the camp, under striking captions like "Death Measured by the Carload." The legend to one such image in the *Washington Post* made an unusual lapse of news language into second-person address: "At first glance," it stated, "the cars seemed to be loaded with dirty clothing. Then you saw feet, hands, and bony fingers."[21]

Territory appeared to work most effectively when its visualization was unnamed, and the press provided scores of shots of unidentified camps. In one rare attempt to repair the generalized presentation of Dachau's liberation, *Time* appended the legend "At Dachau, 32,000 still survived" to a photo showing a dead victim of the camps alongside interred Nazis. The legend suggested that the image had been taken at Dachau. Yet a small asterisk guided readers to the bottom of the page, where they were told that the photograph had been taken "At Belsen, near Stuttgart." This kind of disclosure, however, was problematic, not only because Belsen was nowhere near Stuttgart and had little to do with a story of Dachau, but because it showed how common were the questionable linkages connecting images and texts.[22]

In each of these ways, specific depictions of one camp were made to stand in for the larger terrain the Nazis had occupied. Each concentration camp was interchanged with other localized sites to tell a broader story about suffering under the Nazis. Depictions of the camps' territory thus moved the atrocity story onto a different level of telling, which suggested not only the detail of human suffering but also its magnitude and scope.

IMAGES OF WITNESSING. Images also generalized the witnessing that had been recounted with precision in the verbal narratives of reporters. Photos provided an array of representations of witnessing—different practices of witnessing, targets of witnessing, and types of witnesses. Each kind of depiction generalized witnessing beyond the actual circumstances in which it took place, and the many forms of depiction coaxed the world to take responsibility for what was being witnessed. In that vein, a caption to a picture of one emaciated man told of his request to be photographed so that "the free peoples of the world would know what a German prison-camp does to a man."[23]

More so than with words, the images of witnessing became a separate category of atrocity representation. First, witnessing itself was depicted in stages, with the press initially featuring photos of official delegations on their way to the camps: The *Los Angeles Times* ran a shot of a departing editors' delegation on the steps of a plane, captioned "Editors, Publishers on Way to Reich"; the *New York Times* showed the U.S. congressional delegation landing in France; the *Daily Mail* featured a front-page panel of head shots under the caption "M.P.s Who Will See Horror Camp Secrets"; and the *Saturday Evening Post* portrayed U.S. newspaper editors being briefed by General Eisenhower at his Rheims headquarters. Such pictures provided a frame for contemplating the act of bearing witness before it actually began.[24]

Different targets of witnessing were also depicted: witnesses were shown examining dead bodies, torture settings, and the tools used to bring about death. In what would emerge as a central feature of these photographs, many photos showed witnesses to the atrocities but no atrocities themselves. One such *Newsweek* photo portrayed three U.S. congressional representatives in a somewhat stupefied posture in one of the camps, looking beyond the photographer at an unknown, unpictured horror (fig. 9). The picture, which portrayed Clare Boothe Luce and others gingerly stepping around some unseen tragedy, curiously situated in between them and the photographer, was not identified by place or date, and the caption conveyed in only the most general terms that "Congress Views the Atrocities." No more definitive detail was provided.[25] Yet depicting witnesses to the atrocities without the atrocities was a patterned way of visualizing the activities, and pictures of groups of witnesses—civilians, officials, and editors—proliferated with no visual depiction of the target of their vision. This act of framing made sense primarily because it helped achieve the broader aim of bearing witness.

Depictions of different kinds of witnesses also proliferated. The most frequent depictions were the prisoners and victims, portrayed anonymously and in general terms: for instance, one caption to three glassy-eyed Dachau inmates explained, "They witnessed Nazi culture." Another Buchenwald photo showed worn, emaciated men staring out from four rows of crowded bunks (fig. 10). Originally taken by the Signal Corps in late April, the photo showed bunk beds stuffed with malnourished male survivors, an image whose uniformity was broken only by one male who propped himself up against a post and clutched a piece of prison garb to his nude body. The photo appeared in the *New York Times Magazine* in early May under the caption "Crowded Bunks in the Prison Camp at Buchenwald." Haunting because of the men's pained faces, images such as this one were often used as foils for other pictures—well-fed Germans, civilian witnesses, and even corpses. In most cases, the depicted were not identified, and that anonymity helped to convey powerful nonverbal messages of the effects of depravity.[26]

British Combine

Congress views the atrocities: In addition to the official 12-man mission, the horror camps were visited by Reps. Clare Luce, John Kunkel, and Leonard Hall

Figure 9. U.S. Congress viewing atrocities in Buchenwald, May 1945, by AP/Wide
World Photos.

German nationals were also frequently depicted, and primary here
were German perpetrators. Generally depicted with other collectives,
such as victims or survivors, the press showed them digging graves, staring
down survivors, or walking across camp courtyards. One such picture portrayed the notorious Fritz Klein, wading through a pit of bodies at Bergen-
Belsen (fig. 11). Again, the bodies spilled out of the frame, and his upright
posture in their midst underscored the macabre nature of Nazi deeds. Perpetrators were generally shown at odd angles to the camera, which showed
large uniform bodies—angry stares, colorless prison garb, and, in the case
of women, tightly bound hair. German civilians were also frequently

Figure 10. Former prisoners of Buchenwald, April 16, 1945, by NARA.

depicted witnesses, and they too were photographed in various encounters with the atrocities: reburying the bodies of Nazi victims, looking at cremation ovens, or "being forced to gaze" at stacks of corpses. One frequently circulated shot showed women and young boys from Weimar being forced to look upon the bodies of Buchenwald (fig. 12). The civilians were in various stages of emotional disarray. One clutched a handkerchief to her chin, another looked as if she were about to cry, still another wore an expression of disbelief. Each individual conformed on one point: they looked to the left of the picture, staring at evidence of the atrocities, which were beyond the frame of the camera lens. Taken by the Signal Corps on April 16, the

Figure 11. Fritz Klein in Belsen, April 1945, courtesy of The Imperial War Museum, London.

photo surfaced in numerous newspapers and newsmagazines.[27] This aesthetic—showing witnesses without evidence of the atrocities—forced attention on the act of bearing witness. It froze the act of bearing witness in time and space, inviting readers to attend to what was being witnessed even if it was not shown. By extension, this implied a recognition of the other atrocity photos to make this particular shot understandable, supporting a mutual cross-referentiality across all the shots.

Most shots of German civilians seemed to pronounce a confusion, shock, or bewilderment that complicated the act of bearing witness, as when German children were portrayed in a refusal to bear witness: one shot showed a small boy looking straight at the camera and away from the bodies that took up the majority of photographic space, his glance com-

Figure 12. German civilians in Buchenwald, April 16, 1945, by NARA.

municating an act of witnessing that was in essence not-witnessing; in another photo a boy walked down a road lined with dead bodies in Belsen, his head too averted—again, a refusal to bear witness.[28] Other shots of civilians mirrored the complexity of the German response to atrocity. One such photo showed eight civilians, seemingly aghast at the sight of a dead body, walking gingerly around it. The first woman looked at it and clutched her throat; the second put her hand over her mouth and looked directly at the camera; the woman behind her also looked at the photographer but in a way that suggested she was blinded by the camera. The varying responses not only mirrored Germany's collective discomfort as a nation but complicated the act of bearing witness in the public imagination. Yet they also paradoxically bolstered the authority of the photograph. Looking at the dead body at the same time as readers did, and looking not at the body but at the camera, fit well with the difficulty in forcing the Germans to see the evidence at their doorstep.[29]

Soldiers as witnesses were not featured very prominently in images, perhaps because security made photographing soldiers imprudent. In fact, one of the first atrocity pictures to appear was exceptional, because it showed a U.S. medical officer behind a stack of bodies in Ohrdruf who was identified by name and hometown in the documentation that accompanied the series of photos (see fig. 5, on p. 90). Yet other exceptions involved well-known military figures: a frontal image of Eisenhower topped off the *Illustrated London News*'s detachable supplement on the atrocities, while the *Daily Telegraph* superimposed black arrows with names on an image of Ohrdruf so as to identify the key figures of Generals Eisenhower, Patton, and Bradley. Significantly, each photo offered the same basic shot—dead bodies in the foreground, soldier-as-witness in the background, looking both at the camera and at the bodies. The camera connected with the living across the bodies of the dead.[30]

A final round of witnesses came with the official delegations to the camps, both politicians and editors. One extensively recycled photo depicted the editors' delegation to the camps (fig. 13). The photo portrayed a group of editors in the act of covering the uncovering of corpses in Buchenwald. The editors—all white and male—scribbled into notepads while seeming to avoid looking at the bodies at their feet. A few soldiers at the corner of the frame looked at the bodies, standing in for the act of bearing witness. Released over the wires on May 3, a week after it was taken, the photo appeared in both the *Boston Globe* under the caption "American Editors View Buchenwald Victims" and in the *Los Angeles Times* as "Buchenwald." While the wire service caption identified the editors in the shot by name and newspaper affiliation, that degree of identification was reproduced in neither newspaper. Other photos showed both officials and editors examining the camps' terrain or looking at dead bodies. In fact, authenticity was often established by photographing this version of the act of bearing witness—soldiers, officials, and politicians in front of heaps of bodies. The women officials pictured in these images appeared to play a slightly different role than did the men, in that they supported a gendered expectation of women in the role of consolers, and they were portrayed not only looking at dead victims but talking to survivors.[31]

What did these elaborated portrayals of witnessing accomplish? They provided a representational frame that words could not: they froze witnessing in place. Images prolonged witnessing by separating it from the scenes of horror. Depicting different practices of witnessing, targets of witnessing, and kinds of witnesses, these images underscored the centrality of bearing witness as a response to Nazi terror. Unlike verbal narratives, where bearing witness was only implied in the grounded accounts of lib-

Figure 13. American editors visiting Buchenwald, April, 1945, by NARA.

eration, witnessing here was seen as sufficiently important to merit its own category of representation. While this may not have fit the cadences or aims of daily news, it was well suited to the larger frame of contemplating what had happened in the camps.

Thus, photographs contextualized Nazi atrocity by broadening the two features of the eyewitness report—territory and the activities of witnessing—beyond the contingent instance of violence. Photographs of territory created strong links between one locale and the rest of the depraved Nazi world, links that were denied in reporters' concrete word-tours. Similarly, visual representations underscored variations in the act of bearing witness—stages of the act itself, different targets of bearing witness, different kinds of witnesses, and different kinds of witnessing practices—that not only offered an array of representations but also conveyed a prolonged moment of witnessing that was lost in reporters' narratives. This variance highlighted far more effectively than did words the complications surrounding the act of bearing witness and simultaneously linked the act of witnessing with broader interpretive schema by which it was possible to generalize, contextualize, and symbolize what had happened.

This suggests that the very act of interpretation took shape differently in words and images. With words, the press restricted the act of bearing witness by closing off interpretation and grounding the narratives in the here-and-now. With photos, the press helped the world bear witness more effectively by opening the documents to interpretation.

ATROCITY PHOTOS AS SYMBOLS

The press also provided links between each photo and the larger atrocity story through practices of composition and presentation. Each set of practices helped consolidate the images of the camps as symbols of atrocity.

Practices of Composition: Placement, Number, and Gaze

Though numerous and wide-ranging in their depictions of horror, the atrocity photos were somewhat unusual due to the repetitive scenes reproduced by different photographers, regardless of their degree of professional training. While varying the depiction—by changing the camera position, camera angle, focal length of the lens, light, and length of exposure—might have lent an individualized signature to the photos, this was generally not characteristic of these photos. Instead, near identical images arrived over the wires within hours and days of each other, differing only slightly in focus, distance, exposure, and perspective.

PLACEMENT. The decision of where to place evidence of atrocity in a photo created a layering between the atrocity photos' foreground and background, for the two often communicated different levels of specificity about what was being depicted. Witnesses and bodies were depicted in many of the images, and one was used as context for the other.

Evidence of atrocity usually meant pictures of corpses, and it often alternated with witnesses in either the shot's foreground or background. One widely circulated image portrayed General Eisenhower and other ranking generals at Ohrdruf viewing corpses strewn across the camp's forecourt (fig. 14). Eisenhower and company faced the camera from the back of the shot while they overlooked the dead bodies in its foreground that spilled into the camera. Taken by an unidentified photographer, the photograph appeared in the *Washington Post* on April 16 and resurfaced frequently over the next two weeks. It played in the *Illustrated London News* as a full front-page photo whose legend told readers that "the usually genial General Eisenhower shows by his grim aspect his horror of German bru-

Figure 14. General Eisenhower and other officers examine corpses at Ohrdruf, April 12, 1945, by NARA.

tality." The photo not only heightened the role of the American GI as witness to atrocity but juxtaposed the reader with the GI across the space of the bodies. It was impossible to contemplate the GI's act of witnessing without first contemplating the corpses.[32]

Elsewhere the foreground and background were switched, with the corpses positioned in the back of the shot. The British *News Chronicle* ran a front-page picture of Belsen that showed women cooking and peeling potatoes in the foreground and heaps of dead bodies in the background. Another frequently circulated triangular shot of the Buchenwald courtyard depicted a visual confrontation juxtaposing U.S. soldiers, a stack of dead bodies on a wagon, and the backs of German civilians (fig. 15). The bodies occupied the back right-hand corner of the shot, soldiers the back left-

Figure 15. German civilians view corpses at Buchenwald, April 16, 1945, by NARA.

hand corner, and civilians the foreground. In viewing the shot, the reader had to look over the shoulders of the German civilians in order to see the bodies, creating a layering between the shot's foreground (where the Germans were standing) and the background (where the victims and liberators stood). The effect was magnified by the middle of the shot, where a seemingly impassable white space kept the groups at a distance from each other. That aesthetic was reproduced in other atrocity photos.[33]

NUMBER. A second practice of composition had to do with the numbers of people who were depicted in atrocity photos. The photos oscillated between pictures of the many and pictures of the few. Pictures of the many portrayed mass graves, where bodies had been thrown together so indiscriminately that it was difficult, if not impossible, to discern which appendage belonged to which body; pictures of the few portrayed single

Figure 16. Corpses of civilians killed at Buchenwald, April–May 1945, by NARA.

individual bodies frozen in particularly horrific poses—a starved man stretched out in rigor mortis on the grounds of one of the camps. Taken together, the images portrayed both individual agony and the far-reaching nature of mass atrocity, suggesting that the depiction of each individual instance of horror represented thousands more who had met the same fate. The photos functioned not only referentially but as symbolic markers of atrocity in its broadest form.[34]

On the whole, the press presented collective images of atrocity more frequently than it did those of individuals. Perhaps because the group shots suggested a collective status that helped offset public disbelief, group shots appeared frequently regardless of the type of collective represented—groups of victims, survivors, or witnesses. Group images tended to be less graphic than those of individuals, partly because the rarely visible eyes and faces worked against the possibility of identifying the victims being depict-

Figure 17. Women SS guards at Belsen, April 17, 1945, courtesy of The Imperial War Museum, London.

ed. Foremost here was a famous shot by Margaret Bourke-White, captioned simply "Victims of the Buchenwald Concentration Camp." Unaccredited at the time it originally appeared, the photo portrayed piles of human feet and heads angled away from the camera; the pile gave viewers the impression that it was about to spill over onto the photographer, and that it was barred from doing so only by a length of chain at the bottom of the picture (fig. 16). Other photographs, less renowned than Bourke-White's, showed the same pile of bodies from a long shot, a perspective that revealed them to be stacked atop a wagon in the camp's courtyard. That same wagon, portrayed from an even further distance, was featured in the aforementioned triangular shot of the Buchenwald courtyard.[35]

Images of other kinds of groups—survivors, German civilians, German perpetrators, and official witnesses—also proliferated, each displayed with repeated visual characteristics. Groups of witnesses were nearly always portrayed at one side of the frame, looking sideways at corpses that were either inside or outside the field of the camera. Groups of German perpetrators, for instance, were almost always portrayed at harsh angles to the camera and in rigid and upright postures (fig. 17). These individuals looked

Figure 18. Russian survivor identifies former camp guard at Buchenwald, April 14, 1945, by NARA.

angry and cruel, almost maniacal. That perception was upheld in the captions that accompanied images of this type, as when the *Illustrated London News* labeled a group of perpetrators "The Female Fiends."[36]

Often the shots depicted confrontations between groups—German civilians and victims or news editors and survivors. One image—which circulated under the caption "Slave Laborer Points Finger of Guilt"— depicted a survivor of an unidentified camp pointing at a German guard (fig. 18). The guard stood at the right-hand corner of the image, his contorted face twisting away from both the camera lens and the accusing, outstretched finger of the former prisoner. Although the prisoner was portrayed sideways to the camera, the photographer's empathy with him was clear.[37] Behind the two figures stood other officials, one of whom was witnessing the confrontation.

Figure 19. Two survivors in Bergen-Belsen, April 30, 1945, courtesy of The Imperial War Museum, London.

Thus, in each case framing the depiction as an act of collective, not individual, contemplation reflected a need to collectively address and understand the atrocities. While the emphasis on collective representation may have worked against a recognition of the individual tragedies that lay underneath each photo, the emphasis on groups fit more effectively than did an individual focus on Eisenhower's aim to use the photos as persuasive tools for the war effort. Groups, more than individuals, let the war effort urgency. Understanding the scope and magnitude of atrocity, in this sense, was equally important to recognizing its individual cases.

GAZE. Yet a third compositional practice had to do with the gaze of those being depicted. The gaze of emaciated, near-dead survivors, whose eyes seemed not to comprehend the target of vision, tended to be frontal and appeared to signify frankness—though, as one British Army Film and Photographic Unit photographer of Belsen recalled, many of the same people were "incapable of coherent thought. . . . It was a very quiet, silent business. They sat about, very little movement. Some of them were too far

Figure 20. Corpses of mother and two children at Bergen-Belsen, April 17, 1945, courtesy of The Imperial War Museum, London.

gone to move." The survivors were almost always represented in frontal gazes that stared directly at the camera or at a short distance behind the photographer. In a sense, atrocity survivors appeared to see without seeing. One such photo, which appeared in *PM,* depicted two young adult women in a close shot that echoed their hollowed cheekbones and vacant eyes (fig. 19). "Here's How Nazis Treat Their Captives . . . ," read the caption to the photo, as it implored readers to look at the "faces of these women."[38]

Other photos portrayed the unseeing eyes of the dead. One such photograph, which appeared after Belsen's liberation in *PM* and the *Saturday Evening Post,* portrayed two children, a brother and sister whom readers

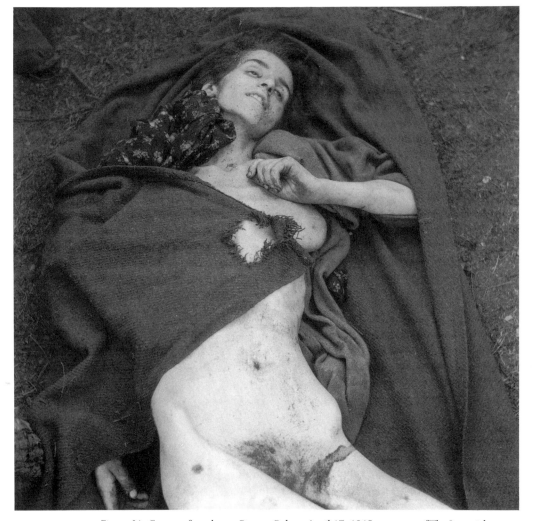

Figure 21. Corpse of mother at Bergen-Belsen, April 17, 1945, courtesy of The Imperial War Museum, London.

were told had died of starvation (fig. 20). The children were depicted lying on the ground, simply clothed and huddled together in death. The specter of the dead children was haunting: both faces were gaunt and drawn, and the eyes of one child were open. Yet lying next to them, bundled in a blanket at the left side of the photograph, was an equally powerful figure—that of the children's dead mother. Although she was not depicted clearly in this photo, she was shown in an accompanying image that was published only later in commemorative literature. There, the woman was depicted alone

Figure 22. Former women guards at Bergen-Belsen, April 1945, courtesy of The Imperial War Museum, London.

and without the blanket, where she was revealed to be nude and beautiful, her long, curly hair spread across her shoulders (fig. 21). The fact that the latter image did *not* make it into the press of the time suggests that it perhaps went against the patterned nature of the photos that did appear.[39]

German perpetrators generally were depicted in side views or three-quarter gazes, their eyes averted and narrowed (fig. 22). Often they were depicted looking sideways at a survivor or soldier, who nearly always stared either directly at them or toward the camera. One such widely circulated image was that of Belsen commander Josef Kramer. It portrayed him walking in Belsen, his mouth pursed and features tight, under a guard's watchful eye, who stared at him intently from the right-hand corner of the photograph. The same figures were portrayed from a greater distance in the *Daily Mail,* where Kramer was shown to be accompanied on his stroll not only by a soldier at his side but by another soldier prodding a rifle into his back.[40]

In composition, then, the published photos depicted a level of horror that went beyond one specific instance of brutality so as to present it as a representative incident. The combination of corpses and witnesses in the photos facilitated both the display of a particular act of barbarism and its more general context of atrocity; the number of individuals depicted in atrocity photos facilitated an emphasis on the collectives involved in atrocity—either as victims, survivors, perpetrators, or witnesses; and the gaze of those associated with atrocity opened the photographic document to the act of bearing witness in different configurations for victims, survivors, and perpetrators. In each case, on the level of composition photographs offered more than just the referential depiction of one specific event, action, or camp. Compositional practices suggested a broader level of the story that went beyond the concrete target of photographic depiction.

Practices of Presentation: Captions, Credits, and Presentational Layout

A similar movement toward the broader atrocity story was achieved in presentation. Many atrocity photos lacked basic identifying attributes, and they were as patterned in the type of information they neglected to provide as in that which they provided. Captions gave little information about what was being depicted. Horrifying for the visual portrayal they offered about death and suffering, they generally omitted any definitive detail about the victims, about which camp had claimed their lives, or about the circumstances by which they died. Detail about the taking of the photograph itself was also often missing, about who had taken the photos, when, or where. In some cases, no name of photographer or photographic agency was given. Still other times, the images existed in questionable relationship with the texts they accompanied, or pictures were used as pieces of news in themselves, with little or no texts to explain what readers were seeing.

The image's referentiality was thus undermined even as the image's symbolic force was underscored. Images were used more to mark general discourse—about atrocity and war—and less as providers of definitive information about certain actions, camps, or victims.

CAPTIONS. Captions were an instrumental way of ensuring that photos invoked the broader atrocity story. Who wrote the captions was not made explicit, despite the fact that captions were typed on the back of nearly all photographs supplied by the U.S. Signal Corps and British Army Film and Photographic Unit. While the press sometimes marked a photo's caption with the phrase "according to caption accompanying this Signal Corps radio photo," more often than not captions were written by people far from the depicted scenes. That distance, rarely made explicit to audiences, generated numerous errors.[41]

Figure 23. Survivors in Bergen-Belsen, April 29, 1945, courtesy of The Imperial War Museum, London.

For instance, readers were told that the same photo of a group of women hovering over dead bodies in Belsen depicted women either stripping the dead corpses of clothing for fuel, stripping them so as to wear the clothes, cleansing them of lice-infested apparel, or stripping them so as to burn the bodies (fig. 23). While all of the cited reasons might have been relevant, it is significant that already at the time of the photo's presentation, the press set in place differential frames for understanding the depicted activity. Various explanations also accompanied an image of an emaciated man who sat amid a pile of rags (fig. 24). In the photo, he appeared bent over the rags, his bones protruding from his body, and other survivors watched from the background. Though the *Sunday Express* explained that the man was "removing his filthy rags," elsewhere he was said to be "overhauling rags of dead prisoners" or picking lice off of his own clothes.[42]

Differences in explanation were problematic, because they set in place a faulty historical record. One aforementioned image of a U.S. Army major crouching behind a stack of lime-covered bodies appeared during the first days of Ohrdruf's liberation (see fig. 5, on p. 90). The same image was claimed, however, to have been taken in a number of camps, including

Figure 24. Survivor in Bergen-Belsen, April 1945, courtesy of The Imperial War Museum. London.

Ohrdruf, Buchenwald, Nordhausen, and the nearby town of Gotha. *Time* wrongly labeled the image as being at Buchenwald, one week after the same image was displayed by *Newsweek,* where it correctly identified the bodies as being at Ohrdruf. On the level of referentiality, the details in *Time*'s caption were simply wrong. Yet in convincing a skeptical world of the atrocities, it mattered little whether a stack of bodies was at Ohrdruf or Buchenwald. What mattered was that it had happened. The image thus functioned to provide proof of atrocity, even if the location of the atrocities was incorrect.[43]

In writing captions, the press adopted a tone that further stripped the pictures of their referential power. One five-page article in *Time,* published in April 1945, brought together a number of vignettes about the camps, all of which were illustrated by generalized images—*a* commandant, *a* mass burial, *a* common grave, *a* charred body, *human* cordwood. One showed an innocuous portrait of Belsen commandant Josef Kramer, with a caption that read simply: "Commandant Kramer: He loved flowers." The other five photographs displayed horrific death scenes—a mass burial at Nordhausen, a common grave at Belsen, a charred body at Erla, human cordwood at Buchenwald, and a starved prisoner at Belsen. The images alternated between representing the many and the few, and their captions were particularly instrumental in negotiating a leap from referential to symbolic representation.

Each of *Time*'s pictures was located in place via a set of parentheses. A picture of an open pit of bodies, accredited to both British Official Pictures and the Associated Press, bore the rather curious caption "Common Grave (Belsen)." Setting off the word *Belsen* in parentheses—and similarly framing the words *Nordhausen, Erla,* or *Buchenwald* in other captions—signaled to readers that the exact location of the atrocities was secondary, almost an afterthought. Where events took place was not only noninstrumental but possibly irrelevant to the image's more universal meaning. When the pictures were taken was not noted at all. Indeed, the captions seemed to suggest that the events depicted could have taken place anywhere in the Third Reich and anytime under its reign. Thus, instead of using captions to anchor the photographs in a precise time and place, the press employed them to mark the photos as symbols of atrocity.

The legends to many of the photographs further facilitated the use of the photos as symbols. One legend observed that the image of a mass burial was "as irrefutable as death." Given that the photograph showed scores of dead bodies lined up in one long grave, readers were left to ponder precisely what was irrefutable about the image. In the text of the article, however, readers learned that the phrase referred to *reporters finding* "the evidence of the camps . . . as irrefutable as death." Comments like these positioned photographs in an uneven balance with text, a balance that worked against the image's referentiality.[44]

CREDITS. Another way of turning images of the camps into symbols of a broader atrocity story was to provide them with few accrediting attributes. Readers often did not know who had taken the pictures they were viewing. At times, the photographic credit lines were presented elsewhere in the journal, as when the *New York Times* presented an image of Buchenwald's crowded bunks with little detail about where, how, or by whom it was

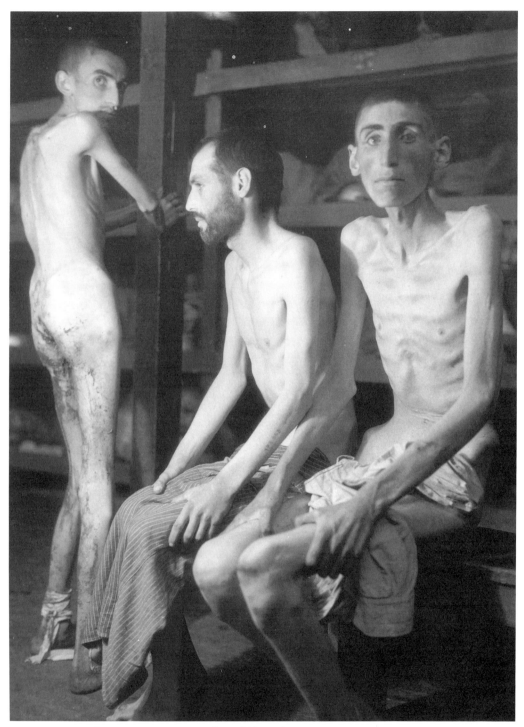

Figure 25. Survivors in Buchenwald barracks, April 16, 1945, by NARA.

taken; readers who skimmed the newspaper learned only on another page that it had been taken by the Associated Press.[45]

The accreditation issue posed numerous problems for British and U.S. photographers. Often, the photographs were printed without credits at all. After the British forces entered Belsen, the *Daily Mail* printed a series of photographs, mostly of camp commandants, and accredited none of them. The *Illustrated London News* printed twenty-two images of the camps in its special supplement on the atrocities, but none of them was accredited. Even photos that are today renowned—such as Margaret Bourke-White's shot of bodies heaped across a wagon—were frequently included without attribution.[46]

When credits were presented, they were brief and tended to include only the name of the official military unit responsible for the image. Thus, the most frequent credit found alongside images of the camps was the phrase, "Photo by U.S. Signal Corps." Names of specific photographic agencies—such as Acme Pictures or Wide World Photos—appeared less frequently. And even less frequently appeared the names of specific photographers. It was only in later years that readers in both the United States and Britain learned which photographers had taken which atrocity photos. And to this day some remain unaccredited.

Most importantly, the press revealed a fundamentally different attitude toward the words and images it used. When *PM* presented a highly referenced and carefully attributed eyewitness report that discussed the Allied War Department's official report on Buchenwald, it did so alongside an unattributed, unaccredited photograph of three ravaged men (fig. 25). In this case the different degree of attribution accorded word and image was striking. The report constituted an indexically powerful narrative that presented verbatim passages from an official report on the camp, including details about camp routines, numbers of prisoners and victims, death counts, and torture procedures. But no attribution accompanied the photograph, no date described when it had been taken, and little identification of the depicted individuals was offered.[47]

LAYOUT. Yet another way of cuing the broader atrocity story through images was via layout. In the press, photos often appeared in photographic spreads or so-called pictorial pages, a presentational format made familiar by the picture-magazine, with four to eight images separated from the verbal text. On April 26, for instance, the *Philadelphia Inquirer* included photographic shots of Buchenwald, Nordhausen, and other locales on its pictorial page.[48]

But because standards then in use for photographic images were inex-

Figure 26. "This Was Nazi Germany," *Stars and Stripes*, April 23, 1945. Reprinted courtesy of *The Stars and Stripes.*

plicit and undeveloped, the press positioned the atrocity photos unevenly. For instance, the military newspaper *Stars and Stripes* regularly printed columns of photographs alongside eyewitness accounts of the camps; one such account described the camps of Gardelegen and Mulhausen, while the accompanying photos presented bodies massacred in Ohrdruf, Nordhausen, and Buchenwald (fig. 26). The images had no specific referential link to the verbal narratives that they were used to illustrate, other than to provide evidence of the same larger story of atrocity, and none of the photographs was dated or attributed to agency or photographer. Similarly, one *Time* column about Germany juxtaposed two photographs—one of three near-naked men under the caption "Buchenwald Survivors: Were They Germany's Hope?" and the other of a German child under the caption "Children." While the captions explained that the men were survivors and the children Germany's future, the accompanying text told of an underground movement at the camp that had planned to build an antifascist Reich. Yet that text was nowhere recognizable in the by-then familiar image of broken, despairing bodies or the less familiar image of the plump, blond German toddler.[49]

This meant that even when the press did not provide precise details about the images it displayed, it was able to link them with the larger atrocity story. This broad interpretive effect of the images made them crucial for underscoring the act of bearing witness as the appropriate response to atrocity. Paradoxically, the usefulness of such images depended on their anonymity. The anonymity through which they made claim to authenticity in fact provided strong visual evidence of atrocity at a generalized level, but uneven documentation of the particular events they were brought in to depict.

One article in *Time* about Belsen illustrates this well. Opposing one picture with another, a small boxed item displayed two photographs: one, without attribution, showed a side view of an angry-looking blonde woman; the other, attributed to Acme Pictures, showed a crowd scene near a spiraling fire and billowing smoke. The caption under both pictures asked, "The End of Belsen?" and in the accompanying text, readers were told that

> these pictures are from the Belsen concentration camp. At left is Hilde Lobauer, known to the prisoners she terrified as "the S.S. woman without a uniform." At right is Belsen burning as the British wiped out the human abattoir by fire.

The descriptive text gave readers definitive information about what they saw—or did not see—in the photographs. Yet the discussion did not end with the images' description, for a second paragraph generalized the information just presented:

> But more than fire was needed to destroy the causes that produced Belsen. For they lay deeper than any tendency to scientific brutality on the part of the German people. They lay in the political philosophy of totalitarianism, which is not the exclusive property of any people. If this was understood, the thousands of men and women who died in anonymous agony at Belsen would not have died completely in vain. Failure to understand this meant that they would have died for absolutely nothing, that the meaning of Belsen would be dissipated in moral revulsion and invective, that other Belsens could recur in history. The meaning of Belsen was the ultimate meaning of all totalitarianism.

The addition of this second paragraph was crucial, for it showed how *Time* transformed the particular images of Belsen and its commander into symbolic markers of a story about human suffering and totalitarianism. Belsen the concentration camp became representative of wartime atrocity.[50]

All of this suggests that by capitalizing on the symbolic dimensions of images, the press set in place a broader interpretive scheme for comprehending and explaining the atrocities. Playing to the symbolic dimensions of these images had an important effect on publics, not only because they may have been the most effective and least uncomfortable way to comprehend the tragedies of Nazi Europe, but also because they framed events in such a way that all who saw the photos could bear witness to the atrocities. Within that frame, the exact details of the atrocities mattered less than the response of bearing witness. For those inundated with a guilt that came from not having responded earlier, this was no small aim.

As with words, the act of bearing witness made the use of images instrumental for setting in place the atrocity record. But using photographs as symbolic markers of atrocity inverted journalistic modes of news presentation. Rather than provide more cues when the information was most unbelievable, less cues were provided when the information stretched belief. Here the more horrific the image, the less detailed the anchoring of the text that accompanied it. In this regard, images were particularly qualified to provide the message that made the act of bearing witness bearable. They also suited the circumstances for coverage that greeted the press in the camps.

Bearing witness thus justified an alternative use of images in news that relied as much on the photo's symbolic dimensions as on its contingent details. Even if reporters had been earlier remiss about recognizing what was happening, bearing witness now enhanced the authority of the image and by extension the press's authority on this specific story. While the photo's muted referentiality may have been typical of most war photos, it had particularly great effect here, for the symbolic nature of photos was well suited to explaining Nazi atrocity in memory.

It is worth noting that this happened in contradiction to what the press expected of photography, for a link between the photo's referential and symbolic dimensions had not been anticipated. Not surprisingly, photographers still faced ambivalence from journalists, despite their valued work in the camps. There was virtually no mention in the press about the photographers who shot scenes of the camps, suggesting that the sense of shared responsibility went far enough to include the photographs as documents but not to include photographers. In fact, when the *Illustrated London News* presented pages of photographic images from Belsen, they were likened to a "Doré *drawing* of Dante's Inferno" (emphasis added). This suggested that the journal's editorial board was still not convinced that photos had done their job of convincing readers of the atrocities. Its solution was to print a series of drawings one week later that depicted many of the camp scenes already shown in photographs, though in the later drawings their details were made less reprehensible. Such ambivalence, which linked to a muted recognition of the value of photographic documents in news, penetrated the core of the record of atrocity.[51]

PICTURE-MAGAZINES AND LIBERATORS

The display of the atrocity photos in the U.S. and British press was enhanced by two additional parties interested in photographing the camps—the picture-magazines and the liberators. Each extended photography's role in bearing witness to the atrocities.

By virtue of the centrality that the picture-magazines accorded images in general, it is no surprise that picture-magazines on both continents, particularly *Life, Look,* and *Picture Post,* played an important role in bringing the atrocity photos home. But their role was secondary to that of newspapers, magazines, and journals, which had already printed most of the photos by the time that they appeared in the picture-magazines. The picture-magazine's main effect was thereby one of repetition more than information. Via its favored presentational format—the depiction of many collected images as parts of a larger picture-story—the picture-magazines bolstered the effect already created by the daily and weekly press, offering more of what had already been presented.

Each picture-magazine published its own photographic spread on the atrocities during the first week of May 1945. The spreads in both the *Pic-*

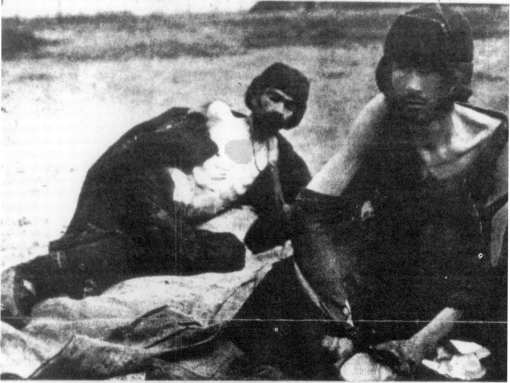

INSIDE THE WIRE: *Hulks of Ruined Humanity Whose Condition Would Make Stones Cry Out*

Inside the wire, horror. But horror that took place within sight or sound of hundreds of thousands of seemingly normal, decent German people. How was it possible? What has happened to the minds of a whole nation that such things should have been tolerated for a day?

THE PROBLEM THAT MAKES ALL EUROPE WONDER

A FLOOD of news-pictures, a crop of unforgettable first-hand accounts of conditions in German concentration camps, have set Europe and the world asking one question. How is it possible that these same Germans, many of whom in pre-war days we have known in this country and their own, should have tolerated the revolting cruelties which have gone on within earshot and eyesight of their homes? What has become, inside Germany, of the common decencies of civilised people? Too much hangs on this question for it to be answered blindly and in the fury of the moment. With the help of qualified psycho-analysts and doctors, German amongst them, we have tried to get nearer to the truth in a series of questions and answers.

AND OUTSIDE

The cover-picture. Just a typical, pleasant-looking German family, to whom what happened inside meant nothing.

(1) *Is the cruelty revealed a racial characteristic of the German people?*

Definitely not. There is cruelty in every nation, though it is almost entirely latent until special circumstances bring it out. War is one of those special circumstances. Not only is the law against killing suspended, but in the waging of war the individual conscience is taken over by the State.

In the case of Germany, the State is represented by the Nazi Party and the national conscience has borne the face of its keeper. For many of these Party men cruelty is an outlet, a reaction against the restrictions and inhibitions which the relatively civilised world before Hitler imposed on them. It is significant that a great many of them, especially those who are the worst thugs of the Party, filling just such jobs as that of concentration camp guard, had never felt themselves a real part of pre-Hitler society. Many were frustrates and throw-outs, the older ones from the last war, who felt a grievance against society which they have been revenging themselves for, by acts of cruelty, ever since.

(2) *An individual may suffer from split personality. Is it possible that a nation can suffer in the same way?*

Continued overleaf

Figure 27. "The Problem That Makes All Europe Wonder," *Picture Post,* May 5, 1945, by Picture Post/Tony Stone Images.

ture Post and *Life* capably wove the horror into picture-essays that were more effective for the combined visual presentation of many images than for the novelty or informative value of any individual picture.

Under the title "The Problem That Makes All Europe Wonder," the *Picture Post* offered a six-page spread of atrocity photos. The first page juxtaposed two images—one of two emaciated, dazed survivors with an image of a plump, well-dressed German woman hugging a blond child (fig. 27). The two sets of figures stared full-faced into the camera's lens, and the captions extended the visual difference between them into verbal cues: one read "Inside the Wire," while the other proclaimed "And Outside." Other images portrayed close-ups of ravaged victims and depictions of a camp roll call, or smaller pictures of drained anonymous faces under a collective caption "These Were Inmates of Prison Camps Set Free in the Allied Advance: For Many We Came Too Late." None of the pictures bore the names of individuals, names of camps, or photographic credits. The photographs were documents of collective authorship, sealed in the anonymity of the photographer and his or her object. Yet another picture in the same article portrayed two men from Nordhausen sitting on a flight of steps staring into the camera. In proclaiming the image to be "The Face, Not of Men, but of Famine," the caption disembodied the image, disconnecting the faces from the men who owned them and rendering them instead symbols of famine.

The spread concluded with a picture that the picture-magazine predicted would be "a picture on which future generations will pass judgment." The picture, which had appeared already ten days earlier in *Stars and Stripes,* showed two dead children, lying at the bottom of a ditch. Their mouths were open, their arms spread-eagled across the dirt on which they rested (fig. 28). A soldier stood at the upper-left-hand corner of the image, looking into the ditch and passing his own judgment. The subhead read, "The Dead Children of Nordhausen Camp." While the subhead offered some degree of explanation for the image, the accompanying text offered little:

> It is not enough to be mad with rage. It is no help to shout about "exterminating" Germany. Only one thing helps: the attempt to understand how men have sunk so far, and the firm resolve to face the trouble, the inconvenience and cost of seeing no nation gets the chance to befoul the world like this again.[52]

The image, in this context, was taken as a cautionary note about the excesses of Nazism. As with the images in the press, the dead children of Nordhausen were invoked as general markers of a discourse about atrocity.

Picture Post ran a second pictorial spread in June, when photographers

Figure 28. Dead children at Nordhausen, April 1945, by NARA.

depicted German civilians exhuming atrocity victims and digging new graves. Eight pictures, documenting the civilians' forced exhumation of dead prisoners, again raised questions about the symbolic currency of images. While the narrative discussed the wisdom and viability of blaming all of Germany for the Nazi deeds, the pictures wove a theme that was by now familiar—voiceless, nameless, unauthored documents attesting to the atrocities. The final picture, captioned "The Silent Witness at Whose Suffering the Earth Has Cried Out Aloud," showed a shrouded, faceless body in a newly dug grave. As a concluding statement, the photograph remained devoid of the physical, geographic, and spatial details that facilitated its placement in real life. Rather, its symbolic aura made it almost better suited to a placement in collective memory.[53]

Life published its photographic spread on the atrocities the same week as *Picture Post*. As had been its custom surrounding other controversial photos, the picture-magazine shared its justification for why it had elected to publish the images:

> Last week Americans could no longer doubt stories of Nazi cruelty. For the first time there was irrefutable evidence as the advancing Allied armies captured camps. . . . With the armies in Germany were four *Life* photographers whose pictures are presented on these pages. The things they show are horrible. They are printed for the reason stated seven years ago when, in publishing early pictures of war's death and destruction in Spain and China, *Life* stated, "Dead men have indeed died in vain if live men refuse to look at them."[54]

Life's defensive posture hinted that audiences were not yet consensual about the need to regard the atrocity photos.

Life titled its photographic spread simply "Atrocities." Atop five pages of graphic photos, the magazine began by declaring that the "capture of the German concentration camps piles up evidence of barbarism that reaches the low point of human degradation." The images depicted a range of Nazi-inflicted horrors, each presented as a generic category of horror, including dazed prisoners at Buchenwald, dying women at Belsen, and burning bodies at Gardelegen. Most of the pictures had appeared already in the daily press.

The spread ended with three full-page, midrange shots, each of which focused on the ravages of war. One, which had appeared previously in the British and U.S. press, depicted bodies lying in the courtyard of Nordhausen (see fig. 8, on p. 99). The second showed a mass of burned bodies at Gardelegen. In both shots, U.S. soldiers walked among the bodies, signifying life rising from the masses of death and decay. The final photograph of the series provided the only midview shot of an individual—a German guard, portrayed with his bowed head angled away from the camera. Readers were told that he was "knee-deep in decaying flesh and bones, [hauling] bodies into place in the Belsen mass grave." Presenting the German guard in mid-distance and using his photograph to conclude the series left a clear message about the irrevocable end of Nazism.[55]

In both *Picture Post* and *Life,* the verbal detail that accompanied the images was sparse. Captions told of unnamed prisoners staring from their bunks or leaning against them. Only sometimes did they inform readers which camp was being depicted. The captions relayed little more than what was made most obvious by the camera. Few images were accredited. This lack of verbal detail, however, mattered little in terms of the broader atrocity story. What was thus initially set in place in the press was bolstered by the picture-magazines.

In using many of the shots already presented in the daily press, the picture-magazines were instrumental in recycling a certain visualization of atrocity. This was central to consolidating the importance of photography, even if picture-magazines played a secondary role. The combined presentation of many familiar images renewed their power. Impact, then, had as much to do with the repeated presentation of certain photographs as with the informative news value of any one image.

If picture-magazines provided one contrast to the photos being printed in the press, images taken by the liberators—that is, amateur photographers—provided another. Members of the liberating forces went in and out of the camps rapidly. Many stopped to take quick snapshots with their private cameras. Photographs constituted a way of extending their fleeting experience in the camps beyond the brief times they spent there. As one soldier recalled, "sometimes we would go in the afternoons and by early morning we had cleared the area and gone on."[56]

Although chaplains, foot soldiers, and individuals in other military roles documented what they were seeing, sometimes their shots were blurred and unclear. The photographs he had taken at one camp, recalled an American GI, were "dim, for I was not a photographer." Other times they were eerily similar to the shots taken by professional photographers. For instance, familiar shots of boxcars of dead bodies outside Dachau, pits of bodies in Belsen, and stacks of bodies in Buchenwald were reproduced by soldiers. The images differed only minimally, such as the addition of a soldier in one corner of the picture. Sometimes the amateur photos were printed in the press, though usually at some delay.[57]

The liberators' photos were important because as amateur documentation they helped secure public belief about what was happening and consolidated the need to bear witness. In fact, belief in the photographs was enhanced when soldiers, not professional photographers, took the images: the public appreciated the amateur shots "in which there could be no doctoring of scenes and no faking of film." But the mission of amateurs in snapping shots of the camps was largely personal, motivated by a desire to record the scenes for posterity. "What I took was there," offered one soldier. "It was fact." Photographs were taken by persons on active military duty in German-occupied territory, were retrieved from dead or captured German soldiers, and were taken by company commanders, who later made duplicates for members of their units. Concern for the pictures reflected a desire to record the scenes for history. As one soldier later put it, "we weren't taking pictures of each other. We were taking pictures of conditions."[58]

The soldiers' pictures were both proof of the horrors and testament to the liberators' presence in the camps. Shots ranging from "skeletons still in the incinerator" to "a pile of bodies still outside" provided depiction of both the atrocities and of soldiers having witnessed them. One chaplain, who photographed the charred bodies still on a pile of wood outside one camp, later said that he "took pictures to make it clear to people at home that the account of German oppression and murder in concentration and labor camps is all too true." The son of General Eisenhower—Lt. John Eisenhower—took a portable camera into Buchenwald. Seeing a group of survivors kicking the dead body of a German guard, he "snapped a couple of pictures and turned to leave with a mumbled word of thanks. The survivors closed back in and resumed kicking the corpses." Former liberator Paul Gumz took a photo of corpses spilling out of one of the train cars at Dachau, with GIs standing in the midspace of the photograph, staring at the bodies (fig. 29). The shot's version of the act of bearing witness also captured the extraordinary length of the train—and hence multiplied the scenes of horror its individual cars contained.[59]

Other shots taken at Buchenwald reproduced the same midview of stacks of corpses that had circulated in the U.S. and British press. One amateur shot differed only with the addition of a soldier in one corner, who stared back at the photographer rather than at the bodies (figs. 30 and 31). On the back of the shot, the liberator had written the following:

> If you starve them, when they die you have less to burn, and the more you burn the more healthy your workmen by replacement. This is just another pile of dead people, America. The Nazis have many more at this place—This is typical on a small scale—Burn!—6,000 one day Jew!—Burn—Dead men.[60]

Figure 29. Paul Gumz Collection, courtesy of The Witness to the Holocaust Project, Emory University.

Both the similarities and differences between the amateur and professional images highlighted how little professional training was needed visually to capture the atrocities. And by implication, the minimal differences somewhat neutralized the role of professional photography in documenting the camps.

In sum, bearing witness through the camera neutralized tensions across different kinds of photographers. The presence of amateur photographers in the camps and the similarity of many of their shots to those taken by semiprofessionals and professionals also minimized the claims of professionals over amateurs. In a sense, the act of bearing witness made a community out of all those who witnessed the atrocities, regardless of their reasons for being there. And the confirmation of what had already been covered became far more important than the coverage itself.

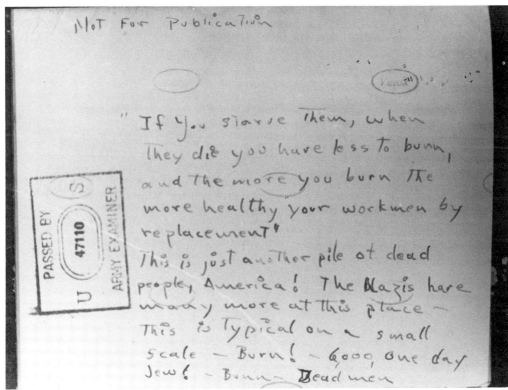

Figures 30 and 31. Dennis Wile Collection, courtesy of The Witness to the Holocaust Project, Emory University.

Figure 32. Civilians looking at pictures, April–May 1945, by NARA.

THE TRIUMPH OF IMAGES

The atrocity photos' emergence as a viable mode of documenting the camps did not go unnoticed by members of the press. In both Britain and the United States, the public discussed the use of images to authenticate what reporters were seeing: the "flood of news-pictures have set Europe and the world asking one question: How is it possible. . . ."[61]

Perhaps the most tangible hint of photography's centrality in delineating the horror of atrocity came with one final wave of representations that depicted the act of looking at the photographs themselves. The so-called denazification campaign required the display of photographs and films to the German population. As the *New York Times* told it, "every German will view the picture of unhumanities practiced on the prisoners at the Buchenwald, Belsen and other Nazi torture camps."[62]

In keeping with that campaign, pictures began to appear that depicted people viewing atrocity photos. Soldiers, civilians, and POWs were all portrayed as witnesses to the photos. These photos were significant, for

Figure 33. Civilians looking at pictures, April–May 1945, courtesy of The Imperial War Museum, London.

they showed numerous additional collectives in the act of bearing witness to photographic documentation. The collectives, like those earlier shots that portrayed groups viewing bodies, now focused on viewing photos. These latter collectives tended to be in a uniform pose that was physically angled toward the evidence of atrocity, in this case, the photos (fig. 32). One such image, displayed in the *New York Times* in June 1945, showed a group of civilians looking at a photographic display. Their backs were to the camera, which focused on them scrutinizing atrocity photos, themselves made clear by the camera's lens. The caption and legend read, "Inside Conquered Germany—civilians examine a photographic display of atrocities committed at a concentration camp." The *Daily Mirror* claimed that photographs were a way of "holding the mirror up to the Huns," and it presented a shot of its own middle pages being displayed to Germans living nearby (fig. 33). Here too, the backs of civilians were captured by the camera, with the atrocity pictures clearly within its frame. Though some journalists and photographers questioned the ease in censorship implied by these officially sanctioned displays of atrocity, the press nonetheless continued to print the photos, prolonging the act of bearing witness beyond its value as a part of news discourse. Thus, photos were set up as a document not only for news but for history too.[63]

In fact, the broader potency of the news photo was strengthened by the response to the atrocity photos. One military newspaper admitted that there "has been no picture story since the invention of photography to match the impact of the layouts now being run on the Nazi atrocities." Soldiers everywhere, it said, know "that within the limits of the printed word and the engraver's art a serious effort is being made to bring home to decent humans the truth of what they found" and that "even the most staid of newspapers are carrying full pages of the brutally grim pictures which came out of the camps."[64]

In contrast to the grounded narratives about the camps, the image-making apparatus in all of its forms thus helped turn collective disbelief into the shock and horror of recognition. Photographic evidence meant that the atrocities of the camps "could not be denied. . . . Buchenwald, Belsen, Dachau—their images were etched in memory forever." Citing "distance, suspicion, what you will," the London-based *World's Press News* said that "something held back full appreciation on the part of the British and American peoples. But these pictures . . ." One newspaper opined that photographic displays of the camps were "revolting and distasteful, but they bring home to a civilized world . . . the cold truth. . . . If anyone ever doubted the animal viciousness of the Nazi mind, he can no longer deny [it]."[65]

More than other types of documentation, photographs offered the certainty needed to appraise the mounting evidence of German atrocities. And both the U.S. and British press were careful to point out the historical role such photographic documentation would play, warning readers of the "photographic evidence of the sadistic brutalities practiced by the Germans. . . . These revelations of coldly calculated massacre and torture are given as a record for all time of German crimes." Even the *Christian Century,* which had stubbornly disbelieved for a longer time than most other journals, admitted that "it will be a long time before our eyes cease to see those pictures of naked corpses piled like firewood or of those mounds of carrion flesh and bones." At least for that journal, "looking at the pictures" became a marker of the experience of Nazism. It was thus no surprise that a full 81 percent of the British population believed the atrocity stories in April 1945, up from a mere 37 percent six months earlier.[66]

Photographs were presented across the Allied front with an authority that underscored their role in muting public skepticism. The black-and-white photos made everyone into a witness, "even those who had remained safely at home far from the stench of the camps." The press seemed to recognize that images had shown themselves capable of conveying the very horror that had incapacitated words. Such was the reigning assumption of the time—that the photograph had helped freeze the camps within a space of undeniability.[67]

Photography's triumph also had to do with the fact that it helped facilitate the act of bearing witness to the atrocities. Unlike words, which concentrated on the details of liberation, images guided publics in both nations to the heart of a story about Nazi atrocity, directing them to the preferred meaning by the fastest route. They offered a vehicle for seeing evidence of Nazi brutality at the same time as they eased the shock of that evidence by broadening its presentation. In this way not only did images uphold military and political aims of "letting the world see," as Eisenhower had mandated, but they did so in a way that bypassed the details of the story of Nazi brutality. In catering to the linkage between the photograph's referential and symbolic dimensions, the press thereby helped focus world attention on the immediate need for a broad political and military response to Nazism.

In representing atrocity in this fashion, photographs challenged traditional journalistic modes of representation and enhanced an alternative aim—that of bearing witness. The more horrific the image, the less detailed the image's anchoring needed to be. In many cases, the images were so devoid of identifiable detail that it was difficult to anchor them in a given physical or geographic place. Yet the broader the story they were used to invoke, the more effective carriers of the collective memory they would be. The transformation of atrocity photos from definitive indices of certain actions to symbolic markers of the atrocity story had to do with a general and urgent need to make sense of what had happened. When images were particularly graphic, the press needed less to explain them and more to link them with broader interpretive themes that lent meaning to the depictions. Images were thus a more effective means of bearing witness than words. Turning verbal chronicles of liberation into a visual story of atrocity directly affected the shape of the recollection that resulted.

No less important, the use of pictures to depict atrocity constituted a turning point in the history of the popular press. While bearing witness took journalism beyond itself by requiring an alternative mode of journalistic practice—one that emphasized cooperation over professional prowess and competition—the reliance on photographs to do so made images the main event of the camps' coverage. Representations of atrocity that were more explicit and unrequited than in previous wars, the lifting of censorship restrictions concerning the coverage of ongoing events of the war, and the upset of professional expectations about how news photography was thought to function were all evidence of such a turning point. While side-stepping journalists' ambivalence about photographs and inverting their long-standing assumption that images functioned most effectively as referential tools, images emerged as a more powerful tool than words for documenting Nazi atrocity. It was no surprise that photography's triumph would permeate the heart of the atrocity story as it was recycled into collective memory.

Forgetting to Remember
Photography as Ground of
Early Atrocity Memories

THE IMAGE'S TRIUMPH IN DOCUMENTING NAZI ATROCITY went straight to the heart of collective memory, where pictures reminded publics of the scenes associated with Nazi terror. While photographic authority persisted over the years that followed, the atrocity photos rose and fell as effective carriers of the memory of Nazi brutality. For those who thought the world would not forget what had happened, it became alarmingly clear that the photos might reach a point at which they would no longer work as carriers of that memory.

In the first years after the war, remembering Nazi brutality drew strength from interpretive trends begun already at the time of the camps' liberation. As the photographs of the newspapers, magazines, and journals of 1945 made their way into other domains of memory production—notably books, films, museums, public viewings, and eventually television retrospectives—images superseded words as the more effective carriers of the atrocity story. As one scholar observed, it was easier to maintain an involvement with the Holocaust "through its translation into symbolic terms." While that involvement, facilitated in part by photography, came to characterize the bulk of memory work on Nazi atrocity, it also eventually facilitated a partial undoing of memory, where bearing witness produced a failure to remember salient points about Nazi atrocity.[1]

WAVES OF MEMORY:
THE LANDSCAPE OF ATROCITY MEMORY

Visual memories of Nazi atrocity were not always predictable, salient, nor viable for those who had experienced the atrocities firsthand. Yet they reflected broader issues in both the United States and Britain that reconfigured and challenged atrocity's relevance in accordance with larger impulses in the cultures at hand.

Three waves of memory work made the Nazi atrocities rise and fall in the public imagination over time: an initial period of high attention persisted until the end of the forties; it was followed by a bracketed period of amnesia that lingered from the end of the forties until the end of the seventies; and that was followed in turn by a renewed period of intensive memory work that has persisted from the end of the seventies until the present day. In the first two periods, photographs lingered as an undeveloped ground to the actual accounts of atrocity; in the most recent wave, photography itself became a figure in retelling the stories of Nazi brutality.[2]

In all three waves, atrocity memory has been shaped by the fact that no tenable structure for understanding the events of the Holocaust has developed over time. As scholar Saul Friedlander has observed, "no compelling framework of meaning seems to have appeared in the public domain." As the atrocity story moved in time away from the events at its core, it failed to reassign the horror of the past into meaningful lessons for the present, raising questions about the limits of historical experience. Remembering thus offered incomplete responses to Nazi brutality. Yet at the same time, the landscape of visual memory, set in place by the photos of 1945, produced a range of capacities for remembering. Its initial thrust toward a broader atrocity story now suited the different aims of interpretive communities trying to come to terms with the act of bearing witness over time.[3]

The First Memory Wave: Photography as Ground

Already in 1945, Nazi atrocity took over public discussion in both Britain and the United States. Despite the fact that millions of people were far from the camps, circulation of the atrocity photos had turned them into witnesses, and the black-and-white photos they had seen were now transformed into a primary "visual symbol of the Holocaust."[4]

Early memory work was wrought by two contradictory tendencies: while most people still needed to bear witness to what had happened, the press was experiencing its own professional ambivalence about how best to remember the atrocities. The press's less than exemplary job of covering the atrocities before the liberation, its difficulties in covering the story at the time of liberation, and a lingering professional ambivalence about the role of photography in documenting the camps all worked against an early need to continually bear witness during the immediate postwar period.

POPULAR MEMORY: THE GROUND FOR
CONTINUING TO BEAR WITNESS. For many U.S. and British citizens, the depictions of the camps of Nazi Europe produced avid discussions of photography's triumph in bringing news of atrocity to the homefront. As one observer later told it, "through pictures the impact of the war was brought home to the people," their publication provoking a lingering "deep

anger." In the eyes of the editor of one photography journal, "the photographs . . . finally awoke the conscience of the world."[5]

Shortly after the atrocity pictures were published, letters to the editor began arriving one after another at most major U.S. and British publications. The majority came from readers who assumed that the images filled a historical function, though a few feared that their display would harm chances for a peaceful settlement. Those who wrote tended to support the images' publication. The press is "doing the world a service in printing the photographs of this horror," offered one reader of the *Manchester Guardian*. "We owe you a debt for printing those terrible photographs which bring home the full meaning of the Nazi concentration camp as none of the verbal descriptions of the past 10 years and more could do," wrote another to the *London Times*. As the *Daily Mirror* published its readers' responses, it declared, "All These Horrors Must Be Known." Readers argued that the atrocities "have got to be shown. The world has to know that they were not dreamed up by newsmen but actually happened"; one reader even suggested to *Life* that it blow up its atrocity photos to mural size so as to adorn the room where the coming peace conference would be held. Additional acts of witnessing were also demanded—sending university representatives to the camps or showing members of the Hitler youth organization photos and films of the camps. As one reader opined, "maybe it would be well to . . . rerun those pictures in 1965 . . . on the 20th anniversary of V-E Day. We are such forgetful people."[6]

Yet not everyone was convinced of what the atrocity photos had depicted. In May 1945, 84 percent of the U.S. public still called the atrocity reports exaggerated, though nearly all believed that atrocity had taken place in some form. While the dissenters were in the minority, two critical discourses emerged that both addressed dimensions of photographic authority: one tackled the photo's ability to reproduce reality, and the other challenged the veracity of photographic documentation. Questions persisted as to whether or not the image was capable of sustaining the news it was expected to bear.[7]

Skepticism derived in part from a lingering professional ambivalence concerning the photograph's documentary capacity. When the task of sending to trial hundreds of Nazi criminals started, *Picture Post* ran a report that began,

> When Belsen concentration camp was liberated on April 15, films were made of the piles of rotting bodies, photographs were taken and horror stories poured out of Press Camps. Horror stories that made the stories of Edgar Allan Poe read like fairy tales. Then the camp was burned, and with the burning it faded out of the news.

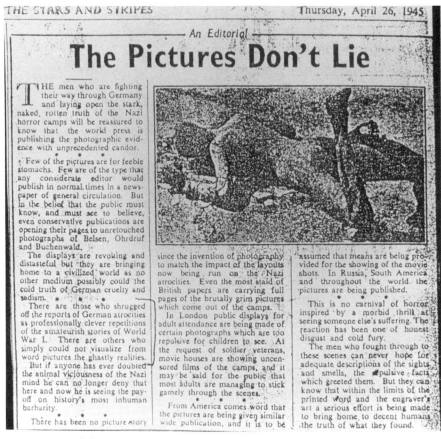

Figure 34. "The Pictures Don't Lie," *Stars and Stripes,* 3 April 26, 1945. Reprinted courtesy of *The Stars and Stripes.*

The piece was remarkable because its author, no mere reporter, was in fact the journal's art editor, and he shared with readers five pages of drawings that he had compiled during three visits to Belsen. While marking the approaching Nuremberg trials in this way suggested how central were images to remembering atrocity, the selection of drawings, not photographs, underscored an ambivalence still being accorded the photographic image. It also showed that drawings were somehow more bearable than the harsher reality provided by the photographic depictions.[8]

A second discourse suggested that the atrocity photos had been faked or forged. On coming home, soldiers were told that their personal photos looked like propaganda, and one claimed that his wife, unable to contain her disbelief, tore up the snapshots he had taken of the camps. The unwillingness to believe in part stemmed from a lack of context for understanding what had happened. For instance, the *Progressive* of May 1945 challenged the authenticity of the photographic evidence, citing "fantastic discrepancies." The "character of the evidence," it said, "including photographs of gas chambers and piles of emaciated bodies, the testimony of liberated prisoners, and the inspections of the scene after the fact—would not be held under ordinary American judicial practice to be sufficient for conviction in a capital crime." The journal thought it worthless to vent vengeance against Germany.[9]

Skepticism was also associated in part with lingering anti-Semitism. A decidedly anti-Semitic letter to the editor of the *Daily Mail* chided the paper for its "one-sided" and "un-English" presentation of the war. It contended that the "emaciated bodies [of atrocity pictures] are more probably evidence of typhus deaths, the result of Allied destruction of habitation." Among declared anti-Semites, the atrocity photos became a target whose authority needed to be undermined, and writers with fascist leanings like Frederick Bowman, Douglas Reed, and Oswald Mosley went on record against the pictures, proclaiming that the "pictorial evidence proves nothing at all."[10]

Among those who had visited the camps, response to criticism of the atrocity photos was swift. An editor with the *Washington Post* bitterly lambasted "people in this country who put down to 'propaganda' the latest reports of murder factories." In "A Report to the American People," *St. Louis Post-Dispatch* editor Joseph Pulitzer complained that people who still doubted the atrocity stories "should have their heads and perhaps their hearts examined." He told them not to "take my word for it, but see the . . . pictures." And one British M.P., writing disbelievingly that "a considerable number of people wish to believe that the photographs are fakes," reasoned that "it would be impossible to persuade large numbers of British and American soldiers, and ten Members of Parliament, to permit their photographs to be super-imposed on fake pictures."[11]

Suspicions about the atrocity photos caused such discomfort among those who had been to the camps that the *Stars and Stripes* ran an editorial in April 1945 entitled "The Pictures Don't Lie." The piece, illustrated with a single atrocity picture, was a proclamation of photographic authenticity (fig. 34). It began by admitting that Allied soldiers would be "reassured to know that the world press is publishing the photographic evidence with unprecedented candor." Yet it cautioned that the pictures brought home "as no other medium possibly could" what was happening in Germany. In its view, both "those who shrugged off the reports of German atrocities as professionally clever repetitions of the amateurish stories of World War I" and "those who could not visualize from word pictures the ghastly realities" had to be convinced by the pictures:

Few of the pictures are for feeble stomachs. Few are of the type that any considerate editor would publish in normal times in a newspaper of general circulation. But in the belief that the public must know, and must see to believe, even conservative publications are opening their pages to unretouched photographs of Belsen, Ohrdruf and Buchenwald.

Significantly, however, although the article discussed the authenticity of photographic evidence, the photo it appended to illustrate its point was an uncaptioned, unattributed atrocity image that showed an unexplained burned human figure sprawled on the ground. The lack of referential data meant that even in an article about the authenticity of images, the paper did not feel it sufficiently important to include such documentation for the image it had selected to bolster its argument.[12]

Despite the naysayers, the vast majority of the U.S. and British publics believed the photos. And within one month of their publication, they were displayed in nearly every possible venue—in the press, handouts, newsreels, even in sidewalk photographic exhibits that blew them up to the size of posters. For some, their extensive display produced audience saturation. "Why, oh why, did you have to print that picture?" asked one reader of *Life's* editorial board. "Why can't we be spared some of it?" Yet the mandate "to see" continued, and the images found their way into nearly all venues of public display.[13]

Volumes of war photographs—taken by the Signal Corps and British Army Film and Photographic Unit, press associations, and other military units—reprinted compilations of atrocity photos, and bookstores displayed large shots of bodies, camp courtyards, and mass burials in their storefront windows. The *Daily Mail* published atrocity photographs in pamphlet form. British newspapers organized sidewalk photographic exhibits, and one U.S. public exhibit of twelve-foot photomurals, put together jointly by the *St. Louis Post-Dispatch* and the *Washington Evening Star,* drew over eighty thousand persons in only twenty-five days.[14]

The Allied forces also distributed booklets bearing photographic evidence of the atrocities across the occupied zones of Europe. The aesthetics of one photographic booklet—*KZ*—are worth describing, because they underscore the centrality of photos for the Allied forces. An abbreviated term for *Konzentrationslagern* (German for "concentration camps"), *KZ* was subtitled *A Pictorial Report from Five Concentration Camps*. It began by telling readers that the "text consists mostly of photographs, for the printed word can never be truly representative of that which was seen." Its first image depicted the triangular shot of the Buchenwald courtyard—which positioned groups of soldiers, bodies, and German nationals staring at each other across an impassable white space—and ended with the shot of General Eisenhower overlooking the bodies of Ohrdruf. The pamphlet itself was thus framed visually as an act of witnessing. Inside was a wide range of photographs that had splashed earlier pages of the press—the bunks and wagons of Buchenwald, women tearing through the clothes of dead inmates at Belsen, German nationals and British parliamentarians viewing stark mounds of bodies, the Nordhausen courtyard, and the picture of the U.S. major atop a heap of lime-covered bodies at Ohrdruf. The message of *KZ* was simple: pictures were central, words were not. Slim, vague phrases only hinted to readers what they were seeing because the images, readers were told, "speak a language which is all too clear." Booklets like *KZ* suggested not only the value that the Allied Forces accorded images in proving that the atrocities had happened, but that they saw them as a continued vehicle of representation about Nazi brutality.[15]

The atrocity photos were such a credible representation of the atrocities that they turned up as reality markers in other modes of Holocaust representation. Artists, for instance, began to use photos of the dead as visual cues: Pablo Picasso's famous painting *The Charnel House* was based on atrocity photos, and Rico Lebrun, who claimed that "the photographic documentation [of the atrocities] gave me the 'facts' which I really must have in order to present a vivid image," gave his versions of the photographed corpses explicit captions like *Buchenwald Cart, Buchenwald Pit,* and *Dachau Chamber.* Early fictional representations of the camps wove in visual scenes that had been already etched in memory by the press; John Hersey's *The Wall,* for example, invoked early atrocity photos as starting points for the seemingly unconnected narrative. And years later, Anatoli Kuznetsov shaped his book on Babi Yar into a "photographically accurate picture of actual events," its scenes recreated in conjunction with the atrocity photos he had seen earlier.[16]

The photos' resonance was so great that liberators of the camps developed their own practices involving them. Often preferring the group's visual memory over their own, individual liberators treated the photos with marked deference. One soldier recalled how his commander had chased the company out of the camp at Nordhausen because of typhoid yet afterward "went back and took a whole series of pictures. He gave each one of us a set. I have them home yet. Every once in a while if you want to refresh your memory, you take those out and look at 'em." Photographic shots taken by soldiers were collectively "passed around from time to time . . . [to] rekindle the nausea that was experienced."[17]

In the immediate postwar period, many liberators published the images in military newsletters and military unit histories. Certain U.S. military units and divisions compiled booklets about the camps that they had liberated. One such booklet, put together by the Seventh U.S. Army and published in 1945 under the simple title *Dachau,* included photos taken both by members of the group and by members of the 163rd Signal Photo Company. Some liberators independently published their images in the press, such as one GI who sent his private photographs to *Look* and requested that they be printed so as to facilitate remembering:

> To the Editor: In these days of tension, I believe it is well to remember the inhumanities suffered by millions only a short time ago. The enclosed pictures of oppressed Polish Jews were confiscated from a German Gestapo officer at Munich in 1945. At that time, I sent the snapshots to my father in New York. . . . Today, I am anxious that your millions of readers may see them—and recall how, in time of war, innocent people become the most tragic victims.

The pictures were not always published, however. In June 1945, the *Toledo Blade* printed a long letter from one liberator but said that his two photographs "taken alongside the prison [of Dachau] and enclosed with the letter were of such shocking nature that the editors refrain from publishing them."[18]

Certain photos found their way into the atrocity films, which were screened in cinemas on both continents. During a two-week presentation of stills and footage taken by the U.S. Signal Corps and the British Army Film and Photographic Unit, one New York City theater chain reported a 25 percent increase in audience attendance. The newsreels mesmerized audiences with their depictions of horror, and no "persons took refuge in shutting their eyes" because nearly all "patrons were determined to see." In a few cases, opposition persisted: Radio City Music Hall refused to show the atrocity newsreels because it "did not want to chance sickening any squeamish persons." And some British citizens walked out of the movie theaters rather than witness the atrocity scenes, only to be immediately turned back by Allied soldiers.[19]

Early efforts to memorialize the horrors of Nazism played to the broad story of atrocity that the images had helped set in place. Already in April 1945, the *Stars and Stripes* reported on proposed memorials that would hold war-related books, magazines, radio broadcasts, films, and papers. Photographs, it implied, would be a primary mode of remembering Nazi horror. Yet such a premise depended on understanding photography as much in terms of its symbolic as its referential force.[20]

The first real test of the atrocity photos' impact came the following autumn with the approach of the Nuremberg trials. Discussions of the trials immediately raised questions as to whether or not photographs of the war criminals' executions should be published. Many who had supported the earlier display of atrocity photos now argued in favor of printing the images of the executions. "The world owes a debt to the camera," said the editor of one photography journal, "for retelling something that cannot, must not ever be forgotten." One reader of the professional organ of the British Institute of Journalists, the *Journal,* lamented that "for years we had the horrors of a criminal war shown us in photographs of mutilated men, women, and babies. The world has as much right to be shown the terrible end of the madmen of the Axis." Polling the U.S. press, the trade journal *Editor and Publisher* found that most editors wanted to print the images. Yet there was no clear agreement about how to do so—on front pages, in detachable supplements, or in certain kinds of newspapers. The discussion displayed a firm recognition of the photograph's cogency but uncertainty about how to accommodate it.[21]

Members of the press responded to the Nuremberg photos in various ways. Although initial announcements predicted that the photographs would be shut away in archives, the Allied Control Council prohibited their printing in Germany but allowed editors elsewhere to make their own decisions about publication. The British government came out against publication, but the *Sunday Pictorial* eluded the ban it suggested and printed a picture of a dead Göring. In the United States, the *New York Times* refused to print the images. Hearst's *Journal-American* advertised in advance that it would print the pictures and advised readers to buy their papers a day ahead. *Newsweek* told its readers that it had decided not to publish "on the basis of taste and public service." And the *Atlanta Journal* "played it both ways: It did not publish the pictures but told its readers . . . 'the pictures will be displayed in a show window for the inspection of anyone interested.'" While the varying practices of image display showed concern for the public's tolerance levels, they also suggested a lingering ambivalence about representation that might evoke sympathy for the Nazis. Much of this had to do with a persistent doubt about the appropriateness of the image itself. Ambivalence involved both the ways in which to play to the image's power and which circumstances merited doing so.[22]

That ambivalence was associated in part with the uneven standards by which the press had used the photos as proof. In fact, recognition of photography's role in documenting the atrocities had not raised discussion over the ways in which the atrocity photos were used in the press. A lack of accreditation, wrong or misleading captions, or a questionable relationship with words faded in importance alongside the success of photos in depicting the atrocities. Not surprisingly, people hailed the image's role in bearing witness and its ability to support a broad story about Nazi atrocity.

Throughout the forties, then, there was a "veritable hemorrhage of expression" about the Nazi atrocities. Stories and pictures of Nazi brutality were everywhere, authenticated in large part through accounts and pictures of the concentration camps so numerous and detailed that they constituted what scholar Sidra DeKoven Ezrahi has called "the testimonial imperative." This first wave of memory was characterized by a continued need to bear witness, even if the act persisted in a more truncated version than in the immediate postwar period.[23]

PROFESSIONAL MEMORY: THE GROUND FOR AMBIVALENCE OVER THE ATROCITIES. The press was more ambivalent than the public about the need to continue bearing witness to Nazi atrocity. On the one hand, the first period after the war was one that glowed in the personal memories of many journalists and photographers. Because those first years shone with the pride accrued from having covered the war, those involved in liberating the camps initially reconstituted their efforts as ones of professional triumph. For them, the experience of having been around to bear witness to the camps had a moral significance. "Not in all its hundred and six years has photography burned such a message into the minds of men," proclaimed one early editorial in the trade journal *Popular Photography*. "Perhaps never before in history has a single transmitted idea kindled such an emotional fire."[24]

Many members of the press made it clear that experiencing the camps constituted a professional badge of honor that needed to be shared. Some wrote war memoirs recounting their experiences, such as British correspondent John D'Arcy-Dawson, who discussed his time at Belsen in nearly ten pages of *European Victory*, or U.S. reporter Martha Gelhorn, who reprinted her essays on the camps, including one from Dachau that was touted by the *Nation* as one of the best attempts to "get at the meaning of the war." Photographer Margaret Bourke-White claimed that her tour of the camps prompted her treatise on the German national character, *"Dear Fatherland, Rest Quietly,"* and she also addressed the camps in her autobiography, where she reprinted one of her atrocity photos. Marguerite Higgins, who reported Dachau's liberation, won the New York Newspapers Women's Club Award for the best correspondence of 1945 and the army campaign ribbon for "Outstanding Service with the Armed Services Under Difficult Conditions." The trade journal *U.S. Camera,* in its yearly review of 1946, devoted five pages to images of the camps, and *Eyes of the War,* billed as a "Photographic Report of World War II," included nearly ten atrocity

photos in its 1945 collection. Finally, in its 1946 overview of the war, the *New York Herald Tribune* juxtaposed copies of its own front pages with atrocity photos that had appeared elsewhere in the press. These photos," remarked the paper somberly, "were history as you saw it happen."[25]

But the glow of professional triumph—as it related to the atrocities—did not apply to all members of the press. For when the Nazi atrocities were discussed in early press retrospectives, little mention was made of photography's role in their documentation. For instance, the U.S. trade journal *Editor and Publisher* found in a 1945 poll of picture editors that photos of the camps were variably and unevenly cited by the press, often reduced to "one of the atrocity pictures" or "a picture from Belsen." Atrocity photos were given no separate notation in discourse about the achievements of war photography, mildly called instead war pictures that "stood out above the others." When Universal Camera Corporation ran advertisements for its equipment that featured reprints of atrocity photos found on dead or captured German soldiers, the journal affixed ironic captions to images of civilians being shot, hanged, and flogged by the Nazis. The resulting impression was that photographic equipment needed to work against the images portrayed—and the text upheld that perception: "Photography is our business," it argued, "but we're working hard to hasten the day when it will be impossible to take photographs—like those above." The advertisement codified photography's critical role much like a dose of preventive medicine and positioned it in the advertisement in a way that did little to enhance knowledge of either the atrocities or of photography.

This was the case even when photographs were centrally involved in the work at hand. Rarely did the early retrospectives credit the work of journalists and photographers equally in telling the story of the war's coverage. One 1945 war retrospective included both short memorable statements by U.S. war correspondents and detailed biographies, while next to the text were three unaccredited and unexplained pictures of the liberation of Paris. Here too photographs were used as secondary documentation that did not need the kind of indexical information required of the text. Similarly, an Associated Press pamphlet called *Reporting to Remember* declared in 1945,

> If the world now is able to learn the bitter lessons of war, and to move on to a better era, it will be in no small measure because of the heroic achievements of the war reporters. Years hence when the historians can begin to appraise World War II more fully, they are certain to lean heavily on the graphic day-to-day accounts, books and recollections of the correspondents.

The "brilliant and courageous work of these Associated Press correspondents," it went on, "truly is reporting *and photography* to remember" (emphasis added). Other than that comment, however, photography was mentioned nowhere in the main text. Rather, the pamphlet appended an unexplained section called "Pictures to Remember" that provided no information on when, where, or by whom the shots had been taken. Thus photography—even for the Associated Press, whose photographers had braved the front lines—was codified as an afterthought to the achievements of reporters.[26]

Many early press retrospectives displayed an additional pattern of memory work that discouraged remembering the atrocities: they separated the atrocity story from recountings of the war. Most press wartime recollections mentioned little, if anything, of the concentration camps; anthologies of war reporting offered few reprints of atrocity coverage; and chronicles of war reportage omitted the story of the camps' liberation altogether. Early photographic anthologies also dislocated the atrocity story from the story of the war, printing few or no atrocity photos in their wartime collections: one commemorative volume promised readers "memorably authentic pictures by Signal Corps combat photographers and army artists," yet the book displayed only combat pictures, except for one unexplained, unattributed photo on its final page that depicted a stack of dead bodies. Another retrospective on Margaret Bourke-White—put together by *Popular Photography*—reprinted ten of her most memorable images; yet while Bourke-White mentioned the significance of her having photographed the concentration camps, atrocity photos were nowhere to be found in the retrospective.[27]

Retrospectives issued by the trade associations and the press itself similarly played down the camps. One such volume, issued by NBC in 1945 and entitled *This Is the Story of the Liberation of Europe from the Fall of Rome to Victory,* told readers that the text was as "newsmen played it . . . to American listeners," yet the collection issued not one word about the camps' liberation. Another commemorative volume, issued by the American Newspaper Publishers Association (ANPA) under the title *Victory in Europe,* celebrated the role played by journalism. "Never did newspapers mean so much to so many," it declared, and then launched an extended discussion of the value of the wartime press that mentioned nothing about its reportage of Nazi brutality. Certain scholarly overviews of war reporting and photography mentioned little, if anything, about the camps. In these cases, the Holocaust, and its specific locus of the camps, were simply separated from the story of the war that brought them about. As the story moved on into memory, then, the glory associated initially with having borne witness to the camps was not always upheld; rather, it gave way to a certain amnesia surrounding the issue of Nazi atrocity.[28]

Why did this ambivalence over the atrocity story emerge in the press's early recountings? Beyond a fundamental discomfort caused by the story, the professional ambivalence may have been associated with the press's earlier failure to cover the atrocities in their preliberation stages. Recognizing the liberation of the camps as a notable point of coverage, photographic or reportorial, would have entailed some mention of the failure of coverage before 1945. Moreover, because the press's wartime reportage covered not only the liberation of the camps but also the broader sequence of events of the war, the press may have had little cause to extract it from its coverage of the surrounding flow of wartime events. The resistance toward remembering photography may have also derived from the fact that the press was not ready to elevate images above words, news photographers above journalists. Many journalists remained ambivalent about giving photographic representation its due, even after it had played such a crucial role in showing the atrocities to the world. All of this rendered the atrocities a problematic site of memory for the press. Perhaps, then, it was not surprising that in many of the professional recollections of the period, ambivalence generated uneven retellings of the atrocity story, long before similar gaps of memory appeared in popular recollections.

As with all memory work, there were exceptions. Fervent attempts to remember the atrocities were made already during this period by the picture-magazines. In 1947, the creator of *Picture Post* argued that the atrocities offered a continuing justification to document current events with photographs: "Who can look at the photograph of the thousand Nazi victims killed in the Belsen gas chamber without a deep feeling and the resolve that such a monstrosity should never happen again?" he asked. Similarly, Time-Life's retrospectives of the war, begun in the years immediately following the war, systematically mentioned the camps. Remembering the "close-to-the-bone pictures [that] gave meaning" to what was happening, one *Life* staffer later recounted that the war photographs "gave the magazine a kind of basic human dignity and even grandeur, a tone that spoke of suffering and pity and man's amazing ability to prevail that only war could bring."[29]

Early Time-Life retrospectives—one of which appeared in 1950 under the title *Life's Picture History of World War II*—signaled both the atrocities and photography as important parts of the war story. The 1950 book began with a tribute by Henry Luce and John Shaw Billings to their staff. "The editors of *Life*," they proclaimed, "are proud to salute this gallant band of journalists in general and *our own photographers and reporters in particular* who contributed so generously to the historical coverage in the following pages" (emphasis added). Ignoring the photographers *not* employed by *Life,* the book applauded the achievements of *Life's* staff as it recounted the turning points of the war. But unlike other endeavors of the time, which glossed over the atrocities and the camps, *Life* forced readers to contemplate the scenes of Nazi carnage. Reproducing a set of images under the caption "Prisoners," it portrayed shots mostly taken by *Life* photographers. The shots had been accredited earlier to the Signal Corps due to the rules of the photographic pools but were now accredited to *Life* photographers, such as Johnny Florea and George Rodger. In memory, then, Time-Life retrospectives gained credit for images that it had earlier needed to share with other press organizations. This may explain in part why it began publishing commemorative volumes in earnest.[30]

Thus, the first wave of memory work was characterized by two memorial trends: a continued need to bear witness to the atrocities in popular recollections and a desire to both bear witness and forget the atrocities in professional memories, the latter motivated in part by an ambivalence toward photography. The tension between the two sets of recollections would be somewhat lessened in the second memory wave, when the early press ambivalence was better suited to collective amnesia among the general population.

The Second Memory Wave: The Ground for Collective Amnesia

As the story moved on in memory, the original aim of remembering atrocity—that of bearing witness—took on new meaning. Earlier patterns in the story's telling had already distanced representations from the details of the atrocity's initial recording, and this broader interpretive thrust had particular relevance to collective memory, which thrived on universal and generalizable messages about the past. The shape of bearing witness also changed, as the original need to take responsibility for what had happened began to dissipate in the popular imagination. As Leon Wieseltier commented, "the memory of an event [was itself] an interpretation of the event," and atrocity photos, as vessels of memory, became a ground with limited parameters for pondering, challenging, and rearticulating the atrocity story over time.[31]

Like other popular understandings of World War II, the ground for remembering Nazi horror vibrated with each recollection, as memories transformed atrocity's "taken-for-granted" meanings. Once the initial shock of the atrocity story gave way to a resigned recognition that entire nations had collectively missed the mark by failing to respond to early reports of brutality, U.S. and British citizens began to rearrange their lives around the burden of knowing what had happened in Nazi Germany. Although the press had provided an incomplete picture of events prior to liberation, it nonetheless had offered a way to bear witness after the camps were opened that forced a partial recognition of Nazi atrocity onto the publics of both continents. Images, often more than words, offered for many the "flashbulb memory" that reflected the extent to which humanity had sunk during World War II. As poet A. Alvarez observed two decades later, "while all miseries of World War II have faded, the image of the concentration camp persists." Images helped keep memories of the atrocities alive. For in the words of photography critic Allan Sekula, when photography enters the picture, "all other forms of remembering begin to fade."[32]

Among many who had seen the initial atrocity photos, the act of having borne witness was thought to be a sufficient way of inscribing it in memory forever. The sheer horror of atrocity seemed to be a sufficient reason for demanding that world attention remain focused on Nazi barbarism. Journalist William L. Chenery was firm in his belief that photos would prevail when he wrote in *Collier's* in June 1945 that "many have seen the pictures. And a very good thing, too, to see and to remember." Yet despite the many offhanded public assurances that memory of Nazi brutality would last, no one knew whether having seen the atrocity photos would engender for everyone the same kind of remembering.[33]

For many, the atrocities continued to make sense as a way of compelling support in peacetime. The repair work required in the immediate years after the war demanded a unified public, and keeping Nazi brutality at the forefront of public attention made it easier for members of both the U.S. and British governments to move onto postwar agendas.

But more than one shared memory about the atrocities began to proliferate, and this became particularly so as the collective response to the events of 1945 moved beyond its initial phase of shock. In fact, as the story of Nazi atrocity moved into memory, variations emerged in the levels of public attention it was able to hold, and evidence was reconfigured in ways that had as much to do with broader agendas about bringing the past into the present as with the atrocities themselves. Memories of Nazi atrocity became in a sense a playing field for reconfiguring the past to suit agendas in the present.

Collective memory offered varied options for making sense of atrocity, and as people invoked membership in more than one collective, they by definition shared more than one memory of Nazi brutality. Memories of the camps offered both broad parameters for remembering—parameters that corresponded with Eisenhower's original mandate "to see"—as well as more particularistic recollections of interpretive communities that were constituted and reconstituted along ethnic, racial, religious, age, class, professional, and other lines.

Such memories were shaped by a range of cultural practices, forms, and settings—museums, pilgrimages, retrospectives, anniversaries, commemorations, to name a few—and the parameters for remembering required that what had been presented originally tended to be recycled over time. Thus, representations

> followed very conventional guidelines. Linear chronology, strong empirical evidence at the expense of analysis, and the closure of events within the stories of redemption, American/Soviet liberation, or the founding of the State of Israel (and thus of a return to progress) were the tools used for writing about the Holocaust.

Such guidelines tended to ignore alternative sources on the past, such as those provided by "language, rhetoric and moral choice, or in photography the question of exclusion from the frame of vision."[34]

In such a light, the liberation of the camps was rapidly and simplistically codified. Already transformed at the war's end into a prism for considering Nazi atrocity, it came to be seen as the end of the Holocaust, making the moment of seeing the camps a crystallization of understanding Nazi atrocity. Yet, as Tony Kushner has argued, the Holocaust did not simply "end" with the liberation of the camps on the western front. Rather, viewing it as such fit well within the worldview of Western liberalism, which had no effective way of understanding the camps' horrors: images of atrocity were "limited by the liberal imagination."[35]

Remembering was also often faulty, for errors of coverage and interpretation that had characterized the initial record were solidified as they were recycled. Initial inaccurate characterizations—naming Buchenwald, Belsen, and Dachau "extermination centers," understating the Jewish nature of victimization by the Nazis, evaluating the scenes of the camps as "the worst" of Nazi crimes, or maintaining that the discovery of the camps caught the Allied governments by surprise—all proliferated over the following years. Within the visual account, captions with wrong information and insufficient credits were cemented into the historical record, making it more difficult to ascertain what the images had originally depicted. Even popular treatments of the atrocities in film, fiction, and poetry recycled such errors and gave them a life that persisted for decades. In scholar Robert Abzug's view, the mistakes of the recycled record were crucial, for they placed "the enduring significance of the Allied confrontation with horror in April–May 1945" within the context of "a sobering historical reality" that left gaps in comprehending how the atrocities had occurred.[36]

As time passed, factual accuracy was further dimmed. Critical overviews of the Holocaust began to attend to the diverse agendas for remembering that became implicated in memory work. Terms associated with the camps were broadened to fit wide-ranging agendas. For instance, already by 1979, President Jimmy Carter referred to the eleven million victims of the Nazis rather than the six million Jews. That adaptation, while addressing others who died under the Nazis, such as gays, diverse religious groups, and political opponents, was seen by many Holocaust scholars as a diminishment of the Jewish nature of Nazi victimization. Scholars argued that the Holocaust was losing its uniqueness:

> the enormity of the crimes committed during the Holocaust, as well as the limitless list of current human-rights violations, has led to a drastic and momentous depreciation of specificity. Because there are too many details to know and to remember, meaning can get lost in the immensity of gruesome details. Hence, we look to the larger picture in order to hold onto some reasonable explanations.

For many, remembering worked most effectively by "always moving to the next larger frame . . . [with] the larger the picture, the more meaning we hope to retrieve." By "adopting the always larger framework, the always greater explanation, the always more encompassing paradigm," those remembering dismissed detail in "favor of the belief in abstract principles and historical coherence. We gloss over details in order to arrive at some intelligible and coherent patterns." In novelist Cynthia Ozick's words, "the more narrowly we look into the perplexing lens of Auschwitz, the more painful will the perception be. It is moral ease to slide from the particular to the abstract." Often, moving to broader frames in turn fueled a preference for rational explanations to irrational phenomena.[37]

It was here that different interpretive communities, brought together by common agendas and worldviews, invoked wide-ranging scenarios to explain the broad strokes of what had happened in Nazi Germany. In one view, there was nothing "particularly improper" about the atrocities "having more than one set of meanings." For

> the historical memory is selective; it does not and cannot recall everything. This is what thinking in symbols, or thinking with symbols, is about: To treat part of the history as representative of the whole, to shrink it down to something of a manageable size.[38]

But what remained after the shrinkage was not necessarily the recollection that was needed to move on. Raising alternate specters of failed economic systems, political scapegoats, comparative genocides, and lamentations over the evil in human nature, different communities—including liberators, survivors, journalists, photographers, and members of different nation-states—remembered atrocity not only in conjunction with what had happened but in ways that reflected unfolding issues of identity and community building. Shifting focus from the record of the past to its pertinence in the present bore directly on the act of bearing witness to Nazi atrocity.

Atrocity Images in Memory

The photos used to remember atrocity gave new meaning to the act of bearing witness, as images anchored memory to specific scenes: a set of railroad tracks, a familiar barracks, a gateway into one of the camps. Certain atrocity photos resurfaced time and again, reducing what was known about the camps to familiar visual cues that would become overused with time. As one scholar commented about images of Auschwitz,

> The photo (the positive of a negative of a positive) is clearly acting as a substitute for the memory object. Yet ever since the first photos of Auschwitz, the meaning imputed to it has been encompassed in the symbolic framework of the barbed wire, the ramp, or the famous entrance gate. These things are of course important parts of the camp, yet they are not the camp but only how we wish to keep seeing it.[39]

Images thus continued to do in memory what they had done at the time of the camps' liberation—to move the atrocity story from the contingent and particular to the symbolic and abstract. Now recycled into additional representational formats, photos continued to mark the broad strokes of atrocity memory, where they kept atrocity alive at the same time as they facilitated its transformation in representation.

Images cued different kinds of shared memory, however. For survivors, photographs from 1945 onward served as evidence of their own experiences of suffering. Groups of Buchenwald orphans sent immediately after the war to France showed a continued and intense interest in being photographed—"They often looked at the photographs. It was proof to them that they were alive." Other individuals who had experienced the camps in other ways—liberators, reporters, photographers, and officials—testified too that the photograph's mnemonic power was so great that it displaced individual memories. *Daily Telegraph* reporter Edwin Tetlow later said that he had "to look at photographs taken then to assure myself that I really did see the scenes they depict." Photographer George Rodger maintained that the memory of what he photographed at Bergen-Belsen made him seek out humanitarian work in later years. Soldiers involved in the liberation testified time and again to the photograph's power to anchor what they remembered. One former GI, writing in the *Humanist* nearly fifty years after the camps' liberation, pondered "those images that by now we have seen too many times—too many? too few? can anyone be sure?"[40]

Others who had not seen the atrocity photos on their original display testified to the shock produced by seeing them later. It was with a "mixture of distance, horror, pity, curiosity, and titillation" that one author remembered seeing pictures of the Holocaust dead many years after the camps' liberation. "I recall that pull of fascination, of seduction, that fear that I might keep looking and never be able to stop." Cultural critic Susan Sontag maintained that "nothing I have seen—in photographs or in real life—ever cut me as sharply, deeply, instantaneously." German nationals born after the Holocaust were particularly affected, as one scholar later recalled:

> Black and white images were my most prevailing memory of the Holocaust. The first Jews I met were documented on photographs: slave laborers, inmates, skeletons, corpses. And I remember images of arrests, roll calls; piles of glasses, shoes, and clothes. . . . On these photographs, the Jewish people were dying time and again—eternal victims. They were transformed into a metaphor of dying.[41]

Images of the camps thereby both authenticated personal experience and stood in for the absence of experience, the embodiment of the act of bearing witness.

Not surprisingly, members of the press played a central role in fashioning these visual memories over time. Although numerous ways of remembering Nazi atrocity have evolved in the years since World War II, the press has persisted as an active agent of memory work. Yet that work has had an underside, for it was connected as much to the vested nature of its own involvement in the past as to a concern with its accurate representation. In particular, its recycling of images rested on a story about photographic triumph that it was not necessarily interested in telling, and its ambivalence about that issue helped shape retellings of the atrocity story.

As the story moved on in time, members of the British and U.S. press were well positioned to retell it. Possessing access to diverse storytelling technologies and a rich capacity for storing visual and verbal information about the past, the press was able to address atrocity from many points in time and space. While it could accommodate both broad and differentiated memories of the atrocities, the press's involvement in producing documentation of the camps' liberation also offered a way to stamp memories with a particularistic signature. This increased the likelihood that what had already appeared in the public domain would continue to be recycled.

Picture archives provided an apt way to co-opt familiar photos into new retellings of the atrocity story. Not surprisingly, photos turned up in patterned ways from the file footage: *Newsweek,* for instance, systematically reran images from its own picture archive, while photos that belonged to Time-Life ventures were turned over to a common "picture collection," where they could be used in publishing ventures associated not only with *Life* but with *Time* and *Forbes* too. Over time, photographs also crossed media boundaries, turning up in video and television retrospectives, museums, and films. Their invocation in popular representations, where the diffusion of familiar knowledge was key, gave them renewed visibility in discourse about the Holocaust.[42]

In most cases, the use of photos to illustrate a story about atrocity was restricted to the display of a few recurrent frames. As Julia Kristeva observed decades later, the end of the war temporarily silenced the verbal capacity to account for what had happened under the Nazis; that silencing not only echoed the word's inadequacy in its original reportage but positioned Nazi atrocity in postwar consciousness via "a profusion of images and a withholding of the word." Images thus capitalized on a familiar dimension of the earlier representations, and already in the early years after the war the act of bearing witness began to change so as to accommodate this need for a more truncated visual frame of reference about atrocity. In other words, the visual frame for bearing witness became highly formulaic.[43]

What disappeared from the first visual memories of atrocity? The variety of representations of the immediate postliberation period, which underscored the complexity of the act of bearing witness, was laundered, as a few familiar shots made repeated rounds across the different domains of representation. Images of confrontation between perpetrators and survivors surfaced less and less, as did the depictions of dead bodies that had proliferated at the time of liberation. The impenetrable visages of the Nazi perpetrators surfaced less frequently, and complications of the act of bearing witness—such as depicting witnessing with no evidence of the atrocities—appeared not at all. In other words, each of the variations that had made the act of bearing witness such a rich representational forum in earlier years dried up almost immediately in the postwar period.

What types of images appeared instead? Representations displayed two primary dimensions of the larger atrocity story: survivors and the accoutrements of atrocity. Nazi brutality came to be repeatedly visualized through the depiction of survivors—small groups of survivors who looked full view into the camera, often from behind barbed wire or the barriers of unidentified camps. One such group photo from Ebensee circulated widely, depicting twenty-odd male figures in prison garb and bare legs looking frontally into the camera lens with vacant, unfocused stares (fig. 35). The

Figure 35. Emaciated Jewish survivors at Ebensee, May 7, 1945, by NARA.

emaciated human beings of these photos pointed the story toward a muted sense of hope for the future. The accoutrements of atrocity, on the other hand, reinforced the industrial nature of mass death. Photos repeatedly displayed empty furnaces, hanging ropes, vials of ashes, torture and gas chambers. Emblematic of Nazi brutality, this type of image surfaced particularly when verbal challenges to popular consensus about what had happened in Nazi Germany were being reported. Typical here was a stark portrayal of ovens (fig. 36), their doors left ajar to reveal the human remains and charred clothing inside. In each case, the images reflected simplified and schematic targets of depiction, rather than the more complex linkages suggested by different kinds of groups, different kinds of witnesses, different targets of witnessing, and different witnessing practices, all of which had characterized the earlier photos.

The change in depiction was telling. The new preference for depictions

Figure 36. Human remains in crematoria at Buchenwald, April–May 1945, by NARA.

of survivors and accoutrements of atrocity suggested that the act of bearing witness had changed. Visual depictions of atrocity no longer provided varied representations that could move collectives into taking responsibility for what they saw. Now, the more simplified and potentially less involved encounter with the past cemented only certain dimensions of the atrocity story in the popular imagination. Already by the end of the first decade, the atrocity story had lost many of its visual nuances.

It was thus no surprise that as the forties gave way to the fifties, the act of bearing witness began to lose meaning. The popular need to see and hear of Nazi atrocities waned, as attending to atrocity started to lose significance as an act of public consensus. The atrocity story no longer served the same sanctioned political purpose that it had played when garnering support for either the war effort or the immediate postwar consensus. And so began a period of amnesia concerning the Nazi atrocities.

Amnesia had many origins. Lingering anti-Semitism, guilt over nonaction, and an inability to comprehend what had happened all complicated the act of bearing witness. On both continents publics were "numbed by the onslaught of sordid accounts and by the guilt of their own record of passivity," as people asked themselves what bearing witness had accomplished and to what end. Ambivalence also derived from an oversaturation with the details that had appeared in the immediate postwar period. For some, the stories and pictures of the camps had become too relentless a reminder of what had happened. The surge of accounts and pictures provided a "morass of excruciating detail" that caused many uninitiated readers to flounder; they now wanted simply to eject the atrocities from memory.[44]

Changes in the global political climate—in particular, strong sentiments about accomplishing a postwar unity with the Axis nations and a postwar economic boom—also made the mandate "to see" less relevant. Even among many Jews, the Holocaust raised the issue of particularism in a way that was ill suited to their collective goals of fitting in. Throughout the sixties they made virtually no public mention of the Holocaust's impact on their lives, as the Holocaust, in Edward Linenthal's view, became "virtually invisible." Many Jews developed a "tendency to bleach the Holocaust of its genocidal focus and to find, if possible, a serviceable moral for mankind." Bearing witness to Nazi atrocity thus began to have less and less resonance as time wore on. As Saul Friedlander wrote years later, "From one day to the next, the past was swept away, and it remained gone for the next twenty-five years."[45]

And so began a bracketed period of amnesia toward the atrocities of Nazi Germany. From the end of the forties until the end of the seventies, stories and pictures of the atrocities moved into the background of memory, where it became "hard to distinguish between the figures in [the camps] and the landscape." Press articles on atrocity came to a virtual halt, and in some places the "publication of testimonies dried up" by the beginning of the fifties. A lack of readers and therefore publishers made Holocaust memories into the unpopular evidence of a past that not everyone wanted to hear.[46]

On both continents those connected with the camps—survivors, liberators, reporters, and photographers—learned from the fifties onward to keep their experiences private. In one newsmagazine's view, "the GIs and generals and correspondents who had peered into the abyss wanted to bury their memories along with the dead." As survivors "found it better not to talk about the concentration camps," Auschwitz survivor Kitty Hart observed that "everybody in England would be talking about personal war experiences for months, even years, after hostilities had ceased. But we . . . were not supposed to embarrass people by saying a word."

Liberators also found it difficult, too, to discuss their experiences, though some changed their lives back home—giving up hunting for pleasure or pursuing careers in keeping with the somberness induced by seeing the camps. One member of the British Royal Army Medical Corps unit that had liberated Belsen complained to the *Daily Telegraph* in 1956 about neglect of the camp's memorial. Noting that "old soldiers may never die, but the causes for which they fight are very soon put quietly to death," he claimed that people around the world were "too anxious to forget." Others advised their cohorts not to tell people what had happened in Europe because "people don't believe it when you tell them." Those who had taken photos of the camps were in a particular quandary. Although many at first readily displayed their personal photos as evidence of what they had seen, keeping them in accessible locations and retrieving them to stave off rumors of denial about the atrocities, they now took to hiding them. Snapshots of the camps were concealed in trunks, basements, and attics. Later, it took one liberator three years to locate the prints because "they had long ago been hidden away, put out of sight."[47]

During this period, very little institutional memorial response was made to the victims of Nazi atrocity. Few memorials to the Nazi victims were built in either the United States or Britain, and Holocaust consciousness was restricted to survivor groups and certain academic journals. Even the increasing availability of government documentation and the persistent involvement of refugees and survivors did not change matters. Indifference was so pervasive that by 1975, *Newsweek* ran a story entitled "Facing Up to the Holocaust" that tracked a popular indifference toward the Nazi atrocities. "Only now," it commented, "is the world—Jew and non-Jew alike—beginning to come to terms with the event." The Holocaust "is hardly what one would call an alive issue," said one British editor of the time.[48]

Indifference to the atrocities also extended to the educational system in both the United States and Britain, where, despite the efforts of those seeking better integration, atrocity stories remained generally absent from texts and curricula on European history. Survivors of the camps began to be seen as less credible spokespersons for what had happened; even historians did "not trust them when looking for evidence of the historical truth" surrounding atrocity. As the first histories of the camps and Nazi brutality began to be written, the testimony of those who had experienced the camps as inmates was overlooked. Because "evidence from the victim [was seen as] somehow less persuasive and objective" than information from other sources, the first major Holocaust historians—Leon Poliakov in France and Gerald Reitlinger in England—avoided using the voices of victims and survivors in their accounts. Historian Peter Gay, who coedited the

Columbia History of the World in 1972, was reportedly embarrassed to find later that the enormous volume contained no mention of Auschwitz nor of the murder of six million Jews, an embarrassment exacerbated by the fact that he himself was a Jewish refugee from Germany. As genocide scholars later complained, forgetting the Holocaust and Nazi atrocity fit larger agendas about laundering history:

> The coarseness and brutality of human existence throughout much of history was a subject that hardly ever appeared in our schools' curricula; the good news was reported, the bad news was not. The great massacres of the past lay beyond the range of the telescopes designed to focus upon evidence that justice always triumphed. . . . In other words, the fate of millions of human beings who died unnatural deaths as defenseless civilians was invisible.

As late as 1980, complaints were still being heard that in modern history textbooks "the [atrocity] story is completely glossed over." Even the maps of Europe in such textbooks displayed incongruities with an understanding of World War II: "The maps are silent about Dachau and Buchenwald and other camps where the Germans imprisoned and destroyed Jews." There were, of course, certain exceptions: in 1966, *American Heritage*'s *Picture History of World War II* included atrocity photos within its story of the war, but it was not accidental that a declared emphasis on pictures—made evident by its self-named label of "picture history"—paralleled atrocity's mention.[49]

Not surprisingly, the U.S. and British press maintained much of their earlier ambivalence toward the atrocity story. Events surfaced as news briefs, rapidly surfacing and receding from view: for instance, a series of articles about the Katyn massacre was published in the press over a six-month period during 1951–52, while articles on the Auschwitz trials appeared in the midsixties; yet both stories used few or no visual cues from the camps. It is important to note that the ambivalence over the atrocity story paralleled a waning interest in photography, which by the sixties was beginning to lose its grip to television. Photographic journals began to close down—*Picture Post* in 1957, *Look* in 1971, and *Life* in 1972—and the photograph, particularly the photo-essay, "suffered a beating." Thus, not surprisingly, the few visual cues to atrocity that did surface did not constitute a body of material that addressed Nazi atrocity in an ongoing fashion.[50]

In instances that photos did resurface, they were used much as they had been at the time of the camps' liberation—unaccredited, unevenly captioned, and with an unclear relationship to the texts at their side. The place of the text was rarely the place of the image. One picture of Auschwitz illustrated the account of a survivor from another camp who returned to

Germany in 1964, while photos of Dachau accompanied a soldier's contemporary recollections about his experiences with the U.S. Army Ordnance Corps in Europe and North Africa. In these images, large groups of survivors resurfaced more frequently than did corpses, often as frontal views of large groups whose pictures had been taken at the time of liberation. One such photo of Ebensee survivors had already been recycled in late 1945 in the military newspaper *Army Talks,* where it was said to depict the "effects of planned starvation" (see fig. 35, on p.161). The theme of starvation persisted into the sixties, when *Time* captioned the same image "Starving Jewish Prisoners" in an article about the Eichmann trial, but by that point Ebensee itself was not mentioned.[51]

When the trade and professional press addressed the topic, it did so in ways that hailed its own earlier coverage. Anthologies and chronicles of war coverage made little mention of the atrocities and rarely depicted them; when they did so, they often reprinted Edward R. Murrow's radio broadcast from Buchenwald; for rarely were the words of press reporters reprinted or the images of photographers recycled. Time-Life, however, did continue to systematically connect the atrocities with photography, and it included a Bourke-White photo of men behind the barbed wire of Buchenwald in its 1960 collection marking twenty-five years of *Life* (fig. 37).[52] This photo portrayed an unself-conscious group of prison-garbed males, who appeared somewhat out of touch with reality as they posed behind the iconic barbed wire.

In popular discourse the atrocity story met an uneven response. Prose recollections of the camps were at best a sporadic reminder of what had happened in Nazi Germany. While fictional and poetic accounts appeared from writers like Leon Uris and Nelly Sachs, others only indirectly addressed the atrocities and rarely made explicit the Jewish nature of victimization. Realistic portrayals of atrocity, such as Alain Resnais's 1955 film *Night and Fog,* structured around images of corpses and open graves, were problematic: the film visually upheld existent errors within the story of Nazi atrocity, understating the targeting of Jews as victims and collapsing vital differences between the various kind of camps in its harsh sequencing of images.[53]

Disinterest in some cases was palpable. Elie Wiesel's much-acclaimed novel about Auschwitz—*Night*—was "passed from publisher to publisher before a small house was willing to take a chance on it." In his view, "'nobody wanted to hear about Auschwitz.'" Readers of the unpublished diaries of Anne Frank found little initial interest among Dutch publishers, and even after the book became a best-seller in the fifties, the Anne Frank House in Amsterdam barely escaped demolition.[54]

Figure 37. Buchenwald, April 1945. Margaret Bourke-White, Life Magazine ©Time Inc.

In other cases, the brutality of Nazi atrocity was highly laundered and presented in antiseptic fashion. For instance, the play *The Diary of Anne Frank*—seen by some as the major piece of memory work of the time period—stressed the girl's "belief in the good of all men" over her Jewishness and focused on her odyssey through adolescence in an Amsterdam attic rather than the macabre end she met in Bergen-Belsen. In fact, her father, who edited the diary on which the play was based, wanted it to "shed its particularity and become a call for universal tolerance. . . . and he deleted details that made Anne's references to her Jewishness seem too pronounced."[55]

In art, there was a movement away from realism, and artists broadened their targets of depiction associated with Nazi atrocity. Buchenwald artist Boris Taslitzky substituted a dramatic and expressionist style for what was called his earlier "objective reportage" of the camp. Others gave "the dead symbolic implications and turned the corpses into Everyman": Lasar Segall's 1950–51 painting *The Condemned* showed no indication of the cause of condemnation he depicted and instead suggested a "need to forget and to generalize"; by the following decade, Gerhart Frankl's depiction of a photo of Buchenwald was generically titled *Sleeping Berths,* and other artists consciously "refrained from using Holocaust titles," preferring instead "neutral names—such as 'Nude' or 'Figure'—which [did] not even hint at the associations immediately aroused by the image."[56]

The effect of such memory work was predictable. In some cases, the lack of attention to atrocity generated a more complicated kind of amnesia, targeting reputable individuals who too quickly forgot what had happened in Nazi Germany. For instance, already in 1951, Harry Truman characterized the killing and mutilation of U.S. soldiers during the Korean War as "the most uncivilized thing that has happened *in the last century*" (emphasis added). His selective forgetting of the atrocities that had come to light a mere six years earlier showed how unmindful the enlightened world had become already over Nazi brutality. In other cases, the unevenness of the recollections broadened the story beyond repair, with the brutality of Nazi atrocity "generalized to the point at which it [was] not only no longer recognizable but had no significance," its images suggesting "man's condition in the post-war world, his anxiety because of pending (rather than past) catastrophes, and his fear of technology."[57]

In most cases, then, Nazi atrocity more or less disappeared from the U.S. and British public imagination for approximately three decades. As Holocaust scholar Berel Lang later told it, these were "years of silence," in which

> those who had been directly affected but survived took the opportunity to leave behind a clamor constituted of so many different sounds that together they would have seemed less like sounds than like noise. . . . Much of it was a reflex, an exclamation without sound: history, for once, was at a loss for words.[58]

Vehicles of memory—words, photographs, artifacts—did not disappear, but they continued to exist as the background of unactivated memories.

Not surprisingly, during the period of amnesia toward Nazi atrocity, the gaps of memory earlier set in place by the press became here a signature trait of more general recollections. As amnesia about the atrocities grew, the atrocity story was severed from the larger story of the war. While the war was reconfigured into adventure stories and tales of glorious pursuits against Fascism, its underside—the story of the atrocities—undermined the broad strokes of those stories. Atrocities thus came to be seen as a hindrance to the larger war narrative. Their retelling was ghettoized as an event of narrow moral importance, restricted to activities associated with

Holocaust-related agendas—curricula in Jewish religious schools, studies of war victimage, and survivor organizations.

It is thus no surprise that the professional ambivalence about photography's role in documenting the atrocities persisted. Because images were a particularly potent representation of the atrocity story, they continued to take a back stage during this period of amnesia, and books of photographic documentation on the war rarely displayed pictures of the camps. When atrocity photos did appear, they were presented as broad reminders of Nazism, not precise depictions of the camps. And events surrounding other wars of the time, notably the Korean War, appeared to have little effect on the ongoing discussions of Nazi atrocity: although graphic images of dead U.S. soldiers were printed in the first days of that war, the military soon censored explicit images of both atrocities and wounded soldiers in battle areas; the failure of its action to generate protest suggested that the U.S. public perhaps had seen enough atrocity in World War II.[59]

Thus, this second wave of atrocity memory produced responses that attended to ongoing agendas about cultural identity, technology, and professionalism at the same time as they reconfigured the act of bearing witness to Nazi atrocities. As one writer recently formulated the pattern, all kinds of memorials, including photographs, monuments, and museums, are an "event in the process of mourning. . . . We make memorials so that we can begin at last to forget." It is possible that during those first three decades, people were not ready to transpose their memories into memorial objects. Bits and pieces of the story needed to settle before being processed into the kind of memories that could work as a collective means of representation about the past. In that view, vessels of memory, photographs chief among them, lingered as the background of memory work until such issues could be settled.[60]

In sum, the first two waves of Holocaust memory were an instance of forgetting to remember. Memory work positioned photographs as a ground against which early visual encounters with the atrocities took place. While the act of bearing witness persisted, by the fifties and onward it had lost much of its resonance, producing instead considerable popular ambivalence about atrocity.

In the first wave of memory, photography offered a ground against which to position the initial experience of Nazi brutality. That ground was splintered already in the early years between a popular need to bear witness and a professional ambivalence in the press over how to remember the story. In the second wave, the atrocities became almost nonexistent, their photographed depictions an unarticulated background to atrocity memory.

By the end of these two memory waves, however, photography would take on a different role. From the late seventies and onward, memory work became primary, and photography—as one of its carriers—became the figure rather than the ground of Holocaust representation. By the eighties, there was, to cite scholar Geoffrey Hartman, a "shift from scarcity to excess," from an "inauthentic silence" to what often seemed like an obsession with the very work of memory.[61] In implicating the practices of remembering as a variable in memory work, such a move foreshadowed a renewed interest not only in the content of what was being remembered but in its form as well. It also renewed the act of bearing witness, but in a way that complicated its resonance as a response to the barbarism of other events.

Remembering to Remember
Photography as Figure of
Contemporary Atrocity Memories

THE CAMPS OF NAZI EUROPE CHANGED IN POPULAR
consciousness as the seventies ended. As the indifference of the previous three decades began to wane, there was a resurgence of memory work that renovated the act of bearing witness in the popular imagination. Photography became the figure rather than the ground of Holocaust representation, and World War II brutality became more, not less, central to contemporary recollections of the past.

THE THIRD MEMORY WAVE:
PHOTOGRAPHY AS FIGURE

By the end of the seventies, the Holocaust drifted to the forefront of public consciousness, making its recollection increasingly at issue. In scholar Lawrence Langer's words, the public began "to enter the [next] stage of Holocaust response, moving from what we know of the event to how we remember it," and the atrocities of Nazi Europe remerged in the public sphere as a source of cues about a receding past. Bearing witness became a frame of attention to events that were no longer on the public's doorstep, and people began to attend not so much to events as to their representation in memory. Bearing witness had become a case of remembering to remember.[1]

Holocaust memory captured the public imagination from the late seventies through the nineties. Press articles ran routinely about remembering and forgetting the atrocities of World War II; attention surged in the early eighties to Holocaust commemoration, motivated largely by the rise of Holocaust deniers; and by 1995, a review of Elie Wiesel's book was tellingly titled "Remembering as a Duty to Those Who Survived." During this memory wave, memorialization took shape as a concerted undertaking, the Holocaust newly established as both an academic subject and in more popular cultural representations. Such a "re-elaboration" of the past" drew attention as much to the act of remembering as to the issue of what was being remembered.[2]

A number of events preceding this time period repositioned the Holocaust as the target of memory work, ending the earlier period of amnesia. The thrust to remember was ignited by events that both increased public self-reflection and facilitated the ability to mourn the past.

Certain events had direct relevance to the Holocaust. Public trials—including the Eichmann trial in Jerusalem in 1961–62 and the Auschwitz trial in Frankfurt in 1964–65—introduced a certain closure for those struggling to deal with the atrocities. Books like Hannah Arendt's *Eichmann in Jerusalem,* Lucy Dawidowicz's *The War against the Jews: 1933–1945,* and Raul Hilberg's *Destruction of the European Jews* gave a jump start to inquiry about life under the Nazis from the sixties onward. Issues of Jewish national identity were crystallized through events such as the Six-Day War in 1967 and the Yom Kippur War in 1973, drawing one group of indifferent remembers—the Jews—toward active memory work. The creation of the U.S. Office of Special Investigations drew public attention to ongoing efforts to bring to trial Nazi war criminals living in the United States. A growing interest in ethnic origins—sparked in the United States by television's screening of *Roots* in 1977 and *Holocaust* in 1978 and in Britain by the 1975 screening of *Genocide* in the *World at War* series—brought Nazi atrocity increasingly to the forefront of Jewish national consciousness. And most importantly, the aging and death of survivors lent an urgency to memory work.[3]

Other events had less relevance to the Holocaust yet prompted an interest in all breaches of the moral order. The Holocaust became relevant to those concerned with national and international justice in both the United States and Britain, unrest surrounding Vietnam, and issues of racism and poverty. In 1978, a threatened march in Skokie, Illinois, by neo-Nazis "brought the principle of free speech into conflict with what seemed common decency, the recognition of survivors' feelings." Issues of agency now began to be highlighted in addressing the atrocities, and they pushed publics to consider what had happened in conjunction with ongoing agendas about identity and collective solidarity. Equally important, they shifted attention to the "how" of memory and made the consideration of memory's workings a precondition for considering "what" memory was.[4]

Still other developments fostered a parallel recognition of photography and particularly photojournalism, which in turn focused attention on the atrocities. A change in the aesthetic of war photos took place with Vietnam, which now depicted the plight of civilians within the larger context of the war. Although television could never be as explicit as still photos, television's coverage of atrocity facilitated the increasingly frequent display of explicit front-page pictures, "war photographs which earlier would have been suppressed as being too shocking." In fact, as Susan Moeller has argued, the chief icons of the Vietnam War, such as Nick Ut's portrayal of a naked napalmed girl running down a street in a Vietnamese village, were those still photographs that portrayed civilian atrocity. Their display and cultural resonance gave renewed life to the atrocity photos of World War II.[5]

Reintegrating the Atrocities

The interest in the Holocaust that reemerged in the late seventies crystallized across settings as wide-ranging as museums, official commemorations, and media retrospectives. In 1979, the United States began officially commemorating the Holocaust in national ceremonies, at the same time as the concentration camps of Europe became pilgrimage destinations for those seeking to remember Nazi atrocity. Churches began adding services memorializing the Holocaust to their liturgical calendars, while the U.S. Holocaust Memorial Council, charged with "the task of keeping alive the memory of the Holocaust," convened its first International Conference of Liberators in late 1981. Memoirs, scholarly studies, films, and novels started "gushing forth as numbing silence gave way to a passion for remembrance."[6]

The surge of memory practices took place earlier in the United States than in Britain. In Tony Kushner's view, the Jewish-U.S. involvement in remembering World War II helped make Nazi atrocity topical in the United States, and "by the late 1970s and certainly by the early 1980s, the subject had become one of almost obsessive interest in American society. In contrast, George Steiner suggested that in Britain the Holocaust was 'not our patch.'"Yet by the late eighties and early nineties, memory had become the rule on both continents. As the revolutions of 1989 "forced open the East European past," to cite Tony Judt, memories of the war came under increased public scrutiny for both countries. After "being swept under the rug for nearly four decades," the Holocaust became topical once again.[7]

The new emphasis on Holocaust memory—not as a secondary issue in discourse but as a primary one—had direct bearing on the shape of discussions about Nazi atrocity. By the early nineties Holocaust-related books abounded with titles that incorporated notions of memory. Titles such as Elie Wiesel's *Between Memory and Hope*, James Young's *The Texture of Memory*, or *Memory Offended*, a volume about the establishment of a convent at Auschwitz, all signaled the relevance of memory work when addressing the atrocities. *A Surplus of Memory*, a translation of Yitzhak Zuckerman's memoirs about the Warsaw ghetto uprising, appeared in 1993, and the same year, the *New Republic* ran a cover story on the Holocaust entitled "After Memory." Holocaust deniers were labeled "assassins of memory" and "enemies of memory"; denial itself was framed as "an assault on truth and memory," and testimonies "the ruins of memory." As Elie Wiesel noted in his 1995 memoirs, "memory is a passion no less powerful or persuasive than love. . . . What does it mean to remember? It is to live in more than one world, to prevent the past from fading and to call upon the future to illuminate it." In the *New York Times*'s view, Wiesel's use of a "wide-angled lens" addressed familiar issues of remembering the Holocaust but broadened them to look at memory itself as a form of representation.[8]

Interest in Nazi atrocity renewed use of its terms and images and reconfigured them as vessels of memory. The Holocaust became a shorthand way of signifying the atrocities of World War II, "a symbol [that] summarizes and condenses within a single term the enormous and complex process in many different countries and circumstances, by which six million Jewish lives were brought to nothing." Emerging as an identifiable category broaching a range of specific experiences related to life under the Nazis, it began to be used "as a metaphor for tragedy as well as a valuable lesson to prevent further tragedy." Yet in becoming a reference point for contemporary tragedy, it also accommodated rather than resisted the partiality of its own representation. As one scholar observed,

> the use of symbols often means that people do not necessarily know precise detailed answers to normal, logical questions: When did the Holocaust begin? When did it end? Where did it happen? Why did it happen? The whole point about a symbol is that it allows one to possess cultural knowledge without having the totality of the facts.

In other words, by broadening the detailed accounts of the camps into the more wide-ranging Holocaust story, people were now able to attend to the issue of Nazi brutality without a full understanding of how or why the atrocities happened.

As Holocaust consciousness grew to accommodate the atrocity story with less visible discomfort, those originally associated with the camps who had kept silent drew attention. Survivors saw a new willingness from others to see and hear their testimony. Soldiers who had themselves been involved in the liberation of the camps began to offer public lectures on their experiences. Some displayed photos. Memoirs appeared from former liberators who, quiet for decades, "could no longer keep what I had seen locked inside me." One former liberator wrote a letter to the *New York Times,* where he hailed the plans to teach the Holocaust in the public schools of Philadelphia and New York City, noting that he was "still shocked by what I saw during my 16 hours" liberating Dachau.[9]

During the seventies and eighties, Nazi brutality actively claimed the imagination of writers, poets, playwrights, and filmmakers on both continents. Writers such as Philip Roth, William Styron, Saul Bellow, and Isaac Bashevis Singer addressed Nazi atrocity in books that met public acclaim. Films such as *The Sorrow and the Pity, The Tin Drum, The Boys from Brazil, Lacombe Lucien,* and *The Last Metro* capitalized on a growing interest in the topic. The screening of Claude Lanzmann's *Shoah* in 1985 lent renewed cogency to the centrality of memory and to the role of survivors in shaping that memory, though the camps were featured through their absence rather than their presence: *Shoah* was acclaimed precisely because it did *not* feature visual depictions of the atrocities. Television broadcasts such as "Playing for Time" brought camp scenes straight into U.S. living rooms. Within each of these instances, memory itself remained at issue.[10]

Changes also began to integrate the Holocaust in secondary and higher educational frameworks in both Britain and the United States. Holocaust education was mandated in certain secondary schools, and courses on the Holocaust were added to university curricula. New journals appeared—such as *Holocaust and Genocide Studies* and the *British Journal of Holocaust Education,* begun in 1992. Endowed chairs in Holocaust education were set up in universities.[11]

Interest in Nazi atrocities grew to such an extent that it produced inappropriate memory work: simulation games like "Gestapo: A Learning Experience about the Holocaust" appeared; vacations in Nazi-style camps were billed as "complete with barbed wire, search lights, watch towers, and fifty guards in SS uniforms"; and Nazi-inspired retro fashion graced the clothing racks of stores on both continents. In 1995, the *New York Times*'s travel section ran a tourism article on "Poland's Holocaust sites." These examples suggest, however, that popular culture was actively shaping the story of Nazi atrocity—as when *Schindler's List* won awards for best movie in 1993, making the subject of the Holocaust "accessible to ordinary people." All of these examples suggested that popular culture was giving new life to the act of bearing witness, sometimes eroding it via its recontextualization. Remembering became less a mode of piecing together holes in consciousness than a legitimate way of framing—and processing—the present through the past. Bearing witness, then, took on a retrospective quality that allowed publics to move back and forth in time, attending both to the atrocities and to contemporary agendas: people were remembering to remember.

While the emphasis on memory's mechanics redirected attention to the devices and strategies by which memories were set in place, it also generated suspicion about their use. As Geoffrey Hartman observed, "the very means that expose truth, the verbal or photographic or filmic evidence, [become] tainted by suspicion. All evidence is met by a demystifying discourse or charges of manipulation."[12] In other words, the new emphasis on the vessels of memory relativized the representations of the past that they produced.

Reviving Atrocity Photos: The Centrality of Visual Memory

Photography fared well in the renovation of atrocity memory. From the late seventies through the nineties, collective memories played to a revival of the atrocity photos, which reconstituted photography as a figure in Holocaust remembrance. In large part, the photos' reemergence derived from their ability to support the renewed interest in the Nazi atrocity story, and the press capitalized on that linkage in recycling the images. Although interest in the photos extended beyond the press—in fact, two scholarly books of the eighties and nineties addressing the camps' liberation, *Inside the Vicious Heart* and *The End of the Holocaust: The Liberation of the Camps,* made extensive use of the photos as historical documentation— their wide accessibility facilitated the story's retelling in a way unmatched by other agents of memory.[13]

The press was able to help revive the atrocity photos because it was adept at working around the presentation of familiar material—storing, recycling, and reconfiguring the original presentations of an event. Visual cues were particularly valuable in suppressing, maintaining, and altering a wide range of rhetorical claims about the propriety, cogency, and appropriateness of its images, and the photos appeared in schematic and conventionalized presentations, depicting familiar shots of groups of survivors and accoutrements of atrocity. Rarely did the other types of depictions, central to the original act of bearing witness, appear here.

From the seventies onward, the atrocity photos began to reappear in numerous public domains—in museums, cultural exhibits, book readings, magazine and television retrospectives, all of which capitalized on what Leon Wieseltier later called their "tart objectivity." The photos, wrote the *Manchester Guardian* in 1975, lingered "in memory as persistent ghosts." They provided

> ways of giving meaning to what is no longer accessible. This multiple role is made abundantly clear by the recurrence of those images for 'plain' documentary and propaganda purposes immediately after the war, and their later reappearance in manifold forms, including illustrating books on the challenge of the Holocaust to Christian theology, the sensational fetishization of the same images in popular war

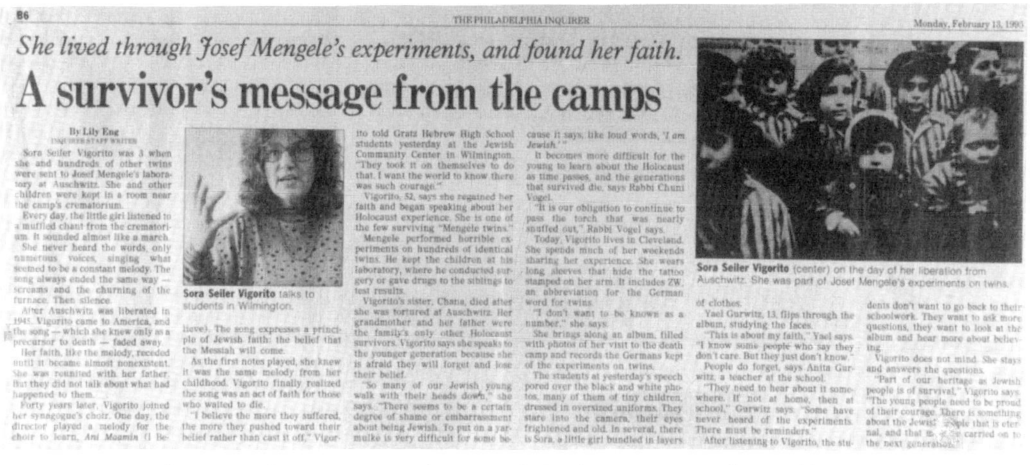

B6 THE PHILADELPHIA INQUIRER Monday, February 13, 1995

She lived through Josef Mengele's experiments, and found her faith.

A survivor's message from the camps

By Lily Eng
INQUIRER STAFF WRITER

Sora Seiler Vigorito was 3 when she and hundreds of other twins were sent to Josef Mengele's laboratory at Auschwitz. She and other children were kept in a room near the camp's crematorium.

Every day, the little girl listened to a muffled chant from the crematorium. It sounded almost like a march.

She never heard the words, only numerous voices, singing what seemed to be a constant melody. The song always ended the same way — screams and the churning of the furnace. Then silence.

After Auschwitz was liberated in 1945, Vigorito came to America, and the song — which she knew only as a precursor to death — faded away.

Her faith, like the melody, receded until it became almost nonexistent. She was reunited with her father. But they did not talk about what had happened to them.

Forty years later, Vigorito joined her synagogue's choir. One day, the director played a melody for the choir to learn, *Ani Maamin* (I Believe). The song expresses a principle of Jewish faith: the belief that the Messiah will come.

Sora Seiler Vigorito talks to students in Wilmington.

As the first notes played, she knew it was the same melody from her childhood. Vigorito finally realized the song was an act of faith for those who waited to die.

"I believe the more they suffered, the more they pushed toward their belief rather than cast it off," Vigorito told Gratz Hebrew High School students yesterday at the Jewish Community Center in Wilmington. "They took it on themselves to do that. I want the world to know there was such courage."

Vigorito, 52, says she regained her faith and began speaking about her Holocaust experience. She is one of the few surviving "Mengele twins."

Mengele performed horrible experiments on hundreds of identical twins. He kept the children at his laboratory, where he conducted surgery or gave drugs to the siblings to test results.

Vigorito's sister, Chana, died after she was tortured at Auschwitz. Her grandmother and her father were the family's only other Holocaust survivors. Vigorito says she speaks to the younger generation because she is afraid they will forget and lose their belief.

"So many of our Jewish young walk with their heads down," she says. "There seems to be a certain degree of shame or embarrassment about being Jewish. To put on a yarmulke is very difficult for some because it says, like loud words, 'I am Jewish.'"

It becomes more difficult for the young to learn about the Holocaust as time passes, and the generations that survived die, says Rabbi Chuni Vogel.

"It is our obligation to continue to pass the torch that was nearly snuffed out," Rabbi Vogel says.

Today, Vigorito lives in Cleveland. She spends much of her weekends sharing her experience. She wears long sleeves that hide the tattoo stamped on her arm. It includes ZW, an abbreviation for the German word for twins.

"I don't want to be known as a number," she says.

She brings along an album, filled with photos of her visit to the death camp and records the Germans kept of the experiments on twins.

The students at yesterday's speech pored over the black and white photos, many of them of tiny children, dressed in oversized uniforms. They stare into the camera, their eyes frightened and old. In several, there is Sora, a little girl bundled in layers of clothes.

Sora Seiler Vigorito (center) on the day of her liberation from Auschwitz. She was part of Josef Mengele's experiments on twins.

Yael Gurwitz, 13, flips through the album, studying the faces.

"This is about my faith," Yael says. "I know some people who say they don't care. But they just don't know."

People do forget, says Anita Gurwitz, a teacher at the school.

"They need to hear about it somewhere. If not at home, then at school," Gurwitz says. "Some have never heard of the experiments. There must be reminders."

After listening to Vigorito, the students don't want to go back to their schoolwork. They want to ask more questions, they want to look at the album and hear more about believing.

Vigorito does not mind. She stays and answers the questions.

"Part of our heritage as Jewish people is of survival," Vigorito says. "The young people need to be proud of their courage. There is something about the Jewish people that is eternal, and that must be carried on to the next generation."

Figure 38. "A Survivor's Message From the Camps," *Philadelphia Inquirer*, February 13, 1995. Reprinted courtesy of *The Philadelphia Inquirer*.

accounts, and the romanticized postcards that one can purchase at the museum. . . . The fact that the same photos are frequently used in different contexts shows how the very context of the photo changes its meaning.[14]

Atrocity photos began to surface as authenticators once the story of Nazi brutality appeared with increasing regularity. When anniversaries of Holocaust-related events needed to be publicly remembered, the press presented depictions of the camps that set in place a sense of "now and then" that visually authenticated the retellings. Contemporary images were often positioned alongside earlier photos, so as to accentuate the passage of time to readers, such as marking the anniversary of the camps' liberation with a picture from fifty years earlier or contextualizing Holocaust TV specials with photos from the 1940s. Anthologies, chronologies, and overviews of the period began to document the Holocaust through atrocity photos. Old photos of Holocaust survivors were displayed alongside verbal accounts of earlier events: the *Philadelphia Inquirer* depicted a middle-aged woman alongside an earlier portrait of her in a group of twin children experimented on by Josef Mengele (fig. 38). In each case, the images' ability to signal both "now" and "then" contemporized the narratives about days long past, offering a stopover in the past by which the speaker was authorized to speak in the present.[15]

Remembering coincided with a larger recognition of photography that resurrected the photographic image. The revival of the atrocity photos did not occur independently of larger discourses about the ability of representational vehicles to do justice to Nazi atrocity. In fact, images brought such sentiments to a head, producing a "word and image overload" that drew attention away from the fact that all representational vehicles were ill equipped for the task of representation. Some argued that the "thoughtless and repetitive overuse [of images] reduced the atrocities to an almost commonplace sight in the press and on television," whereby the atrocity photos became the "sum of knowledge about the Holocaust and its survivors. Too often the point of departure for the 'popular study' of the Holocaust begins and ends with these images alone." As Marianne Hirsch has said,

> We respond with horror, even before looking at the caption or knowing the context of the image. . . . The viewer fills in what the picture leaves out: The horror of looking is not necessarily in the image but in the story we provide to fill in what is left out of the image.[16]

For many, this made photos even less sufficient vehicles of representation. In Saul Friedlander's words:

> Why do we feel that Picasso's 'Guernica' forcefully expresses the horrors of the death and destruction brought about by the German attack on this peaceful Spanish town, whereas we do not know of any visual expression, nor can we clearly think of any that would adequately express the utter horror of the extermination of the Jews of Europe?[17]

Against such a recognition of the fragility of memory work, the atrocity photos continued to be invoked as vehicles of the Holocaust's popular memorialization.

The atrocity photos were so resonant that they also resurfaced in other modes of representation. Photos were displayed in Art Spiegelman's *Maus I* and *Maus II,* a cartoon representation of his father's journey to and from Auschwitz. Eyewitness memoirs from the camps such as Erich Kulka's *Escape from Auschwitz* and Filip Mueller's *Eyewitness Auschwitz* used photos to "authenticate and to increase the authority of actual eyewitness accounts." Still photos of the camps became a favored way to depict the atrocities in both documentary films and in movies such as *Schindler's List.* Novels—such as Don DeLillo's *White Noise* and D. M. Thomas's *The White Hotel*—depicted Holocaust-related scenes in ways that configured directly with the frequently recycled atrocity photos; the latter case involved an evocative description of Babi Yar that described photographs taken by members of the SS Einsatzgruppen in December 1941.[18]

Figure 39. "Untitled" by Robert Morris, courtesy Sonnabend Gallery, New York, © 1992.

Artists began to incorporate the atrocity photos in new representational setups. Robert Morris, for instance, painted an erotic gloss around a photograph of the corpse of Bergen-Belsen woman (see fig. 21, on p.116), whose nude body was depicted alongside those of her dead children. In its 1987 renovated form, the woman looked as if she had innocently fallen asleep under neon and strobe lights, and the title—*Untitled*—offered little to offset that impression (fig. 39). Others combined identifiable Holocaust themes with contemporary concerns about inhumanity—the Biafra famine or the Algerian war. As one artist said of his own turn to Holocaust art, "everything must appear in its own good time. . . . How often did we say in Dachau that such things should never be repeated in this world? They are being repeated."[19]

Enhancing Atrocity Memory

As the atrocity photos reappeared in new venues of the nineties, atrocity memory was enhanced by two particularly prominent practices: event-driven memory, memory attached to the commemoration of certain events; and rupture-driven memory, memory that involved ruptures in the ongoing consensus about the atrocity story. Both types of memory were facilitated by the press's involvement.

USING ATROCITY PHOTOS TO ENHANCE MEMORY: EVENT-DRIVEN MEMORY. The press's role in reviving the atrocity photos played off of its prior coverage of events related to the Holocaust. As the years passed between the atrocities and their recollection, the press spawned a cottage industry of Holocaust recollections. From anniversaries of *Kristallnacht* and the fall of the Warsaw ghetto to the appearance of new eyewitness testimonies about other events of the Holocaust, event-driven memory gave publics in both the United States and Britain a predictable and patterned way of marking the past.

In activating its memory work, the press provided numerous settings in which to display photos: accounts of the liberation of specific camps, the liberation of all camps, other events of the war, and general Holocaust commemorations—all on routinized schedules. Around each event, numerous books, articles, films, and videos appeared, such as a *MacLean's* cover story on the bombing of Dresden or a *Newsweek* column commemorating D-Day, both of which invoked the camps as a tangible memory site from which war-related discourses could spring. Photographs were used to represent a wide range of events, not all of them directly related to what was being depicted, such as when *Time* used a picture of Belsen victims to illustrate an article commemorating V-E Day. Photographs functioned as memory pegs: the visual information that they conveyed tended to remain the same, while its verbal contextualization changed over time. This had the effect of linking readers to the past through visuals, while the narratives at their side traveled on various tangents into the present. One *Philadelphia Inquirer Magazine* cover story used the fiftieth anniversary of Ohrdruf's liberation to fashion a narrative about Eisenhower's decision to embark on his denazification campaign of Germany. The article, entitled "Witness," began by telling readers that "We are looking through the eye of an old 35 mm. movie camera. The scene is a Nazi concentration camp." It probed the general's response to a ragpile of bodies in the courtyard, the lime-covered corpses in the shed, and the burned remains of bodies in the woods, all simulated through the camera's eye.[20]

In event-driven memory, certain photographs became popular candidates for recycling. The U.S. and British press somewhat differed over which photos they recycled, though both tended to choose frontal group shots of survivors. Each nation generally replayed those photos of the camps that were most central to its collective memories, with photos of Belsen, liberated by the British forces in 1945, surfacing more frequently in Britain. Conversely, photos of Buchenwald—liberated by the U.S. forces—resurfaced in the United States more frequently than did images of Belsen. For instance, Margaret Bourke-White's close-up shot of the wagonload of bodies in Buchenwald appeared in numerous U.S. retrospectives on World War II.[21]

One image that resurfaced on both continents depicted a group of emaciated, half-clothed prisoners as they stood at the gates of Ebensee in May 1945 (see fig. 35, on p. 161). Already in the sixties the photograph had come to signify liberation, and that cue persisted to the present day, where it came to be captioned, simply, "Concentration Camp Survivors," "Prisoners on Liberation Day," or, wrongly, "Death-Camp Survivors." In few instances was it mentioned that the photograph had been taken in Ebensee, and little, if any, information was provided about the circumstances facing liberators when they had entered the camp. The same photo also frequently turned up in other domains of public expression, where it was used as the cover photograph for the United States Holocaust Memorial Museum's 1995 exhibit on the liberation of the camps. There, it was captioned "Liberation, 1945."[22]

Another recurrent image that resurfaced in both the United States and Britain depicted male prisoners clutching the barbed-wire fence of Buchenwald, newly neutralized of its electric current (see fig. 37, on p. 167). Taken by Margaret Bourke-White and captioned "Survivors behind Barbed Wire, Buchenwald 1945," the image was recycled in dozens of Holocaust retrospectives—in anniversary issues of journals, magazines, and overviews of photojournalism. Considered a candidate for inclusion in a Leonard Baskin memorial to FDR in the late seventies, in 1989 *Time* selected the photo as one of the ten great iconic images of photojournalism because it "informed the world about the true nature of the Holocaust." The photo was also used as the starting point of depiction for other modes of representation: Audrey Flack's *World War II (Vanitas)* of 1976–77

Figure 40. "World War II (Vanitas)" by Audrey Flack, incorporating a portion of the Margaret Bourke-White photograph "Buchenwald, April 1945" copyright Time Inc., courtesy Louis K. Meisel Gallery, New York.

positioned the photo inside an opulent still-life of butterflies, roses, and carefully decorated pastries, an odd juxtaposition that embedded the male survivors behind the barbed wire but also behind the objects of the still-life (fig. 40). Flack noted that the portrait was supposed to show "memory receding in space: My idea was to tell a story, an allegory of war. . . . I wanted to shock."[23]

Significantly, this same image, lauded and imitated in so many different quarters, was not published at the time of the camps' liberation.[24] Its use as a commemorative tool—despite its not having been published at the time of the event—reveals crucial features about memory work, signaling how an event's constitutive features can be blurred or rearranged in order to make memory effective. It also suggests, yet again, how images can work better in memory—where they are frequently positioned within alternative interpretive schema—than as a tool of news relay.

In each of these cases, the original disjunctions between the event in text and the event in image multiplied as event-driven memory provided new opportunities for remembering the past. The original forms of visual documentation—by which the event depicted was not necessarily the event discussed—produced new forms of visual memory that further differentiated the record from the remembered event. Event-driven memory thus offered additional ways to use atrocity photos that were irrelevant to their original recording.

Disjunctions between the image of recording and the image of memory, however, did not occur at random or without limit, and these boundaries of event-driven memory can best be seen by examining the uses of one atrocity photo that circulated widely in the United States and Britain—a U.S. Signal Corps photo of the Buchenwald barracks (see fig. 10, on p. 103).

The image, which originally appeared in both the *New York Times* and the *Los Angeles Times* in 1945, depicted prisoners lying in the bunks of Buchenwald. Already at that time, the picture had moved from signifying Buchenwald's liberation to signifying the liberation in general, with readers told that they were looking at freed slave laborers in an unidentified camp. It is thus not surprising that the same image turned up in later Holocaust literature that marked the liberation story but not Buchenwald. For instance in 1995, *Newsweek* published a cover story on the fiftieth anniversary of the liberation of Auschwitz in which the text spoke of Auschwitz but the picture depicted Buchenwald (fig. 41). The familiar discrepancy between the place of the text and the place of the image was in this case transported into memory.[25]

Over time, this particular image moved even farther from the scene it originally depicted, as atrocity's visualization invoked a wide range of treatments of the war. It illustrated numerous Holocaust-related topics, including articles about Holocaust deniers, Holocaust education, and so-called Holocaust politics. One journal repeated earlier errors of interpretation when it used the photo to illustrate a 1982 article on British Holocaust revisionist David Irving. While the text told of Irving's thesis that Hitler had not condoned or ordered the Jews' systematic extermination, the photograph was wrongly captioned as a depiction of "death-camp survivors." Repetition

Figure 41. Survivors at Auschwitz, © 1995, Newsweek, Inc. All rights reserved. Reprinted by permission. Auschwitz photo reprinted by permission of Sovfoto/Tass.

of the earlier inaccurate representation of Buchenwald, now within an article about Holocaust revisionism, underscored how little those using images
in news had developed a critical eye on their own practices.[26]

Other problematic presentations of this photo, underscoring a similar
linkage between image and text, appeared regularly. The image was repeatedly captioned wrongly as "death-camp survivors" and mistakenly associated with Dachau in one publication. One 1979 *MacLean's* story used the
bunkmates of Buchenwald to illustrate an account of a reunion of former
Buchenwald prisoners in which the photo was juxtaposed with a second
picture, depicting four men in their sixties, smiling and mugging for the
camera. The juxtaposition implied that the reunited former prisoners were
in fact depicted in the earlier photo, though it depicted none of the men
seen in the more recent image. Rather, the juxtaposition set in place an
additional historical inaccuracy, for the men pictured at the reunion had
been incarcerated as non-Jewish Allied POWs, while the picture presumably portrayed Jewish inmates. Because different treatment was accorded
the two groups of prisoners, the visual comparison between "then" and
"now" was invalid not only on historical grounds but on representational
ones too: the "then" and "now" comparison set in place a far crueler analogy between "them" and "us," and the photograph's seemingly innocuous
invocation as a piece of memory work inadvertently vulgarized at least one
premise about how Nazi brutality was inflicted.[27]

Not surprisingly, the photo also resurfaced in other modes of representation. It adorned a 1995 advertisement for the Church of Scientology that
called for increased German compensation to Nazi victims. It provided a
reality marker of a 1993 art installation by Judy Chicago, who embroi-
dered pastel-colored creatures atop the forlorn black-and-white male faces
in the barracks (fig. 42). In this context entitled *Double Jeopardy,* the photo
enabled Chicago to address the issue of gender in the camps, and she juxtaposed the painted experiences of women to the "black and white photographs of male experiences: The men's activities [provide] the historical
context for the women's, a metaphor for the fact that women are generally impacted by the historic events that men orchestrate."[28]

Thus, in each case the photo allowed its users to move beyond a simple
reminder of Buchenwald's liberation. Not only did it help them recall the
camps but recalled the atrocities and the Holocaust too. In many cases, this
contemporary placement signaled a surrender of the image's referentiality
to its symbolic status, even in cases where it consolidated old errors and
introduced new ones. This, then, was the new shape of bearing witness,
where the target of attention was memory and memory's invocation for
present-day agendas.

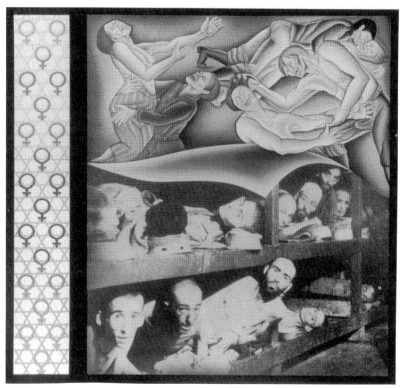

Figure 42. "Plates 7 and 8 Double Jeopardy," from *Holocaust Project: From Darkness Into Light,* by Judy Chicago. Copyright © 1993 by Judy Chicago, text and original artwork; Copyright © 1993 by Donald Woodman, photographs. Used by permission of Viking Penguin a division of Penguin Books USA Inc.

Interestingly, this particular photograph received an additional referential life years after the liberation. Following its publication and recycling, two of its depicted individuals took on public identity—noted author Elie Wiesel and Los Angeles businessperson Mel Mermelstein, both of whom identified themselves as prisoners in the depicted bunks. Mermelstein, who in the eighties successfully challenged the claims of the revisionist Institute for Historical Review in court, was portrayed in a U.S. newsmagazine holding a framed copy of the original photograph (fig. 43). In keeping with the thrust toward using the story to mark memory, in the more recent image the original photograph's attribution and captioning were both displaced to accommodate those of the more recent image.[29]

What do these uses of the Buchenwald barracks photograph tell us? Like other cases, perhaps less illustrative but no less central, each twist to memory underscores memory's fundamentally variable nature. Memory

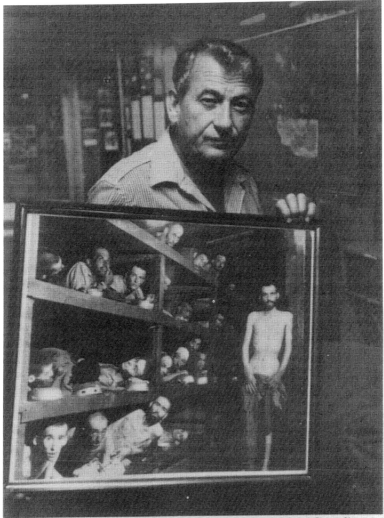

Lester Sloan—NEWSWEEK

Mermelstein with photo of Buchenwald inmates (he is barely visible at far right, top rack): A painful victory

Figure 43. "Footnote to the Holocaust," *Newsweek,* October 19, 1981, by *Newsweek*— Lester Sloan. © 1981, Newsweek, Inc. All rights reserved. Reprinted by permission.

worked both unexpectedly and in many simultaneous temporal directions. Photos were reprinted not necessarily because they supported a photo's original publication but because they helped launch new rhetorical arguments. Photos thereby spawned a simultaneous before-and-after life as memory tools, invoking Holocaust recollections on many different levels. Yet in an age where the press cogently recycles historical information at will, this raises questions about the use of photos to remember. For underlying the recycling of the Buchenwald barracks photograph was an event that came over time to resemble less and less its original presentation.

USING ATROCITY PHOTOS TO STABILIZE MEMORY: RUPTURE-DRIVEN MEMORY. The U.S. and British press have also used the atrocity photos to stabilize contested moments in the ongoing discourse about the original record of Nazi brutality. As the story of Nazi atrocity was retold from an increasing range of points in time and space, contemporary agendas threatened to rupture the story and rearrange memories of it. Memory work responded to such tensions by altering hitherto intact patterns of representation, creating new events around the ruptures. As Edward Linenthal has suggested, "the commemorative membrane is so sensitive to any perceived act of desecration, it immediately becomes an event."[30]

Eruptions occurred whenever the invocation of memory cues lacked workability or resonance for groups with vested interests in a memory's shaping and maintenance. Often associated less with the event itself than with challenges over the right to address it, ruptures emerged around the question of how to remember the atrocities—in debates over whether Ronald Reagan should place a wreath at the graves of Wehrmacht soldiers at Bitburg or how to commemorate in Poland the fiftieth anniversary of the liberation of Auschwitz. In the case of Bitburg, hundreds of observers streamed to the scene to be present, in *Newsweek*'s words, to "bear witness" to Reagan's act of "wounding Holocaust survivors," much as their forebears had borne witness to the acts of Nazi atrocity; in the case of Auschwitz, Jewish groups invited to the ceremony complained that it had been poorly planned and that its Polish "nationalist" flavor obscured Jewish victimization. Implicit in the question of how to remember were secondary questions concerning which vehicle of memory could most effectively do the work. Thus, debates over whether to censor Nazi materials from the Internet and whether to let Nazi deniers have a platform in U.S. college newspapers moved Holocaust memory to new levels of elaboration that addressed memory's "how."[31]

Visual evidence here was crucial. The press used atrocity photos to stabilize the discourse when it was most shaky, presenting visual evidence so as to cut remaining ambivalence. Depictions of accoutrements of atrocity—gas chambers, crematory ovens, and hanging cells—appeared whenever ruptures chipped away at the popular consensus about what had happened. Such was the case with historian Arno Mayer's book, *Why Did the Heavens Not Darken?,* attacked by scholars invested in the record that it challenged. An Associated Press photograph of the charred remains of human bodies was set inside the accompanying article to visually rebut the discursive eruption that Mayer's book had generated. In a similar fashion, depictions of the Dachau ovens resurfaced in 1993 to offset articles on Holocaust denial. Significantly, images were used to stave off the deniers as well, and the press tended to select particularly grotesque scenes for display when illustrating textual discussions about the deniers. For instance, when Jean-Claude Pressac published *The Crematoriums of Auschwitz* in September 1993—where, despite his own rumored linkage with Holocaust deniers, he provided documentation of the gas chambers—*Newsweek* illustrated the piece with a photograph showing a body protruding from an oven in Dachau. The graphic image, in this case, was employed to refute the claims of denial elaborated in the text. In other words, the greater the vibrations caused by the discourse, the more explicit about atrocities the image needed to be. Even the "rediscovery" of the so-called Auschwitz album—a photo album depicting the selection process for extermination at Auschwitz found in the midfifties and rediscovered decades later—brought photography again to the foreground of discourse about Holocaust memory. But it did so by emphasizing the uses and abuses of photographic documentation.[32]

The press also used photography to stabilize the popular response to the 1992 film *Liberators,* which created a rupture in the United States over its representation of the liberation of Buchenwald and Dachau. The film, produced by William Miles and Nina Rosenblum for the PBS series *The American Experience,* portrayed the experiences of an African-American regiment of U.S. soldiers, the 761st Tank Battalion, which, it claimed, had helped liberate both camps. Although the film was initially lauded for improving relations between the Jewish and African-American communities, surviving members of the battalion later contended that "the producers twisted the history of [the] Army unit to make their film more dramatic and more politically pleasing." Not only did the 761st not help liberate the camps, but members of the battalion had never even been there.[33]

Response to the film was swift, and both veterans and survivors attacked it for misrepresenting the camps' liberation. Veterans of the battalion denied that they had been in either Dachau or Buchenwald and feared that their actual accomplishments—liberating Gunskirchen, a satellite of the Mauthausen concentration camp, and fighting at the Battle of the Bulge—would now be smudged in the historical record. White veterans credited historically with liberating the camps were miffed about being unmentioned in the film. At stake in the discussions was the popular consensus about how the camps had been liberated.

Articles about the film responded to the rupture by presenting visual documentation of the camps' liberation. Atrocity photos helped the press take a stand either for or against *Liberators*. Numerous newspapers displayed photos of white liberators in the camps; one complicated popular memory by showing Leon Bass, an African-American liberator who had been in Buchenwald, though it was unclear at what point in its liberation. In many cases, the liberators' presence in the camps was authenticated by the presence of corpses, suggesting a revival, however temporary, of the more common representation of the forties that had brought together victims and witnesses in the act of bearing witness.[34]

In February 1993, the American Jewish Committee critiqued the film in a thirteen-page report, much of which focused on the persistence and believability of visual documentation of the camps. Maintaining that "the film has serious factual flaws, well beyond what can be written off as 'artistic license,'" the report argued that "we live in a time where there are people questioning the very existence of the Holocaust" and lamented the wrongful visual impressions that the film provided both about what happened and about who participated. Woven through the film's formal discussion were references to photographic images: "There is no question," the report admitted, "that Leon Bass was in Buchenwald while the dead bodies were still in piles: *there is a picture*. Likewise, there is no question that Paul Parks [another African-American soldier] was in Dachau. Nor is there question that other black soldiers were in these camps—*there are photographs*" (emphases added). Issues arose in the linkages between the images and the claims that they were upholding. As scholar and film adviser Robert Abzug later observed, "Some of the images identified as Buchenwald and Dachau were actually other camps." Abzug's response to the use of images was interesting because the practice of using images of one place to stand in for others was, of course, a common practice for representing atrocity. Unusual here was the naming of images that contradicted what they in fact represented, raising questions as to whether the images themselves were problematic or the naming procedures surrounding them. In either case, the atrocity photos stabilized the rupture sufficiently so as to neutralize the claims of *Liberators* and reinstate popular consensus about what happened.[35]

Reviving Atrocity Photos and Additional Memory Agents

Bearing witness to memory has required attention beyond that of the press, and the act of remembering to remember engaged professional forums, liberators, museums, and picture-magazines, each of which has helped revive the atrocity photos as memory cues. Holocaust deniers also tried to rework the resonance of photos as cultural documents. Each agent of memory facilitated a renewed interest in the atrocity photos in ways that both challenged and supported existing commemorative efforts.

PROFESSIONAL FORUMS AND ATROCITY PHOTOS. For professional forums, the revival of the atrocity photos coincided with another development—the further recognition of photojournalism. That is to say, as one surfaced in professional memory, so did the other.

From the seventies onward, photography began to redefine itself in conjunction with the competition posed by television, and photographic publishing reasserted its presence. *Life* reemerged in 1978, when photographic books flooded the market, and "photographic historians and photographers began to look closely at the iconography of war. Another set of memories, often those of photojournalists, began to imprint themselves on our minds." Books on photojournalism soon filled the shelves of libraries and bookstores, at the same time as new changes in technology— such as electronic cameras and the satellite transmission of images in the eighties—changed perceptions of photography. The earlier surge of interest in television that had helped temporarily bury still photographs now came to be seen in perspective. As one photography scholar saw it,

> Few three-minute reports on the network news or even special documentaries on late-night television can make the kind of sustained complex statement that it is possible to make using a combination of still images and printed text—and without VCR technology. None can make the kind of report that a viewer can go back to and linger over. With this knowledge gained after two decades of network news broadcasts, the still photograph and the photographic essay have come back.

The ability to linger over photos made them particularly well suited for memory work and the act of bearing witness. And with the consolidation of interest both in general photography and in photojournalism as a profession, attention now began to be paid to the events that photography had documented well.[36]

It is thereby no surprise that by the late seventies and early eighties photographic books turned their attention to Nazi atrocity. In a marked turn from the past, books that traced the history of the news image now included atrocity photos as part of their repository of good photojournalistic images. Marianne Fulton's *Eyes of Time: Photojournalism in America,* Jorge Lewinski's *The Camera at War,* and Vicki Goldberg's *The Power of Photogra-*

phy—all published in this time period—devoted pictorial space to the photos in their overviews of the profession. Interestingly, each book reprinted Margaret Bourke-White's photograph of men behind the barbed wire of Buchenwald despite the fact that it had not appeared at the time of the camp's liberation, suggesting an attentiveness to photography as a cue of memory as much as a documenter of current events. The same photo also appeared in *Reporting the War: The Journalistic Coverage of World War II,* where it topped a chapter on World War II photographers. [37]

The resurgence of the atrocity photos took shape in numerous commemorative volumes and histories of news organizations, which paid renewed attention to photography's role in documenting atrocity. One early account that tied the history of a specific type of journalism and photography to the camps was Philip Knightley's *The First Casualty,* whose historical overview of the work of war correspondents included substantial discussion of the camps' coverage, in both word and image. The camps merited their own chapter, entitled "Never Again." Knightley's account became the model for other treatments of the atrocities, and by the eighties, press accounts of the war regularly mentioned the atrocities. Typical here were the *Boston Globe*'s *World War II: From D-Day to V-J Day, 40 Years Later* and *The World at War,* issued in 1990 by the *Illustrated London News.* In cataloging the paper's role in documenting British history, the latter book issued its own view of the war and reprinted a full page of its supplement on atrocity pictures exactly as it had appeared in the newspaper in April 1945. In fact, such pictorial spreads frequently resurfaced, useful ways of depicting a large number of images in a small space. [38]

Retrospectives of the war thus began to regularly include atrocity pictures. One new book on British war photography began its text with a discussion of what photographers had found at Belsen. In 1995, the *New York Times Book Review* reviewed two current anthologies on war reporting, skimming the accounts of John Hersey, Dorothy Thompson, and William Shirer, mentioning that "various reporters offer ghastly descriptions of the Maidanek, Dachau and Buchenwald concentration camps" and appending a picture of a young Margaret Bourke-White on her way to photograph the war. The inclusion of Bourke-White's photo in an anthology on war reportage differed markedly from earlier efforts in which the photographer's role had been largely missing. [39]

LIBERATORS AND ATROCITY PHOTOS. Liberators of the camps played a key role too in reviving the atrocity photos. Although many liberators for decades had hidden their snapshots of the camps from public sight, as Holocaust consciousness grew during the eighties and nineties they began to pull their amateur images from their hiding places. They attended liberator conferences and displayed albums of photographs taken decades earlier. As one liberator later said, "What I can remember of this particular time is spelled out right here in these pictures." This was curious, because the camera and the photograph were hardly their own professional tools; they "belonged," as it were, to photographers. In a sense, however, the memory work implemented by soldiers set straight one of the less addressed facts about the photographic record of the camps: the role played by nonprofessional picture-takers. The photos were proof of their having been there and upheld the centrality of bearing witness as a response to atrocity.[40]

The thrust to remember visually had its origins in a mission to make people believe. One observer recounted how he had taken out his pictures to show a neighbor who told him he did not believe that the camps had ever existed. As he recalled, "After seeing my pictures, he said 'Well, I guess it did happen.'" In 1978, a former liberator responded to a review of a book on Dachau by sending a letter and photographs to his local newspaper, which then printed them with a caption reading "Photos Taken at Dachau by Carlton Raper." Other newspapers printed pictures of former GIs alongside earlier photographs, such as one that showed a former liberator peering into the ovens of Dachau.[41]

As time moved on, the liberators were increasingly interviewed by the press, where they recounted their experiences with the aid of photos. "You could hardly call them souvenirs," one former GI said of his seven or eight photographs of Ohrdruf. "But I've shown them to people." Another GI, interviewed in a newspaper about his role in liberating Dachau, pulled out "five photographs he took at the time. Each showed dozens of bodies piled at last six feet high, twisted grotesquely." Yet another soldier's face "screwed up in a grimace as he looked at the grainy black and white photos he had taken so long ago. 'Sometimes even now, if I look at these pictures,' he said sadly, 'I still smell that odor.'"[42]

This coupling of amateur practitioners and the tools of the press upheld the revival of the photos. But it also upheld the atrocity photos as tools of bearing witness. While the soldiers' words differed little from what had been reported at the time of the liberation—with former liberators speaking of corpses "stacked like cordwood," a phrase taken directly from the reportage of Buchenwald—the similarity between professional and amateur images was striking. Many amateur shots were nearly identical to photos that had originally appeared in the U.S. and British press. Each representation—the open pits of Belsen, the stacks of bodies at Buchenwald, the train cars loaded with corpses outside of Dachau—

was pictorially depicted by amateurs in much the same way as the press had originally displayed them.

The phenomenon of soldiers' amateur photographs grew as the atrocities faded in time. By the nineties, their public display became a familiar cultural practice: when the U.S. Holocaust Memorial Council sponsored its International Conference on Liberators, former GIs pulled out their worn and fraying snapshots to show what they had seen. One such GI sat at the conference displaying his album of photographs in a State Department lobby. As one observer told it,

> The album, the ex-G.I. explained to me, contained just some of the thousands of photographs he had around his house; he had once had the negatives but they had been lost. After thirty-four years he could still remember much of what they portrayed, the names of the Nazi officers in them, the story of this or that survivor. What would happen to that memory in ten years? He didn't know.

In the early nineties the National Museum of American Jewish Military History organized an exhibit called "G.I.s Remember," which addressed the story of Jewish soldiers who had served as Allied liberators of the camps and included photos that were "not professional photographers' [but] tiny black-and-white pictures often taken in the grisly first moments after the Americans arrived at concentration camps." Pictures even circulated that showed former GIs examining their own photographs.[43]

In memory, then, as at the time of the liberation, the liberators neutralized the boundaries separating the professionals from the nonprofessional photographers. They created a common community in which many agents of memory continued to bear witness to the atrocities, regardless of the different circumstances that had brought them together in the first place.

MUSEUMS AND ATROCITY PHOTOS. The museum boom of the eighties and nineties created an additional memory agent that helped revive the atrocity photos. Museums generated additional venues in which to visually contemplate the Holocaust. In his engaging account of the establishment of the U.S. Holocaust Memorial Museum, Edward Linenthal recounted the ways in which photography helped resolve the larger issue of where and how to commemorate the Holocaust. Questions about which photographs to use and how and where to display them were central to figuring out the visual shape of memory work in museums.[44]

On both continents, the atrocity photos were seen as central to museum work. A concerted effort to address the Holocaust, begun in the late 1980s, produced a 1991 permanent photographic exhibit on the liberation of Belsen and a 1993 exhibit on the Warsaw Ghetto Uprising, both at London's Imperial War Museum. Both exhibits were organized in large part through exhibits of atrocity photos that provided a recycled visual record of events. At the United States Holocaust Memorial Museum, curators found that they preferred so-called dirty photographs—those marred by scratches, dust, dirt, and generations of copying—that gave the photograph a badge of authenticity. The museum also showed a regard for images when it installed Yaffa Eliach's three-story tower of photographs, which reproduced the prewar lives of the Jews of a Lithuanian town. Those involved in museum work on both continents found themselves in the midst of discussions about whether to include the visual representation of other atrocities—in Bosnia, Rwanda, Armenia, and elsewhere—alongside those of Nazi Europe.

Not surprisingly, photos were seen by the public as a central tool of memory within the museum experience. Visitors toured the Holocaust museums with cameras, taking shots of the photographic displays that they could later examine in their homes. The press regularly displayed photos of museum visitors looking at photographs—depictions of the act of bearing witness to images of atrocity, in a revived state—and in some cases, the museum's display raised problems. In the words of a former chairman of the National Endowment of the Arts, a Holocaust photograph

> might be inappropriate for display in the entrance of a museum where all would have to confront it, whether they chose to or not, but would be appropriate in a show which was properly labeled and hung so that only those who chose to confront the photographs would be required to do so.

Such an issue came to a head in 1995, surrounding a photographic exhibit of the camps in Israel's Holocaust museum, Yad Vashem. The long-standing exhibit of images showed naked women and generated a debate over whether the pictures violated ultrareligious Orthodox notions of modesty. When the Orthodox Jews demanded that the photographs be taken down, questions persisted as to whether removing the graphic images in effect sanitized Nazi atrocities. Yad Vashem formally rejected the protests, invoking familiar claims about photographic realism: "We have no reason [nor] authority to cover up the terrible truth or to beautify it." At heart, claimed some observers, the issue was less the photographs and more the contest of different voices—secular and Orthodox—in shaping collective memory of the Holocaust. But it was significant that the debate took place on the backs of photographic images.[45]

The museum boom also produced a slew of commemorative volumes on the Holocaust that highlighted the salience of photography. In 1991, a commemorative book on the liberation of Belsen, issued by the British Imperial War Museum as *The Relief of Belsen,* organized the volume's text around extensive and explicit photos that had been taken at the time of the camp's liberation. The Victoria and Albert Museum of London staged an exhibit that formed the basis for *Warworks*—a volume on women, photography, and the iconography of war. Yad Vashem's *Pictorial History of the Holocaust,* the United States Holocaust Memorial Museum's *The World Must Know,* and memorial books put out by the Auschwitz-Birkenau State Museum—tellingly titled *Auschwitz: A History in Photographs* and *Representations of Auschwitz: 50 Years of Photographs, Paintings, and Graphics*—all appeared during the early nineties. Each superimposed its own chronology onto the events of the Holocaust, highlighting institutional claims to its memory. The U.S. Holocaust Museum's book was in fact subtitled "The Story of the Holocaust *as Told* in the United States Holocaust Memorial Museum" (emphasis added). The Yad Vashem book, issued in 1990, used photos taken at the camps' liberation to illustrate a chapter on mass murder, a chapter on the death camps, and a chapter on the end of the war. They included the by-now familiar images of the bunks of Buchenwald, heaps of bodies at Dachau, and pits of bodies at Belsen.[46]

Pictorial spreads were popular in this regard. A book issued by the United States Holocaust Memorial Museum, entitled *1945: The Year of Liberation,* included three reprints of full-page pictorial spreads on the atrocities that had originally appeared in the *Illustrated London News.* The emphasis on pictorial spreads, however, created an additional disjunction concerning memory of the initial recording of the camps' liberation: it helped highlight the role originally played by picture-magazines. This perhaps helps explain the commonly held view that it was picture-magazines, rather than the daily or weekly press, that gave publics their original visualization of the atrocities. In fact, that initial visualization was provided first by the daily and weekly press.[47]

In each of these cases, photographs became memory vehicles that distanced them from their original presentation, particularly the aura of verisimilitude and referentiality. Photo credits regularly documented the ownership of the photographs rather than their original construction. In the 1990 Yad Vashem book, none of the photographs was accredited, although a copyright, signaling that they belonged to Yad Vashem, appeared up front. This displacement—of the image's authorship to its ownership—indicated the transformative nature of the museum's claims to visual memory. It also suggests yet again how inconsequential were both the contingent details of an image and details about its original construction.

Significantly, that trend was upheld by the press too: when one news-magazine's retrospective on Auschwitz, commemorating the fifty years since its liberation, incorporated thirteen original photos, none of the accompanying credits delineated the circumstances in which the photos had been taken but rather told readers which archive or museum owned them. Photos thus became regularly identified by their institutional own-ership, suggesting that the image's original construction was less important than which institution owned it. Such a practice also upheld the photo as a memory cue rather than a tool of information relay.[48]

PICTURE-MAGAZINES AND ATROCITY PHOTOS. The picture-magazine also played a crucial part in reviving the atrocity photos. Time-Life was instrumental in reviving atrocity recollections as photographic pub-lishing became more popular. In the decades after the war, Time-Life com-mitted large sums of money for high-quality reproductions and large pho-tographic spreads and published works of its own photographs. In characteristic fashion, Time-Life—the parent company of *Life* and *Time* mag-azines—tackled the atrocities from the late seventies onward.[49]

In keeping with its pattern of reflecting positively on its own corre-spondents' earlier coverage of main news events, Time-Life recalled the liberation by highlighting its own original liberation photographs, present-ed in *Life* in May 1945. Building in a highly organized fashion on that pho-tographic record, Time-Life contextualized its verbal discussions of the lib-eration generally in line with the visuals. Not surprisingly, then, the impression emerged that "the images of World War II came home primari-ly because of *Life*." While this was not the case at the time of the camps' lib-eration—where the pictures had been provided by the daily and weekly press well before *Life*—a high degree of institutional effort and organiza-tion helped make it so in memory.[50]

From the late seventies through the nineties, Time-Life produced a cot-tage industry of material related to World War II that focused on the atroc-ities. Reprinting the camps' depictions originally displayed in *Life,* special issues and books commemorated both Time-Life and the events reported by its subsidiary journals. Most combined the story of the camps with the story of the war; for instance, *Life* issued war retrospectives in 1985, 1991, and 1995, all of which incorporated the camps, and one even used atroci-ty photos to illustrate a collector's edition on Pearl Harbor. In 1989, Time-Life published *WWII: Time-Life Books History of the Second World War.* Offering careful accounts of the military events of the war, the book presented an entire section entitled "The Holocaust," where in over twenty pages of text and thirty photographs, the book documented both verbally and visually the atrocities before and after the liberation of the camps. Its liberation photographs appeared in a section called "Telling the Truth to the World," which recounted how journalists and photographers had accompanied the troops to view the horrors of the camps. Not surprisingly, the photographs, many of them taken by *Life* photographers in Buchenwald and Belsen, were portrayed without much of the referential data that had originally accompanied them. Even one well-known photograph of Belsen's infamous doctor—Fritz Klein—portrayed him wading knee-deep through a pit of dead bodies but did not bother to identify him, and the caption instead spoke of preparing bodies for burial in a mass grave (see fig. 11, on p. 104). In 1991, Time-Life devoted an entire book to the atrocities on the eastern front, primarily Auschwitz. Called *The Apparatus of Death,* it visually documented the atrocities before liberation by circulating primarily Russian images of the camps after they were liberated.[51]

Atrocity photos also turned up in organizational overviews about *Life* that focused on its accomplishments as a picture-magazine but bore no obvious connection to the war. In 1979, *Life: The First Decade, 1936–1945* reprinted atrocity photos as part of its reconstruction of the decade. Originally taken by *Life* photographers and featured in *Life*'s atrocity spread of May 7, 1945, the photographs included Margaret Bourke-White's famous shot of the wagonload of bodies at Buchenwald. Uncharacteristically, however, *Life* also appended the photographer's own words to the images, as they had been written to the editors years earlier. Bourke-White, for instance, wrote,

> The sights I have just seen are so unbelievable that I don't think I'll believe them myself until I've seen the photographs. . . . The important thing about today was not just the camp itself but the fact that the German civilians WERE BEING FORCED TO LOOK AT WHAT THEIR PARTY LEADERS HAD DONE.

Shots from Buchenwald also figured in *Time*'s special edition, "150 Years of Photojournalism."[52]

Although it is impossible to ascertain the precise effect of these retrospectives on the shaping of atrocity memory, it is clear that Time-Life's efforts played an important part in setting a certain visual memory in place. Time-Life recycled the images of the camps perhaps more than any other professional news organization. Not only did this make Time-Life an active player in the field of memory production, but it enabled Time-Life to claim for itself a role in memory that far exceeded the role it originally played in recording the event. This retrospective elevation of Time-Life's status may have also helped set in place the notion that the photographic

record of the camps in fact came from *Life*. In other words, Time-Life created its own place in memory by working backward to reshape the historical record.

DENIERS AND ATROCITY PHOTOS.   The Holocaust deniers constitute one of the most problematic agents of memory associated with the
atrocity photos. Their invocation of images as proof sometimes had positive
consequences—as when Austrian chancellor Kurt Waldheim denied his
Nazi past until presented in 1986 with a photograph depicting him in a
Nazi uniform. But when co-opted by the Holocaust deniers, the issue
became not one of proof but of manipulation—that is, propaganda under
the guise of representation.

In the years following the camps' liberation, publics were initially
agreed about one aspect of the coverage—that the atrocities of Nazism
would never be denied. So absolute was the force of the photographic
image in recording the atrocities that observers firmly predicted that the
atrocities would live forever in historical record. Yet mere decades following the liberation of the camps, the deniers attempted to refute precisely
what was thought to be an untouchable part of the collective memory. In
claiming that the Holocaust never happened, they challenged all vehicles of
memory about Nazi atrocity, including photographs.[53]

The deniers' claims posed an additional challenge to the authority of the
photographic image. For many of the premises that they set forth concerning the Holocaust's denial went to the heart of the issue of photographic realism and the authenticity of the atrocity photos. The photographs, in the deniers' view, were simply faked depictions of
concentration camp victims, and photos were said to be mislabeled, composite, to be paintings, to evince a "contradictory" use of light and shadow
that suggested tampering with the images. For instance, one issue of the
revisionist newspaper *Spotlight* claimed that a picture of bodies in Dachau
in fact portrayed corpses of Germans who had died in the bombing of
Dresden. Many deniers questioned the motives of those who took and
recycled the photos: as one denier saw it, "what would one expect from the
people who operate Hollywood? They have the means, the ability and obviously the will to confuse and lie to the world with their faked 'evidence'
which has brought hundreds of billions of dollars to Zionist coffers." In the
early eighties, one of the larger centers for Holocaust denial began publishing its own journal, the *Journal of Historical Review,* and the issue of "photographic truth" became a recurrent theme on its pages. The journal discussed frequently what it saw as the so-called truth-value of a number of
Holocaust-related images, including the famous shot of a boy in the War-

saw ghetto with his hands stretched above his head, and it focused on inaccurate data in captions to atrocity photos that had appeared in the daily and weekly press.[54]

The deniers' apparent interest in photographic documentation generates questions about the original loosening of the photograph's referentiality. It may be that the thrust to use the photograph as symbol, set in place at the time of the liberation, over time deprived the atrocity photos of too much of their referential data, facilitating the deniers' claims. While it is fair to assume that if the deniers had no problematic photographs through which to advance their claims of denial they would have found other venues, the invocation here of photographs as a tool of rhetorical persuasion and propaganda nonetheless bears contemplation.

RECYCLING THE PAST INTO THE FUTURE. Today our public space is plastered with grim reminders of the documented horror of the Nazi regime. From the U.S. Holocaust Memorial Museum to the movie *Schindler's List* and debates over Holocaust denial—the atrocity photos of World War II continue to occupy the corridors of our collective life, reminding us of the evil and horror witnessed but half a century ago. As one observer recently said, "they sit in our consciousness as half-repressed photographs and newsreels, the first images—always present reminders of what is now called the Holocaust."[55] They are one bearing wall of the house that contains Holocaust memory.

Yet the positioning in memory of the visual record of Nazi atrocity and its invocation in ways that undermine, challenge, distort, and taint collective memories of the past raise a number of important questions. Not only does visual memory reveal disturbing limits to the resonance of visual images as historical documentation but it casts doubt upon the ability to use photos in bearing witness to events of the past. It suggests that remembering to remember may have outlived its usefulness. Film scholar Anton Kaes has suggested that at a certain point in time the vehicles of memory—films, photographs, narratives—stop energizing and become instead energized by memory itself.[56] In such a scenario, memory breathes life into the photographs rather than the other way around. It is possible that we have reached that point with the memory of Nazi atrocity, in that the photos have been depleted as effective markers of that horrific past. Bearing witness to memory, then, may be inadvertently losing all force, with the cues which set memory in place no longer moving publics to respond.

This is not a new notion. Susan Sontag said long ago that the atrocity photos had lost their power as vessels of recollection, reaching "a saturation point" and revealing that "'concerned' photography has done at least as much to deaden conscience as to arouse it." This suggests that in facilitating the act of bearing witness decades past the event, photography may have lost its linkage with the events that it first depicted. Thus, the problem with Holocaust imagery, as Andreas Huyssen has claimed, is "not forgetting, but rather [its] ubiquitousness, the excess." For the continuous and repeated recycling of images has its underside too. The original thrust toward a broader story that the atrocity photos helped set in place may have facilitated an act of bearing witness that is questionably linked with the events at its core. In empowering both those who seek authentication of Nazi atrocities and those who deny them, atrocity photos thereby threaten to become a representation without substance.[57]

Remembering to Forget

Contemporary Scrapbooks of Atrocity

A S WE NEGOTIATE OUR ENTRY INTO THE TWENTY-FIRST century, we find ourselves relying increasingly on visual memory to help us make sense of the past and present. We leave the twentieth century looking backward. From whole museum villages, retro fashions, history channels on cable television, and even videotapes of experiments with collective memorialization, we are "struck not by signs of amnesia, but rather by a veritable obsession with the past." Our fascination with the past, however, may be less than satisfying, for "the impulse to memorialize events like the Holocaust may actually spring from an opposite and equal desire to forget them," making our attempts to remember an effort to "divest ourselves of the obligation to remember."[1] It may be, then, that at times we have begun to remember so as to forget.

Though still tentative, recent changes in the act of bearing witness seem to bear this out. This book has shown how over the past fifty years the act of bearing witness to atrocity has changed in accordance with larger cultural impulses at hand. An initial need to take responsibility for what was being witnessed, experienced directly after the Holocaust, soon gave way to a period of amnesia—the forgetting to remember that stretched from the 1950s through the 1970s. It was replaced by an obsession with Holocaust memory—a period of remembering to remember that has lasted till the present day. But as memory proliferates in the public imagination, the act of bearing witness is growing thin, and our often empty claims to memory work render us capable of little more than remembering so that we may forget in its shadow.

Remembering to forget creates numerous potholes in the journey between past and present. Uncertain of where one memory ends and another begins, we blur events with the tools by which we remember them. As scholar Andreas Huyssen has aptly observed, "the simply remembered past may turn into mythic memory . . . , a stumbling block to the needs of the present rather than an opening in the continuum of history."[2]

When our memories concern atrocity, remembering to forget is particularly troublesome. On the one hand, we leave the twentieth century with scrapbooks that are cluttered with snapshots of horror. Those snapshots have taken us on a macabre journey around the globe, depicting genocide and barbarism that have ended the lives of an estimated 50 to 170 million civilians since the century began. Atrocities as wide-ranging as the liquidation of a reported two million Cambodians by the Khmer Rouge, Saddam Hussein's genocidal actions against the Kurds of Iraq, acts of brutality against the Bahai in Iran, 30 million killed by intentional famine in Mao's China, massacres in Rwanda and nearby Burundi, mass barbarism in Bosnia, and killings in Algeria, add new leaves to our scrapbooks, each of which stretches further the cumulative sum of deaths caused by this particular category of violence. No wonder, then, that the contemporary age has earned such dubious titles as "the age of genocide" and "the most murderous century in history."[3]

While contemporary atrocities appear more far-reaching than the barbarism of yore in scale, frequency, geographical spread, methods, and the manipulation of bureaucracy, science, and technology, they also depend more directly than in previous eras on the media for their public representation. Much of this has had to do with photography, which over the years has been instrumental in helping publics bear witness to atrocities that they did not personally see. This means that the media can and do ferret out new instances of barbarism around the globe and that their contemporary display differs from the days in which we saw little or nothing of atrocity. Yet coverage has not prevented atrocity's recurrence. And unlike the atrocities of World War II, when whole populations claimed that they did not know what was happening, today we do know and still have not done enough to stop the recurrence of sanctioned barbarism. Despite ample evidence of atrocity as it is taking place, our response to pictures of horror often produces instead helplessness and indifference, by which we do little more than contextualize each instance of horror against those which come before and after.[4]

Is the barrage of snapshots of atrocity desensitizing us to the pain of others? Remembering to forget suggests that at times this may be the case. Breaking down the consensus on which the act of bearing witness was originally founded, remembering to forget ruptures the connection between representation and responsibility. While this book has shown how photography helps us remember, it also helps us remember to forget. And forgetting through images is an idea with a long history, discussed by critics as wide ranging as Roland Barthes, Marguerite Duras, and Susan Sontag.[5] It thus should come as no surprise that picturing atrocity may sometimes push it from memory.

THE MEDIA AND SCRAPBOOKS OF ATROCITY

Remembering to forget teaches us that the indifference to human suffering displayed in World War II was "not so incomprehensible, after all." In scholar Geoffrey Hartman's words, the media capitalize on familiarity, by which new acts of atrocity easily become news stories. They work through "a desensitizing trend, one that keeps raising the threshold at which we begin to respond," while "use of the old, the expected, secures the creation of the new by making its novelty nevertheless recognizable for meaning." In both the words and images that comprise atrocity stories, violence and brutality are so commonplace that a new case of politically sanctioned barbarism seems to pop up just as an old one fades. Nearly every time we pick up a newspaper, turn on the television, or listen to the radio, we learn of another instance that has been added to the repertoire of horrific acts. The predictable arrival of iconic images of barbarism adds new residents to already-populated categories of visual representation: as soon as we see the agonized collectives of survivors and victims, gaunt faces behind barbed wire, vacant stares of the tortured, and accoutrements of torture, we recognize the atrocity aesthetic. And the media help us respond to that aesthetic by showing us where to position new horrors rather than understand them—how to classify, categorize, and in many cases forget what we are seeing.[6]

Verbal Cues of Atrocity

In words, the media order the public's experience of new atrocities by recycling key phrases—Holocaust, genocide, massacre, ethnic cleansing. To an extent, this revolving lexicon of terms contextualizes barbarism against its antecedents and keeps atrocity alive by reminding us of what came before. As *Newsweek* asked in a 1992 column about genocide:

> Would there have been such a furor over the war in Bosnia if *New York Newsday* had not used the phrase "death camps" in its front-page headline? . . . In Western society, there is something uniquely evocative, and politically potent, about the image of a concentration camp and the charge of genocide. The ghosts of Hitler, Stalin, and Pol Pot flit through Western consciences. And once again, the world is haunted by the vow "Never Again."

Boosted by a lingering belief that "extreme situations are somehow more revealing of the human condition," the resonance of the past generates numerous second-generation titles related to atrocity: the Vietnamese village of My Lai earned comparisons with Lidice, the Czech village destroyed by the Germans in 1942; atrocities in Cambodia of the seventies merited the title "Auschwitz of Asia," while mass slaughter in East Timor became "another Cambodia"; El Salvadorean guerrillas were called the "Pol Pot Left"; and brutality in Burundi earned the nation the nickname of "the next Rwanda." The continuum of terror is ongoing, and it sometimes even works backward, as when the *New York Times* proclaimed that Cambodia offered terror "Before Rwanda, before Bosnia" or Pol Pot was called "Cambodia's Saddam."[7]

More specific verbal cues are also recycled. The Khmer Rouge's meticulous record-keeping practices in Cambodia were likened to those of Hitler's henchmen. A church in Ntarama, Rwanda, where hundreds of men, women, and children were hacked to death, was said to house the remains of "Rwanda's own Auschwitz." In the Balkans, the Albanians were accused of practicing a "Nazi policy" of persecution, and the war called a "parish-pump Holocaust." New categories of personhood arose, as in "genocide orphans"—a name affixed by the Rwandan government to infants born from the rape of Tutsi women by Hutu militiamen. There were also categories of reporters: *Guardian* correspondent Ed Vulliamy, who uncovered the Bosnian concentration camp of Omarska, earned comparisons with World War II correspondent William Shirer and his reportage of Nazi horror.[8]

But while the continual references keep atrocity in the public imagination, they also abandon it there. Employing familiar terms in so many new contexts of barbarism flattens the original term's resonance and denies the complexity of the events to which it refers. In other words, the media may fail to clarify the meaning of each new instance of brutality they cover. As reporter Meg Greenfield recently lamented, an overuse of these verbal cues blunts meaning: "it hides it, blurs it, or at least makes it remote by several degrees from immediacy and truth."[9]

This is vividly seen in the recycling of two terms most directly associated with atrocity—*Holocaust* and *genocide*. The term *Holocaust* has been widely overused, to the point that it no longer displays a direct link with the events that originally thrust it into the public eye. Now invoked "by people who want to draw public attention to human-rights abuses, social inequalities suffered by racial and ethnic minorities and women, environmental disasters, AIDS, and a whole host of other things," the word "has become flattened [so that] any evil that befalls anyone anywhere becomes a Holocaust." The word *Holocaust* describes arguments for and against issues as wide-ranging as free speech, arms sales, and activities against terrorism. In a sense, then, the failure to invoke lexical choices to describe atrocity is forcing an emptying of the original term.[10]

Similarly, the term *genocide*—originally used in 1944 and defined by the

United Nations Genocide Convention as acts carried out "with a specific intent to destroy in whole or part a national, ethnic, racial, or religious group"—is regularly used to describe an array of barbaric acts. It is invoked both for the systematic wholesale slaughter of nations or ethnic groups and less generalized cases of brutality, such as those associated with Sri Lanka, Nigeria, and Tibet. Accusations of genocide are leveled too at circumstances even more far-reaching, such as the cry of African-Americans over a rising murder rate among teens and the lamentations of Panama's Manuel Noriega concerning the U.S. invasion of his country. Paradoxically, genocide is so powerful a label that sometimes considerable action is taken to avoid its use. U.S. officials at first refused to append *genocide* to Rwandan barbarism, so as "to avoid the rise of moral pressure to stop the mass killing."[11]

Subtle lexical changes—such as the transformation of *Holocaust* to *holocaust* and of *genocide* to *genocidal*—further flatten the term's original referent. The term *final solution* became a plural reference—as in *final solutions*—to signify the barbarism of regimes as wide-ranging as those of Pol Pot and Papa Doc. The term *ethnic cleansing*—which lost its quotation marks in the early 1990s—was used in discussions of the Balkans to denote the "mass expulsion of population from coveted areas by the deliberate use of terror" and later applied to clashes in Burundi and Rwanda.[12]

It is thus no surprise that at times the need to contextualize horror promotes curious lexical choices: the *London Times* pronounced the Rwandan atrocities "the worst atrocities taking place in the world *today*" (emphasis added), while the *Washington Post* selected the misnomer "Double Genocide" to refer to mass killings in Burundi. In each case, the media give meaning to new instances of horror by contextualizing them against earlier brutality. Yet in so doing, they flatten the complexity of the original event and create a macabre continuum of barbaric acts that both mainstreams atrocity and shocks much of the public into stupefied inaction. In the *Washington Post*'s view, at each "new ethnic eruption, the cry of 'never again'—never another uncontested genocide—rings weaker."[13] All of this suggests that the act of bearing witness may no longer compel responsibility.

Visual Cues of Atrocity

The role of photographs in helping the public remember to forget is crucial. To begin with, the ongoing display of visual evidence of atrocity is undoing the popular premise that depiction promotes response. The role photographs might have played in creating a responsive public in the past has been discussed in conjunction with far-ranging brutality in the Korean War, the Stalinist regime, and the Armenian genocide.[14] In each case, the assumption has been that a lack of depiction promoted a lack of response.

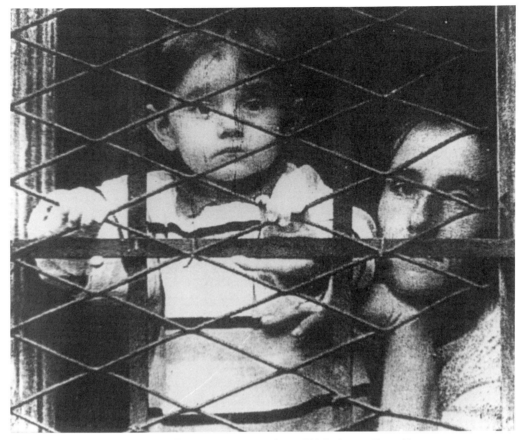

Figure 44. Child behind barbed wire, *London Times,* July 9, 1993, by Agence France Presse.

The most recent transformation in the act of bearing witness, however, may challenge that assumption. Why, for instance, has there been insufficient response surrounding atrocities that *were* visually depicted, such as Rwanda or Bosnia? That photographic depiction suggests that even had the world known of atrocities under Stalin or Armenia, it may not have acted differently, testament to much of the world's helplessness and inaction in the face of horror. In Susan Sontag's view, "the genocide of the Bosnian people has taken place in the glare of worldwide press and TV coverage. No one can plead ignorance of the atrocities." Or, as experts commented recently on PBS's *MacNeil-Lehrer NewsHour,* had CNN's cameras been able to show the plight of German Jews in the 1930s, "instant TV images would not have changed the course of history then, as they have failed to do today."[15] Recognition, then, may not move us to respond

Figure 45. Cambodian woman and skulls, *New York Times,* May 27, 1996, by *New York Times* Permissions.

so much as to forget, and bearing witness is undoing the public's ability to respond at all.

Part of the nature of contemporary response has to do with the eerie familiarity of contemporary atrocity photos. Some show agonized faces behind barbed wire, as in the *London Times*'s depiction of a wide-eyed visage of one child in the Balkans (fig. 44). Captioned "Bleak Outlook," the photo pictured the child alongside her mother, both of them clutching what appeared to be barbed wire but what was in fact a safety netting strewn across a window. Others show stacks of skulls and body parts, as in the *New York Times*'s portrayal of a Cambodian woman and an enormous mound of human skulls (fig. 45). The woman, situated in the right-hand corner of the shot, looked away from the skulls yet pointed readers back to them. Yet others display pits of human carnage (fig. 46). One such shot in the *Economist* portrayed Rwandan civilians staked alongside a pit of human corpses, in much the same way as civilians had been portrayed around the rim of open graves in Belsen.

In each case, the photos depict moments of agony that

> extort the maximum concern [but] are discontinuous with all other moments. They exist by themselves. The reader who has been arrested by the photograph may tend to feel this discontinuity as his own personal moral inadequacy. And as soon as this happens even his

At the end of the road

Figure 46. Rwandan dead, *The Economist,* July 23, 1994, by Corrine
Dufka/Reuters/Archive Photos.

sense of shock is dispersed. [The atrocity behind the image is] effectively depoliticized. The picture becomes the evidence of the general human condition. It accuses nobody and everybody.[16]

While picturing atrocity creates an opportunity for bearing witness to
atrocity, it also molds the kind of witnessing that takes place. Over the past
fifty years depictions of horror have moved from a variegated array of representations, as experienced in 1945, to overused icons of atrocity. The initial visual repertoire for depicting the act of bearing witness, which pictured
varieties of witnessing practices, witnesses, and targets of witnessing, has
been narrowed to a meager selection of repeatable stock shots. Like their
predecessors, photos of contemporary atrocity are presented in ways that
facilitate little knowledge about what is being depicted—with little relation
to the accompanying texts, little or no credits, and captions that play up a
generalized aura of horror over the specific instance of violence. But unlike
their predecessors, they refill an insatiable category of atrocity, a standard
against which new cases of mass slaughter can be judged, evaluated, and

made sensical. And it is here that the atrocity photos of earlier decades come into play.

The photos of Nazi atrocity—of survivors, victims, courtyard horror, accoutrements of terror, and witnesses—have all resurfaced in depictions of East Timor, Cambodia, Bosnia, and Rwanda, where they count as evidence of the more recent brutality. While the Holocaust was not the first case of genocide and mass slaughter, it has become the archetypal case, facilitating the replay of the lingering images of Nazi brutality in depicting contemporary atrocity. As the *London Times* recently observed in an article about Bosnia:

> Something about the scene seems terribly familiar when you stroll through Sarajevo in a misty twilight. The shattered central European facades, the charred innards of officers spilling into the street, the mangled buses, the sandbags and sniper barriers are of course the decor of [images] from the Second World War.[17]

Our memory bank of atrocities thus works backward in time—using the past to stand in for the present. Ultimately it reaches the first major killing fields to have been extensively and elaborately depicted in photos in the daily press—the concentration camps of World War II—and it is those killing fields that are replayed in discussions of contemporary atrocity.

This act of bearing witness has a peculiar shape vis-à-vis the atrocities it brings us. The shared memory of atrocities rests—in clear, vivid detail—in the scrapbooks of atrocity photos from other eras. The atrocity photos of World War II thus constitute an initial mental step to appropriating the killing fields of today. Those first atrocity photos remain the starting point, standard, and background for depicting contemporary atrocity in its many forms around the globe. It is thus no surprise that the atrocities of 1945 are now positioned as only "one stage of development in the history of genocide and not in any way its epilogue."[18] The popular assumption is that atrocity today just comes in bigger, more sophisticated, and increasingly outrageous forms, and seeing it facilitates habituation, an habituation entrenched on moral, political, and technological grounds.

THE PAST IN THE PRESENT:
THE CHANGING ACT OF BEARING WITNESS

This book has shown how the backward and forward temporal movement of vessels of collective memory produces a variety of messages about both the past and present. Often this occurs with little predictability about where a given marker will resurface, which kind of event it will illustrate, or which association will emerge as a resonant cue for bringing the past into the present. The linkage between vehicles of memory and events of the past instead follows somewhat unpredictable pathways back into the present, bearing different meanings and sets of associations. And even though we probably today have more tools and devices for retaining images than ever before, the result does not always display fidelity to the events being depicted. For with our powerful capacity to visualize the past comes a cogent ability to entertain not one but many agendas in its representation. Authoritatively documenting the visual past becomes instead an endangered resource, captured in what Susan Sontag called "neat slices of time" that bear no predictable relevance, proximity, or congruence to the larger context or picture from which they have been excised.[19] No wonder, then, that much of the enlightened world remains helpless and overwhelmed when faced with the evidence of barbarism against others.

The vacant nature of contemporary acts of bearing witness has been facilitated by changing perceptions about how we think of war, shifting with notions about what it means to bear witness. War has gone largely from being seen as a glorious and heroic pursuit to an unpleasant and even unnecessary task, and with the changing perception of war come new standards for visualizing atrocity. On the one hand, we have been told repeatedly how extensive the visualization of contemporary atrocity has been. "Shocking images from Bosnia put pressure on Bush to decide what America should do," said *Newsweek* in 1992. "Pictures sear the conscience of the world." Or, as *Time* phrased it, "the cruelty captured in powerful pictures of dead children and imprisoned adults succeeded in arousing moral outrage."[20]

But did it? To begin with, the burst of depictions surrounding the atrocities of World War II has not been reproduced in more recent atrocities. In range of representation, explicitness of representation, number of photos, display of photos, and prominence of photos, the uneven repository of contemporary atrocity photos shows us far less of the ravages of war on civilians than we saw fifty-odd years ago. As George Rodger, who captured the horror of Belsen, declared, "the world must know the pits of such depravity to ensure that they are never descended to again." Yet, in his view, "the world has not seen to it. From Indonesia to the former Soviet Union, from Latin America to Africa, genocide has persisted with similar ferocity and depravity."[21]

In some cases, the visual representation of atrocity has been slight. For instance, two recent wars—the Falklands War and the Persian Gulf War—offered the British and U.S. publics cleansed depictions of antiseptic warfare with virtually no depiction of atrocity. The Falklands War's depiction totaled a meager two hundred individual shots, while the photos of both

British dead and nearly two thousand Argentine casualties were simply absent from the record: the war remained "unbelievably clean," raising hypothetical questions about the effects of shocking photos because "there was none to be seen. . . . The absence of the lurid war let in the illusion of a clean war."[22] Similarly, the scarcity of photographs in the 1991 Persian Gulf War called into question the conflict's reportage. Sparse visual depictions favored shots of combat activity that overstated the technology and presence of U.S. military personnel and underplayed human suffering; even on CNN, the cable-driven camera shots that tracked the doors of bombed-out buildings with no depiction of the damage outside offered a peculiar visual construction of the war's brutality. Thus, it is no surprise that years later we have not yet seen the still photographs that faithfully recorded the atrocities caused by that war. It remained a war "censored into invisibility, void of images of real violence and suffering."[23] While this may have much to do with both the changing nature of photography, the difference between then and now should give pause.

In other situations, the visual representation of atrocity has been subject to debate, facilitated by changes in image-making technologies. The progressive advent of television, cable, computer graphics, and fiber optics has changed the technical grounds for bearing witness, creating an image-conscious culture that, in media critic Kiku Adatto's words, overattends to the "artifice of the image: our culture blurs the distinction between realism and artifice almost to the vanishing point."[24] While that might pose important questions for all events, in the act of bearing witness it raises moral questions of the first order—not only for those whose tragedies are depicted but for the world that proclaims itself a witness to their pain. For if not to show the authentic pain of those beyond immediate reach, what *is* the value of the media's presentations of atrocity? And if not to take responsibility for what it sees, why *does* the world continue to bear witness to that pain? In other words, what does the act of bearing witness accomplish in the contemporary age? What role does the photographic depiction of atrocity fill, if not to stop atrocity from recurring?

This book argues that photography may function most directly to achieve what it ought to have stifled—atrocity's normalization. It may be that the act of making people see is beginning to take the place of making people do, and that witnessing—even if it involves a narrowed representation of atrocity and little real response—is becoming the *acte imaginaire* of the twentieth century. In fact, the contemporary hollowness of bearing witness may not be a new phenomenon. Nearly half a century ago sociologists Paul Lazarsfeld and Robert Merton warned of what they called "narcotization," cautioning that people would become so overwhelmed with information that they would no longer be able to act. Although they spoke then of political campaigns, their words today ring true about all modes of information relay. In 1994, when ABC's *Nightline* looked closely at the parallels between Bosnia and the Holocaust, two of the three "expert" guests admitted that they did not sufficiently understand the nuances of the barbarism occurring in the former Yugoslavia. As one TV critic asked mournfully, "is it possible that the more we watch, the less we know?"[25]

Such words ring particularly true in atrocity's visual depiction, where the photograph's concomitant qualities of truthfulness, verisimilitude, and a sense of "having been there" define its shape in the public imagination. In some cases, viewing images may now stand in for action itself, raising crucial questions about the shape of public response in the contemporary era. Bearing witness, then, may have turned into an act carved out of the shadows of habituation, a mere outline of the call for substantive action that it seems to have played at the end of World War II. It is within such a scenario that the lingering effect of atrocity photos makes sense. For the photos—as powerful vehicles of memory about atrocities—reconfigure what is seen versus what is remembered. Their overuse may create a situation in which much of the public is content *not* to see—looking so as not to see, and remembering so as to forget.

HAVING MORE BUT SEEING LESS:
HABITUATION AND THE DEPICTION OF ATROCITY

As the technologies for depicting mass atrocity have become increasingly available, the emphasis on seeing as a sufficient response to atrocity threatens to loom larger. We live in a minefield of atrocity representations, which blur the temporal and spatial playing fields of memory. In technologies like CNN's twenty-four-hour-a-day video camera and cable-driven images or devices of relay like slow motion, freeze frames, and instant replays, moments are temporally frozen into still photographs, giving us an extensive technical capacity to see more.[26]

Yet many of us may end up "seeing" less. Technological, political, and moral issues all dull the linkage between what we see and what we attend to. In such a scenario, the media contribute

> to the breakdown of the barriers of citizenship, religion, race, and geography that once divided our moral space into those we were responsible for and those who were beyond our ken. . . . It makes us voyeurs of the suffering of others, tourists amidst their landscapes of anguish. It brings us face to face with their fate, while obscuring the distances—social, economic, moral—that lie between us.[27]

Seeing less thus comes from a fundamental ambivalence about the degree to which we are willing today to regularly confront visual depictions of atrocity.

Technological Habituation: The Diminished Truth-Value of the Photograph

Responding to atrocity through the lens of habituation appears to have many origins. While the initial response to depictions of atrocity traditionally was one of disbelief, that disbelief was shaped in conjunction with prevailing sentiments about the truth-value of photographs at the time. The changing nature of photographic representation—and its changing importance in our culture—were uppermost here. For instance, the public response to the graphic photos of the My Lai atrocities in 1969—which showed frontal views of a massacre of Vietnamese men, women, and children lying dead on a dirt road—differed from that accorded the atrocity photos of World War II. At first people stridently protested their publication and accused those who printed them of being unpatriotic. "Enormous numbers of people simply refused to believe any of the reports, including the photographs. . . . Some believed that the press had exaggerated the whole thing." Only substantially later, after the photos continued to appear, did "editors and readers [begin] to feel reasonably convinced that the episode had occurred at all." While the atrocity images eventually became so powerful that they helped plant public doubt about the U.S. war effort in Southeast Asia, it took time. In other words, the citizenry of the late sixties was far from being persuaded of atrocity in the manner that had greeted the photos of World War II. In critic Vicki Goldberg's view, this was because in the earlier era

> people had still been fully convinced by photographs. Although distrust of written accounts had long been rampant, trust in the camera was then intact. In the twenty-four years since the war, and particularly in the 1960s, television, world events, and the American administration had changed the climate of belief.[28]

That difference may be even more pronounced today.

The popular notion has it that as images became increasingly sophisticated, their power grew, shrinking, in George Steiner's words, the "world of words."[29] This book suggests that the opposite may be the case. As images become more complex and multimediated, their truth-value is communicated in configurations that allow us to see less: in some cases it dissipates; in others it is reconfigured; in still others it completely disappears. Pro-

claimed vehicles by which we bear witness to events of the present and past, images in some cases become deceptively ambivalent, communicating contradictory messages about their ability to replicate slices of reality and their ability to aggressively reconstruct it, often to the point of fabrication.

This has various effects on the public status of photographic representation. Some critics argue that "seeing and believing have come unglued" in the contemporary age: today much of the public no longer accepts photography's truth-value and instead recognizes alternatives to photographic truth facilitated by retouching, cropping, montage, setup, and collage. In that light, the *London Times* recently noted about Somalia that the "camera may not lie, but by concentrating on Mogadishu, it has given American viewers a highly disoriented picture of the truth." Similarly, in discussing Bosnia, British foreign secretary Douglas Hurd commented that "the camera is an actor. Cameras provoke their subjects to perform differently." In fact, Hurd's comments underscore the camera's ability to intervene in the depiction of unfolding atrocities.[30]

Regardless of the degree to which publics are knowledgeable about photography's workings, the ability to capitalize on the photograph's truth-value for different aims makes it easier to move beyond the simple photographic authentication of a real-life event. Thus, in Vietnam, where capitalizing on the image's assumed truth-value was a crucial part of challenging the administration, atrocity photos and the act of bearing witness took a turn once photographs appeared of a naked napalmed Vietnamese girl running down a road in the South Vietnamese village of Trabang. The still photograph, taken by Associated Press photographer Nick Ut, appeared on both ABC and NBC News on June 8, 1972; the next day it was spread across four and five columns of the front pages of the *Washington Post,* the *New York Times,* and the *London Times,* eventually becoming "the last major icon of the [antiwar] movement." Similarly, Eddie Adams's photograph of General Loan, the South Vietnamese chief of police, became an iconic critical representation of the atrocities of Vietnam at the moment that he executed an anonymous Vietcong prisoner. In both cases, authentication had little to do with official aims.[31]

This does not mean that the truth-telling aura of the photographic image in news is disappearing. Truth-value—and its concomitant traits of denotation, referentiality, and indexicality—persists even in cases that question the authenticity of the depicted object. And regardless of the numerous possible reasons to distrust photography, the fundamental belief in photographic images as visual corollaries of news remains. But the near-automatic force of the image has not persisted. As one critic maintained, it's hard to think of recent images that had as large an international impact, even as large a national impact, as the pictures of Birmingham, Dachau, or General Loan's curbside execution. . . . There is no single photograph that has become common mental property, no lone image or sequence that summarizes the Nicaraguan conflict, the Palestinian uprising, or the breakup of the Berlin Wall.

Today, many contemporary discussions of photography admit some notion of its protractability and constructed nature, an admission that may generate doubts about the role of image as authenticator. Some critics argue that the looming issue may be "what will be believed once a wide public is convinced that photographs are no longer a reliable means of communication." To quote critic Fred Ritchin, "photography's relationship with reality is as tenuous as that of any other medium. . . . It constitutes a rich and variegated language, capable, like other languages, of subtlety, ambiguity, revelation, and distortion."[32] If this is so, then the events which we have remembered in conjunction with that technology may be rearranged in accordance with the more tentative appraisals through which we understand the technology itself.

Political Habituation: The Diminished Political Mandate to See Atrocities

Another reason for the response of habituation toward contemporary atrocities has to do with the failure to mandate more recent atrocities to be seen as politically important. While restrictions on the presence of journalists and photographers in areas where acts of brutality are taking place have some relevance, political habituation has much to do with an official ambivalence about mandating which events can and will be seen. As *Newsweek* noted, the misleading frame of one often-invoked political argument—the "either-or" scenario that promises military involvement or nothing—supports a "convenient fiction" that military action is "the only alternative to the politically and militarily pitiful way in which the Western nations as a group, along with much of the rest of the world, have up till now reacted."[33] This may render photographs of many atrocities unnecessary due to the fact that they lack corresponding political aims.

This does not mean that political authorities have demanded that certain atrocities be shown. In some cases, the opposite has occurred. For instance, following media criticism over British policy in Bosnia, British foreign secretary Douglas Hurd accused the media of "tunnel vision"—of "distorting foreign policy-making by focusing public attention on conflicts such as Bosnia at the expense of less accessible tragedies just as harrowing, such as

Sudan and Liberia." Arguing that media coverage did not operate "with the even and regular sweep of a lighthouse," Hurd contended that organizational and practical concerns—such as getting reporters to the coverage site or finding the money and technology to beam the reports back to London—played a large part in determining which atrocity went under the "searchlight of media coverage."[34]

That lack of attention describes atrocities in both Cambodia and East Timor, neither of which received extensive photographic coverage. Despite the hundreds of thousands of lost lives, neither set of atrocities commanded media attention. East Timor—which lost two hundred thousand persons, or one-third of its population, when Indonesia invaded in the midseventies—was called the "untelevised terror," while the atrocities that killed over one million Cambodians by the Khmer Rouge between 1975 and 1978 were then labeled "the most thorough instance of genocide" but were "no longer front page news" by the nineties. Two decades later, the *Nation* lamented the continuation of atrocities in that country, reducing them to the title of "Killing Fields II."[35]

In keeping with the media's efforts to classify atrocities with other accounts of barbarism, it is no surprise that the attention to atrocity has had much to do with which atrocities elsewhere simultaneously demanded public attention. Because atrocity's depiction works by a substitutional rule, with each new instance of atrocity taking the place of preceding atrocities, publics have been able to absorb only small doses of the story. In that light, the *New Statesman and Society* lamented the fact that "while Bosnia bleeds to death with cameras and phones standing by, Cambodia's unfashionable demise is not news; clearly, the end must come before the headlines return." Lack of coverage similarly characterized atrocities in East Timor, when the Timorese deaths went largely unnoticed until the early 1990s, once an additional one hundred East Timorese were gunned down in the early 1990s in full view of Western reporters. Yet even then, televisual and photographic coverage of the event made little impact. When photos did address both atrocities, they followed predictable lines, such as the *Economist*'s shot of a Cambodian boy clutching himself in agony, under unaccredited captions posing rhetorical questions like "Does Anybody Care?" There was virtually no referential detailing appended to the photographs.[36]

Yet the coverage was aptly contextualized, if not reported or photographed fully, and the parallel with the Holocaust offered the most compelling context: Khmer Rouge leader Pol Pot was labelled a reincarnation of Adolf Hitler, with names like "Asia's Hitler" or "Adolf Hitler revisited." The crimes of the Khmer Rouge were called the "worst to have occurred anywhere in the world since Nazism." Indonesia's Suharto was labeled one of a "network of thugs with Hitlerian tendencies." Photos reproduced a narrowed but familiar World War II atrocity aesthetic: groups of victims and survivors, shots of the killing fields, guards keeping watch over Cambodian refugees. While no sanctioned or mandated act made it necessary to view either the atrocities of Cambodia or East Timor, the Holocaust's invocation as a background for both instances created an ability to bear witness even in the highly truncated versions. [37]

Thus, the fact that bearing witness continues to be an action of choice today for publics may obscure the possibility that it now offers only the barest contour of political involvement. Rather than prod us on to action, public discourse splits open with "euphemisms, sophistry and avoidance" that call for little more than "self-involved and self-deceiving busywork." As columnist Meg Greenfield wrote in 1993,

> You'd think that with only a few years left to go in this genocidal century, we'd at least by now have figured out some rudimentary way to confirm the recurring horror. But we haven't. We have only gotten better—more subtle—at looking the other way. [38]

Moral Habituation:
The Diminished Moral Need to See Atrocities

A third reason for the habituation toward atrocity may have the most far-reaching effect: people may feel so helpless from seeing repetitive shots of horror that they do not want to see more than they are already seeing. "Even without looking," said an editorial about Rwanda in the *Washington Post,* "we know what is going on there." The "resistance to atrocities" partly derives from the fact that we gain comfort the less that we see, suffering from what Anthony Lewis called "compassion fatigue." Reports of new atrocities—in Cambodia, East Timor, Rwanda, Somalia, Bosnia—bring on a sense of moral resignation, of knowing that it is happening again yet feeling powerless to act. And given the additional variables that may complicate our ability to "see"—such as racism, prejudice, and indifference toward atrocities in certain parts of the world—the lack of response implicit in habituation can become a default reaction. As the *Christian Science Monitor* said in an editorial about the Bosnian carnage,

> In a century where as many as 167 million people died in two world wars, over a hundred lesser wars, and the final solutions and cultural revolutions of Hitler, Stalin, Mao Zedong, Pol Pot, Saddam Hussein—not to mention all the Shining Paths and Papa

Docs—one more atrocity may seem like just an angry echo as the century ends.

There may be, then, a shutoff point, a point at which even photographs no longer matter. As the *Washington Post* commented on Rwanda, "at first the world was riveted to scenes of carnage. . . . At a certain point, however, the eyes of the world closed, the cameras clicked off. . . . the capacity to absorb such a living nightmare shut down."[39]

It is no surprise, then, that unlike the 1940s, today we tend to disagree about how atrocity photos should be displayed or even about the place that they should take in public discourse. Graphic images of death and suffering in Somalia initially produced claims of yellow journalism, protests that they upset family sanctity, and a recognition of their limited strategic usefulness; consequently, the images were limited in what they depicted. In the midnineties, the *Philadelphia Inquirer's* depictions of the execution of a Liberian man drew over 250 letters of complaint and prompted an ombudsman's column apologizing for the picture's display. In August 1995, a California newspaper drew protest over its decision to publish a front-page color image of a woman who had hanged herself in war-torn Bosnia, with readers complaining that the photo forced unwanted public discussion of the atrocities. Other newspapers, magazines, and journals, perhaps anticipating protest, displayed the same image more gently: the *New York Times* printed it in black and white only on an interior page, while the *Washington Post* did not use the photograph but ran a front-page story describing it. Each case markedly contrasted with the circumstances of 1945.

Even when associated with terrorist actions, atrocity is visualized in a tepid fashion that does not match the World War II depictions. When a Pan Am jet blew up over Lockerbie, Scotland, in 1988, the U.S. and British press showed "a gap between the written and pictorial records. The photos of corpses that were published either were taken from a distance or showed them draped and flagged by the police." Yet reporters described "shattered bodies," "scraps of flesh," and "mangled remains," none of which was depicted by the images. Similarly, when a Hamas terrorist blew himself up alongside a Tel Aviv shopping center in March 1996, the words recorded the grisly details of burial-society members gathering the remains of shattered bodies. But the pictures were another matter. Though graphic photos were readily available, the media opted to carefully publish only contained images of human carnage. For instance, the *Philadelphia Inquirer* displayed one front-page photo of the commercial square filled with dead and wounded but appended an explanation of its decision to publish:

Though images of such graphic violence will be disturbing to some readers, the *Inquirer,* after careful consideration, decided to publish the photograph on the front page because it so powerfully illustrates the misery and the waste of human life that have resulted from the campaign of terrorist bombings in Israel.

One week later, the newspaper's ombudsman justified the display yet again, proclaiming that the photo's sensitive nature had signaled a change in editorial policy, by which the *Inquirer* would routinely explain its decision-making process to readers.[40]

In part, moral habituation may have to do with an inability to develop representational forms in news that nourish moral response. In fact, there seems to be a growing capacity for absorbing pictures of atrocity in Hollywood films, such as *The Killing Fields, Schindler's List, Apocalypse Now,* and *Full Metal Jacket,* that in some ways provide a more explicit depiction of atrocity than does the news. In that vein, one recent discussion of the Bosnian atrocities even maintained that they resembled "less the black and white flashback over half a century [and] more a screenplay from all those films of the post-nuclear apocalypse."[41]

THE BACKDROP OF MEMORY:
THE HOLOCAUST IN CONTEMPORARY ATROCITY

This book has suggested that photographs can prolong the memory of an event so powerfully that representation undoes the ability to respond. Such has been the case with the atrocity photos of World War II. Their recycled appearances in the discussion of contemporary atrocities constitute a backdrop for depiction that neutralizes much of the potential response to other ravages against humanity. While the surfacing of the atrocity photos fits well with the ongoing political instrumentalization of the Holocaust in both the United States and Britain, each new invocation raises an old question in new forms: how is it possible to extrapolate from the Holocaust beyond the event itself? For the images of Nazi atrocities are invoked not only within the boundaries of Holocaust discourse but in the representation of other atrocities. Holocaust images have turned up in the art installations of Leon Golub on Vietnam, Yigael Tumarkin on Israel, and Antonio Antunes Moreira on Lebanon, who in 1982 turned the famous boy from the Warsaw ghetto into a kaffiyehed Palestinian. In *Time's* view, the linkage between images of then and images of now is so clear that the temporal bridge is becoming void of significance, overdrawn by the "ghastly images in newspapers and on television screens [that] conjure up [the] discomfiting memory" of Nazi atrocity.[42]

Editorial and Op-Ed pages, 12-13
Education Advertising
Careers in Education and
Health Care Employment

The New York Times

Sunday, January 14, 1996

Week in Review

Section **4**

Never Again, Again

After the Peace, the War Against Memory

Figure 47. Trnpolje Camp, Bosnia, Yugoslavia, *New York Times,* January 14, 1996, by Ron Haviv/Saba.

The Holocaust cues atrocity memory in three ways—through the words that guide us through the images, through parallels in the images, and through a pattern of substitutional representation. The words surrounding the image traditionally contextualize new atrocities with the Holocaust, just as words were used to broaden a depicted act of barbarism in World War II into a larger story of Nazi atrocity. In that light, in discussing the atrocities in Vietnam during the late 1960s, the *New York Times* recalled that the Vietnamese atrocities were contrasted with "one of the most awful visual images . . . that of a storm-trooper leading a child who could barely walk into the gas chambers." The Bosnian concentration camp of Omarska, presented in photos in numerous newspapers and journals, was labeled "Belsen 1992." A headline in the *New York Times* captioned a large picture of Bosnian prisoners, "Never Again, Again" (fig. 47). Here was the familiar Holocaust aesthetic—the gaunt, malnourished faces of two male, unclothed figures, looking into the camera's lens [43]

A second way of cuing memory through Holocaust photos is through parallels in the image itself. In such cases, Holocaust photos linger by virtue of their repeated aesthetic, even when they are not represented. The

THE KILLING FIELDS
Above left, the suspiciously level and rectangular
clearing in the woods near a livestock farm outside
Brcko. Witnesses say it contains a mass grave.
The spot closely matches the location of this
macabre pit of corpses photographed in 1992

Figure 48. "Unearthing Evil," *Time,* January 29, 1996, by AP/Wide World Photos.

Before Rwanda, Before Bosnia

Waiting for Justice in Cambodia

On the killing fields, more than a million were left dead. Newer estimates are approaching two million.

Figure 49. Cambodian skulls, *New York Times,* February 25, 1996, by SIPA.

emaciated bodies alongside barbed wire, vacant gazes of survivors who stare directly into the camera, and neatly stacked corpses and skulls underscore atrocity in its most contemporary form. As *Time* put it,

> the shock of recognition is acute. Skeletal figures behind barbed wire. Murdered babies in a bus. Two and a half million people driven from their homes in an orgy of "ethnic cleansing." Detention camps, maybe even concentration camps. Surely these pictures . . . come from another time.

Corpses are depicted in ways that range from pits of bodies on Balkan livestock farms to macabre displays of tidily arranged Cambodian skulls (figs. 48 and 49).[44] These photos—one from the Balkans and one from Cambo-

Figure 50. UN envoy in Srebenica, *New York Times,* April 7, 1996, by *New York Times* Permissions; Reuters/Archive Photos.

dia—respectively recalled the open graves of Bergen-Belsen and the neatly stacked corpses of Buchenwald.

What is missing from these representations suggests much about the contemporary form of bearing witness. These recent photos lack the nuances and complications of earlier representations to such an extent that in none of the recent atrocities do publics see the extent of horror displayed in the 1940s. Gone from these more recent depictions are the number of photos displayed in World War II, the primacy of the photos, and the constant discussion of the photos—in both the press and the professional literature. Gone is the variety in the targets of witnessing, types of witnesses, and types of witnessing activity. Also gone are the depictions of witnesses looking at evidence of atrocities, such as photos, and at evidence beyond the frame of the camera. Equally important, gone in large part are the collectivities who were earlier shown bearing witness to atrocity. They have generally been replaced by individuals, such as the *New York Times*'s depiction of a UN official overlooking newly excavated corpses in Bosnia (fig. 50). In this picture, unlike the collectives who bore witness in earlier days, here a lone figure is shown scrutinizing skulls. The individual bearing witness overlooks the evidence of atrocities in much the same way that col-

Figure 51. "Watching for a Judgment of Real Evil," *New York Times,* November 12, 1995, by David Van Der Veen / *New York Times* Permissions.

lectives—groups of congressional representatives, government officials, and journalists—did during the 1940s: the aesthetic is thereby reproduced but without the insistence on collective action that was implicit in depictions of the earlier era.[45]

In the third case, the Holocaust photos actually replace the depictions of contemporary atrocities. In these cases, the photo's iconic, conventionalized, and simplified nature collapses the distance between then and now, with substitutional representation extending the earlier disjunction between the place of text and the place of image beyond the event itself. Such was the case of the *New York Time's* discussion of Bosnian war crimes (fig. 51). The article on the Bosnian war crimes tribunal featured two photos: one a small image of one of the accused, the other, which stretched over half a page, the Nuremberg trials; the juxtaposition and unequal size of the two photos suggested visually how memory crowded out the ability to attend to the event. The article also proclaimed that "as Court TV prepares for its next 'trial of the century,' Nuremberg is the point of reference." Yet it is curious that that point of reference occupied a far larger visual portion of the page than did the corresponding picture of the Bosnian Serb about to go on trial. Elsewhere, images of Jews in the Warsaw ghetto illustrated a contemporary discussion of Bosnia, positioned alongside photos of a Serb execution of Muslims. Similarly, in May 1993 a Belgrade TV news report carried a graphic report of a Croat attack on a Serbian village in Bosnia. "The report," commented a correspondent for the *New Statesman and Society,* "was substantially true, but the reporter had omitted one detail. The massacre took place over 50 years ago, during the second world war."[46]

References to the images of the Nazi camps thus activate a memory bank that allows viewers to visualize contemporary acts of atrocity in conjunction with what they remember from the recycled images of World War II. The decision to leave hundreds of clothes-draped skeletons as a reminder of the barbarism that took place outside a Rwandan church was called by the *Economist* "a snapshot of terror" that connected the event with the public display of corpses during World War II. Other comparisons arose following the excavation of mass graves in Cambodia, where mounds of newly covered skulls and bones were piled on building ledges as reminders of the Khmer Rouge atrocities, touted as the Asian version of Holocaust memorials. Bearing witness to contemporary atrocity is thus being accomplished in part by bearing witness to Nazi barbarism.[47]

But in providing the visual category for depicting more recent acts of barbarism, the overuse of the photos may diminish the need to "see" more contemporary instances of brutality. The images provided long ago—on the killing fields of World War II—offer a context that undermines the events that it contextualizes. Our helplessness toward these more contemporary atrocities may thereby derive from our sense that we already know what they look like.

All of this suggests the degree to which habituation may be entrenched as the default response to atrocity. For as long as there is skepticism about the truth-value of the tools we depend on to bring us the news, as long as there is no political gain that mandates these more recent events to be more fully seen, and as long as we have no moral imperative that forces a linkage between depiction and action, habituation may remain the preferred response to atrocity. And the collective memories of the Holocaust may continue to persist as the backdrop of contemporary acts of barbarism.

This is problematic, for the collapse of distance between then and now is precarious, overused, and paradoxical. It is precarious because Holocaust memory lingers like the ground floor of a partially demolished building. The past cannot be cleared away, but neither can it be salvaged. It is overused because it reconfigures not only what we see versus what we remember but also what we remember of the events of yore versus what we need to see of the events of now. And it is paradoxical because our capacity for action may lie in an altered linkage with the Holocaust: we may need to remember it less so as to remember contemporary atrocities more. When recently considering the increasing atrocities in Burundi, the *New Yorker* sardonically observed, "the West remembers Rwanda, but does nothing."[48] The insistence on remembering earlier atrocities may not necessarily promote active responses to new instances of brutality. This book has argued that the opposite, in fact, may be true: we may remember earlier atrocities so as to forget the contemporary ones.

European Atrocities: The Holocaust in Bosnia

We can consider what we have seen in Bosnia. Parallels to the Holocaust here have been ongoing, offering numerous verbal and visual linkages between the events of the Balkans and the ravages of World War II. While the atrocities of World War II were not the only memory by which it was possible to make sense of Bosnia—its events, for instance, gave rise to frames as wide-ranging as the U.S. Civil War and Vietnam—the gross barbarism inflicted on civilians of the former Yugoslavia nonetheless made the Holocaust analogy particularly apt.

Although there were some cases of exemplary reporting, most coverage revealed neither the extent of the Balkan violence nor the scale and magnitude of its recurring barbarism. While by mid-1995 a UN tribunal on war crimes had collected over one thousand photographs documenting atrocities, few actually appeared in the media in either the United States or Britain. Atrocity coverage instead became what the *New York Times* called "the war that can't be seen," whose stories and pictures were "lost in the fog of second-hand reporting," and whose "journalists, almost without exception, [were] unable to get there." In comparison with the World War II atrocity photos, the pictures of Bosnia were troubling for their lack of detail. Thus, even when the United States released satellite photos in August 1995 suggesting that Bosnian Serbs had buried thousands of Bosnian Muslims in mass graves, visual evidence of the atrocities did not appear until much later.[49]

Photos that did appear adopted representational practices used with earlier atrocities—a lack of referential detailing in captions and texts, a lack of credits, a thrust to accommodate the broad story of atrocity rather than the contingent details of the photo. Most photos displayed the generic captions seen in earlier years, recounting people "Lost in Grief" and "Captives in Detention Camps." The *New Statesman and Society* featured a half-page unaccredited image of a dozen bodies covered in a blanket with the caption "Slaughter in Vukovar"; two shots of groups of refugees and prisoners were captioned simply "The Free and the Caged" in *Time;* one photograph depicting a man behind barbed wire was unilaterally presented to readers as "An Icon of Barbarism"; and photos were presented without captions, credits, or explanations.[50]

Not surprisingly, problems with documentation ensued, with the same atrocity pictures presented as evidence of both Serbian and Croatian barbarism. Captions described military personnel as Serbs when the insignia on their uniforms identified them as Croats; complaints centered on whether or not the malnourished detainees were Serbian tubercular patients arrested for looting. The *New York Times* accused television crews of staging an eerie visual replay of Holocaust photographs, by pleading for staged "bang bang pictures" from Bosnia commanders, and the media became so "mesmerized by [its] focus on Serb aggression and atrocities that many became incapable of studying or following up numerous episodes of horror and hostility against Serbs."[51]

Practices similar to those of World War II also persisted in accreditation and linking photos to texts. The vast majority of photos on Bosnia were unaccredited, even when the issue of veracity was raised. There was also considerable borrowing from other agents of documentation, such as Balkan photos that were frozen television stills. The *New York Times,* for instance, replayed photos that had appeared a full week earlier on ABC's *Nightline,* and the *Washington Post* reprinted an image of a grieving woman at her husband's funeral, taken from a photography exhibit at the U.S. Holocaust Memorial Museum. In linking photos to texts, the photos of Bosnia facilitated a symbolic interpretation of the event rather than depicted contingent details of the photo: a *New York Times* article about the difficulties of reportage was illustrated by an image of Serb soldiers, while the *New Statesman and Society* illustrated an article about the destruction of Bosnia with a photo of an identified man crouching and holding a rifle. Again, errors abounded: photos neglected to show dead Serbs or destroyed Serbian property.[52]

The media were more effective, however, in contextualizing these acts of carnage, and here the parallel with the Holocaust was unstintingly anchored in place. In words, the media countered the story of now with the story of then, reminding readers "that the clock has been turned back a half-century." "Fifty years after Hitler's fall," *Time* told its readers, "war crimes are being committed in the Balkans on a level reminiscent of Nazi Germany." The newly released survivors of Bosnian detention camps were described as "victims of Nazi concentration camps," the camps themselves "echoes of the Reich." The *Nation* observed that the warring sides were "running concentration camps along Nazi lines." In the *Washington Post*'s view, much of the "nightmare of killing, destruction, and forced exile . . . fosters unavoidable images of World War II," because the "horrors of the conflict in Bosnia recall the Nazi nightmare of a half-century ago." "The Holocaust analogy is too true," offered the *Los Angeles Times*. A 1993 report argued that fifty thousand Muslims had been herded "into a squalid area that evokes images of the ghetto in which the Nazis imprisoned Warsaw's Jews during World War II": the town of Mostar was headlined "a Warsaw Ghetto in Bosnia." By 1996, an account of the partition of Bosnia was labeled "The Double Anschluss." And readers were reminded that "the number of Muslims tortured, killed, and crudely buried near a once cheer-filled Bosnian soccer stadium doesn't compare in scale to the Holocaust." In each case, the absence of photos directed publics to familiar visual memories that are no longer required for depiction.[53]

When images did appear, the parallel was more subtle but potentially more powerful. The presentation of photos from Bosnia used the practices set in place in World War II, but without the repetitiveness, explicitness, number, prominence, and centrality that the earlier photos had merited. And while the photos' referential documentation was uneven, their contextualization with the Holocaust was overused.

The photographic aesthetic reproduced that of the earlier atrocity images in many ways. Already in mid-1992, pictures reproduced iconic shots of distraught women holding fearful children, imprisoned men behind barbed wire, and corpses strewn across the ground. Close-up shots of fearful and distressed women and children appeared frequently, with one of them—depicting weeping women in Bosnia—captioned "Out of the Past" (fig. 52). The grief-stricken women, one in tears, stared frontally beyond the camera's frame. Nothing in the shot identified the figures as contemporary. Images of the dead ranged from the corpses downed by snipers' bullets to the mass graves of hundreds of victims reduced to skeletons. The *Washington Post* ran pictures of Muslim men lying in cattle sheds, and the *London Times* showed grief-stricken women clutching their faces and men rolling water carts past burned building shells. As with the 1940s, children with wide and imploring eyes gazed at the photographers through barbed wire.[54]

Many shots connected readers with the photographer across the bodies of the dead. Lines of corpses depicted in the forefront of shots mimicked the aesthetic of World War II atrocity photos, and courtyard scenes of the dead and incarcerated in the Balkans reproduced the carnage of the World War II camp courtyards (fig. 53). In one shot from *Newsweek*, male prison-

Out of the past

Figure 52. Weeping women, *The Economist,* August 10, 1991.

ers lined up in rigid lines as they waited to have their heads shaved. The photo was captioned "The Casualties of War." Distressed women and children gazed at photographers, while gaunt men peered from behind barbed wire. In *Time,* pits of corpses on livestock farms outside the village of Brcko recalled the pits of the Belsen dead (see fig. 48, on p. 222).[55]

Sometimes actual Holocaust images set in place the visual context for contemporary photos. The *New York Times* showed Jews being lined up for execution in Poland of the 1940s in a piece on Serb executions of Muslims (fig. 54). The heading—"Does the World Still Recognize a Holocaust?"—juxtaposed photos of the 1940s alongside those that appeared half a century later, and the article was titled "Ever Again," a play on the Holocaust phrase "Never Again." A 1993 *Time* article on rape in Bosnia used a World War II photograph of what it said was a Jewish girl who had been raped in Poland. That photo's use, however, provoked over 750 readers' letters questioning the newsmagazine's identification of the girl; their intervention forced *Time* to conduct additional research into the photo, and it later concluded that "despite our best efforts, we have not been able to pin down exactly what situation the photograph portrays."[56]

ANDREE KAISER—SIPA

The casualties of war: Prisoners line up to have their heads shaved at Manjaca, a Serb-run detention center; mourner at a Muslim funeral

Figure 53. "The Casualties of War," *Newsweek,* August 17, 1992, by SIPA.

Figure 54. "Does the World Still Recognize a Holocaust?" *New York Times,* April 25, 1993, by *New York Times* Permissions; from the Archives of The Yivo Institute for Jewish Research; Bojan Srdjan/Reuters/Archive Photos.

Interestingly, there was considerable discussion of how much the pictures failed to change policy. U.S. and British publics were assumed to have seen evidence of the contemporary atrocities and to have noticed the historical parallels, with the events in Bosnia stirring "an agonizing echo of past horrors," as *New York Times* correspondent Leslie Gelb wrote. It is "as if we were given the chance to replay history and confront Hitler as his troops marched into the Rhineland in 1936—knowing all we now know—and once again simply scolded him and shrugged." But at some level, there was a recognition of the fact that seeing was not promoting sufficient action to stop the atrocities. The Balkans had become, in the *Economist*'s view, "a war that gets harder to watch." Particularly in Britain, where the conflict in Bosnia was called "Europe's first television war," the images did not have considerable impact: the "European public [seemed] eerily silent." As late as 1994, Europeans were criticized for ignoring the first major war on their continent since 1945: "The electronic images from Bosnia have yet to shake any European government to its foundations." Even the Srebenica death march, said to be the "worst massacre in Europe since the Nazi era," did not earn extensive photographic depiction. There was "an element of shame involved in merely *watching* such things happen." As one legislator asked unabashedly about the atrocities in Bosnia, "what still has to happen for us to finally decide no longer to just watch. . . . How can one just watch when people are slaughtered?"[57]

African Atrocities: The Holocaust in Rwanda and Burundi

Perhaps in no other contemporary instance of atrocity did the sense of "otherness" apply so brutally as in Rwanda and Burundi. Limitations on the depiction of African atrocities have flattened a story whose events produced parallel slaughters of Tutsis by Hutus in Rwanda and of Hutus by Tutsis in Burundi. Pictures of ravaged and agony-stricken men and women, slain corpses sprawled across the ground, and neat stacks of skulls and bones replenished the ongoing inventory of visual depictions of atrocity, but they did little to push the act of bearing witness beyond its default frame of habituation.[58]

Like that of Bosnia, coverage of Rwanda was uneven. It varied from stories offering a simplistic "tribal war" frame to serious and thoughtful reportage that appeared in certain journals. Here too, attempts to derail discussions of the atrocities were rampant. By not drawing the public into the economic and political ramifications of the story, and framing it instead as tribal warfare, the "media legitimated the sense that with people like these (you know: savages), nothing can be done." On the week after ten thousand people were killed in Rwanda, *Newsweek* devoted three pages to

Kurt Cobain's suicide and one to Rwanda: "the media [were] at a loss over what to report."Yet, as the *Progressive* noted, "there is a racism here so thorough, so naturalized, and so subtle, that it takes work to recognize it. It is a racism that justifies moral resignation."[59]

As with the atrocities in Bosnia, the pictures of Rwandan and Burundi brutality were presented with the same practices used in World War II. The same iconic and largely overdetermined images of barbarism resurfaced—maimed and bandaged children, group shots of survivors in cordoned-off areas, neat stacks of skulls and bones. Photos connected with the readers across the bodies of the dead, as in a tidy slew of Rwandan skulls that took up the shot's foreground (fig. 55). The background inclusion of the church in Ntarama, Rwanda, reminded readers of the mass killings that took place on the church's doorstep. Captions—either broadly framed, irrelevant, or missing altogether—upheld the symbolic dimension of the photos, as in "Nowhere to Run" and "Everyday Slaughter." The *Economist* labeled one photo of a dead body in a river "Deadly Water," while another showed an unidentified, uniformed man wielding a knife under the caption "On a Knife's Edge." One photo from the *London Times* was captioned, "Ugandan fishermen lining up Rwandan bodies for burial."The piece discussed the history of the region and had nothing to do with the depicted bodies in the photo—other than the more general atrocity story. Even the *Washington Post*'s one-page 1994 pictorial spread of images of Rwanda—which included eight photographs of horror under the collective title "Death Knows No Borders"—were titled generically with phrases such as "White Badges of Courage,""Final Refuge," and "Keeping Out the Cold."[60]

At times, there was no systematic attempt to accredit the photos that appeared. Photographs of Tutsi refugees in Rwanda and of Tutsi civilians had no credit in the *London Times*. Pictures of Rwandan refugees lacked both definitive captions and credits in the *Economist*. A photo of two bandaged sisters left for dead in a pile of corpses graced the front page of the *London Times* but bore no credit. Many of these pictures also bore no linkage whatsoever to the texts at their side. One photo showed a group of refugees huddling under a blanket for warmth, while the accompanying piece discussed a UN endeavor in the region. Images of bandaged child survivors of the atrocities illustrated articles about the implications of the atrocities in Rwanda and Burundi. In one *London Times* photo, Tutsi civilians peeked out from behind barbed wire in a refuge in the town of Kabgayi, yet the text conveyed in detail the account of a mother of six in Musha who had slaughtered her neighbor's children. Similarly, the *Washington Post,* in an article on Rwanda massacre figures, displayed a "man

BY MOLLY BINGHAM FOR THE WASHINGTON POST

This church in Ntarama, Rwanda, was the scene of the April 15, 1994, massacre of 2,500 Tutsis by Hutu militiamen who blasted their way inside.

Figure 55. Skulls in front of a church in Ntarama, Rwanda, *The Washington Post,* January 27, 1996. Photo by Molly Bingham, 1994.

who wanted to be identified only as Mudi" on his return to a devastated Kigali neighborhood. Many combined the atrocious with the mundane: a picture of a corpse, labeled as that of a schoolmaster, spread out below a map of Africa; another corpse was sprawled before a church entrance, underneath the spread-eagled arms of a statue of Christ.[61]

There were numerous complaints about the media's performance. The *London Times* reported that Rwandan refugees "grew tired of being told to wait in orderly lines for hours while being photographed by the world's press." Elsewhere, the same reporter noted that the "press thirsts for corpses, mutilations and misery and all can be provided." And one journal caustically observed that Nazi atrocity photos were replayed more effectively in certain contemporary instances of barbarism than in others. It is a "political fact that the sight of bone-thin men behind barbed wire in the Balkans, on the doorstep of the West, resonates more deeply with Americans than the many horrors of Asia and Africa."[62]

The atrocities in Rwanda and Burundi, however, merited more extensive coverage than did nearby acts of barbarism. For earlier atrocities in other parts of Africa—the ethnic war and starvation of Somalia or the relocation of refugees in Zaire—received even less mention. Yet in the former instance, the lingering memory of shots of the corpse of a U.S. serviceman being paraded through the Mogadishu streets and videotape of a frightened U.S. serviceman offered snapshot memories that made much of the U.S. viewing world turn away from the African savagery. A front-page story about Reuters correspondents who were killed by a Somali mob had similar effect. As the *London Times* said in an editorial, "news pictures showing the corpses of UN peacekeepers being trampled by jubilant, blood-hungry mobs of the people they are there to protect would have been almost unthinkable a few years ago."[63]

Against this lack of referential detailing, it is perhaps no surprise that the coverage of African atrocities did little to offset growing habituation among the U.S. and British publics. As the *Progressive* noted, "the media treated black Africa as a 'dark continent,' where nothing happens except coups, massacres, famines, disease, and drought." Such an agenda had meaning back home: "for when we ignore and dehumanize black people from Africa, it's easier to ignore and dehumanize them here."[64]

Yet here too, the media's efforts to contextualize the atrocities was ongoing, and the Holocaust's resurfacing in discussions of Rwanda and Burundi was vast. Discussions referenced Rwanda's own "Holocaust museum at its own Auschwitz." Machete-wielding villagers were said to be "like the Nazis." The *Washington Post* noted how "the heads and limbs of victims were sorted and piled neatly, a bone-chilling order in the midst of chaos

Figure 56. "Pall of Death," *Time,* June 13, 1994, © Newspix International.

that harked back to the Holocaust." And the epithet of "bodies stacked like cordwood"—a phrase relentlessly repeated following the liberation of the Nazi camps—resurfaced in discussions of Rwandan terror, specifically to describe the methodical piling of body parts in public spaces following that country's 1994 massacres.[65]

Photos of Rwanda and Burundi also reproduced the Holocaust aesthetic, where corpses spilled into the camera's lap (fig. 56). Under the caption "Pall of Death," *Time* portrayed a spread of human bodies that recalled the photos of 1945. Ugandan fishermen were depicted lining up Rwandan corpses for burial much like German townspeople had done with the victims of the concentration camps. Pictures of Rwandans walking among scores of dead corpses recalled the depictions of GIs stepping across hundreds of bodies at the massive courtyard at Nordhausen fifty years earlier. Angled pictures of long rows of Rwandan militiamen repeated the depiction of lines of captured Nazi guards, their heads averted from the camera. In one photo that surfaced frequently, the camera showed scores of dead clothed bodies sprawled across the foreground of a shot in eastern Rwan-

In Rwanda, tribunal is dragging along

More than two years after the slaughter, no trials have started. Many suspects are sought.

By Andrew Maykuth
INQUIRER STAFF WRITER

ARUSHA, Tanzania — George P. Challe is one of the few officials who is pleased that the United Nations International Tribunal for Rwanda is moving so slowly to put anyone on trial.

Challe is the jovial city manager for Arusha, a tourist center near the Kenyan border with eight gas stations and four-digit telephone numbers. It has undergone a boom since the United Nations chose to locate the tribunal here.

The United Nations has leased office space for four years, but it is widely assumed in Arusha that the tribunal may become a permanent fixture, providing a steadier cash flow than the seasonal tourists attracted by Mount Kilimanjaro and the Serengeti plains.

"With the hunt for criminals going very slowly, they could be here a long time," Challe said, smiling.

More than two years after half a million ethnic Tutsis and moderate Hutus were slaughtered largely by

The Philadelphia Inquirer / ANDREW MAYKUTH

Forensic anthropologist William D. Haglund, an investigator for the United Nations International Tribunal, looks at excavations in a Kigali junkyard where bodies were buried after tribal massacres.

Figure 57. Forensic anthropologist views bodies in Kigali, Rwanda, *Philadelphia Inquirer*, July 8, 1996, by Andrew Maykuth/ *The Philadelphia Inquirer.*

da; *Time* told its readers that it depicted "hundreds of corpses, victims of a massacre that took place in April." The shot, again reminiscent of the aesthetic of earlier photos from the courtyards of Nordhausen, showed lines of corpses stretching from the shot's foreground into its background. Yet other photos depicted neat lines of skulls that recalled the images from World War II: the church in Ntarama, where thousands of Tutsis had been massacred the previous spring, became an accoutrement of atrocity. In these pictures too, there were the familiar eyes of survivors: agonized faces stared straight into the camera from behind barbed-wire fences.[66]

Here too, there were depictions of the act of bearing witness. Sometimes the witnesses were UN soldiers. Individuals were shown in solemn acts of witnessing. A number of newspapers portrayed an individual U.S. forensic anthropologist staring at newly unearthed bones in both Kibuye and Kigali, Rwanda (fig. 57). These pictures placed him in the act of bearing witness to the Rwandan atrocities much like the official delegations that had toured the Nazi concentration camps half a century earlier. Officials viewed the skulls of victims, and readers connected with the witnesses above the remains of the dead, much as they had done in World War II. But as with Bosnia, these were largely individual acts of bearing witness. There were few or no depictions of collectives bearing witness; of witnessing without atrocity; or of bearing witness to photos.[67]

MEMORY THROUGH THE CAMERA'S EYE:
FROM THE PAST TO THE FUTURE

Visualizing atrocity lends perspective, positions boundaries, and concretizes standards of appropriate behavior in a so-called civilized world. This book has examined the ways in which images have kept those standards vivid. Photographs of atrocities are like tombstones: they create a visual space for the dead that anchors the larger flow of discourse about the events that motivated their death. Yet tombstones, like the cemeteries that house them, are significant only insofar as they merit attention from the living. Without memorial ceremonies, manicured lawns, flowers, and general practices of maintenance, tombstones—and the deaths that they mark—fade away.

Perhaps nowhere is this as evident as in the ongoing discourse—both verbal and visual—about atrocity. The unevenness of contemporary Western response to that discourse calls into question the viability of generating public action. The *New Republic* wrote in 1995 that "the United States seems to be taking a sabbatical from historical seriousness, blinding itself to genocide and its consequences, fleeing in the moral and practical imperatives of its own power." And columnist George Will pondered not long ago, "the West—what exactly does that noun now denote, given the non-response to genocidal aggression?" The resting place of discourse about atrocity is presently overshadowed by habituation, exacerbated over time and the fact that there may "never again be a time when self-extinction is beyond the reach of our species."[68]

This book has argued that photography has critically shaped our understanding of atrocity. And although we reside today in a culture infused with visual artifacts, the power of images is no longer one only of creation but of reconstitution. While our images of this past, the tools by which we remember, have become highly conventionalized and simplified, they are also much of what we have left. Photographs, said writer Lance Morrow, are "history's lasting visual impression. . . . But sometimes the power they possess is more than they deserve."[69]

All of which brings us back to the questions with which this book began: What is an image? What is a memory? And how do the two link together? In discussing Auschwitz, Holocaust scholar Jonathan Webber argued that "the past becomes present only through representation," for "we cannot know the past in any other way." He complained, however, that "all too often we ignore the medium of representation and assume that it gives us immediate and unmediated access to the past." Perhaps nowhere has this been as evident as with photography:

> photographs focus only on the visual, providing icons too one-dimensional to convey the reality properly: So-called "documentary" photos document only part of reality. But these images are what people remember. They know the photos, and they think they know everything. In a sense, photos really do represent the past, [but] . . . even so, they never show more than part of an event.[70]

There is need, then, to closely consider what has been wrought by the visualization—however momentary and fleeting—of atrocity. The linkage of images and words in sustaining certain collective memories over others has depended on the media, suggesting that their role in setting up the background against which collective memory can prosper deserves closer attention. To paraphrase Lance Morrow, the question is not "is it evil to forget?" or "is it necessary to remember"[71] but in what forms can we change memory? Who allows us to do so? Who sanctions the changes? Who alarms us when memories change? And most importantly, how do we offset the voyeurism and habituation that takes over our acts of remembering when they are distanced from responsibility?

In offering us broader parameters for visualizing carnage and a less explicit depiction of its details, photography raises important questions about documentation in all times of need. In times of crisis, should we demand less detail and more sense from those details? While the changing shape of the act of bearing witness accommodates a lessened attention to detail over time, bearing witness wrests images free of details so that they can be effectively utilized to tell a story larger than that of the scenes they depict. That slicing into the affairs of public life raises additional questions about the ease with which we may be abdicating responsibility for the pain of others. The media's use of images is inadvertently creating a breach between representation and responsibility, in that the less grounded an image's original use, the more misused it can become in memory. The act of attending through memories has come to stand in for real action.

This book has questioned the image's role in both representing the past and remembering the past into the present. The very tools by which we assume to remember may in fact be helping us remember to forget. As Michael J. Sandel wrote recently, "if politics is to recover its civic voice, it must again find a way to debate questions we have forgotten how to ask."[72] That issue is nowhere as salient as in the visual coverage of atrocity.

NOTES

BA   British Archives
NA   Pictorial Archive, National Archives, College Park, Maryland
HIA   Hoover Institution Archives, Stanford University
USHMM   United States Holocaust Memorial Museum, Washington, D.C.
WHP   Fred R. Crawford Witness to the Holocaust Project, Emory University
YVPA   Yad Vashem, Jerusalem

CHAPTER ONE

1. Walter Benjamin, "Theses on the Philosophy of History," in *Illuminations,* ed. Hannah Arendt, trans. Harry Zohn (New York: Schocken, 1969), p. 255.

2. Saul Friedlander, *Reflections of Nazism: An Essay on Kitsch and Death,* trans. Thomas Weyr (Bloomington: Indiana University Press, 1993), p. 105.

3. Susan Sontag, *On Photography* (New York: Anchor Books, 1977), p. 20; Patrick Hutton, "Collective Memory and Collective Mentalities: The Halbwachs-Aries Connection," *Historical Reflections / Réflexions Historiques* 15, no. 2 (1988): 314. For the classic work on collective memory, see Maurice Halbwachs, *The Collective Memory* (New York: Harper and Row, 1980); originally published as *La memoire collective* (Paris: Presses Universitaires de France, 1950).

4. John Gillis, "Memory and Identity: The History of a Relationship," in *Commemorations: The Politics of National Identity,* ed. Gillis (Princeton, N.J.: Princeton University Press, 1994); Geoffrey H. Hartman, "Introduction: Darkness Visible," in *Holocaust Remembrance: The Shapes of Memory,* ed. Hartman (Oxford: Basil Blackwell, 1994), p. 15. These issues are discussed at length in Barbie Zelizer, "Reading the Past against the Grain: The Shape of Memory Studies," *Critical Studies in Mass Communication* 12, no. 2 (June 1995): 214–39.

5. Barbie Zelizer, "America's Past in Israel's Present: The Assassinations of Yitzhak Rabin and John F. Kennedy," in *The Rabin Assassination,* ed. Yoram Peri (forthcoming).

6. Iwona Irwin-Zarecka, *Frames of Remembrance: The Dynamics of Collective Memory* (New Brunswick, N.J.: Transaction Publishers, 1994), p. 67.

7. Interpretive communities are "united through their collective interpretations of key events." See Barbie Zelizer, "Journalists as Interpretive Communities," *Critical Studies in Mass Communication* 10, no. 3 (September 1993): 223; the term "memory communities" comes from Robert N. Bellah, Richard Madsen, William M. Sullivan, Ann Swidler, and Steven M. Tipton, *Habits of the Heart* (New York: Harper and Row, 1985), pp. 152–55; Hans Kellner, "'Never Again' Is Now," *History and Theory* 2 (1994): 140.

8. Robin Wagner-Pacifici, "Memories in the Making: The Shape of Things That

Went," *Qualitative Sociology* 19, no. 3 (1996): 301–21; David Thelen, "Memory and American History," *Journal of American History* 75, no. 4 (March 1989): 1125.

9. W. J. T. Mitchell, *Picture Theory* (Chicago: University of Chicago Press, 1994), p. 4; Jefferson Hunter, *Image and Word* (Cambridge, Mass.: Harvard University Press, 1987), p. 6.

10. The same image was featured in 1996 at the New York Museum of Modern Art in a special exhibit on news photography, called "Photos of the *Times,*" at The Sixth Floor (the Dallas JFK assassination museum), and in the famous Andy Warhol poster.

11. Interestingly, these three events have been visualized through three image-making technologies—the Emmanuel Leutze painting of Washington, which reconfigured memories of the American Revolution (David Lowenthal, *The Past Is a Foreign Country* [Cambridge: Cambridge University Press, 1985], p. 307); Joe Rosenthal's photographic depiction of the flag raising on Iwo Jima (Karal Ann Marling and John Wetenhall, *Iwo Jima: Monuments, Memories, and the American Hero* [Cambridge, Mass.: Harvard University Press, 1991]); and the Zapruder film and television in Kennedy's death (Barbie Zelizer, *Covering the Body: The Kennedy Assassination, the Media, and the Shaping of Collective Memory* [Chicago: University of Chicago Press, 1992]).

12. James Fentress and Chris Wickham, *Social Memory* (Oxford: Basil Blackwell, 1992), pp. 47–49; James Halloran, Philip Elliott, and Graham Murdock, *Demonstrations and Communication: A Case Study* (London: Penguin, 1970); Fred Ritchin, *In Our Own Image* (New York: Aperture, 1990).

13. Fentress and Wickham, *Social Memory,* pp. 47–48; Catharine A. Lutz and Jane L. Collins, *Reading National Geographic* (Chicago: University of Chicago Press, 1993); Wendy Kozol, *Life's America: Family and Nation in Postwar Photojournalism* (Philadelphia: Temple University Press, 1994); Paul Fussell, "Images of Anonymity," *Harper's,* September 1979, p. 76.

14. This lack of knowledge about the event was somewhat corrected in November 1996, when the child in the photo made a conciliatory gesture to the U.S. government at ceremonies marking Veteran's Day. See Elaine Sciolino, "A Painful Road from Vietnam to Forgiveness," *New York Times,* November 12, 1996, p. A1.

15. Vicki Goldberg, *The Power of Photography: How Photographs Changed Our Lives* (New York: Abbeville, 1991), p. 135.

16. Jonathan Webber, foreword to *Representations of Auschwitz: Fifty Years of Photographs, Paintings, and Graphics,* ed. Yasmin Doosry (Oswiecim: Auschwitz-Birkenau State Museum, 1995), p. 10; Kellner, "'Never Again' Is Now," p. 129.

17. This view was upheld as recently as June 1996, when former *New York Times* editor Abe Rosenthal told a symposium on news photography that in news, "pictures are created by and for the word" (lecture at Museum of Modern Art, New York, June 27, 1996).

18. Goldberg, *The Power of Photography,* p. 250.

19. Walter Lippmann, *Public Opinion* (New York: Macmillan, 1922), p. 92; John Taylor, *War Photography: Realism in the British Press* (London: Routledge, 1991), p. 13.

20. Paul Messaris, *Visual Literacy,* (Boulder, Colo.: Westview Press, 1994), p. 121; Goldberg, *The Power of Photography,* p. 21; Roland Barthes, "The Photographic Message," in *Image / Music / Text,* (New York: Hill and Wang, 1977), p. 31.

21. Alan Trachtenberg, *Reading American Photographs: Images as History, Mathew Brady to Walker Evans* (New York: Hill and Wang, 1989), pp. 72–73; John Tagg, *Grounds of Dispute: Art History, Cultural Politics, and the Discursive Field* (Minneapolis: University of Minnesota Press, 1992), pp. 103–4.

22. Shoshana Felman, "The Return of the Voice: Claude Lanzmann's *Shoah,*" in *Testimony: Crises of Witnessing in Literature, Psychoanalysis, and History,* ed. Felman and Dori Laub (New York: Routledge, 1992), p. 204; James E. Young, *Writing and Rewriting the Holocaust* (Bloomington: Indiana University Press, 1988), p. 15.

23. Young, *Writing and Rewriting,* p. 17; Julia Kristeva, "The Pain of Sorrow in the Modern World: The Works of Marguerite Duras," *PMLA* 102 (1987): 139; Annette Wieviorka, "On Testimony," in Hartman, *Holocaust Remembrance,* p. 24.

24. Sontag, *On Photography,* pp. 17–19.

25. Pierre Sorlin, "War and Cinema: Interpreting the Relationship," *Historical Journal of Film, Radio, and Television* 14, no. 4 (1994): 362.

26. Bjorn Krondorfer, "Innocence, Corruption, Holocaust," *Christianity and Crisis,* August 11, 1986, p. 276; Harry James Cargas, "Holocaust Photography," *Centerpoint,* fall 1980, p. 141.

27. Janet Maslin, "Imagining the Holocaust to Remember It," *New York Times,* December 15, 1993, p. C19.

28. Leon Wieseltier, "After Memory," *New Republic,* May 3, 1993, p. 20.

29. Benjamin, "Theses on History," p. 255.

CHAPTER TWO

1. Photographers and journalists did share a history that dated back to the camera's invention in the mid-1800s. However, as late as the 1940s, photography's accommodation in the popular press was still accompanied by residual tensions. For a discussion of the evolution of modern photojournalism, see Wilson Hicks, *Words and Images: An Introduction to Photojournalism* (New York: Harper Brothers, 1952).

2. Kent Cooper, "Report of the General Manager," in *The Associated Press Thirty-Second Annual Report of the Board of Directors* (New York: Associated Press, 1932), p. 6.

3. Arthur J. Dalladay, "Photography Today," *British Journal Photographic Almanac,* 1940, p. 99; Aled Jones, "The British Press, 1919–1945," in *The Encyclopedia of the British Press, 1422–1992,* ed. Dennis Griffith (New York: St. Martin's, 1992), p. 48; "People Are Picture Nuts," *Editor and Publisher,* April 24, 1937, p. 5. Traditional and critical scholars have constructed different histories of the photograph. Traditionalists see pictures moving toward providing an accurate reflection of the world, while the critical view argues against the notion that pictures reproduce reality and assumes that photographs use artificial conventions, often borrowed from painting, that have been labeled natural by society.

4. Barbie Zelizer, "Journalism's Last Stand: Wirephoto and the Discourse of Resistance," *Journal of Communication* 45, no. 2 (spring 1995): 78–92; Marianne Fulton, "Bearing Witness: The 1930s to the 1950s," in *Eyes of Time: Photojournalism in America* (New York: New York Graphics Society, 1988), p. 118.

5. George Brandenburg, "Huge Gains in Use of Pictures Shown in Survey of Dailies," *Editor and Publisher,* February 19, 1938, p. 8; Roscoe Drummond, "Keeping Pace with the Picture Parade," *Quill,* June 1937, p. 11; "Press Photography," *Newspaper World,* July 17, 1937, pp. 25–33.

6. *Time* editors, *Four Hours a Year* (New York: Time, Inc., 1936), p. 20, with similar comments made at the British Institute of Journalists, the National Union of Journalists, the ASNE, and the American Association of Teachers of Journalism. Cited in Basil L. Walters, "Pictures versus Type Display in Reporting the News," *Journalism Quarterly* 24, no. 3 (September 1947): 193.

7. N. Howard, "A Critical and Constructive Review of Our Wire and Picture Ser-

vices," in *Problems of Journalism,* Proceedings of the 1936 Convention of the American Society of Newspaper Editors, April 16–18, 1936 (Washington, D.C.: ASNE, 1936), pp. 102, 104; Robert Blanchard, "News and Pictures—Cameras and Reporters," in *Problems of Journalism,* Proceedings of the 1935 Convention of the American Society of Newspaper Editors, April 18–20, 1935 [Washington, D.C.: ASNE, 1935], p. 54; J. L. Brown, "Picture Magazines and Morons," *American Mercury,* December 1938, pp. 404, 408.

8. Frederick J. Higginbottom, "Work of News Photographers Is Not Journalism," *Journal,* August 1935, p. 119; C. E. Brand, "Two Professions," *Journal,* March 1935, p. 54; Edmund Grimley, "Not Journalists," *Journal,* March 1935, p. 54.

9. Jack Price, "Reporters Train to Be Photographers," *Editor and Publisher,* April 1, 1944, p. 52; "Gannett Reporters Will Carry Cameras," *Editor and Publisher,* June 11, 1932, p. 18; Blanchard, "News and Pictures," pp. 57, 58.

10. Frank Hause, "News and Pictures—Cameras and Reporters," in *Problems of Journalism,* 1935, p. 60.

11. E. K. Bixby, "New Angles and New Fangles in News and Pictures," in *Problems of Journalism,* 1936, p. 148; M. Komroff, "The Little Black Box," *Atlantic,* October 1938, p. 471; Edward Stanley, "This Pictorial Journalism," *Quill,* November 1937, p. 5; Kent Cooper, "Report of the General Manager," *The Associated Press Thirty-Fifth Annual Report of the Board of Directors* (New York: Associated Press, 1935), p. 8; "This Is the *Life* Story," *Quill,* May 1938, p. 10.

12. Duane Featherstonhaugh, *Press Photography with the Miniature Camera* (Boston: American Photographic Publishing Company, 1939), p. 9; A. Spencer, "Photography with a Miniature Camera," *Photographic Journal,* December 1936, p. 582; "For the Pictures That Won't Wait," advertisement, *Camera,* February 1941, p. 16; A. J. Mason, "With a Camera in Spain," *Photographic Journal,* March 1939, pp. 112–14.

13. T. Welles, "What Makes a News Picture?" *Camera,* January 1941, pp. 48–51; Duane Featherstonhaugh, "You Can't Take That!" *American Photography,* July 1942, pp. 8–10; G. T. Eaton and J. I. Crabtree, "Washing Films and Papers in Sea Paper," *American Photography,* June 1943, pp. 12–15; F. J. Mortimer, "Photography's Part in the War," *Photographic Journal,* April 1943, p. 98.

14. Alexander M. Meyers, "The Camera: A Silent Witness," *American Photography,* June 1943, p. 20; J. Drew, "What about Army Photography?" *Camera,* April 1941, p. 51; Thurlow Weed Barnes, "Seeing Is Believing in Newspictures," *Photo-Era Magazine,* March 1926, p. 129.

15. For a discussion of wartime cooperation, see Arthur Marwick, "Print, Pictures, and Sound: The Second World War and the British Experience," *Daedalus* 111, no. 4 (fall 1982): 152.

16. Robert W. Desmond, *Tides of War: World News Reporting, 1931–1945* (Iowa City: University of Iowa Press, 1990), p. 450. Type and headlines were also reduced to accommodate more text on a page, and the white "gutter" space in the margins was used to publish radio logs. See Jones, "The British Press, 1919–1945," p. 53, and "Small Papers Make Special Problems," *World's Press News,* March 6, 1941, p. 3.

17. R. H. Turner, "Photographers in Uniform," in *Journalism in Wartime,* ed. Franklin Luther Mott (Washington, D.C.: American Council on Public Affairs, 1943), p. 77. The U.S. Still Picture Pool, which included twenty-eight accredited photographers from the Associated Press, Acme Newsphotos, International News Photos, and *Life* magazine, worked as follows: Pictures from the war theaters were wired to Washington or London, where they were inspected by officials of the army, navy and OWI

before being released. The wire-distribution agencies—AP Wirephoto, Acme Tele-photo, and INS Soundphotos—then transmitted the images onto the wires, with the assistance of British Combine and Keystone, on a simultaneous-release basis. The entire process could be completed in less than two hours. See Bruce Downes, "From Battlefield to Front Page," *Popular Photography,* August 1945, p. 86; F. A. Resch, "Photo Coverage of the War by the Still-Picture Pool," *Journalism Quarterly,* December 1943, p. 311; and Jack Price, "Enlisted Photographers Aided by New Army Policy," *Editor and Publisher,* June 10, 1944, p. 58.

18. "Do Service Chiefs Block Free Flow of British Army Pictures?" *World's Press News,* April 19, 1945, p. 1. As one observer saw it, "when any place on the Western front becomes hot news, we get a selection of American pictures within 24 hours. We don't expect any British for at least two or three days" ("Do Service Chiefs Block," p. 11); "Is British Photo Pool Worth While?" *World's Press News,* April 12, 1945, p. 4; "Is Photographic Skill Lacking?" *World's Press News,* May 3, 1945, p. 8.

19. Margaret Bourke-White, *Portrait of Myself* (New York: Simon and Schuster, 1963), p. 258; Jack Price, "Picture Story of Invasion Well-Planned," *Editor and Publisher,* October 7, 1944, p. 30; "War Photography: Past and Present," *Camera,* March 1943, p. 39.

20. Howard L. Kany, "Experts Eye Pictures: Photographer as Reporter," *Quill,* April 1947, pp. 8, 10; "The Institute's Four Agreements with the Newspaper Society," *Journal,* January 1944, p. 6; Jack Price, "Cameramen Launch National Organization," *Editor and Publisher,* June 23, 1945, p. 28.

21. Jack Price, "'Doormat' Label Develops Ire of Cameramen," *Editor and Publisher,* March 10, 1945, p. 44; Roger Butterfield, "The Technique of Wrapping It Up," *Saturday Review,* March 16, 1946, p. 26; Kany, "Experts Eye Pictures," p. 10; cited in Jack Price, "Credit Line Asked for Photographers," *Editor and Publisher,* October 28, 1944, p. 64.

22. Susan Moeller, *Shooting War* (New York: Basic Books, 1989), pp. 150, 135; John Taylor, *War Photography: Realism in the British Press* (London: Routledge, 1991), p. 50.

23. Hicks, *Words and Images,* p. 27. Many editors compensated for the lack of standards for using news images by modeling themselves on the picture-magazines. But this exacerbated an already problematic situation, for few attempts were made to address the differences between the picture-magazine and the rest of the popular press.

24. Cited in Philip B. Kunhardt Jr., *Carl Mydans: Photojournalist* (New York: Harry N. Abrams, 1985), pp. 23–24.

25. Frank R. Fraprie, "The Editor's Point of View," *American Photography,* September 1945, p. 7; John R. Whiting, *Photography Is a Language* (Chicago: Ziff-Davis, 1946), pp. 97, 139. This had in fact been the case since the mid-1800s, when photographs arrived at the magazine's editorial office "without one word of explanatory matter." Cited in Michael J. Carlebach, *The Origins of Photojournalism in America* (Washington, D.C.: Smithsonian Institution Press, 1992), p. 65.

26. War Department Pamphlet no. 11-2, *Standing Operating Procedures for Signal Photographic Units in Theaters of Operations,* April 20, 1944, cited in Peter Maslowski, *Armed with Cameras: The American Military Photographers of World War II* (New York: Free Press, 1993), p. 145; transcript in the archives of the Imperial War Museum, London, cited in Martin Caiger-Smith, *The Face of the Enemy: British Photographers in Germany, 1944–1952* (Berlin: Nishen, 1988), p. 8; James C. Kinkaid, *Press Photography* (Barton: American Photographic, 1936), p. 255; Downes, "Battlefield to Front Page," pp.

34–35, 86–87. Photographer George Rodger, for instance, regularly wrote his own captions, a habit he acquired during his stint at the Black Star Photographic Agency (interview with George Rodger, in Paul Hill and Thomas Cooper, *Dialogue with Photography* [New York: Farrar, Straus and Giroux, 1979], p. 57).

27. Kany, "Experts Eye Pictures," p. 11; *APME Inc., 1948: Reports and Discussions of the Continuing Study Committees of the APME Association* (New York: Associated Press, 1949), pp. 93–94; M. W. MacPherson, "News Picture Captions," *American Photography,* September 1946, p. 46; Walters, "Picture versus Type Display," p. 194.

28. Maslowski, *Armed with Cameras,* p. 27; Herbert Giles, cited in Mary Ellen Slate, "The Magazines," *Popular Photography,* October 1945, p. 104.

29. Fulton, "Bearing Witness," p. 143; see Price, "Credit Line Asked," p. 64; Jack Price, "More about Photographic Credits," *Editor and Publisher,* March 4, 1944, p. 53; and Slate, "The Magazines," p. 104. Similar discussions in Britain over the copyrighting of news photos met no resolution. See "Copyright of Photographs," *Newspaper World,* April 1939, p. 12; "Photographic Copyright," *Journal,* January 1937, p. 6, and February 1937, p. 26.

30. Cited in Price, "Credit Line Asked," p. 64; Jack Price, "Are Photographers Newspapermen, Like Reporters?" *Editor and Publisher,* September 30, 1994, p. 46; "Is the Photographer the Forgotten Man?" *U.S. Camera,* February 1944, p. 28; "What about the Poor Photographer?" *U.S. Camera,* December 1943, p. 38; Kany, "Experts Eye Pictures," p. 11.

31. Text of an address by William J. White, Jr. to the September 10, 1943, meeting of the Associated Press Managing Editors, published as "The Daily Routine of a 'Picture Newspaper,'" *Journalism Quarterly,* December 1943, p. 310; Welles, "What Makes a News Picture?" p. 51; "Leslie Burch's Forecasts of Post-War Press Photography," *Newspaper World,* November 13, 1943, p. 12; Fulton, "Bearing Witness," p. 135. There is also some question as to how widespread the use of pictorial pages really was. In an analysis of 108 studies of the Advertising Research Foundation's *Continuing Study of Newspaper Readers, 100 Year Summary,* only twenty picture-pages were counted (cited in Bert W. Woodburn, "Reader Interest in Newspaper Pictures," *Journalism Quarterly,* September 1947, p. 201).

32. Butterfield, "Technique," p. 26; Jack Price, "Combat Graphics May Be Adopted for News Use," *Editor and Publisher,* September 16, 1944, p. 62; Frederic B. Harvey, "The Picture Editor," *Newspaper World,* April 13, 1940, p. 5. Here too, the default case was the picture-magazine.

33. Walters, "Picture versus Type Display," p. 194; "Wanted: Picture Editors," letter to editor, *Saturday Review of Literature,* November 8, 1947, p. 21.

34. Daniel D. Mich, "The Rise of Photojournalism in the United States," *Journalism Quarterly,* September 1947, p. 206; Dalladay, "Photography Today," p. 94.

35. "Phony Planes," *Time,* August 19, 1940, p. 56; "The 'Sunday Pictorial' Makes a Mistake," *Picture Post,* April 10, 1943, p. 18.

36. Laura Vitray, John Mills Jr., and Roscoe Ellard, *Pictorial Journalism* (New York: McGraw-Hill, 1939), p. 4.

37. William F. Thompson, *The Image of War: The Pictorial Reporting of the American Civil War* (Baton Rouge: Louisiana State University Press, 1944), pp. 86–98; Philip Knightley, *The First Casualty: From the Crimea to Vietnam: The War Correspondent as Hero, Propagandist, and Myth Maker* (New York: Harcourt Brace Jovanovich, 1975), pp. 55–56, 75. Not much attention, however, was paid the issue of British concentration camps.

38. Cited in Taylor, *War Photography,* p. 79; Knightley, *The First Casualty,* pp. 105–6; Moeller, *Shooting War,* p. 108.

39. In a *New York Times* story of the Vilna massacre, for instance, the reporter noted that "the Polish refugee's story of the Vilna massacre, of which he said he was an eyewitness, is impossible to confirm now" (Bernard Valery, "Vilna Massacre of Jews Reported," *New York Times,* June 16, 1942, p. 6).

40. Knightley, *The First Casualty,* p. 15; Thompson, *The Image of War,* pp. 91–97; "Further Proofs of Rebel Inhumanity," *Harper's,* June 18, 1864, p. 387. One photograph was displayed for months in the window of a New York City bookseller, and the U.S. Congress reacted to that display in discussing retaliation against the South (Vicki Goldberg, *The Power of Photography: How Photographs Changed Our Lives* [New York: Abbeville, 1991], pp. 21–24); Knightley, *The First Casualty,* p. 73; Moeller, *Shooting War,* p. 31. Similarly, Frederick Barber used atrocity photos to display his own pacifist views in *The Horror of It: Camera Records of War's Gruesome Glories* (New York: Brewer, Warren, and Putnam, 1932). Barber used terse captions to ironically shock readers with his depictions of human carnage: for instance, the word "Silent" was affixed to a picture of a decomposing body and "Field of Glory" explained a view of a field of dead corpses (pp. 44, 50).

41. Moeller, *Shooting War,* pp. 125–26.

42. William A. Frassanito, *Gettysburg: A Journey in Time* (New York: Charles Scribner's Sons, 1975), pp. 186–95; "Real War Pictures—and the Other Kind," *Collier's,* January 26, 1918, pp. 12–13. An extreme case of image alteration was the composograph, which required individuals to reenact events for the camera; that image was then pasted together with other images.

43. Hause, "News and Pictures," pp. 59–61. The printing of pictures of dead corpses was discussed at length during the 1935 meetings of the ASNE. "Pictures We Would Rather Not Publish," *Picture Post,* December 11, 1943, p. 19.

44. "America at War: The First Year," *Newsweek,* December 14, 1942, p. 20; "Pearl Harbor Damage Revealed," *Life,* December 14, 1942, pp. 36–37; Moeller, *Shooting War,* pp. 199, 235, 237. The photographs appeared in a wide span of newspapers on August 12 and 13, 1945. Vincent Leo argues that the timing of the Hiroshima and Nagasaki photographs' release turned them into pictures of victory. See Vincent Leo, "The Mushroom Cloud Photograph: From Fact to Symbol," *Afterimage* 13 (summer 1985): 6–12. The captions were less evocative: respectively, they read "Hiroshima: Atom Bomb No. 1 Obliterated It," and "Nagasaki: Atom Bomb No. 2 Disemboweled It" ("The War Ends," *Life,* August 20, 1945, pp. 26–27).

45. Paul Fussell, "Images of Anonymity," *Harper's,* September 1979, p. 76; Maslowski, *Armed with Cameras,* p. 82.

46. Picture appended both to John R. Wilhelm, "They Killed Sick Prisoners in Nazi Death Camp," *PM,* April 9, 1945, p. 5, and to Richard Wilbur, "Wave of Anger Sweeps U.S. as Nazi Horror Stories Unfold," *Stars and Stripes,* April 23, 1945, p. 5. Florea, who took the photograph, was later that year hailed as one of the "21 war photographers who worked up in the front lines, who paid a price in injury and illness and who finished the job of reporting war as no war before has ever been reported." See "War Photographers," *Life,* November 5, 1945, p. 108.

47. The practice of *re*-presenting an image seems to have been associated with marking certain images beyond their function as a document of daily news. The *Daily Sketch,* for instance, re-published a photograph of Neville Chamberlain returning from

Munich, but the second time it was embellished with the caption "Lest We Forget" (December 20, 1939, p. 1).

48. "If any excuse were given," he said, "that it was unnecessary to publish these pictures of outrage in order to bring home to the British public the horror of what is taking place in China, I think those who were responsible for those publications greatly mistake the feelings of our people." See "'Shocking' and 'Terrible' War Pics Deplored by Minister," *Newspaper World,* November 6, 1937, p. 6.

49. William L. Chenery, *So It Seemed* (New York: Harcourt Brace and Company, 1952), pp. 278–79. The memo, entitled "Release of Pictures" and written by Lt. Col. Curtis Mitchell, chief of the Pictorial Branch, Bureau of Public Relations, was cited by Maslowski, *Armed with Cameras,* p. 81; "Photo with a Message," *Newsweek,* May 24, 1943, p. 27; "War Photo Confusion," *Newsweek,* October 11, 1943, p. 12.

50. The first picture was captioned "On the Beach Near Gela an American Soldier Stands Guard over a Fallen Comrade," *Life,* August 2, 1943, p. 23; the second image was "Three Americans," *Life,* September 20, 1943, p. 34; "Realism for Breakfast," *Newsweek,* September 20, 1943, p. 98; "Gallup Says Readers Want Grim Photos," *Editor and Publisher,* January 29, 1944, p. 20.

51. "Front Page Pictures," *Newspaper World,* May 9, 1942, p. 6; "Where Are the Pictures?" *Picture Post,* July 15, 1944, p. 3; "Do Service Chiefs Block," p. 11.

52. An articulate discussion of this issue is found in Deborah Lipstadt, *Beyond Belief: The American Press and the Coming of the Holocaust, 1933–1945* (New York: Free Press, 1986). For an analysis of the British side, see Andrew Sharf, *The British Press and Jews under Nazi Rule* (London: Oxford University Press, 1964).

53. Tony Kushner, *The Holocaust and the Liberal Imagination: A Social and Cultural History* (Oxford: Basil Blackwell, 1994), pp. 18–20.

54. Edgar Ansel Mowrer, *Triumph and Turmoil: A Personal History of Our Times* (New York: Weybright and Talley, 1968), pp. 216–17, 224; William Zuckerman, "Jews at the Crossroads," *Harper's,* January 1935, p. 218; "Passion versus Reason," *Time,* September 18, 1939, p. 59; "Concerning the Atrocities," *Christian Century,* February 16, 1944, p. 200.

55. George H. Gallup, *The Gallup Poll: Public Opinion, 1935–1971,* vol. 1 (New York: Random House, 1972); Vernon McKenzie, "Atrocities in World War II—What Can We Believe?" *Journalism Quarterly,* September 1942, p. 268. McKenzie predicted that there would be "appalling documentation after the war" to validate the atrocity stories then circulating; Lipstadt, *Beyond Belief,* pp. 9, 27.

56. See, for instance, Tosha Bialer, "Behind the Wall," *Collier's,* February 20, 1943, pp. 17–18 and "Behind the Wall: Part II," *Collier's,* February 27, 1943, pp. 29–32. In some accounts, bylines remained anonymous, as in "Death in Dachau," *National Jewish Monthly Magazine,* April 1939, pp. 262–63, whose author was identified only as "A Survivor." The author of "The Nazis Got Me" (*Collier's,* June 18, 1938, pp. 12–13, 62–64) was an "anonymous Aryan survivor" whose tale, "As Told to Samuel T. Williamson," included illustrations of Nazi thugs and emaciated bodies. The introductory note told readers that the illustrator had also spent six months in Nazi concentration camps. "To illustrate this article with such photographs as the Nazis see fit to release would be dull, inadequate and flat. What we wanted was a good artist who knew what he was drawing. We found him" (p. 12). This was one of the few instances in which drawings of the camps were preferred to photographs. Lipstadt, *Beyond Belief,* pp. 135, 16.

57. Templeton Peck, Evening Editorial, American Broadcasting Station in Europe,

April 19, 1944, taken from papers of Templeton Peck, Box 1, HIA; Lipstadt, *Beyond Belief,* pp. 20, 26, 139.

58. For example, see "Foreign News," *Time,* April 24, 1939, p. 26; William Barkley, "Savagery as in the 'Darkest Ages of Man,'" *Daily Express,* October 31, 1939, p. 5; "Stories of Nazi Brutality," *Manchester Guardian,* October 31, 1939, p. 1; "Horrors of the Nazi Camps," *Daily Telegraph,* October 31, 1939, p. 1; "Cabinet Brands Torturers," *Daily Herald,* October 31, 1939, pp. 1, 6; and Raymond Daniell, "Nazi Tortures Detailed by Britain: Concentration Camp Horrors Told," *New York Times,* October 31, 1939, p. 1. No pictures accompanied any of these articles except in the *Daily Herald,* which portrayed Nazi functionaries facing down inmates at Sachsenhausen.

59. Frederick Oechsner, *This Is the Enemy* (Boston: Little Brown, 1942), pp. 131, 137; Louis B. Lochner, *What about Germany?* (New York: Dodd, Mead, 1942), pp. 53–57; Sigrid Schultz, *Germany Will Try It Again* (New York: Reynal and Hitchcock, 1944), p. 186; "We Must Stop It," editorial, *New York Daily Mirror,* February 22, 1943, p. 19. "It is a documented record," the editorial flatly stated: "Documented with fact after sickening fact." The War Refugee Board's report was actually released in November 1944, but it repeated information from the earlier news reports, such as "Poles Report Nazis Slay 10,000 Daily," *Washington Post,* March 22, 1944, p. 2, and "50,000 Executed in Poland," *New York Herald Tribune,* March 22, 1944, p. 3.

60. Arthur Koestler, "The Nightmare That Is a Reality," *New York Times Magazine,* January 9, 1944, pp. 5, 30; Fred Eastman, "A Reply to Screamers," *Christian Century,* February 16, 1944, pp. 204–6.

61. Jan Karski, "Polish Death Camp," *Collier's,* October 14, 1944, pp. 18–19, 60–61. The report was accompanied not by a photograph but by an unaccredited drawing that portrayed anonymous, terror-stricken faces and arms stretched upward. In circumstances requiring difficult access, drawings were often far easier to produce than photographs, and some journals, such as the *Picture Post,* sometimes used illustrations to portray what was taking place behind inaccessible enemy lines.

62. "Life inside a Nazi Concentration Camp," *New York Times Magazine,* February 14, 1937, p. 16; "Nazi Germany Reveals Official Pictures of Its Concentration Camps," *Life,* August 21, 1939, pp. 22–23. The magazine reprinted seven of the images with their captions, yet underscored in text how unrepresentative they were. See Sybil Milton, "The Camera as Weapon, Voyeur, and Witness: Photography of the Holocaust as Historical Evidence," in *Visual Explorations of the World,* ed. Martin Taureg and Jay Ruby (Aachen, Germany: Edition Herodot, 1987), pp. 80–114.

63. "Where Germans Rule: Death Dance before Polish Mass Execution," *Illustrated London News,* March 22, 1941, p. 387.

64. Pictures titled "Inside Poland: Smuggled Pictures Show Nazi Persecution," *PM,* February 5, 1941, pp. 15–19; picture appended to Koestler, "Nightmare That Is Reality," p. 30. Significantly, the article's front page was illustrated by a cartoon of victims hanging from ropes near a crowd of Nazi officers in conversation. The cartoon reflected similar photographs taken by Nazis themselves of their victims, yet it is possible that no such photograph had as yet appeared in the press. The latter photograph, captioned "The Women Want to Be Photographed," was appended to "Eighth Army Breaks Open a Concentration Camp in Italy," *Picture Post,* October 23, 1943, p. 7. The shot's civility was a painful contrast to the grotesque images of the camps that would be released in later years.

65. This estimate was provided by Sybil Milton, "Images of the Holocaust—Part II," *Holocaust and Genocide Studies* 1, no. 2 (1986): 195. It is worth mentioning that from

the beginning the photographs of the camps were problematic documentation. Many were in poor condition at the end of the war, damaged by moisture, mildew, or fire; others simply disappeared: some were appropriated by soldiers as souvenirs. Some were burned by the retreating German army, and Allied officers dismantled intact files so as to accommodate different intelligence-related tasks. Moreover, many images were mislabled.

66. Officers in the German army did attempt to confiscate all amateur photographs of atrocities, arguing that "it is beneath the dignity of a German soldier to watch such incidents out of curiosity," but the orders never took hold. The commandant in the picture was Kurt Franz. See Sybil Milton, "The Camera as Weapon: Documentary Photography and the Holocaust," *Simon Wiesenthal Center Annual* 1, no. 1 (1984): 47. Gerhard Schoenberner's *The Yellow Star* (London: Corgi Books, 1969) is a classic on photography and the Holocaust. My thanks to Froma Zeitlin of Princeton University for acquainting me with it. The quote appears on p. 6.

67. These questions are posed in Sybil Milton, "Images of the Holocaust—Part I," *Holocaust and Genocide Studies* 1, no. 1 (1986): 27–61, and "Images of the Holocaust—Part II."

68. See, for instance, Barkley, "Savagery," p. 5. Also see Nazi images of Russians being hanged, as in "War Pictures We Have to Print," *Daily Sketch,* February 1942.

69. Picture appended to "Nazi Frenzy Threatens to Murder 5 Million Jews by End of Year," *New York Post,* February 23, 1943, p. 26; Patrick G. Walker, "The Terror in Europe," *Picture Post,* October 11, 1941, overleaf. Other documents that trickled to the West—such as *The Camp of Death,* a pamphlet on Auschwitz issued by the Polish underground in 1944—displayed drawings, not photographs, of women being herded to the gas chambers at Birkenau and Auschwitz (*The Camp of Death* [London: Liberty Publication Series, 1944]); Milton, "Images of the Holocaust—Part I," p. 32.

70. Walker, "The Terror in Europe," pp. 7–13. The 1933 photograph appeared on p. 7, the picture of the Polish women on p. 9. No credit was given for any of the photographs. Appended to the article was also a series of head shots of key personalities sympathetic to the Nazis.

71. Walker, "The Terror in Europe," pp. 9, 8.

72. "Nazi Atrocities," *New Republic,* April 30, 1945, p. 572.

CHAPTER THREE

1. The history of the liberation of the camps is complicated by numerous discrepancies over when a camp was liberated, whether it was actually liberated, which military units were involved, and so on. I have tried to adopt the most consensual master narrative, though variations from the account I provide can be found elsewhere. In that vein, my analysis does not claim to be a comprehensive examination of coverage of the liberation of all the camps. Rather, I focus primarily on Buchenwald, Bergen-Belsen, and Dachau as "strategically-chosen examples" of the coverage afforded the camps of the western front (see Barney Glaser and Anselm Strauss, *The Discovery of Grounded Theory* [New York: Aldine, 1967]) and on discussion of Majdanek's liberation as a dress rehearsal for that coverage. The first three camps were liberated within weeks of each other and received considerable coverage from the U.S. and British media. Dates and details concerning the liberation have been taken from Jon Bridgman, *The End of the Holocaust: The Liberation of the Camps* (Portland, Ore.: Areopagitica Press, 1990) and Konnilyn G. Feig, *Hitler's Death Camps: The Sanity of Madness* (New York: Holmes and Meier, 1981).

2. Even when the War Refugee Board published its report on Auschwitz, one news-paper—the *Chicago Tribune*—skeptically commented that "no pictures were released to corroborate the atrocity story released today" (Hal Foust, "Nazi Brutality in Camps Told by 3 Who Fled," *Chicago Tribune,* November 26, 1944, pt. 1, p. 1). This response did not consider the American aerial-reconnaissance images of the Auschwitz-Birke-nau complex, taken between June and December 1944. Nor did it mention that Auschwitz was still in German hands, a fact that made photographing the camp virtu-ally impossible.

3. "Poland: *Vernichtungslager,*" *Time,* August 21, 1944, pp. 36–37; "Lublin Funeral," *Life,* August 28, 1944, p. 34.

4. Ilya Ehrenburg, "Something I Can Never Forget," *New York Times Magazine,* December 26, 1943, p. 5. Ehrenburg pleaded with the U.S. public to believe him: "I want to tell America what I have seen," it began. "The Germans have outdone them-selves." See Philip Knightley, *The First Casualty: From the Crimea to Vietnam: The War Cor-respondent as Hero, Propagandist, and Myth Maker* (New York: Harcourt Brace Jovanovich, 1975), pp. 246, 329.

5. "Atrocity Pictures from Polish Camp," *Chicago Tribune,* November 26, 1944, pt. 1, p. 14.

6. Paul Winterton, "Biggest Murder Case in History," *News Chronicle,* August 30, 1944, p. 4.

7. Cited in Bridgman, *End of the Holocaust,* p. 20; "Murder, Inc.," editorial, *Messen-ger,* October 30, 1944, pp. 5–6; "Biggest Atrocity Story Breaks in Poland," *Christian Century,* September 13, 1944, p. 1045.

8. The Editors, "This Is Why There Must Be No Soft Peace," *Saturday Evening Post,* October 28, 1944, p. 18; W. H. Lawrence, "Nazi Mass Killing Laid Bare in Camp," *New York Times,* August 30, 1944, p. 1. Lawrence's article, published some days after he toured Majdanek, was marked with the simple term "Delayed." The editorial appeared the following day ("The Maidanek Horror," *New York Times,* August 31, 1944, p. 16); Lawrence later chided the *Times* for its overzealous confirmation of his reportorial skills. Its attempt to legitimate him came because "much of what I reported from Poland that day met skeptical eyes and minds, people who were not convinced of the German guilt because they had not seen the evidence personally as I had seen it." Lawrence later suggested that his ability to believe what he saw in Majdanek in part derived from his having earlier downplayed the story of the massacre at Babi Yar. Lawrence admitted that he had consciously played down that story, reporting both "the enormous crime of which I had been told and the small amount of supporting evi-dence I had been able to find to verify it" (Bill Lawrence, *Six Presidents, Too Many Wars* [New York: Saturday Review Press, 1972], pp. 92, 102).

9. Edgar Snow, "Here the Nazi Butchers Wasted Nothing," *Saturday Evening Post,* October 28, 1944, p. 18. Snow made the comments to justify why he, as a magazine writer, was reporting on a topic "fully reported in the daily press."

10. "The Lublin of Alsace: The Nazi Order as It Operated in France," *New York Times,* December 18, 1944, p. 3.

11. John Taylor, *War Photography: Realism in the British Press* (London: Routledge, 1991), p. 7.

12. Winterton, "Biggest Murder Case," p. 4.

13. Snow, "Nazi Butchers Wasted Nothing," p. 18; Lawrence, "Mass Killing Laid Bare," p. 9; "Merchants of Murder," *Newsweek,* September 11, 1944, p. 64. Unlike other

dispatches, the latter report never named its author but simply introduced him as "*Newsweek*'s Moscow correspondent [who] sends an eyewitness account."

14. Snow, "Nazi Butchers Wasted Nothing," p. 19; Richard Lauterbach, "Murder, Inc.," *Time,* September 11, 1944, p. 36; Maurice Hindus, "Lublin Inquiry Lays 1,500,000 Deaths to Nazis," *New York Herald Tribune,* August 30, 1944, p. 4.

15. "Merchants of Murder," p. 67; "German 'Death Factory,'" *Daily Telegraph,* August 14, 1944.

16. Uncaptioned pictures, *Daily News,* August 15, 1944, p. 11; "Atrocity Pictures," pt. 1, p. 14. Other more gruesome Russian pictures appeared not to reach the Western press.

17. Pictures appended to Snow, "Nazi Butchers Wasted Nothing," pp. 18–19; "The Most Terrible Example of Organized Cruelty in the History of Civilization," *Illustrated London News,* October 14, 1944, p. 442.

18. Picture appended to Snow, "Nazi Butchers Wasted Nothing," p. 19; pictures appended to "Most Terrible Example," p. 443.

19. Picture appended to Snow, "Nazi Butchers Wasted Nothing," p. 18; "Most Terrible Example," p. 443.

20. Captain D. McLaren, cited in Martin Gilbert, *Auschwitz and the Allies* (London: Michael Joseph, 1981), p. 334; Edward Folliard, "Skeptic Yanks See Proof of Nazi Atrocities," *Washington Post,* April 16, 1945, p. 1; Bridgman, *End of the Holocaust,* pp. 21, 17.

21. Knightley, *The First Casualty,* p. 328.

22. Uncle Dudley, "Bedeviled Germans," *Boston Globe,* April 24, 1945, p. 10.

23. See, for instance, A. M. Sperber, *Murrow: His Life and Times* (New York: Bantam, 1986), pp. 248–53, and Edwin Tetlow, *As It Happened: A Journalist Looks Back* (London: Peter Owen, 1990).

24. I employ the term *liberation* here hesitantly. *Liberation* tends to conjure images of drunken street scenes and unrestricted expressions of public joy, but when used here it invokes more sober images. Considerable literature has attested to the difficulties surrounding the notion of liberation: technically, some of the camps had already been abandoned by the Germans by the time the liberating forces reached them, and most "liberated" survivors were not fully free but entered a new phase of their own deprivation, encountering the magnitude of their individual tragedies. For many survivors, only on liberation did they realize the full scope of their loss. Nonetheless, the liberation deserves marking, for it shifted largely abstract discussions about the atrocities onto an identifiable target, the site of the camps. I therefore use the term as a conscious choice among less viable alternatives.

25. Eisenhower wrote, "The visual evidence and the verbal testimony of starvation, cruelty, and bestiality were so overwhelming. . . . I made the visit deliberately in order to be in a position to give firsthand evidence of these things if ever, in the future, there develops a tendency to charge these allegations to propaganda" ("M.P.s Report on Horrors of Buchenwald," *Manchester Guardian,* April 28, 1945, p. 3).

26. See, for instance, John M. McCullough, "Publicity Given Atrocities in Reich Stirs Speculation," *Philadelphia Inquirer,* April 24, 1945, p. 16.

27. Tetlow, *As It Happened,* p. 75.

28. Tetlow, *As It Happened,* p. 78.

29. M. E. Walter, "Nazi Camp Ex-Prisoners Still Dying from Effects," *Los Angeles Times,* April 24, 1945, pt. 1, p. 3.

30. Jan Yindrich, "9,000 Died at Dachau Camp in Three Months," *News Chronicle,* May 1, 1945, p. 3.

31. These remarks were made respectively by *Life* correspondent George Rodger, *Time* correspondent Bill Walton, and *Time* correspondent Percival Knauth, cited in "Foreign News: Germany," *Time,* April 30, 1945, p. 38; Martha Gelhorn, "Dachau: Experimental Murder," *Collier's,* June 23, 1945, p. 25.

32. The first postliberation news of the camps came from Ohrdruf. See, for example, Robert Richards, "Nazis Butcher Yank, 30 Other Prisoners," *Washington Post,* April 9, 1945, p. 2. Articles began appearing with a Buchenwald dateline a few days later.

33. Cited in Vicki Goldberg, *Margaret Bourke-White: A Biography* (Reading, Mass.: Addison-Wesley, 1987), p. 290; Harold Denny, "Despair Blankets Buchenwald Camp," *New York Times,* April 20, 1945, p. 3.

34. William Frye, "Thousands Tortured to Death in Camp at Belsen," *Boston Globe,* April 21, 1945, pp. 1, 3; Christopher Buckley, "Burgomasters at Belsen Say 'We Didn't Know,'" *Daily Telegraph,* April 26, 1945, p. 5.

35. Howard Cowan, "39 Carloads of Bodies on Track at Dachau," *Washington Post,* May 1, 1945, p. 2; Antoinette May, *Witness to War: A Biography of Marguerite Higgins* (New York: Beaufort Books, 1983), pp. 89, 90.

36. Saul Friedlander, introduction to *Probing the Limits of Representation: Nazism and the "Final Solution,"* ed. Friedlander (Cambridge, Mass.: Harvard University Press, 1992), p. 3.

37. Victor O. Jones, "This Ends for All Time Notion That Only Small Groups Guilty," *Boston Globe,* April 21, 1945, p. 3.

38. John McDermott, "How the S.S. Burned 22 Prisoners Alive," *New York Daily Worker,* April 21, 1945, p. 2; William Frye, "Dead, Living Almost Alike in Nazi Starvation Camp," *Philadelphia Inquirer,* April 21, 1945, p. 8; R. W. Thompson, "S.S. Women Tied Dead to Living," *London Sunday Times,* April 22, 1945, p. 5.

39. See Cowan, "39 Carloads of Bodies," 2.

40. Denny, "Despair Blankets Buchenwald Camp," p. 3; "The Horrors of Buchenwald: A Conducted Tour of the Camp," *Manchester Guardian,* April 18, 1945, p. 5.

41. Ronald Monson, "Smug Guards Marched Out," *London Evening Standard,* April 20, 1945, p. 3; R. M. McKelway, "Clergy Were Used as Guinea Pigs; Dogs Were Turned on Prisoners for Sport," *Boston Globe,* May 8, 1945, p. 10; Sidney Olson, "Foreign News: Dachau," *Time,* May 7, 1945, p. 35; Gelhorn, "Dachau," p. 28.

42. "British M.P.s See Buchenwald," *London Observer,* April 22, 1945, p. 1; Colin Wills, "Belsen Camp: The Full, Terrible Story," *News Chronicle,* April 19, 1945, p. 1; "Forced Tour of Buchenwald," *London Times,* April 18, 1945, p. 3.

43. Robert Chandler, "Horrors Recalled," *ASNE Bulletin,* June 1, 1945, n.p.

44. William Frye, "S.S. Forced to Bury Horror Camp Dead," *Los Angeles Times,* April 21, 1945, p. 3; Monson, "Smug Guards Marched Out," p. 3; Tetlow, *As It Happened,* p. 78.

45. These categories of witness differ somewhat from those more generally invoked in Holocaust literature—that is, perpetrators, victims, and bystanders (see Raul Hilberg, *The Destruction of the European Jews* (New York: Holmes and Meier, 1985)]. Journalistic accounts did not so much attempt to offer *different* performances of the act of seeing but were instead pieced together with the seemingly omniscient authority of the journalist. They do, however, somewhat correspond to what Laub has suggested concerning the levels of witnessing activity: "the level of being a witness to oneself

within the experience; the level of being a witness to the testimonies of others; and the level of being a witness to the process of witnessing itself" (Dori Laub, "An Event without a Witness," in *Testimony: Crises of Witnessing in Literature, Psychoanalysis, and History,* ed. Shoshana Felman and Laub (New York: Routledge, 1992), p. 75.

46. Hal Boyle, "Nazi Horrors Too Awful for Belief," *Philadelphia Inquirer,* April 26, 1945, p. 14; Frederick Graham, "Three Hundred Burned Alive by Retreating S.S.," *New York Times,* April 22, 1945, p. 12; Buckley, "Burgomasters at Belsen."

47. Edward T. Folliard, "German Civilians Forced to See S.S. Horror Camp by Patton," *Washington Post,* April 18, 1945, p. 1; Gene Currivan, "Nazi Death Factory Shocks Germans on a Forced Tour," *New York Times,* April 18, 1945, p. 8.

48. Ivan H. Peterman, "Nazis Kill 51,000 in Single Camp," *Philadelphia Inquirer,* April 22, 1945, p. 1. He went on to say that he had an urge to see the S.S. "dragged by and to that meat hook on the wall and [I] would have watched with good heart their expiration" (p. 3); Howard Cowan, "Dachau, Most Dreaded Prison Captured," *Los Angeles Times,* May 1, 1945, pt. 1, p. 5.

49. Harold Denny, "'The World Must Not Forget,'" *New York Times Magazine,* May 6, 1945, p. 8; George Rodger, "Belsen," *Time,* April 30, 1945, p. 40; Peter Furst, "Freedom Fighters Liberate Dachau Camp," *PM,* April 30, 1945, p. 1.

50. Denny, "Despair Blankets Buchenwald Camp," p. 3; Gene Currivan, "Germans Murder 5,000 Prisoners Removed from Buchenwald Camp," *New York Times,* April 30, 1945, p. 5; Colin Wills, "Belsen Victim," *News Chronicle,* April 23, 1945, p. 1.

51. Percival Knauth, "Buchenwald," *Time,* April 30, 1945, p. 44; John R. Wilhelm, "German Villages Forced to Bury Jewish Victims," *PM,* April 30, 1945, p. 9; Edwin Tetlow, "Belsen: The Final Horror," *Daily Mail,* April 20, 1945, p. 1; Denny, "Despair Blankets Buchenwald Camp," p. 3.

52. Knauth, "Buchenwald," pp. 41, 42; Wade Jones, "Yanks Make Germans Dig Up Murdered Prisoners by Hand," *Stars and Stripes,* April 23, 1945, p. 4; Folliard, "Skeptic Yanks See Proof," p. 4.

53. "Piles of Bodies Found in Camp," *Los Angeles Times,* April 19, 1945, pt. 1, p. 2; "Nazi Barn Murders," letter to the editor, *Newsweek,* June 11, 1945, p. 10.

54. "Buchenwald Tour Shocking to M.P.s," *New York Times,* April 23, 1945, p. 5; "To Look at Horror," *Newsweek,* May 28, 1945, p. 34; Knauth, "Buchenwald," p. 44; "There Is a Camp Worse Than Buchenwald," *News Chronicle,* April 23, 1945, p. 1.

55. "Woman, M.P. to See Horror Camps," *Daily Telegraph,* April 20, 1945, p. 1; "3,500,000 Were Slain at Auschwitz," *PM,* April 23, 1945, p. 7; "Camp Worse Than Buchenwald," p. 1; "Congressmen See Buchenwald," *New York Times,* April 22, 1945, p. 13. No such comment was made about the male members of the delegation, despite the headline. For more on women and the atrocity photos, see Barbie Zelizer, "Gender and Atrocity: Women in Holocaust Photographs," collection in preparation, ed. Stephen Browne.

56. For example, see "Editors Inspect Buchenwald," *New York Times,* April 26, 1945, p. 12; "2 Pamphlets Contain Views on Nazi Camps," *Editor and Publisher,* June 23, 1945, p. 28; Norman Chandler, "Stories of Nazi Prison Horrors Substantiated," *Los Angeles Times,* April 28, 1945, pt. 1, p. 1.

57. Walker Stone, "Words Cannot Describe Horrors," *ASNE Bulletin,* June 1, 1945, n.p.

58. "To Look at Horror," p. 35; Clare Boothe Luce, "German People Must Answer for Their Crimes," *PM,* April 27, 1945, p. 11.

59. "Nazi Murder Camp," *New York Times,* April 22, 1945, sec. 4, p. 1E; "For the

Record," *London Evening Standard,* April 20, 1945, p. 3; "Nazis Deliberately Starved, Neglected Yank Prisoners," *PM,* April 19, 1945, p. 10.

60. Edward R. Murrow, "They Died 900 a Day in 'the Best' Nazi Camp," *PM,* April 16, 1945, p. 4; "Gazing into the Pit," *Christian Century,* May 9, 1945, p. 575; Edwin Tetlow, "The Most Terrible Story of the War," *Daily Mail,* April 19, 1945, p. 1; headline reprinted in *Daily Mail,* April 20, 1945, p. 1.

61. "Press Exposure of German Horror Camps," *Newspaper World,* April 28, 1945, p. 1; Chandler, "Horrors Recalled"; E. Z. Dimitman, "Lest We Forget Dachau!" *Quill,* July–August 1945, p. 5.

62. Victor H. Bernstein, "I Saw the Bodies of 3,000 Slaves Murdered by Nazis," *PM,* April 17, 1945, p. 15; Jones, "This Ends Notion," p. 3; Cowan, "Dachau, Most Dreaded Prison," pt. 1, p. 5. This obviously continued beyond the three camps at focus here, when Mauthausen, liberated during the first week of May, was labeled "another Buchenwald" (William H. Stoneman, "Yanks Killed by Gas at Camp in Austria," *Boston Globe,* May 9, 1945, p. 8), and when the Russians released their report on Auschwitz, said to make the atrocities "at the Buchenwald, Dachau, Maidanek, and Babi Yar Nazi camps pale into insignificance" ("4 Million Killed in German Camp in Poland, Soviets Report," *Washington Post,* May 8, 1945, p. 3).

63. See Robert H. Abzug, "The Liberation of the Concentration Camps," in *Liberation, 1945* (Washington, D.C.: United States Holocaust Memorial Council, 1995), p. 35.

64. Tony Kushner, *The Holocaust and the Liberal Imagination: A Social and Cultural History* (Oxford: Basil Blackwell, 1994), p. 126. Kushner provides an eloquent discussion of how liberalism limited moral obligation toward the Jews. A lack of attentiveness to sites of industrialized mass murder furthered mischaracterization of the camps.

65. Tetlow, *As It Happened,* p. 77.

66. Frye, "Eyes of Breathing Cadavers," p. 3; Tetlow, *As It Happened,* p. 77. Most reporters did not at the time attempt identification of the victims who perished in the camps. This may have ultimately worked against a recognition of Jewish victimization during the Holocaust.

67. Tetlow, *As It Happened,* p. 81.

68. "Belsen—World Must Know These Facts" (text of radio dispatch by Patrick Gordon Walker on Luxembourg Radio; released by Office of War Information), *PM,* April 25, 1945, p. 11. Interestingly, as if to heighten the contrasting degree of importance lent the attribution of reporters and photographers, two photographs (both of Belsen inmates) were appended to the article. Yet neither was identified by photographer or photographic agency, and the captions beneath each image spoke of suffering only in highly generalized terms.

69. Richard Collier, *The Warcos: The War Correspondents of World War II* (London: Weidenfeld and Nicolson, 1989), pp. 187–88; May, *Witness to War,* p. 88; Templeton Peck Papers, Box 1, HIA; Leonard Miall, ed. *Richard Dimbleby, Broadcaster: By His Colleagues* (London: British Broadcasting Corporation, 1966), p. 47.

70. Peterman, "Nazis Kill 51,000," p. 1; Denny, "World Must Not Forget," p. 9.

71. Richard J. H. Johnston, "Yanks Bare Prison Horror, 'Ghosts' Fight over Food," *New York Times,* April 4, 1945, p. 7; Knauth, "Buchenwald," p. 41; Ben Hibbs, "Journey to a Shattered World," *Saturday Evening Post,* June 9, 1945, p. 22; Edward Murrow, "Buchenwald," *London Evening Standard,* April 18, 1945, p. 3; Edward R. Murrow, "Buchenwald Was a Living Death," *Stars and Stripes,* April 17, 1945, p. 4. Murrow's piece was also broadcast on the BBC before that of its own reporter, because the words

of a U.S. reporter were thought more effective in compelling belief (Kushner, *Holocaust and Liberal Imagination,* pp. 214–15). CBS veteran Fred Friendly later called Murrow's radio broadcast "the best piece of television journalism ever done and obviously there are no pictures. . . .Your mind's eye [transports] you to Buchenwald swifter and with more accuracy than any television camera, electronic or film could ever do" (Fred Friendly/Edward R. Murrow Tape, 1961, No. 0315264,YVPA).

72. Julius Ochs Adler, "Buchenwald Worse Than Battlefield," *New York Times,* April 4, 1945, p. 6; Knauth, "Buchenwald," p. 40; Harry J. Ditton, "Prison Camp Horrors Will Be Shown to Germans," *News of the World,* April 22, 1945; "How Will Kremer [*sic*] Die? Victims Ask," *Washington Post,* April 22, 1945, p. 5; "This IS the Enemy," *PM,* April 26, 1945, p. 13.

73. Tetlow, "Most Terrible Story," p. 1; "Real Horror of Nazi Camps 'Unprintable,'" *Stars and Stripes,* April 30, 1945, p. 3; Denny, "Despair Blankets Buchenwald Camp," p. 3; Edward R. Murrow, "Despatch by Ed Murrow—CBS," transcription, April 15, 1945, pp. 1, 3 (Templeton Peck Papers, Box 1, HIA); Uncle Dudley, "Evil Strips Down," editorial, *Boston Globe,* April 29, 1945, p. 4.

CHAPTER FOUR

1. Jack Price, "'Doormat' Label Develops Ire of Cameramen," *Editor and Publisher,* March 10, 1945, p. 44.

2. Interview with Sgt. W. Lawrie, Department of Sound Records, IWM; cited in Martin Caiger-Smith, *The Face of the Enemy: British Photographers in Germany, 1944–1952* (Berlin: Nishen, 1988), p. 11.

3. "Europe's Problem: What M.P.s Say of the Nazi Horror Camps," *Picture Post,* May 12, 1945, p. 25; Edward R. Murrow, "Despatch by Ed Murrow—CBS," transcription, April 15, 1945, p. 2 (Templeton Peck Papers, Box 1, HIA).

4. Margaret Bourke-White, *Portrait of Myself* (New York: Simon and Schuster, 1963), pp. 160, 259–60; Vicki Goldberg, *Margaret Bourke-White: A Biography* (Reading, Mass.: Addison-Wesley, 1987), p. 290; Bourke-White, *"Dear Fatherland, Rest Quietly"* (New York: Simon and Schuster, 1946), p. 77.

5. Jorge Lewinski, *The Camera at War: A History of War Photography from 1848 to the Present Day* (New York: Simon and Schuster, 1978), p. 14; interview with George Rodger, in *Dialogue with Photography,* ed. Paul Hill and Thomas Cooper (New York: Farrar, Straus and Giroux, 1979), pp. 59–60; Amanda Hopkinson, "You Have Been Framed," *New Statesman and Society,* June 30, 1995, pp. 32–33.

6. Cited in Anthony Penrose, ed., *Lee Miller's War* (Boston: Bullfinch Press, 1992), pp. 161, 182, 187.

7. Cited in Goldberg, *Margaret Bourke-White,* p. 291.

8. "Press Exposure of German Horror Camps," *Newspaper World,* April 28, 1945, p. 1; "Slain Internees Found in German Camp," *Washington Post,* April 20, 1945, p. 3; also appended to John M. Mecklin, "I Saw Men, Women, Children Slain by Nazis," *PM,* April 10, 1945, p. 5.

9. Accredited in both cases to the U.S. Signal Corps, in the former case the image appeared alongside an article on a Nazi murder mill near Limburg; in the latter, it accompanied a report of a fire in a Polish ghetto. In neither case was the linkage between the three events made explicit. But the data accompanying the image in both cases were highly detailed. "More Brutality!" proclaimed the caption in the *Washington Post:* "Major John Scotti of Brooklyn, New York, a medical officer in the Fourth Armored Division, United States Third Army, inspects naked bodies of slain internees,

as they were found in a woodshed of a concentration camp at Ohrdruf, Germany, nine miles south of Gotha."

10. The photos' publication was discussed in "To Print or Not to Print?" *Newspaper World,* April 14, 1945, p. 6; "Britain's Anger," *Daily Mail,* April 23, 1945, p. 2; "Press Exposure," p. 1.

11. Picture captioned "They Witnessed Nazi Culture," *Washington Post,* May 2, 1945, p. 3, and picture appended to R. M. McKelway, "Clergy Were Used as Guinea Pigs; Dogs Were Turned on Prisoners for Sport," *Boston Globe,* May 8, 1945, p. 10.

12. Photo appended to "Foreign News: Germany," *Time,* April 30, 1945, pp. 38–45.

13. "This Is the Enemy—Horror Unequalled throughout the Centuries," *Daily Telegraph,* April 19, 1945, p. 5. None of the pictures was accredited.

14. "World Demands Justice," *Daily Mirror,* April 19, 1945, pp. 4–5. According to Signal Corps files, it was taken on April 12 (Document #SC-203545, file "Atrocities," NA); picture appended to "Torture Camps: This Is the Evidence," *Daily Mail,* April 19, 1945, p. 2; picture appended to Captain C. A. Burney, "Prisoner Describes Horrors of Buchenwald in Broadcast," *PM,* April 19, 1945, p. 11; "Lest We Forget! Some Examples of German Sadistic Inhumanity," *Illustrated London News,* April 14, 1945, p. 404; "British Prisoners of War Regain Freedom," *Illustrated London News,* April 21, 1945, p. 435.

15. "Atrocity Pictures," *Editor and Publisher,* May 5, 1945, p. 40. The piece went on to say that while Americans "have built up such immunity to what they call propaganda" that they refuse to believe even the pictures, now was not "the time to be squeamish—print the pictures and lots of them." Also see John R. Whiting, "Candid Shots," *Popular Photography,* July 1945, p. 16; "To Print or Not," p. 6.

16. Penrose, *Lee Miller's War,* p. 161; "German Atrocities in Prison Camps," *Illustrated London News,* April 28, 1945, supplement, p. i; cited in "Press Exposure," p. 14.

17. "Pictures of Germans' Victims," *London Times,* April 19, 1945, p. 4; uncaptioned picture appended to Ronald Clark, "1,800 Airmen Prisoners in Torture March," *Daily Telegraph,* April 21, 1945, p. 3; Edwin Tetlow, "The Most Terrible Story of the War," *Daily Mail,* April 19, 1945, p. 1; "Nazi Barbarism," *Philadelphia Inquirer,* April 26, 1945, p. 14; "Indisputable Proof," *News Chronicle,* April 19, 1945, p. 1; "Heaped Evidence . . . ," *Daily Mirror,* April 18, 1945, p. 5.

18. For a discussion of these Holocaust symbols in art, see Ziva Amishai-Maisels, *Depiction and Interpretation: Visual Arts and the Holocaust* (Oxford: Pergamon, 1993), pp. 131–34.

19. For example, picture appended to "Buchenwald Factory for Extermination," *Washington Post,* April 29, 1945, p. 8M; "Nazi Policy of Organized Murder Blackens Germany for All History," *Newsweek,* April 30, 1945, pp. 56–57; pictures appended to "The Problem That Makes All Europe Wonder," pp. 7–11. Of eleven images, only two (from Nordhausen) were identified by location.

20. The earlier image appeared as a picture captioned "Bodies in Nordhausen Gestapo Concentration Camp," *Boston Globe,* April 17, 1945, p. 16; and "At Nordhausen," *London Times,* April 19, 1945, p. 6. The second shot appeared as a picture captioned "Bodies of Slave Laborers Await Burial at German Camp," *Boston Daily Globe,* April 26, 1945, p. 15.

21. Picture captioned "Death Measured by the Carload," *Washington Post,* May 2, 1945, p. 3.

22. Picture appended to "Foreign News: Dachau," *Time,* May 7, 1945, p. 35.

23. Picture appended to "Problem Makes Europe Wonder," p. 11.

24. Picture captioned "Editors, Publishers on Way to Reich," *Los Angeles Times,* April 26, 1945, pt. 1, p. 3; picture captioned "American Legislators in Europe to Investigate Atrocities," *New York Times,* April 25, 1945, p. 3; "M.P.s Will See Horror Camp Secrets," *Daily Mail,* April 21, 1945, p. 1; picture appended to Ben Hibbs, "Journey to a Shattered World," *Saturday Evening Post,* June 9, 1945, p. 20.

25. Picture appended to "To Look at Horror," *Newsweek,* May 28, 1945, p. 35, and to "German Civilians Made to See for Themselves," *News Chronicle,* April 19, 1945, p. 4.

26. "Dachau—a Grisly Spectacle," *Washington Post,* May 2, 1945, p. 3. The image was taken on April 16 (Document #208AA-206K-31, file "German Concentration Camps–Buchenwald and Dachau," NA) and appeared as "Crowded Bunks in the Prison Camp at Buchenwald," *New York Times Magazine,* May 6, 1945, p. 42. One exception to the anonymity rule was a Dachau survivor named Margit Schwartz, who insisted on being photographed in the same upright pose she had assumed in her only prewar possession—a photograph of herself standing. Despite the protestations of those around her, she dragged herself to her feet and prodded the photographer to take her image. British Official Photo (Document #208-AA-129G-3, file "Atrocities–Germany–Belsen," NA).

27. Picture appended to Harold Denny, "'The World Must Not Forget,'" *New York Times Magazine,* May 6, 1945, p. 8; picture appended to "World Demands Justice."

28. Unnumbered document in file entitled "Jews–Antisemitism–Germany, World War II," archive of Columbia University School of Journalism; picture appended to "Atrocities" file, p. 32.

29. Photo by U.S. Signal Corps (Document #208-AA-207B-10, file "German Concentration Camps, Wobbelin," NA).

30. Aforementioned picture captioned "Slain Internees Found in German Camp," p. 3; picture appended to "German Atrocities"; uncaptioned picture appended to "'Take Hitler Prisoner Unless He Resists,'" *Daily Telegraph,* April 20, 1945, p. 5.

31. "American Editors View Buchenwald Victims," *Boston Globe,* May 4 1945, p. 4; "Buchenwald," *Los Angeles Times,* May 4, 1945, pt. 1, p. 3; picture captioned "M.P.s View Hun Cruelty," *Daily Mirror,* April 24, 1945, p. 5; Clare Boothe Luce, "What Angered Me Most at Buchenwald," *London Evening Standard,* April 27, 1945.

32. Picture captioned "'Ike' at Scene of Atrocity," *Washington Post,* April 16, 1945, p. 4; picture appended to "German Atrocities."

33. "There Was Fuel in Plenty," *News Chronicle,* April 21, 1945, p. 1. The British photographer who snapped this shot later wrote home of the difficulties he experienced in doing so. "There were hundreds of bodies lying about, in many cases piled 5 or 6 high," he wrote. "Amongst them sat women peeling potatoes and cooking scraps of food. They were quite unconcerned when I lifted my camera to photograph them. They even smiled" (letter from Sgt. Midgley, IWM, cited in Caiger-Smith, *Face of the Enemy,* p. 14). The triangular shot of Buchenwald, taken on April 16, appeared in numerous newspapers, including a picture captioned "At Buchenwald," *London Times,* April 19, 1945, p. 6, and a picture captioned "German Civilians See Truckload of Bodies," *Boston Globe,* April 25, 1945, p. 13.

34. Such pictures were typical of a two-page pictorial spread entitled "When You Hear Talk of a Soft Peace for the Germans—Remember These Pictures," *PM,* April 26, 1945, pp. 12–13. The journal displayed an additional page of atrocity photos the next day.

35. Picture appended to "This Was Nazi Germany—Blood, Starvation, the Stench of Death," *Stars and Stripes,* April 23, 1945, pp. 4–5. A long shot of the same wagon was used by photographers to depict the witnessing activities of different groups, such as Weimar civilians facing Allied troops in the aforementioned triangular shot of Buchenwald or official delegations inspecting the bodies. See "Nazi Barbarism," *Philadelphia Inquirer,* April 26, 1945, p. 14, and "Penna. Congressman Sees Evidence of Foe's Cruelty," *Philadelphia Inquirer,* April 26, 1945, p. 14.

36. Shot captioned "Study in Evil: The S.S. Women of Belsen," *Daily Mail,* April 23, 1945, p. 3; picture appended to a set of pictures entitled "Like a Doré Drawing of Dante's Inferno: Scenes in Belsen," *Illustrated London News,* April 28, 1945, supplement, p. iii.

37. Picture captioned "Slave Laborer Points Finger of Guilt," *Washington Post,* April 26, 1945, p. 9.

38. Interview with Sgt. M. Lawrie, cited in Caiger-Smith, *Face of the Enemy,* p. 11; picture appended to "Here's How Nazis Treat Their Captives . . . ," *PM,* May 1, 1945, p. 8.

39. Picture appended to Peter Furst, "Anti-Nazi Bavarians Helped to Seize Munich," *PM,* May 1, 1945, p. 12, and to Hibbs, "Journey to Shattered World," p. 21; *Lest We Forget: The Horrors of Nazi Concentration Camps Revealed for All Time in the Most Terrible Photographs Ever Published* (London: Daily Mail, 1945), p. 73.

40. Picture captioned "Belsen's Commandant," *London Times,* April 21, 1945, p. 8; picture captioned "The Beast of Belsen," *Daily Mail,* April 21, 1945, p. 4. In reference to the earlier picture of the seated Nazi, the legend asked readers, "Remember this man's face, pictured in yesterday's *Daily Mail?*"

41. The documentation that actually accompanied many of the photographs, particularly those wirephotos sent by the U.S. Signal Corps, bears mention. Affixed to the back of many of these images was detailed information about who took the photograph, where it was taken, and how. Additionally, the Signal Corps provided extensive background information about the circumstances that preceded the photograph, and the images were often grouped according to the background information that might be most relevant in explaining the broader circumstances surrounding a given event. Yet very little, if any, of this information was picked up by the news organizations using the shots.

42. The first picture was captioned "Like a Doré Drawing of Dante's Inferno"; "Horror, Starvation, Death in German Concentration Camps Revealed by Allies' Advance," *Stars and Stripes,* April 30, 1945, p. 4; also as *KZ: Bildbericht aus funf Konzentrationslagern* (prepared under the supervision of the American Office of War Information for the Commander-in-Chief of the Allied Forces, 1945), p. 31. The second picture was appended to *Lest We Forget,* p. 23; to "Horror, Starvation, Death in German Concentration Camps Revealed by Allies' Advance," *Stars and Stripes,* April 30, 1945, p. 4; to "The Murder Gang of Belsen Spread This Horror in the Name of the Germans," *Sunday Express,* April 22, 1945, p. 9; to "Like a Doré Drawing of Dante's Inferno," p. ii, and to *KZ,* p. 6.

43. The photograph appeared appended to Percival Knauth, "Buchenwald," part of the larger section entitled "Foreign News: Germany," p. 42; as a picture captioned "Victims of the Beast" appended to Al Newman, "Nordhausen: A Hell Factory Worked by the Living Dead," *Newsweek,* April 23, 1945, p. 52; and as a picture appended to "This Was Nazi Germany," pp. 4–5. In the last two cases, the bodies were correctly identified as being at Ohrdruf. The location was identified as Nordhausen in a pam-

phlet issued in April 1945 by the British Communist Party (see *Fascist Murders: Pictures of the Concentration Camps You Must Never Forget* [London: Communist Party, April 1945], n.p.; taken from file #K4H, WL). The photograph was actually part of a series taken by the war pool photo, jointly attributed to British Combine and Acme Photos, and was taken sometime between April 4 and April 8, 1945 (Photo 1460/41, F 15476, YVPA). It was in fact the same image that had appeared two to three weeks earlier, on April 10, in both the *Washington Post* and *PM,* as a picture captioned "Slain Internees Found in German Camp," p. 3 and as a picture appended to Mecklin, "Men, Women, Children Slain," p. 5.

44. Picture appended to "Foreign News: Germany," pp. 38–40. This picture was appended to a series of eyewitness reports from Erla, Belsen, and Buchenwald, but there was no such report from the camp outside Nordhausen. The photograph thus served as the *only* marker of Nordhausen in the *Time* account.

45. Picture appended to Denny, "World Must Not Forget," p. 42. We need only consider how unusual it would be to find a reporter's byline situated elsewhere in a newspaper.

46. See pictures printed in the *Daily Mail,* April 20, 1945, p. 1; *Daily Mail,* April 21, 1945, p. 4; *Daily Mail,* April 23, 1945, p. 3; pictures appended to "German Atrocities."

47. Picture appended to "Official Report on Buchenwald Camp," *PM,* April 30, 1945, p. 9. In an atypical move, the caption identified the figure in the foreground as a "Hungarian Jew." On the whole, however, Jewish victimization in the Holocaust was rarely mentioned in the press. The same image, for instance, appeared in the *Saturday Evening Post* with the legend, "The editors saw these living caricatures of human beings, and hundreds like them, at Buchenwald" (picture appended to Hibbs, "Journey to Shattered World," p. 21).

48. "Daily Feature and Pictorial Page," *Philadelphia Inquirer,* April 26, 1945, p. 14.

49. "This Was Nazi Germany," pp. 4–5; picture appended to "Foreign News: Germany," *Time,* May 14, 1945, p. 43.

50. "The End of Belsen?" *Time,* June 11, 1945, p. 36.

51. See Bryan de Grineau, "As Doré Might Have Conceived It: Belsen Death Camp," *Illustrated London News,* May 5, 1945, pp. 471–73. The editors told readers that the drawings "throw a further light on the photographs published in our last issue" (p. 471). Unlike the unaccredited photographs, however, the drawings bore the name and signature of the artist who drew them.

52. "Problem Makes Europe Wonder," pp. 7–11, 26.

53. Picture appended to Bertrand Russell, "Whose Guilt? The Problem of Cruelty," *Picture Post,* June 16, 1945, p. 13. The spread ran on pp. 10–13.

54. "Atrocities," *Life,* May 7, 1945, pp. 32–37.

55. "Atrocities," pp. 32–37. Quotes were taken from pp. 33, 37.

56. Interview with John Henry Baker Jr., on Ohrdruf, February 27, 1980, WHP.

57. The writer of the letter actually photographed the liberation of Ohrdruf, but he apparently did so by chance. "The morning Ohrdruf was liberated," he wrote, "I was there. Several days before I had picked up a camera that had about ten pictures left on the film, and I took them there" (letter from Raymond J. Young to John B. Coulston, taken from file "Jews in the American Army Liberation of Ohrdruf," Document B/60; K/15/82, YVPA). We can assume that such circumstances for documenting the camps were common.

58. Cited in Robert H. Abzug, *Inside the Vicious Heart: Americans and the Liberation of*

Nazi Concentration Camps (New York: Oxford University Press, 1985), p. 138; interview with Joseph B. Kushlis, on Ohrdruf, March 30, 1979, WHP; Baker, interview.

59. Interview with William A. Scott, April 9, 1979, WHP; letter from Captain James B. Ficklen, April 15, 1945 (Collection 1986, Document # 031.24a, USHMM); taken from Paul Gumz file, WHP; Tom Infield, "Witness," *Philadelphia Inquirer Magazine,* April 9, 1995, p. 26.

60. Taken from Dennis Wile file, WHP.

61. "Problem Makes Europe Wonder," p. 7.

62. See the *New York Times,* April 24, 1945. The article detailed that "such a plan was being perfected tonight by information services of Britain and the United States in cooperation with Allied Supreme Headquarters. These services are assembling a pictorial layout of scenes of both Buchenwald and Belsen together with pictures of men and women wardens, who were captured at the camps. The photographs will be reproduced on large boards for display in every community in conquered Germany at points where inhabitants will be compelled to view them as they go to and from their homes."

63. Picture appended to Tania Long, "Goering's Home Town—under American Rule," *New York Times,* June 3, 1945, sec. 6, p. 9; picture captioned "Holding the Mirror Up to the Huns," *Daily Mirror,* April 30, 1945, p. 5.

64. "The Pictures Don't Lie," *Stars and Stripes,* April 26, 1945, p. 2.

65. Goldberg, *Margaret Bourke-White,* p. 290; "Public Crowd for Pictures of Atrocities," *World's Press News,* April 26, 1945, p. 1; "The Pictures Don't Lie," p. 2. Crowds of three and four persons deep gathered around a public display in London of enlarged photographs from the camps.

66. "German Atrocities"; "Gazing into the Pit," *Christian Century,* May 9, 1945, pp. 575, 576; "Special Pre-Peace News Questionnaire," April 18, 1945, pp. 14–22; cited in John Taylor, *War Photography: Realism in the British Press* (London: Routledge, 1991), pp. 62–66.

67. Amishai-Maisels, *Depiction and Interpretation,* p. 50.

CHAPTER FIVE

1. Ziva Amishai-Maisels, *Depiction and Interpretation: Visual Arts and the Holocaust* (Oxford: Pergamon, 1993), p. 123.

2. In developing the distinction between figure and ground, I am invoking perception theories common to social psychology; in one familiar example, the figure and the ground alternate in a drawing as one perceives either the sides of a vase or the profiles of two women.

3. Saul Friedlander, *Memory, History, and the Extermination of the Jews of Europe* (Bloomington: Indiana University Press, 1993), p. 45.

4. Amishai-Maisels, Depiction and Interpretation, p. 50.

5. Jorge Lewinski, *The Camera at War: A History of War Photography from 1848 to the Present Day* (New York: Simon and Schuster, 1978), p. 136; Sydney Gruson, "British Anger Deep at Atrocity Proof," *New York Times,* April 20, 1945, p. 3; John R. Whiting, "Candid Shots," *Popular Photography,* July 1945, p. 16.

6. "Supplement to Committee, Letters to the *Times,*" *New York Times,* May 7, 1945, p. 16; "Nazi Camps," letters to the editor, *Manchester Guardian,* April 25, 1945, p. 4; Robert Donington, "Germany and the Camps," letter to the editor, *London Times,* April 24, 1945; "All These Horrors Must Be Known," *Daily Mirror,* April 23, 1945, p. 2; "Atrocities: Letters to Editor," *Life,* May 28, 1945, pp. 2–4. The *London Times* received

so many letters that it published them in two batches—"German Crimes," letters to the editor, *London Times,* April 21, 1945, p. 5, and "Apparatus of Nazism," letters to the editor, *London Times,* April 28, 1945, p. 5.

7. Report on George Gallup's American Institute of Public Opinion, May 1945; cited in "What the Homefront Thinks," *Army Talks,* July 10, 1945, p. 5.

8. Edgar Ainsworth, "Victim and Prisoner," *Picture Post,* September 22, 1945, p. 13.

9. E. Z. Dimitman, "Lest We Forget Dachau!" *Quill,* July–August 1945, p. 138. During World War II, even official photo interpreters "were given no historical or social background by which to judge pictures. . . . They were usually in a hurry to make judgments and often used shortcuts in making them" (Dino Brugioni, cited in Thomas O'Toole, "'44 Photos Showed Auschwitz Camp," *Washington Post,* February 23, 1979, p. A26); Milton Mayer, "Let the Swiss Do It!" *Progressive,* May 14, 1945.

10. "Letter from a British Hitler?" letter to the editor, *Daily Mail,* April 27, 1945, p. 2. For a discussion of Mosley, Bowman, and Reed, see Tony Kushner, *The Holocaust and the Liberal Imagination: A Social and Cultural History* (Oxford: Basil Blackwell, 1994), p. 224.

11. Marquis Childs, "Washington Calling: Victims of Nazism," *Washington Post,* April 27, 1945, p. 14; Joseph Pulitzer, "A Report to the American People," *St. Louis Post-Dispatch,* May 20, 1945, p. 1D; "Europe's Problem: What M.P.'s Say of the Nazi Horror Camps," *Picture Post,* May 12, 1945, p. 25.

12. "The Pictures Don't Lie," *Stars and Stripes,* April 26, 1945, p. 2. The picture had arrived over the wires from the U.S. Signal Corps with extensive documentation about the body of a slave laborer burned and machine-gunned to death by the German troops at Leipzig, Germany, on April 13, 1945. It was not identified as such by the *Stars and Stripes,* despite the fact that the newspaper apparently received such documentation with the photograph (see Massacre at Leipzig, Document #14581/166, SC 203743-S, YVPA). It is possible that years later radio broadcaster John MacVane was describing this photo when he recalled how the victims outside of Leipzig "were only skin and bones, living skeletons, and they lay in grotesque attitudes just as they had fallen asleep when they had been shot. One was up on his knees and elbows, his hands clasped in supplication, stiffened in position as he had been shot down" (John Mac-Vane, *On the Air in World War II* [New York: William Morrow, 1979], p. 313).

13. "Letter to Editor," *Life,* June 4, 1945, p. 3. The photo depicted an Allied flyer about to be beheaded by his Japanese captor. A second letter protested its supposed lack of authenticity and called on *Life* to provide additional background information.

14. Nat Hyman, ed., *Eyes of the War: A Photographic Report of World War II* (New York: Tele-Pic Syndicate, 1945); *Lest We Forget: The Horrors of Nazi Concentration Camps Revealed for All Time in the Most Terrible Photographs Ever Published* (London: Daily Mail and Associated Press, 1945); "Record of the Horror Camps," *Sunday Express,* April 29, 1945. The U.S. exhibition was entitled "Lest We Forget," and persons under the age of sixteen were barred from attending (Robert H. Abzug, *Inside the Vicious Heart: Americans and the Liberation of Nazi Concentration Camps* [New York: Oxford University Press, 1985], p. 134).

15. *KZ: Bildbericht aus funf Konzentrationslagern* (prepared under the supervision of the American Office of War Information for the Commander-in-Chief of the Allied Forces, 1945) was the most widely circulated of the military pamphlets. Reprinted as part of Emory University's Fred R. Crawford Witness to the Holocaust publication series, no. 5, 1983.

16. Lebrun apparently used for inspiration photos displayed earlier in the *U.S. Cam-*

era Annual of 1946, which he kept as a souvenir at the end of the war. Picasso's inspiration for *The Charnel House* presumably came from photos of Majdanek, released earlier than those of the camps on the western front (see Amishai-Maisels, *Depiction and Interpretation,* p. 62); John Hersey, *The Wall* (New York: Knopf, 1950); interview with Anatoli Kuznetsov, "The Memories," *New York Times Book Review,* April 9, 1967, p. 45.

17. Quoted in Studs Terkel, *"The Good War": An Oral History of World War II* (New York: Pantheon Books, 1984), p. 144; interview with Jack D. Hallett, on Dachau, December 26, 1978, WHP.

18. *Badge,* March 1975, pp. 7–8; *45th Division News,* May 31, 1945, p. 1, and *Timberwolf Tracks: History of the 104th Infantry Division, 1942–1945* (Washington, D.C.: Infantry Journal Press, July 1946), both in Dachau File, WHP; "The Seventy First Came . . . to Gunskirchen Lager," 1945; reprinted as part of Emory University's Fred R. Crawford Witness to the Holocaust publication series, no. 1, 1979; "Dachau," 7th U.S. Army, 1945; reprinted as part of Emory University's Fred R. Crawford Witness to the Holocaust publication series, no. 2, 1979; Frank M. S. Miller, *Buchenwald Concentration Camp: A Letter Home* (n.p.: May 5, 1945), Buchenwald File, WHP; John Weitz, "To the Editor," letter to the editor, *Look,* June 6, 1950; Lloyd Marker, "Eyewitness to Scene, Results of Crimes at Dachau," letter to the editor, *Toledo Blade,* June 29, 1945, Dachau File, WHP.

19. "What the Homefront Thinks," p. 6; "Camp Horror Films Exhibited Here," *New York Times,* May 2, 1945, p. 3; "Music Hall Atrocity Film Ban Protested," *Hollywood Reporter,* May 7, 1945, p. 1; "Allied Troops Compel London Audience to View German Atrocities Films," *New York Times,* April 22, 1945, p. 5; "Soldiers Insist Civilians View Atrocity Film," *Washington Post,* April 21, 1945, p. 2. "People walked out from cinemas all over the country," the *Washington Post* reported, "and in many places there were soldiers to tell them to go back and face it." Ambivalence was in fact widespread. When the U.S. Signal Corps released its footage to the major newsreel companies, many questioned the wisdom of showing scenes of the camps, arguing that to do so would increase the difficulties of making peace with the Germans. This seemed "inspired, at least in part, by an unwillingness to confront the scenes themselves" (Abzug, *Inside the Vicious Heart,* p. 135).

20. "Wants Factual Record of German Atrocities," *Stars and Stripes,* April 23, 1945, p. 5.

21. Whiting, "Candid Shots," p. 16; Joseph Upton, "Nuremberg Pictures," *Journal of the British Institute for Journalists,* January 1947, p. 7.

22. "Pictures of Death," *Newsweek,* September 4, 1946, p. 71; "Picture Story," *Time,* November 4, 1946, p. 75.

23. Robert Antelme, cited in Annette Wieviorka, "On Testimony," in *Holocaust Remembrance: The Shapes of Memory,* ed. Geoffrey Hartman (Oxford: Basil Blackwell, 1994), p. 26; Sidra DeKoven Ezrahi, *By Words Alone: The Holocaust in Literature* (Chicago: University of Chicago Press, 1980), p. 21.

24. Whiting, "Candid Shots," p. 16.

25. Margaret Bourke-White, *"Dear Fatherland, Rest Quietly"* (New York: Simon and Schuster, 1946); John D'Arcy-Dawson, *European Victory* (London: MacDonald and Company, 1945); Martha Gelhorn, *The Face of War* (New York: Simon and Schuster, 1959); Joseph Waldmeir, "The Documentation of World War II," *Nation,* November 19, 1960, p. 396; Margaret Bourke-White, *Portrait of Myself* (New York: Simon and Schuster, 1963); cited in Antoinette May, *Witness to War: A Biography of Marguerite Higgins* (New York: Beaufort Press, 1983), p. 91. There was a twist to the honors, because

by the time Higgins left the camp, the road was blocked with convoys, so that her article appeared one day late, with the dateline "April 29 (delayed)"; Tom Maloney, ed., *U.S. Camera Annual* (New York: Duell, Sloan and Pearce, 1946), pp. 227–31; Hyman, *Eyes of the War,* pp. 266–69; *New York Herald Tribune: Front Page History of the Second World War* (New York: Herald Tribune, Inc., 1946), n.p.

26. "'Best Photo' Tags Go to a Jig and a Jerk," *Editor and Publisher,* June 30, 1945, p. 48; untitled advertisement, *Popular Photography,* June 1945, p. 72; National Broadcasting Company, *This Is the Story of the Liberation of Europe from the Fall of Rome to Victory* (n.p.: May 1945), p. 16; Associated Press, *Reporting to Remember: Unforgettable Stories and Pictures of World War II by Correspondents of the Associated Press* (New York: Associated Press, 1945), p. 5.

27. For example, see John C. Oestreicher, *The World Is Their Beat* (New York: Duell, Sloan and Pearce, 1945); Ralph G. Martin and Richard Harrity, *World War II: A Photographic Record of the War in Europe, from D-Day to V-E Day* (Greenwich, Conn.: Fawcett Publications, 1962), n.p; Natalie Canavor, "Margaret Bourke-White—a Retrospective," *Popular Photography,* May 1973, p. 135.

28. National Broadcasting Company, *This Is the Story;* American Newspaper Publishers Association—Bureau of Advertising, *Victory in Europe* (New York: ANPA, 1945), n.p; Joseph J. Mathews, *Reporting the Wars* (Minneapolis: University of Minnesota Press, 1957). Three chapters of the book addressed World War II coverage, but they offered not a word about the camps. This also characterizes history textbooks on World War II, where the Holocaust has been treated as an independent series of events.

29. Stefan Lorant, cited in Robert E. Girvin, "Photography as Social Documentation," *Journalism Quarterly,* September 1947, p. 219; Loudon Wainwright, *The Great American Magazine* (New York: Alfred A. Knopf, 1986), p. 159.

30. *Life's Picture History of World War II* (New York: Time, Inc., 1950), p. v. The pictures appeared on pp. 310–12.

31. Leon Wieseltier, "After Memory," *New Republic,* May 3, 1993, p. 20.

32. The term "flashbulb memory" was popularized by Ulric Neisser, "Snapshots or Benchmarks?" in *Memory Observed,* ed. Ulric Neisser (San Francisco: W. H. Freeman, 1982), pp. 43–48: "memories become flashbulbs primarily through the significance that is attached to them afterwards. Later that day, the next day, and in subsequent months and years. What requires explanation is the long endurance [of the memory]" (p. 45); A. Alvarez, "The Concentration Camps," *Atlantic,* December 1962, p. 70; Allan Sekula, "Reading an Archive: Photography between Labor and Capital," in *Photography/Politics: Two,* ed. Patricia Holland, Jo Spence, and Simon Watney (London: Comedia, 1986), p. 159.

33. William L. Chenery, "I Testify," *Collier's,* June 16, 1945, p. 14.

34. Dan Stone, "Chaos and Continuity: Representations of Auschwitz," in *Representations of Auschwitz: Fifty Years of Photographs, Paintings, and Graphics,* ed. Yasmin Doosry (Oswiecim: Auschwitz-Birkenau State Museum, 1995), p. 27.

35. Kushner, *Holocaust and Liberal Imagination,* p. 311.

36. Robert H. Abzug, "The Liberation of the Concentration Camps," in *Liberation, 1945* (Washington, D.C.: United States Holocaust Memorial Council, 1995), p. 35. Other claims, equally inaccurate, were set in place as the recording of the event gave way to memory. One such claim offered the view that people remembered Belsen because it was the "first concentration camp to be liberated" (S. J. Goldsmith, "Belsen: Chamber of Incredible Horrors," *Jewish Digest,* September 1957, p. 41). It was not the

first, of course, but it was among the most publicized, which may have created the false impression of its having been the first.

37. Alvin H. Rosenfeld, "The Americanization of the Holocaust," *Commentary,* June 1995; Bjorn Krondorfer, *Remembrance and Reconciliation* (New Haven, Conn.: Yale University Press, 1995), pp. 115, 117; Cynthia Ozick, "A Liberal's Auschwitz," in *The Pushcart Press: Best of Small Presses,* ed. Bill Henderson (New York: Pushcart Press, 1976), p. 153.

38. Jonathan Webber, "Personal Reflections on Auschwitz Today," in *Auschwitz: A History in Photographs,* ed. Teresa Swiebocka, English edition prepared by Jonathan Webber and Connie Wilsack (Bloomington: Indiana University Press, 1993), p. 284.

39. Stone, "Chaos and Continuity," p. 27.

40. Judith Heemminger, "The Children of Buchenwald: After Liberation and Now," in *Echoes of the Holocaust,* ed. Shalom Robinson (Jerusalem: Bulletin of the Jerusalem Center for Research into the Late Effects of the Holocaust, July 1994), p. 43; Edwin Tetlow, *As It Happened: A Journalist Looks Back* (London: Peter Owen, 1990), p. 75; George Rodger, "You Have Been Framed," interview by Amanda Hopkinson, *New Statesman and Society,* June 30, 1995, pp. 32–33; Melvin Seiden, "Remembering 1945," *Humanist,* September–October 1994, p. 30.

41. Francine Prose, "Protecting the Dead," *Tikkun,* May–June 1989, p. 50; Susan Sontag, *On Photography* (New York: Anchor Books, 1977), p. 20; Bjorn Krondorfer, "Innocence, Corruption, Holocaust," *Christianity and Crisis,* August 11, 1986, p. 276.

42. Robert R. Littman, introduction, *Life: The First Decade, 1936–1945* (Boston: New York Graphic Society, 1979), n.p.

43. Julia Kristeva, "The Pain of Sorrow in the Modern World: The Works of Marguerite Duras," *PMLA* 102 (1987): 138–52.

44. Ezrahi, *By Words Alone,* p. 22.

45. Edward T. Linenthal, *Preserving Memory: The Struggle to Create America's Holocaust Museum* (New York: Viking, 1995), p. 8; Kenneth L. Woodward, "Facing Up to the Holocaust," *Newsweek,* May 26, 1975, p. 72; Saul Friedlander, *Reflections of Nazism: An Essay on Kitsch and Death* (New York: Harper and Row, 1984), p. 12.

46. Alvarez, "The Concentration Camps," p. 69; Wieviorka, "On Testimony," p. 26. For instance, between 1945 and 1947 the *Reader's Guide to Periodical Literature* mentioned over seventy citations involving the atrocities of World War II. That number shrunk between 1951 and 1954 to only sixteen items on Nazi atrocity, eleven of which concerned the Katyn massacres. For the period between 1957 and 1959, only seven articles were cited.

47. Gerald Parshall, "Freeing the Survivors," *U.S. News and World Report,* April 3, 1945, p. 65; Anton Gill, *The Journey Back from Hell: Conversations with Concentration Camp Survivors* (London: Grafton Books, 1988), p. 152; Kitty Hart, *Return to Auschwitz* (New York: Atheneum, 1985), p. 11; Kushner, *Holocaust and Liberal Imagination,* p. 243; Barry Markowitz, "Saharovici Receives Holocaust Pictures," *Hebrew Watchman,* August 1984, n.p., Dachau File, WHP.

48. Woodward, "Facing Up to Holocaust," p. 72.

49. William H. Honan, "Holocaust Teaching Gaining a Niche, but Method Is Disputed," *New York Times,* April 12, 1995, p. B11; Stella Dong, "Study Criticizes Coverage of Holocaust by 43 Current History Textbooks," *Publisher's Weekly,* August 27, 1979, p. 296; Andrea Reiter, "Literature and Survival: The Relationship between Fact and Fiction in Concentration Camp Memoirs," *European Studies* 21 (1991): 259; Kushner, *Holocaust and Liberal Imagination,* p. 3; Woodward, "Facing Up to Holocaust," p. 72;

Frank Chalk and Kurt Johassohn, *The History and Sociology of Genocide* (New Haven, Conn.: Yale University Press, 1990), p. 7; Gideon Hausner, chairman of Yad Vashem, in an address to the British Yad Vashem Committee, April 30, 1980, cited in Kushner, *Holocaust and Liberal Imagination,* p. 254; Randolph Braham, ed., *The Treatment of the Holocaust in Textbooks* (New York: Columbia University Press, 1987); Gerd Korman, "Silence in American Textbooks," *Yad Vashem Studies* 8 (1970): 188–89; C. Z. Sulzberger and *American Heritage, The American Heritage Picture History of World War II* (New York: American Heritage Publishing Company, 1966).

50. For example, "Katyn Forest Massacre," *Time,* November 26, 1951, p. 25; "Katyn as a Weapon," *New Republic,* April 14, 1952, p. 7; A. Schalk, "Return to Auschwitz," *Commonweal,* July 9, 1965, pp. 498–501; S. Bedford, "Worst That Ever Happened," *Saturday Evening Post,* October 22, 1966, pp. 29–33; Susan Moeller, *Shooting War* (New York: Basic Books, 1989), p. 418.

51. Leon H. Wells, "Living Ghosts of the Concentration Camps," *New York Times Magazine,* January 26, 1964, p. 55; Herbert P. Schowalter, "This Was Dachau—Part I and Part II," *National Jewish Monthly,* September and October 1966; "Crime and Punishment," *Army Talks,* July 10, 1945, p. 4; "The Man in the Cage," *Time,* April 21, 1961, p. 23.

52. M. L. Stein, *Under Fire: The Story of America's War Correspondents* (New York: Julian Messner, 1968); John Hohenberg, *Foreign Correspondence: The Great Reporters and Their Times* (New York: Columbia University Press, 1964); Louis L. Snyder, ed., *Masterpieces of War Reporting: The Great Moments of World War II* (New York: Julius Messner, 1962), pp. 426–36; "Moments Remembered," *Life,* December 26, 1960, p. 100.

53. The two best-known accounts of life in the camps during this period may have been Elie Wiesel, *Night* (New York: Hill and Wang, 1960); and Tadeusz Borowski, *This Way for the Gas, Ladies and Gentlemen* (New York: Viking, 1967). For a discussion of Resnais's film, see Friedlander, *Memory, History,* p. 52.

54. Quoted in Paula E. Hyman, "New Debate on the Holocaust," *New York Times Magazine,* September 14, 1980, p. 67; cited in Kushner, *Holocaust and Liberal Imagination,* pp. 5–6.

55. As Tony Kushner has argued, the *Diary of Anne Frank* was the only major exception to the neglect of the Holocaust during the 1950s and 1960s. First published in 1952, dramatized in 1955, and made into a film in 1959, Anne Frank's story has been instrumental in Americanizing and universalizing the Holocaust (Kushner, *Holocaust and Liberal Imagination*). See also Judith Doneson, *The Holocaust in American Film* (Philadelphia: Jewish Publication Society, 1987). An additional version of the book was published in 1989 in response to denials of its authenticity by the Netherlands State Institute for War Documentation (*The Diary of Anne Frank: The Critical Edition* [New York: Viking. 1989]), and Edward Rothstein, "Anne Frank: The Girl and the Icon," *New York Times,* February 25, 1996, p. H23.

56. Amishai-Maisels, *Depiction and Interpretation,* pp. 8, 46, 48, 73, 90, 66, 123. Some, however, like Zoran Music and Gerhart Frankl, turned back to atrocity photos and titled their art in direct linkage.

57. "Hope for a Speedy Armistice; Anguish from Atrocity Report," *Newsweek,* November 26, 1951, p. 31; Amishai-Maisels, *Depiction and Interpretation,* p. 69, 73.

58. Berel Lang, *Act and Idea in the Nazi Genocide* (Chicago: University of Chicago Press, 1990), pp. 328–29.

59. One graphic image that appeared in the war was a picture of a U.S. soldier with

his legs and arms bound, dead at the side of the road. See "Murdered Yanks," *Newsweek,* July 24, 1950, pp. 12–13.

60. See Lance Morrow, "The Morals of Remembering," *Time,* May 23, 1983, p. 88.

61. Geoffrey H. Hartman, "Introduction: Darkness Visible," in *Holocaust Remembrance,* p. 8.

CHAPTER SIX

1. Lawrence Langer, "Memory's Time: Chronology and Duration in Holocaust Testimonies," *Yale Journal of Criticism* 6, no. 2 (1993): 263.

2. For instance, see C. McConkey, "Forgetting the Holocaust," *Christian Century,* July 20, 1977, pp. 669–70; F. Brown, "French Amnesia," *Harper's,* December 1981, pp. 68–70; Michiko Kakutani, "Remembering as a Duty to Those Who Survived," *New York Times,* December 5, 1995, p. C19.

3. For example, see Gideon Hausner, "Eichmann and His Trial," *Saturday Evening Post,* November 3, 1962, pp. 19–25, November 10, 1962, pp. 58–61, November 17, 1962, p. 6; "Auschwitz Comes Alive Again," *New York Times Magazine,* April 19, 1964, pp. 14–15; Hannah Arendt, *Eichmann in Jerusalem* (New York: Viking, 1963); Lucy S. Dawidowicz, *The War against the Jews: 1933–1945* (New York: Holt, Rinehart and Winston, 1975); and Raul Hilberg, *The Destruction of the European Jews* (New York: Holmes and Meier, 1985).

4. Tony Kushner, *The Holocaust and the Liberal Imagination: A Social and Cultural History* (Oxford: Basil Blackwell, 1994), p. 249; Edward T. Linenthal, *Preserving Memory: The Struggle to Create America's Holocaust Museum* (New York: Viking, 1995), p. 11.

5. Susan Moeller, *Shooting War* (New York: Basic Books, 1989), pp. 402, 410; John Berger, "Photographs of Agony," in *About Looking* (New York: Pantheon, 1980), p. 37.

6. Gerald Parshall, "Freeing the Survivors," *U.S. News and World Report,* April 3, 1995, p. 65.

7. Kushner, *Holocaust and Liberal Imagination,* p. 255; Tony Judt, "The Past Is Another Country: Myth and Memory in Post-War Europe," *Daedalus* 121, no. 4 (fall 1992): 108.

8. Carol Rittner, ed., *Elie Wiesel: Between Memory and Hope* (New York: New York University Press, 1990); James E. Young, *The Texture of Memory: Holocaust Memorials and Meaning* (New Haven, Conn.: Yale University Press, 1993); and Carol Rittner and John K. Roth, *Memory Offended* (New York: Praeger, 1991); Yitzhak Zuckerman (Antek), *A Surplus of Memory: A Chronicle of the Warsaw Ghetto Uprising* (Berkeley and Los Angeles: University of California Press, 1993); Leon Wieseltier, "After Memory," *New Republic,* May 3, 1993, pp. 16–21, 24–26; Pierre Vidal-Naquet, *Assassins of Memory* (New York: Columbia University Press, 1992); Walter Reich, "The Enemies of Memory," *New Republic,* April 21, 1982, p. 20; Deborah Lipstadt, *Denying the Holocaust: The Growing Assault on Truth and Memory* (New York: Free Press, 1993); Lawrence L. Langer, *Holocaust Testimonies: The Ruins of Memory* (New Haven, Conn.: Yale University Press, 1991); Kakutani, "Remembering as a Duty," p. C19.

9. Kushner, *Holocaust and Liberal Imagination,* p. 248; Lewis H. Weinstein, "The Liberation of the Death-Camps," *Midstream,* April 1986, p. 20; Walter J. Fellenz, "Holocaust: I Am Still Shocked by What I Saw at the Liberation," letter to the editor, *New York Times,* December 22, 1977.

10. Philip Roth, *The Ghost Writer* (New York: Farrar, Straus, and Giroux, 1979); Saul Bellow, *Mr. Sammler's Planet* (New York: Viking, 1970); Isaac Bashevis Singer, *Ene-*

mies:A Love Story (New York: Farrar, Straus, and Giroux, 1972); *The Sorrow and the Pity,* directed by Marcel Ophuls, 1972; *The Tin Drum,* directed by Volker Schloendorff for Franz Seitz Films, 1979; *The Boys from Brazil,* directed by Franklin J. Schaffner for the Producer Circle, 1978; *Lacombe Lucien,* directed by Louis Malle, 1974; *The Last Metro,* directed by Francois Truffaut for Les Films du Carosse, 1980; *Playing for Time,* directed by Daniel Mann for CBS, 1980.

11. A unit on Holocaust education was made mandatory in some U.S. secondary schools in the late 1970s, and university courses began in the early 1980s. The situation somewhat lagged in Britain, but by the end of the eighties, Holocaust education there was equivalent if not better than that in the United States (see William H. Honan, "Holocaust Teaching Gaining a Niche, but Method Is Disputed," *New York Times,* April 12, 1995, p. B11; Kushner, *Holocaust and Liberal Imagination,* p. 263).

12. Geoffrey Hartman, "Public Memory and Its Discontents," *Raritan* 13, no. 4 (spring 1994): 28.

13. Robert H. Abzug, *Inside the Vicious Heart: Americans and the Liberation of Nazi Concentration Camps* (New York: Oxford University Press, 1985); and Jon Bridgman, *The End of the Holocaust: The Liberation of the Camps* (Portland, Ore.: Areopagitica Press, 1990). Unlike previous treatments, both books examined the record of liberation camp after camp and illustrated their narratives with photographs taken at the time. Abzug, in particular, included nearly ninety photos of the camps.

14. Wieseltier, "After Memory," p. 19; Val Williams, "Prints of Darkness," *Manchester Guardian,* January 22, 1995, p. 26; Dan Stone, "Chaos and Continuity: Representations of Auschwitz," in *Representations of Auschwitz: Fifty Years of Photographs, Paintings, and Graphics,* ed. Yasmin Doosry (Oswiecim: Auschwitz-Birkenau State Museum, 1995).

15. Pictures appended to Lily Eng, "A Survivor's Message from the Camps," *Philadelphia Inquirer,* February 13, 1995, p. B6.

16. Saul Friedlander, *Reflections of Nazism: An Essay on Kitsch and Death* (New York: Harper and Row, 1984), p. 96; Sybil Milton, "The Camera as Weapon: Documentary Photography and the Holocaust," *Simon Wiesenthal Center Annual* 1 (1984): 60; James E. Young, *Writing and Rewriting the Holocaust* (Bloomington: Indiana University Press, 1988), p. 163; Hirsch, "Family Pictures," p. 7.

17. Saul Friedlander, *Memory, History, and the Extermination of the Jews of Europe* (Bloomington: Indiana University Press, 1993), p. 58. In fact, Picasso's own response to the Nazi atrocities—*The Charnel House*—evoked little of the response that *Guernica* had marshaled into the public imagination.

18. Art Spiegelman, *Maus I* (New York: Pantheon, 1986), and *Maus II* (New York: Pantheon, 1986); Marianne Hirsch, "Family Pictures: *Maus,* Mourning, and Post-Memory, *Discourse* 14, no. 1 (winter 1992–93); Young, *Writing and Rewriting,* p. 60; Erich Kulka, *Escape from Auschwitz* (South Hadley, Mass.: Bergin and Garvey, 1986); Filip Mueller, *Eyewitness Auschwitz* (New York: Stein and Day, 1979); *Nightmare's End: The Liberation of the Camps,* directed by Rex Bloomstein for Discovery Channel, 1995; Don DeLillo, *White Noise* (New York: Viking, 1985); D. M. Thomas, *The White Hotel* (New York: Viking, 1981). This is also discussed in Young, *Writing and Rewriting,* p. 57. As Young states: "Contemporary documentary novelists now conflate their narratives with rhetorically factual materials, like photographs, newspaper articles, and eyewitness testimony to lend them a certain factual authority" (p. 62).

19. Ziva Amishai-Maisels, *Depiction and Interpretation: Visual Arts and the Holocaust* (Oxford: Pergamon, 1993), pp. 91, 96, 360.

20. "The Faces of War," *MacLean's,* September 4, 1989, pp. 36–39; Meg Greenfield, "Misusing World War II," *Newsweek,* June 6, 1994, p. 86; "A Gigantic Death Camp," *Time,* April 29, 1985, p. 21; Tom Infield, "Witness," *Philadelphia Inquirer Magazine,* April 9, 1995, pp. 12–15, 24–31.

21. Sybil Milton has suggested that the disorganization of photographs in archival settings may be responsible for what she calls the "limited and repetitive use of certain images." Many images today remain dispersed, unlabeled, and without supplementary information, which increases the risk of losing their visual documentary value. See Milton, "The Camera as Weapon," p. 62. Photos also resurfaced in museum work, as in the Imperial War Museum's commemorative book, *The Relief of Belsen* (London: Imperial War Museum, 1991), pp. 5, 14, and 15, and literature on the exhibit "Warworks" at the Victoria and Albert Museum, London, in 1995.

22. The photograph appeared in Jerry Adler, "Hitler and the Holocaust," *Newsweek,* May 2, 1983, p. 62; Kenneth L. Woodward, "Facing Up to the Holocaust," *Newsweek,* May 26, 1975, p. 72; Kenneth L. Woodward, "Debate over the Holocaust," *Newsweek,* March 10, 1980, p. 97; the cover photo to *Liberation, 1945* (Washington, D.C.: United States Holocaust Memorial Council, 1995).

23. The photo appeared in *1945: The Year of Liberation* (Washington, D.C.: United States Holocaust Memorial Council, 1995), p. 10; "25 Years of *Life,*" *Life,* December 26, 1960, where it was cited one of the magazine's eighteen "Great Photos" of all time; "*Life:* 50 Years," *Life,* special anniversary issue, fall 1986, p. 192; "*Life* Celebrates 1945," *Life,* special collector's edition, June 5, 1995, pp. 30–31; "150 Years of Photojournalism," *Time,* fall 1989, p. 47; Malcolm N. Carter, "The FDR Memorial: A Monument to Politics, Bureaucracy, and the Art of Accommodation," *Art News,* October 1978, p. 56; and Audrey Flack, *On Painting* (New York: Harry N. Abrams, 1981), pp. 78–80.

24. See Vicki Goldberg, *The Power of Photography: How Photographs Changed Our Lives* (New York: Abbeville, 1991), p. 37.

25. The image originally appeared as a picture captioned "Hitler's Slaves," *Los Angeles Times,* April 24, 1945, pt. 1, p. 3 and appended to Harold Denny, "'The World Must Not Forget,'" *New York Times Magazine,* May 6, 1945, p. 9. Later, it appeared in Andrew Nagorski, "The Last Days of Auschwitz," *Newsweek,* January 16, 1995, pp. 58–59, alongside Holocaust recollections by Elie Wiesel.

26. Walter Goodman, "The Politics of the Holocaust," *Newsweek,* September 27, 1982, p. 33.

27. Martin Gilbert, *Atlas of the Holocaust* (London: Pergamon, 1988), p. 239; Kenneth L. Woodward, "Hitler and the Holocaust," *Newsweek,* July 11, 1977, p. 77; "Buchenwald Remembered: They Were Not Alone," *MacLean's,* September 24, 1979, p. 12.

28. "No Remorse, No Recourse," advertisement, *New York Times,* January 18, 1995, p. A17; "Double Jeopardy," Judy Chicago, *Holocaust Project: From Darkness into Light* (New York: Penguin, 1993), p. 175, overleaf. The quote is on p. 126.

29. Melinda Beck, "Footnote to the Holocaust," *Newsweek,* October 19, 1981, p. 73.

30. Cited in Gustav Niebuhr, "Whose Memory Lives When the Last Survivor Dies?" *New York Times,* January 29, 1995, p. 5.

31. Niebuhr, "Whose Memory Lives?" p. 5; Barbara Nemick, "Auschwitz Is Yielding New Anger," *Philadelphia Inquirer,* January 26, 1995, p. 1; Jeffrey R. Young, "U.S. Campuses Debate German Censorship of Nazi Materials on Internet," *Chronicle of Higher Education,* February 16, 1996, p. A26.

32. Tamar Jacoby, "The Holocaust: Why the Jews?" *Newsweek,* May 15, 1989, p. 64; Laura Shapiro, "Denying the Holocaust," *Newsweek,* December 20, 1993, p. 120; Lipstadt, *Denying the Holocaust.* Also see Pierre Vidal-Naquet, *Assassins of Memory,* and his "Theses on Revisionism," in *Unanswered Questions: Nazi Germany and the Genocide of the Jews,* ed. François Furet (New York: Schocken, 1989); Randolph L. Braham, "The Photographer as Historian: The Auschwitz Album," *Shoah,* fall–winter 1983–84, pp. 20–23; Jo Thomas, "'Holy Document' at Auschwitz Found," *New York Times,* August 14, 1980.

33. Jeffrey Goldberg, "The Exaggerators," *New Republic,* February 8, 1993, pp. 13–14; Stephen J. Dubner, "Massaging History," *New York,* March 8, 1993, p. 48.

34. Interview with William A. Scott, April 9, 1979, Emory University, WHP.

35. Kenneth S. Stern, *Liberators: A Background Report* (New York: American Jewish Committee, 1993), p. 2; Dubner, "Massaging History," pp. 49, 51.

36. Val Williams, *Warworks* (London: Virago Press, 1994), p. 13; Moeller, *Shooting War,* p. 418.

37. Marianne Fulton, *Eyes of Time: Photojournalism in America* (Boston: New York Graphic Society, 1988), p. 162; Jorge Lewinski, *The Camera at War: A History of War Photography from 1848 to the Present Day* (New York: Simon and Schuster, 1978), pp. 18, 20, 98, 134, 135; and Goldberg, *The Power of Photography,* pp. 32–37. Atrocity photos also appeared in Ken Baynes, ed., *Scoop, Scandal, and Strife: A Study of Photography in Newspapers* (London: Lund Humphries, 1971), p. 138; Frederick S. Voss, *Reporting the War: The Journalistic Coverage of World War II* (Washington, D.C.: Smithsonian Institution Press for the National Portrait Gallery, 1994), p. 40.

38. Philip Knightley, *The First Casualty: From the Crimea to Vietnam: The War Correspondent as Hero, Propagandist, and Myth Maker* (New York: Harcourt Brace Jovanovich, 1975); Thomas F. Mulvoy Jr. and William T. Stewart, eds., *World War II: From D-Day to V-J Day, 40 Years Later* (Boston: Globe Newspaper Company, 1986). The series reprinted the picture of a trench of bodies at the camp near Nordhausen, which had originally appeared in the paper in April 1945, pp. 30–31; *The World at War, 1939–1945* (London: Bracken Books, 1990), p. 169: the page displayed seven of the most grotesque images, including that of a "usually genial General Eisenhower" examining bodies at Ohrdruf. Captions were reproduced exactly as they had appeared originally in the newspaper. Here, as in the original reporting, nowhere in the book were credits given for the photographs recorded therein.

39. See, for instance, "The Faces of War": of twelve images, one depicted children in Buchenwald (p. 38); Martin Caiger-Smith, *The Face of the Enemy: British Photographers in Germany, 1944–1952* (Berlin: Nishen, 1988); Malcolm W. Browne, "Reporters at War," *New York Times Book Review,* August 27, 1995, pp. 22–23.

40. Reich, "The Enemies of Memory," p. 21; interview with John Henry Baker Jr., February 27, 1980, WHP.

41. Arthur C. Dietrich, cited in Infield, "Witness," p. 28; Carlton Raper, "Dachau," letter to the editor, *Greensboro Daily News,* December 20, 1978, Dachau File, WHP; Bill Varner, "Holocaust Horror Part of This Coach's Life," *Rockland County (New York) Journal-News,* October 7, 1979, p. 3D, Dachau File, WHP.

42. Arthur C. Dietrich, cited in Infield, "Witness," p. 28; Bill Wallace, quoted in Dan Hardy, "50 Years Later, Horrors of Dachau Lingers with One Who Saw It," *Philadelphia Inquirer,* April 23, 1995, p. MD1; Hardy, "50 Years Later," p. MD4.

43. Reich, "The Enemies of Memory," p. 21; Leigh Rivenbark, "Faith in the Field,"

Army Times, May 22, 1994; Barry Markowitz, "Saharovici Receives Holocaust Pictures," *Hebrew Watchman,* August 1984, n.p., Dachau File, WHP.

44. Linenthal, *Preserving Memory,* particularly pp. 171–210.

45. Philip Gourevitch, "In the Holocaust Theme Park," *Observer Magazine,* January 30, 1994, p. 24; Clyde Haberman, "In a Museum of Hell, Qualms about Decorum," *New York Times,* March 7, 1995, p. A4; John E. Frohmayer, quoted in Andrea Liss, "Trespassing through Shadows: History, Mourning, and Photography in Representations of Holocaust Memory," *Framework* 4, no. 1 (1991): 33; Haberman, "In Museum of Hell," p. A4; Allyn Fisher, "Holocaust Photos Cause Rift," *Philadelphia Inquirer,* February 10, 1995, p. A14.

46. *The Relief of Belsen;* Williams, *Warworks;* Yitzhak Arad, *The Pictorial History of the Holocaust* (New York: Macmillan, 1990); Michael Berenbaum, *The World Must Know: The History of the Holocaust as Told in the United States Holocaust Memorial Museum* (Boston: Little, Brown, 1993); and Teresa Swiebocka, ed., *Auschwitz: A History in Photographs,* English edition prepared by Jonathan Webber and Connie Wilsack (Bloomington: Indiana University Press, 1993), and Doosry, *Representations of Auschwitz.*

47. *1945: The Year of Liberation,* pp. 118–19, 122–23, 126, and 140.

48. Arad, *Pictorial History of Holocaust;* Nagorski, "Last Days of Auschwitz"; pictures appended to Woodward, "Debate over the Holocaust," p. 97.

49. Wendy Kozol, *Life's America: Family and Nation in Postwar Photojournalism* (Philadelphia: Temple University Press, 1994), p. 7.

50. Dora Jane Hamblin, *That Was the Life* (New York: W. W. Norton, 1977), p. 33. One novelist, recalling the first time she saw the atrocity photos, laid claim to the uncertainty with which she remembered *Life*'s role: "I remember seeing the [photos] in *Life* magazine—although this is a vague memory and may not be true" (see Prose, "Protecting the Dead," p. 51).

51. See, for instance, "World War II: 40 Years Later," *Life,* special issue, spring–summer 1985; "Pearl Harbor: December 7, 1941–December 7, 1991," collector's edition, *Life,* fall 1991, and "*Life* Celebrates 1945"; *WWII: Time-Life Books History of the Second World War* (New York: Prentice Hall Press, 1989), p. 351; Editors of Time-Life Books, *The Apparatus of Death* (Alexandria, Va.: Time-Life Books, 1991).

52. "25 Years of *Life,*" and "*Life:* 50 Years," *Life: The First Decade, 1936–1945* (Boston: New York Graphic Society, 1979), p. 171; "150 Years of Photojournalism."

53. See Lipstadt, *Denying the Holocaust,* and Vidal-Nacquet, *Assassins of Memory.*

54. Linda Marie Delloff, "Revising Holocaust History: Malice in the Mails," *Christian Century,* July 16–23, 1980, p. 725; Frank Tompkins, "$50,000 Offered for Proof of Gassed Jews," *Spotlight,* September 24, 1979, n.p., WHP. Also see "Famous 'Victims' Emerge as Public Figures," *Spotlight,* December 24, 1979, pp. 4–5, WHP; Mark Weber, "The 'Warsaw Ghetto Boy,'" *Journal of Historical Review,* March–April 1994, pp. 6–7. Also see Mark Weber, "Inaccurate *Time* Magazine Photo Caption Defames Ukranians," *Journal of Historical Review,* March–April 1994, p. 8.

55. Abzug, *Inside the Vicious Heart,* p. ix.

56. Anton Kaes, *From Hitler to Heimat: The Return of History as Film* (Cambridge, Mass.: Harvard University Press, 1989), p. 179.

57. Susan Sontag, *On Photography* (New York: Anchor Books, 1977), p. 21; Andreas Huyssen, *Twilight Memories* (New York: Routledge, 1996).

CHAPTER SEVEN

1. Andreas Huyssen, "Monument and Memory in a Post-modern Eye," *Yale Journal of Criticism* 6, no. 2 (fall 1993): 254; James E. Young, *The Texture of Memory: Holocaust Memorials and Meaning* (New Haven, Conn.: Yale University Press, 1993), p. 5.

2. Huyssen, "Monument and Memory," p. 250.

3. See Tony Kushner, *The Holocaust and the Liberal Imagination: A Social and Cultural History* (Oxford: Basil Blackwell, 1994), pp. 270–71; Eric Markusen and David Kopf, *The Holocaust and Strategic Bombing: Genocide and Total War in the Twentieth Century* (Boulder, Colo.: Westview Press, 1995), p. 242.

4. Kushner, *Holocaust and Liberal Imagination,* p. 271. Popular belief about atrocity representation holds that what we represent prefigures whether we will intervene. "What is not pictured is not real. Much of routinized misery is invisible; much that is made visible is not ordinary or routine. The very act of picturing distorts social experience in the popular media and in the professions under the impress of ideology and political economy. So entailed, even personal 'witnessing' is compromised. We are living through a great historical transformation in the imaging and therefore perhaps also in the experience of social adversity" (Arthur Kleinman, Veena Das, and Margaret Lock, introduction to special issue "Social Suffering," *Daedalus* 125, no. 1 [winter 1996]: xiii).

5. Roland Barthes, *Camera Lucida,* trans. Richard Howard (New York: Hill and Wang, 1981), p. 91; Marguerite Duras, *Practicalities: Marguerite Duras Speaks to Michel Beaujour* (New York: Grove Press, 1990), p. 89; Susan Sontag, *On Photography* (New York: Anchor Books, 1977), p. 21.

6. Geoffrey Hartman, "Public Memory and Its Discontents," *Raritan* 13, no. 4 (spring 1994): 25; Hans Kellner, "'Never Again' Is Now," *History and Theory* 2 (1994): 140.

7. Michael Burleigh, "Synonymous with Murder," *Times Literary Supplement,* March 3, 1995, p. 13; Anthony Lewis, "What Are We Doing to Ourselves?" *New York Times,* November 22, 1969, p. 36; "Help for the Auschwitz of Asia," *Time,* November 5, 1979, p. 47; Morton Kondrake, "Another Cambodia," *New Republic,* November 3, 1979, pp. 13–14; Robert White, cited in Ed Herman and Noam Chomsky, *Manufacturing Consent* (New York: Pantheon, 1988), p. 302; Samir El Khalil, "The Republic of Fear and the Killing Fields," *Institute for the Study of Genocide Newsletter* 7 (spring 1991): 3–4; Eric Gillet and Alison Des Forges, "The Next Rwanda," *New York Times,* August 11, 1994, p. A23; Mary Gray and Sarah Milburn Moore, "Next Arena for Genocide," *Washington Post,* August 24, 1994, p. A19; Ben Kiernan, "Cambodia's Saddam: Pol Pot Is Still Ignored," *Australian Left Review* 129 (June 1991): 7–8; Barbara Crossette, "Waiting for Justice in Cambodia," *New York Times,* February 25, 1996, p. E5.

8. David Hawk, "The Killing of Cambodia," *New Republic,* November 15, 1982, p. 18; Donald G. McNeil Jr., "At Church, Testament to Horror," *New York Times,* August 4, 1995, p. A4; Roger Cohen, "Yugoslavia's Disintegration, from All Angles," *New York Times,* December 24, 1995, p. H37; Ed Vulliamy, *Seasons in Hell: Understanding Bosnia's War* (New York: St. Martin's Press, 1994), p. xiii; Donatella Lorch, "Wave of Rape Adds New Horror to Rwanda's Trail of Brutality," *New York Times,* May 15, 1995, p. A1; Robert D. Kaplan, "Introduction: The Meaning of History," in Vulliamy, *Seasons in Hell,* p. xiii.

9. Meg Greenfield, "The Bosnia Example," *Newsweek,* April 26, 1993, p. 74.

10. Yehuda Bauer, quoted in Alvin H. Rosenfeld, "The Americanization of the Holocaust," *Commentary,* June 1995, p. 1.

11. Helen Fein, "Genocide: A Sociological Perspective, *Current Sociology* 38, no. 1

(spring 1990): 1; Douglas Jehl, "Officials Told to Avoid Calling Rwandan Killings 'Genocide,'" *New York Times*, June 10, 1994, p. A8.

12. "No Excuses," editorial, *Christian Science Monitor*, August 18, 1995, p. 20; Jonathan S. Landay, "Mostar: A Warsaw Ghetto in Bosnia," *Christian Science Monitor*, September 14, 1993, p. 2; Russell Watson, "Where the World Can Draw the Line," *Newsweek*, January 4, 1993, p. 35; Andrew Purvis, "Specter of Genocide," *Time*, February 5, 1996, p. 34.

13. Michael Binyon, "Children Murdered at Red Cross Home," *London Times*, May 4, 1994, p. 1; "Double Genocide," editorial, *Washington Post*, April 14, 1995, p. A20.

14. Hyman Letger, "The Soviet Gulag: Is It Genocide?" in *Toward the Understanding and Prevention of Genocide: Proceedings of the International Conference on the Holocaust and Genocide*, ed. Israel W. Charny (Boulder, Colo.: Westview Press, 1984), pp. 60–66; Richard G. Hovamisian, "The Armenian Genocide," in *Genocide: A Critical Bibliographic Review*, ed. Israel W. Charny (London: Mansell, 1988), p. 99.

15. Susan Sontag, "A Lament for Bosnia," *Nation*, December 25, 1995, p. 819; Warren P. Strobel, "TV Images May Shock but Won't Alter Policy," *Christian Science Monitor*, December 14, 1994, p. 19.

16. "Bleak Outlook," *London Times*, July 9, 1993, p. 12; "Cambodian Woman and Skulls," *New York Times*, May 27, 1996, p. 6; "At the End of the Road," *Economist*, July 23, 1996, p. E1; John Berger, "Photographs of Agony," in *About Looking* (New York: Pantheon, 1980), pp. 39–40.

17. Charles Bremner, "Bosnia Stages High-Tech Armageddon," *London Times*, January 22, 1993, p. 11.

18. Kushner, *Holocaust and Liberal Imagination*, p. 270.

19. Sontag, *On Photography*, p. 17.

20. Russell Watson, "Ethnic Cleansing," *Newsweek*, August 17, 1992, p. 16; J. M. O. McAllister, "Atrocity and Outrage," *Time*, August 17, 1992, p. 21.

21. Amanda Hopkinson, "You Have Been Framed," *New Statesman and Society*, June 30, 1995, pp. 32–33.

22. John Taylor, *War Photography: Realism in the British Press* (London: Routledge, 1991), pp. 94, 97, 110, 112–13; David E. Morrison and Howard Tumber, *Journalists at War* (London: Sage, 1988); Deborah Cherry and Alex Potts, "The Changing Images of War," *New Society*, April 27, 1982, pp. 172–74.

23. Michael Griffin and Jongsoo Lee, "Picturing the Gulf War: Constructing an Image of War in *Time, Newsweek,* and *U.S. News and World Report,*" *Journalism and Mass Communication Quarterly* 72, no. 4 (winter 1995): 813–25; Kevin Robins, "The War, the Screen, the Crazy Dog, and Poor Mankind," *Media, Culture, and Society* 15 (1993): 325.

24. Kiku Adatto, *Picture Perfect: The Art and Artifice of Public Image-Making* (Cambridge, Mass.: Harvard University Press, 1993), p. 175.

25. Paul F. Lazarsfeld and Robert K. Merton, "Mass Communication, Popular Taste, and Organized Social Action," in *The Communication of Ideas*, ed. Lyman Bryson (New York: Institute for Religious and Social Studies, 1948); Danny Schechter, "A Failure of Journalism," *Progressive*, April 1994, p. 26.

26. In picturing atrocity in the contemporary age, photography's role in an increasingly diverse image-making environment has been one of anchoring and concretizing the more fluid images of other image-making technologies. Yet perhaps because their recycling capacity is more accessible and ever-present than that of cinematic or televisual images, their ability to help publics bear witness—that is, by extending the event beyond itself—is primary.

27. Michael Ignatieff, "Is Nothing Sacred? The Ethics of Television," *Daedalus* 114, no. 4 (1985): 59.

28. Vicki Goldberg, *The Power of Photography: How Photographs Changed Our Lives* (New York: Abbeville, 1991), p. 234. The pictures were brought back by a combat photographer from Cleveland, Ronald Haeberle, and published in the *Cleveland Plain Dealer* on November 20, 1969. They played elsewhere the next day—including the *London Times, New York Times, Life,* and the *New York Post*—and were shown—still photo by still photo—on CBS News. While the My Lai photographs differed from the photos of Nazi atrocities in the important respect that the former represented U.S.-inflicted atrocities rather than atrocities committed by the enemy, their play on television and elsewhere was revealing for what they suggest about the potency of still images: "Six seconds on one picture, ten on another, twenty-two seconds of utter silence on that image of heaped-up bodies. No voice-over, no music, nothing but pictures of death" (Goldberg, *The Power of Photography,* p. 232).

29. George Steiner, *Language and Silence* (New York: Penguin, 1969), p. 45.

30. Goldberg, *The Power of Photography,* p. 222; "What Somalia Needs," *London Times,* October 11, 1993, p. 15; cited in Michael Binyon, "Media's Tunnel Vision Is Attacked by Hurd," *London Times,* September 10, 1993, p. 13.

31. Goldberg, *The Power of Photography,* p. 243. This photo received somewhat of an afterlife when one of the children in the photo in 1996 made a conciliatory speech at the U.S. Vietnam Veteran's Memorial in celebration of Veteran's Day. The original photo was redisplayed on numerous newspapers alongside coverage of the ceremonies. See, for instance, Elaine Sciolino, "A Painful Road from Vietnam to Forgiveness," *New York Times,* November 12, 1996, pp. A1, A20.

32. Goldberg, *The Power of Photography,* pp. 247, 259; Fred Ritchin, *In Our Own Image* (New York: Aperture Books, 1990), p. 1.

33. Greenfield, "The Bosnia Example," p. 74.

34. Cited in Binyon, "Media's Tunnel Vision," p. 13. The *Times* responded by calling the foreign secretary "naive" and "at war with the media" ("At War with the Media" [editorial], *London Times,* September 11, 1993, p. 17).

35. Sven Bergman, "Timor's Untelevised Terror," *Washington Post,* March 14, 1993, p. C2. The subhead read, "As the World Looks Elsewhere, a Small Island Suffers in Hideous War." The estimate of killed Timorese was provided in John Pilger, "East Timor Rises Up," *New Statesman and Society,* November 25, 1994, p. 16; Keith B. Richburg, "The World Ignored Genocide, Tutsis Say," *Washington Post,* August 8, 1994, p. A11; cover trailer appended to John Pilger, "Reseeding the Killing Fields," *Nation,* October 2, 1995, p. 342.

36. John Pilger, "Another U.N. Triumph (Cambodia)," *New Statesman and Society,* July 21, 1995, Arnold S. Kohen, "Making an Issue of East Timor," *Nation,* February 10, 1992, pp. 162–63; picture appended to "Blood, Bullets, and Chinese Beans," *Economist,* March 12, 1994, p. 68.

37. John Pilger, "Pol Pot's Safe Haven," *New Statesman and Society,* April 26, 1991, p. 10; John Pilger, "The West's Lethal Illusion in Cambodia," *New Statesman and Society,* July 9, 1993, p. 15.

38. Greenfield, "The Bosnia Example," p. 74.

39. "The Next Genocide," editorial, *Washington Post,* November 21, 1994, p. A24; Strobel, "TV Images May Shock," p. 19; Anthony Lewis, "The Hidden Horror," *New York Times,* August 12, 1994, p. A23; "No Excuses," p. 20; Jennifer Parmelee, "Fade to Blood," *Washington Post,* April 24, 1994, p. C3.

40. "Fatal Neglect," editorial, *New Statesman and Society,* August 21, 1992, p. 5; John V. R. Bull, "Execution Photo Should Not Have Been on Page One," *Philadelphia Inquirer,* May 12, 1996, p. E4. As a response to the outcry, the newspaper initiated a new feature called "Reader Reaction" to address issues that evoked "unusually intense reaction; M. L. Stein, "News Value versus Gore," *Editor and Publisher,* August 12, 1995, p. 12; discussed in Taylor, *War Photography,* p. 160; uncaptioned picture appended to Dan Perry, "Suicide Bomber Kills 14 in Tel Aviv," *Philadelphia Inquirer,* March 5, 1996, p. 1. In fact, one week later, the *Philadelphia Inquirer* also published an ombudsman's report that discussed the decision making that had led to the display of the graphic photo (John V. R. Bull, "Israel Photo Caption Is the Start of a New Policy," *Philadelphia Inquirer,* March 13, 1996, p. A14).

41. For a discussion of this notion and television, see Ignatieff, "Is Nothing Sacred?" pp. 57–78; Bremner, "Bosnia Stages Armageddon," p. 11.

42. Ziva Amishai-Maisels, *Depiction and Interpretation: Visual Arts and the Holocaust* (Oxford: Pergamon, 1993), p. 341; McAllister, "Atrocity and Outrage," p. 21.

43. Lewis, "What Are We Doing?" p. 36; cited in Vulliamy, *Seasons in Hell,* p. xii; Chris Hedges, "Never Again, Again: After the Peace, the War against Memory," *New York Times,* January 14, 1996, p. E1.

44. McAllister, "Atrocity and Outrage," p. 21; picture appended to James Walsh, "Unearthing Evil," *Time,* January 29, 1995, pp. 46–47; picture appended to Crossette, "Waiting for Justice," p. E5; and uncaptioned picture appended to "Ethnicity Masks Politics in Rwanda and Burundi," *Washington Post,* January 27, 1996, p. A15.

45. Picture appended to Mike O'Connor, "Harvesting Evidence in Bosnia's Killing Fields," *New York Times,* April 7, 1996, p. D1.

46. Alex Ross, "Watching for a Judgment of Real Evil," *New York Times,* November 12, 1995, p. H37; John Darnton, "Does the World Still Recognize a Holocaust?" *New York Times,* April 25, 1993, sec. 4, p. 1; Paul Sieveking, "Forteana," *New Statesman and Society,* August 27, 1993, p. 47. The Europeans, he wrote, "each evening confront a relentless, deeply disturbing conflict whose very ugliness flies in the face of the values they profess."

47. "Sin and Confession in Rwanda," *Economist,* January 14, 1995, p. 53; picture appended to Seth Mydans, "Skulls Still Speak in Cambodia to Both Victim and Victimizer," *New York Times,* May 27, 1996, p. 6. The photograph was discussed in David Hawk, "The Photographic Record," in *Cambodia, 1975–78,* ed. Karl Jackson (Princeton, N.J.: Princeton University Press, 1989).

48. Philip Gourevitch, "Is Burundi Next?" *New Yorker,* February 19, 1996, p. 7.

49. See, for instance, Cohen, "In Bosnia, the War That Can't Be Seen," *New York Times,* December 25, 1994, p. E4; David Rohde, "Evidence Indicates Bosnia Massacre," *Christian Science Monitor,* August 18, 1995, p. A1; and Rohde, "How a Serb Massacre Was Exposed," *Christian Science Monitor,* August 25, 1995, p. 1.

50. Picture appended to Tim Judah, "Struggle for Water and Life Saps the Spirit of Sarajevo," *London Times,* July 14, 1993, p. 9; picture appended to Misha Glenny, "The Wheel of History Turns Full Circle," *New Statesman and Society,* August 28, 1992, pp. 10–11; picture appended to Bruce W. Nelan, "Rumor and Reality," *Time,* August 24, 1992, p. 47; picture appended to McAllister, "Atrocity and Outrage," pp. 20–21; picture appended to "Bosnia's Dismal Endgame," *Economist,* August 7, 1993, p. 33.

51. Schechter, "A Failure of Journalism," p. 26; Kevin Weaver, "Body Counts,"

New Statesman and Society, July 31, 1992, p. 13; picture captioned "A Defining Event," appended to Watson, "Ethnic Cleansing," pp. 16–17; Cohen, "In Bosnia," p. E4; Brock, "Dateline Yugoslavia," p. 156.

52. See, for instance, picture captioned "Icon of Barbarism," appended to McAllister, "Atrocity and Outrage," p. 20. It was accredited to ITN/REX and showed a frontal view of a male face behind barbed wire. Also see pictures appended to Roger Cohen, "Yugoslavia's Disintegration," p. H37, which reproduced stills from the Discovery Channel's screening of the BBC documentary, *Yugoslavia: Death of a Nation; New York Times,* April 15, 1996; Judith Weinraub, "The Bosnia Question," *Washington Post,* September 23, 1994, p. F1; picture appended to Cohen, "In Bosnia," p. E4; uncaptioned picture appended to Tihomir Loza, "A Victory for Genocide," *New Statesman and Society,* July 16, 1993, p. 12; Brock, "Dateline Yugoslavia," p. 163.

53. Michael Getler, "In Europe, a New Savage Age," *Washington Post,* December 21, 1992, p. A18; James O. Jackson, "No Rush to Judgment," *Time,* June 27, 1994, pp. 48–49; David B. Ottaway, "'I Didn't Know When It Was Day or Night,'" *Washington Post,* September 11, 1993, p. A11; Vulliamy, *Seasons in Hell,* p. 98; Alexander Cockburn, "Beat the Devil," *Nation,* August 31–September 7, 1992, p. 198; Getler, "In Europe," p. A14; Henry Siegman, "The Holocaust Analogy Is Too True," *Los Angeles Times,* July 11, 1993, p. M9; Landay, "Mostar," p. 2; Thomas L. Friedman, "The Double Anschluss," *New York Times,* March 27, 1996, p. A21; "No Excuses," p. 20.

54. Picture appended to Watson, "Ethnic Cleansing," p. 18, captioned "Horror Stories," with a legend that stressed the photo's broader interpretive force rather than its contingent details, "A Distraught Mother Holds Her Son in Northern Bosnia"; undated picture appended to Joel Brand, "Life and Death in the Camps," *Newsweek,* August 17, 1992, p. 22, and captioned "The Casualties of War: Prisoners Line Up to Have Their Head Shaved at Manjaca, a Serb-Run Detention Center"; Joann Byrd, "The Power of One Child's Story," *Washington Post,* August 22, 1993, p. C6; picture captioned "Water Run," appended to Judah, "Price of Water," p. 8; photo captioned "Bleak Outlook," *London Times,* July 9, 1993, p. 12. The apparent barbed wire was, in fact, a safety netting strewn across the window behind which the child stood, but the effect neatly conjured up memories of the barbed-wire images from World War II.

55. Picture appended to "Bosnia's Dismal Endgame," p. 33; picture appended to Watson, "Ethnic Cleansing," pp. 16–17; reprint of a 1992 photo appended to Walsh, "Unearthing Evil," p. 47.

56. Darnton, "Does World Still Recognize?" p. 1; picture appended to Helene Despic-Popovic, "Judging Bosnia's Carnage," *Liberation,* November 8, 1994. The piece was reprinted in *World Press Review,* February 1995, pp. 19–20; picture captioned "Traditions of Atrocity," appended to Lance Morrow, "Unspeakable," *Time,* February 22, 1993, p. 50. The follow-up comments appeared in bold print in the readers' letters section, under "Wartime Atrocities," *Time,* April 19, 1993, p. 8.

57. Darnton, "Does World Still Recognize?" p. 1; Leslie Gelb, "Never Again," *New York Times,* December 13, 1992, p. E7; "A War That Gets Harder to Watch," *Economist,* August 8, 1992, p. 27; Tyler Marshall, "Faced with a TV War, Europeans Switch Off," *Los Angeles Times,* March 19, 1994, p. A16; Rod Nordland, "A Death March in the Mountains," *Newsweek,* July 31, 1995, p. 26; Christopher Hitchens, "The Death of a Nation," *Washington Post,* March 20, 1994, p. G8; German legislator Stefan Schwarz, cited in Marshall, "Faced with TV War," p. A17.

58. For example, see Leo Kuper, *The Pity of It All: Polarization of Racial and Ethnic*

Relations (Minneapolis: University of Minnesota Press, 1977). These battles had earlier reverberations in 1965 and 1972, when between one hundred thousand and three hundred thousand Hutu were killed. See, for instance, Charny, *Genocide: A Critical Bibliographic Review,* p. 7. Also see Frank J. Parker, "The Why's in Rwanda," *America,* August 27, 1994, pp. 6–9.

59. Gourevitch, "Is Burundi Next?"; Susan Douglas, "A Three-Way Failure," *Progressive,* July 1994, p. 15; James Martin, "Media Camouflage," *America,* August 27, 1994, p. 9; Douglas, "A Three-Way Failure," p. 15.

60. See, for example, pictures appended to Eric Ransdell, "Why Is Rwanda Killing Itself?" *U.S. News and World Report,* May 23, 1994, pp. 46–48; pictures appended to Purvis, "Specter of Genocide," pp. 34, 35; picture appended to "Land of the Dead and Dying," *Economist,* July 30, 1994, p. 50; picture appended to "Danger Ahead," *Economist,* August 27, 1994, p. 46; picture appended to Eve-Ann Prentice, "UN Envoy to Fly In after Cancelling Risky Kigali Round Trip," *London Times,* May 24, 1994," p. 13; Michael Williamson, "Death Knows No Borders," *Washington Post,* May 13, 1994, p. A39.

61. Uncaptioned picture appended to James Bone, "UN Chief Hits Out at Response to Rwanda Plea," *London Times,* May 26, 1994, p. 14; picture appended to "Telling Tales," *Economist,* August 13, 1994, p. 49; picture appended to "Girls Left for Dead in Pile of Corpses," *London Times,* May 9, 1994, p. 1; Bone, "UN Chief Hits Out," p. 14; uncaptioned pictures appended to Sam Kiley, "U.N. Dooms Its Rwandan Peace Force to Failure," *London Times,* May 21, 1994, p. 14; picture captioned "Tutsi Civilians," appended to Mark Fritz, "Rwandan Mother of Six Tells How She Killed Neighbors' Children," *London Times,* May 16, 1994, p. 11; uncaptioned picture appended to Richburg, "World Ignored Genocide," p. A1; picture appended to "Rwandan Killers Leave a Village of the Dead," *New York Times,* May 14, 1994, p. C3; picture appended to "This Life and the Next: Sin and Confession in Rwanda," *Economist,* January 14, 1995, p. 53.

62. Tom Walker, "Hutu Refugees Loot Food Lorries after Press Keeps Them Waiting," *London Times,* May 4, 1994, p. 14; Tom Walker, "Rwandans Eke Out Life of Daily Misery," *London Times,* May 9, 1994, p. 12; Lane, "When Is It Genocide?" p. 27.

63. Parmelee, "Fade to Blood," p. C3; Martin Fletcher and Eve-Ann Prentice, "Gloating Somalis Parade Corpses of U.S. Servicemen," *London Times,* October 5, 1993, p. 13; Philip Willan and Jonathan Ewing, "Western Newsmen Die in Somali Mob Attack," *London Times,* July 13, 1993, p. 1; "Clinton's Choice," editorial, *London Times,* October 8, 1993, p. 19.

64. Douglas, "A Three-Way Failure," p. 15.

65. McNeil, "At Church," p. A4; Fritz, "Rwandan Mother of Six," p. 11; Parmelee, "Fade to Blood," p. C3.

66. Uncaptioned picture appended to Prentice, "UN Envoy to Fly," p. 13; picture appended to Stephen Buckley, "Afraid to Leave, Rwandans Camp with the Dead," *Washington Post,* April 28, 1995, p. A32; unaccredited picture captioned "Who Did Just What?" appended to "Rwanda's Mass of Murderers," *Economist,* October 29, 1994, p. 77; picture captioned "Pall of Death," appended to Andrew Purvis, "All the Hatred in the World," *Time,* June 13, 1994, p. 36; picture appended to Steven Buckley, "Tribal Label Masks African Power Struggle," *Washington Post,* January 27, 1996, p. A15; uncaptioned picture appended to Fritz, "Rwandan Mother of Six," p. 11.

67. Uncaptioned picture appended to Donatella Lorch, "Rwanda Calls for Others to Join Massacre Inquiry," *New York Times,* April 28, 1995, p. A12; uncaptioned picture

appended to Maykuth, "In Rwanda," p. A3. Also see uncaptioned picture appended to James C. McKinley Jr., "From a Grave in Rwanda, Hundreds of Dead Tell Their Tale," *New York Times,* February 16, 1996, p. A4; picture appended to McNeil, "At Church," p. A4.

68. Cited in George F. Will, "Worthy of Contempt," *Washington Post,* August 3, 1995, p. A31; Jonathan Schell, *The Fate of the Earth* (New York: Alfred A. Knopf, 1982).

69. Anton Kaes, *From Hitler to Heimat: The Return of History as Film* (Cambridge, Mass.: Harvard University Press, 1989), p. ix; Lance Morrow, "Imprisoning Time in a Rectangle," *Time,* fall 1989, p. 76.

70. Jonathan Webber, foreword to *Representations of Auschwitz: Fifty Years of Photographs, Paintings, and Graphics* ed. Yasmin Doosry (Oswiecim: Auschwitz-Birkenau State Museum, 1995), p. 10.

71. Lance Morrow, "The Morals of Remembering," *Time,* May 23, 1983, p. 88.

72. Michael J. Sandel, "America's Search for a New Public Philosophy," *Atlantic,* March 1996, p. 58.

SELECTED BIBLIOGRAPHY

SOURCES ON JOURNALISM

Cooper, Kent. "Report of the General Manager." In *The Associated Press Thirty-First Annual Report of the Board of Directors.* New York: Associated Press, 1931.

Desmond, Robert W. *Tides of War: World News Reporting, 1931–1945.* Iowa City: University of Iowa Press, 1990.

Jones, Aled. "The British Press, 1919–1945." In *The Encyclopedia of the British Press, 1422–1992,* ed. Dennis Griffith. New York: St. Martin's, 1992.

Keating, Isabelle. "Reporters Become of Age." *Harper's,* April 1935, pp. 601–12.

Knightley, Philip. *The First Casualty: From the Crimea to Vietnam: The War Correspondent as Hero, Propagandist, and Myth Maker.* New York: Harcourt Brace Jovanovich, 1975.

Mathews, Joseph J. *Reporting the Wars.* Minneapolis: University of Minnesota Press, 1957.

Mott, Frank Luther, ed. *Journalism in Wartime.* Washington, D.C.: American Council on Public Affairs, 1943.

Riess, Curt. *They Were There: The Story of World War II and How It Came About by America's Foremost Correspondents.* New York: G. P. Putnam and Sons, 1944.

Voss, Frederick S. *Reporting the War: The Journalistic Coverage of World War II.* Washington, D.C.: Smithsonian Press for the National Portrait Gallery, 1994.

TRADE PERIODICALS AND PUBLICATIONS ON JOURNALISM

Associated Press Annual Reports of the Board of Directors

Editor and Publisher

The Journal

Newspaper World

Problems of Journalism (proceedings of the yearly conventions of the American Society of Newspaper Editors)

The Quill

SOURCES ON PHOTOGRAPHY

Barnhurst, Kevin. *Seeing the Newspaper.* New York: St. Martin's, 1994.

Barthes, Roland. *Camera Lucida.* Trans. Richard Howard. London: Hill and Wang, 1981.

———. "The Rhetoric of the Image." In *Image/Music/Text,* trans. Stephen Heath. New York: Hill and Wang, 1977.

Carlebach, Michael. *The Origins of Photojournalism in America.* Washington, D.C.: Smithsonian Press, 1992.

Evans, Harold. *Eyewitness.* London: Quiller Press, 1981.

Fulton, Marianne. "Bearing Witness: The 1930s to the 1950s." In *Eyes of Time: Photo-*

journalism in America, ed. Marianne Fulton. New York: New York Graphics Society, 1988.

Gidal, Tim. *Modern Photojournalism: Origin and Evolutions, 1910–1933.* New York: Macmillan, 1972.

Goldberg, Vicki. *The Power of Photography: How Photographs Changed Our Lives.* New York: Abbeville, 1991.

Hall, Stuart. "The Determinations of News Photographs." In *The Manufacture of News,* ed. Stanley Cohen and Jock Young. London: Sage, 1974.

Hicks, Wilson. *Words and Images: An Introduction to Photojournalism.* New York: Harper Brothers, 1952.

Hunter, Jefferson. *Image and Word.* Cambridge, Mass.: Harvard University Press, 1987.

Lewinski, Jorge. *The Camera at War: A History of War Photography from 1848 to the Present Day.* New York: Simon and Schuster, 1978.

Maslowski, Peter. *Armed with Cameras: The American Military Photographers of World War II.* New York: Free Press, 1993.

Messaris, Paul. *Visual Literacy.* Boulder, Colo.: Westview, 1994.

Mitchell, W. J. T. *Picture Theory.* Chicago: University of Chicago Press, 1994.

Moeller, Susan. *Shooting War.* New York: Basic Books, 1989.

Newhall, Beaumont. *The History of Photography.* New York: Museum of Modern Art, 1982.

Sekula, Allan. "On the Invention of Photographic Meaning." In *Photography against the Grain.* 1974; rpt. Halifax: Press of the Nova Scotia College of Art and Design, 1984.

Sontag, Susan. *On Photography.* New York: Anchor Books, 1977.

Szarkowski, John, ed. *From the Picture Press.* New York: Museum of Modern Art, 1973.

Tagg, John. *The Burden of Representation: Essays on Photography and History.* London: Macmillan, 1988.

Taylor, John. *War Photography: Realism in the British Press.* London: Routledge, 1991.

Thompson, George Raynor, and Dixie R. Harris. *The Outcome, Mid-1943 through 1945.* Vol. 3 of *The Signal Corps.* Washington, D.C.: Office of the Chief of Military History, United States Army, 1966.

Thompson, George Raynor, Dixie R. Harris, Pauline M. Oakes, and Dulany Terrett. *The Test, December 1941 to July 1943.* Vol. 2 of *The Signal Corps.* Washington, D.C.: Office of the Chief of Military History, Department of the Army, 1957.

Trachtenberg, Alan. *Reading American Photographs: Images as History, Mathew Brady to Walker Evans.* New York: Hill and Wang, 1989.

Zelizer, Barbie. "Words against Images: Positioning Newswork in the Age of Photography." In *Newsworkers: Toward a History of the Rank and File,* ed. Hanno Hardt and Bonnie Brennen. Minneapolis: University of Minnesota Press, 1995.

TRADE PERIODICALS AND PUBLICATIONS ON PHOTOGRAPHY

American Photography
British Journal Photographic Almanac
British Journal of Photography
The Camera
Photo-Era Magazine
Photographic Journal

SOURCES ON COLLECTIVE MEMORY

Bodnar, John. *Remaking America: Public Memory, Commemoration, and Patriotism in the Twentieth Century*. Princeton, N.J.: Princeton University Press, 1992.

Casey, Edward S. *Remembering: A Phenomenological Study*. Bloomington: Indiana University Press, 1987.

Connerton, Paul. *How Societies Remember*. Cambridge: Cambridge University Press, 1989.

Fentress, James, and Chris Wickham. *Social Memory*. Oxford: Basil Blackwell, 1992.

Halbwachs, Maurice. *The Collective Memory*. New York: Harper and Row, 1980.

Hobsbawm, Eric, and Terence Ranger, eds. *The Invention of Tradition*. Cambridge: Cambridge University Press, 1983.

Huyssen, Andreas. *Twilight Memories: Marking Time in a Culture of Amnesia*. New York: Routledge, 1996.

Irwin-Zarecka, Iwona. *Frames of Remembrance: The Dynamics of Collective Memory*. New Brunswick, N.J.: Transaction Publishers, 1994.

Johnson, Richard, Gregor McLennan, Bill Schwarz, and David Sutton, eds. *Making Histories: Studies in History-Writing and Politics*. Minneapolis: University of Minnesota Press, 1982.

Kammen, Michael. *Mystic Chords of Memory: The Transformation of Tradition in American Culture*. New York: Alfred A. Knopf, 1991.

Le Goff, Jacques. *History and Memory*. New York: Columbia University Press, 1992.

Maier, Charles. *The Unmasterable Past: History, Holocaust, and German National Identity*. Cambridge, Mass.: Harvard University Press, 1988.

Nora, Pierre. *Realms of Memory*. New York: Columbia University Press, 1996.

Schudson, Michael. *Watergate in American Memory: How We Remember, Forget, and Reconstruct the Past*. New York: Basic Books, 1992.

Schwartz, Barry. "The Reconstruction of Abraham Lincoln." In *Collective Remembering*, ed. Drew Middleton and Derek Edwards. Beverly Hills, Calif.: Sage Publications, 1990.

————. "The Social Context of Commemoration: A Study in Collective Memory." *Social Forces* 61, no. 2 (1982): 347–402.

Zelizer, Barbie. *Covering the Body: The Kennedy Assassination, the Media, and the Shaping of Collective Memory*. Chicago: University of Chicago Press, 1992.

————. "Reading the Past against the Grain: The Shape of Memory Studies." *Critical Studies in Mass Communication* 12, no. 2 (June 1995): 214–39.

COLLECTIVE MEMORY AND THE HOLOCAUST

Friedlander, Saul. *Memory, History, and the Extermination of the Jews of Europe*. Bloomington: Indiana University Press, 1993.

————, ed. *Probing the Limits of Representation: Nazism and the "Final Solution."* Cambridge, Mass.: Harvard University Press, 1992.

Hartman, Geoffrey, ed. *Holocaust Remembrance: The Shapes of Memory*. Oxford: Basil Blackwell, 1994.

Krondorfer, Bjorn. *Remembrance and Reconciliation*. New Haven, Conn.: Yale University Press, 1995.

Langer, Lawrence. *Holocaust Testimonies: The Ruins of Memory*. New Haven, Conn.: Yale University Press, 1991.

Miller, Judith. *One, by One, by One*. New York: Touchstone Books, 1990.

Young, James E. *The Texture of Memory: Holocaust Memorials and Meaning*. New Haven, Conn.: Yale University Press, 1993.

Zelizer, Barbie. "Every Once in a While: *Schindler's List* and the Shaping of History." In *Spielberg's Holocaust: Critical Perspectives on "Schindler's List,"* ed. Yosefa Loshitzky. Bloomington: Indiana University Press, 1997.

JOURNALS ON COLLECTIVE MEMORY

"Between Memory and History." *History and Anthropology* 12, no. 2 (1986).

History and Memory: Studies in Representation of the Past, 1991–.

"Memory and American History." *Journal of American History* 75, no. 4 (March 1989).

"Memory and Counter-Memory." *Representations* 26 (spring 1989).

"Monumental Histories." *Representations* 35 (summer 1991).

"Social Memory." *Communication* 11, no. 2 (1989).

SOURCES ON THE HOLOCAUST AND THE LIBERATION OF THE CONCENTRATION CAMPS

Abzug, Robert. *Inside the Vicious Heart.* New York: Oxford University Press, 1985.

Amishai-Maisels, Ziva. *Depiction and Interpretation:Visual Arts and the Holocaust.* Oxford: Pergamon, 1993.

Atrocities and Other Conditions in Concentration Camps in Germany (Report to U.S. Congress). Washington, D.C.: United States Government Printing Office, 1945.

"Belsen." *British Zone Review Supplement,* October 13, 1945, pp. 1–8.

Bridgman, Jon. *The End of the Holocaust:The Liberation of the Camps.* Portland, Ore.: Areopagitica Press, 1990.

Buchenwald Camp:The Report of a Parliamentary Delegation. London: His Majesty's Stationery Office, April 1945.

Caiger-Smith, Martin. *The Face of the Enemy: British Photographers in Germany, 1944–1952.* Berlin: Nishen, 1988.

Chamberlin, Brewster, and Marcia Feldman, eds. *The Liberation of the Nazi Concentration Camps, 1945.* Washington, D.C.: United States Holocaust Memorial Council.

Eliach, Yaffa, and Brana Gurewitsch, eds. *The Liberators.* Brooklyn: Center for Holocaust Studies Documentation and Research, 1981.

Feig, Konnilyn G. *Hitler's Death Camps:The Sanity of Madness.* New York: Holmes and Meier, 1981.

Kushner, Tony. *The Holocaust and the Liberal Imagination:A Social and Cultural History.* Oxford: Basil Blackwell, 1994.

Lipstadt, Deborah. *Beyond Belief:The American Press and the Coming of the Holocaust, 1933–1945.* New York: Free Press, 1986.

Milton, Sybil. "The Camera as Weapon: Documentary Photography and the Holocaust." *Simon Wiesenthal Center Annual* 1, no. 1 (1984): 45–68.

———. "Images of the Holocaust." *Holocaust and Genocide Studies* 1, nos. 1 and 2 (1986): 27–61, 193–216.

"Official Report on Buchenwald Camp." *PM,* April 30, 1945, p. 9.

Ross, Robert W. *So It Was True:The American Protestant Press and the Nazi Persecution of the Jews.* Minneapolis: University of Minnesota Press, 1980.

Selzer, Michael. *Deliverance Day:The Last Hours at Dachau.* Philadelphia: J. B. Lippincott, 1978.

Sharf, Andrew. *The British Press and Jews under Nazi Rule.* London: Oxford University Press, 1964.

United States Holocaust Memorial Council. *1945:The Year of Liberation.* Washington, D.C.: United States Holocaust Memorial Museum, 1995.

INDEX

The letter *f* attached to a locator refers to an illustration.